Suicide: Biopsychosocial Approaches

Edited by:

Alexander J. Botsis
University Mental Health Research Institute
Athens, Greece

Constantin R. Soldatos
University of Athens Medical School
Athens, Greece

Costas N. Stefanis
University Mental Health Research Institute
Athens, Greece

1997

ELSEVIER

Amsterdam – Lausanne – New York – Oxford – Shannon – Singapore – Tokyo

International Congress Series No. 1145
ISBN 0 444 82755 2

This book is printed on acid-free paper.

Published by:
Elsevier Science B.V.
P.O. Box 211
1000 AE Amsterdam
The Netherlands

Printed in the Netherlands

Preface

Suicide cannot be fully understood as an isolated phenomenon. In fact it merely represents the tip of an iceberg, one of many manifestations admittedly the most dramatic one — of the human self-destructive behavior in its many facets and consequences, at the individual and social level. Regarded even in isolation, suicide constitutes one of the most serious public health problems and a major challenge to our societies, to understand it and to effectively prevent it.

In recent years, research in the area of suicidality is burgeoning and significant advances have been made in clarifying the phenomenological and clinical profile of the potential suicide victim as well as in identifying some of the biological, psychological and sociological risk factors for self-destructive behavior. The accumulated body of knowledge has shed light on many aspects of suicidal behavior and provides a sound ground in answering the question, what leaves the person with no other choice but to terminate his life?

The strong links between suicide and self-destructive behavior in general with psychopathology — depression in particular — is by now well-established and not only on the clinical level. Biological markers associated with both conditions are being currently identified and offer a new perspective in unraveling the common neurobiological mechanisms underlining psychopathology and suicidality. On the other hand, recent systematic epidemiological research, while indicating that suicide is an almost universal phenomenon, has also shown that its occurrence varies considerably across countries and cultures with 2- and even 3-fold differences in rates of incidence, a finding that strongly supports the view that neurobiology and psychopathology alone can neither fully account for, nor can explain the phenomenon. Social and cultural variables have to also be involved and their interaction with the biological and psychological risk factors need to be further investigated. Obviously, suicide represents a complex and multifactorial human behavior and as such, raises a variety of theoretical, clinical, ethical and legal issues, which can only be successfully addressed by concerted multidisciplinary research efforts.

Despite progress being made in the field of suicidality, the available knowledge is still deficient and far from adequate to allow for the formulation of unified and comprehensive hypothesis on the etiology and pathogenesis of suicidal behavior. Even more significant is that clinical practice and preventive policies do not adequately benefit from the available body of research findings. Rates of suicide in most countries do not decline, and in some others, a steady increase over time is observed. This further indicates the need for bridging the gap between researchers and clinical practitioners in the field of suicidology and/or initiating public awareness programs on suicidal and associated behaviors.

In the past, research on suicide was mainly focused on psychopathology by assigning the victims to the various diagnostic groups and linking the suicide composite phenomenon with the psychological and psychobiological dimensions with each of the nosological entities. Currently, although the strong association between suicidal behavior and diagnostic groups of patient populations is widely acknowledged, research on suicidology has largely been expanded and in addition to investigating the distinguishing features of suicidal and nonsuicidal individuals within the same diagnostic group, it integrated into its scope the study of the psychobiological and social correlates of human aggression. The expanded view of suicidality and its disentanglement from the strictly nosological frame has contributed to the accumulation of new knowledge and provided new insights that greatly facilitated the identification of risk factors as an essential part of suicide prevention.

The presentation in a book of such a multifaceted, multidimensional, age-long human enigma is a difficult task and a stimulating challenge. In this book, which is based on a selection of papers presented at the International Conference on Suicide which took place in Athens in 1996, we tried to satisfy competing demands on the one hand to cover in a comprehensive way the wide range of issues currently related to suicide and on the other, to select out of the many topics the most central presentations and sequence them in a way to secure a cohesive text. To this end we relied mostly on material drawn from the lectures presented at the conference by widely renowned researchers in the field as well as chapters contributed by colleagues who were chosen by the editors of the book on the basis of their innovative studies on suicide and were, therefore, invited to fill in thematic gaps within each section of the book. The material gathered according to these constraints was arranged in four sections:
— epidemiology in general and special populations,
— etiopathogenetic considerations,
— clinical issues, and
— conceptual and ethical issues.
It is our hope that we have succeeded to provide the reader with an integrative perspective on current approaches in the understanding of suicide, a major problem in public health and a challenging enigma of human nature. The diversity that appears in the authors' approach as well as their mode of writing was both expected and welcome. On behalf of the editors, I wish to express my gratitude to them for their valuable contribution. Last but not least I would like to thank Ms. Helen Kavadias for her devoted and skillful input to this project.

Professor C.N. Stefanis
Director
University Mental Health Research Institute

DATE DUE

Suicide: Biopsychosocial Approaches

Contents

Clinical issues

Conceptual and ethical issues

Epidemiology in general
and special populations

Suicide trends in Europe, 1984–1990

D. Wasserman[1], M. Dankowicz[1], A. Värnik[2] and L. Olsson[1]

[1]*National and Stockholm County Centre for Suicide Research and Prevention at the National Institute for Psychosocial Factors and Health, Karolinska Institute in Stockholm, Sweden; and* [2]*Estonian-Swedish Suicidological Institute, Tallinn, Estonia*

Abstract. The purpose of this study was to identify changes in the suicide rates of European countries between 1984 and 1990. It was found that suicide rates in 22 European countries decreased between 1984 and 1990 by 11.1%, or 8.4% for men and 17.0% for women, breaking from the increasing trend which was previously observed between 1972 and 1984. In the Baltic and Slavic regions of the former USSR, in contrast to the rest of Europe, a sharp 28.6% decline in suicide rates was observed during the period of perestroika, 31.6% for men and 19.1% for women, between 1984 and 1990. Decreases in suicide rates between 1984 and 1986–1988 were particularly strong in the Baltic and Slavic regions, at 35.6%, or 40.3% for men and 17.8% for women. At the same time in the 22 European countries, suicide rates dropped by 2.6% for men and 6.7% for women, or 4.3% overall.

Keywords: 1984–1990, age, Baltic region, Europe, mortality, perestroika, sex, Slavic region, USSR.

Introduction

WHO collects annual suicide figures from approximately 60 countries. According to the WHO data, suicide is among the 10 leading causes of death in the world [1]. In some countries suicide is among the top three causes of death for people aged 15–34 years, and in Sweden suicide is the most common cause of death for males aged 15–44 years [2].

In the study of suicide mortality, the reliability of suicide statistics has often been questioned. Reliability seems to vary between different countries. This can be judged by the number of cases which are reported by WHO [3] as death, when it is uncertain if the death was accidental or purposely inflicted (E980-E989 according to ICD-9 classification). Some countries, such as Sweden, France, Poland and Denmark, use E980-E989 diagnoses to a much larger extent than countries such as Greece, Spain, Italy, Norway and Portugal. Studies from Sweden [4] show that 75% of all cases in this category are actually certain suicides. There are many reasons for believing that suicide is underreported, such as the negative sanctions and attitudes towards people who commit suicide and towards their families, as well as different registration procedures used in different countries.

Despite the above-mentioned problems with suicide statistics, the WHO data

Address for correspondence: Danuta Wasserman, National Centre for Suicide Research and Prevention, P.O. Box 230, S-171 77 Stockholm, Sweden.

4

are used because they, for the time being, are the only source for comparisons of suicide rates within and between different countries.

The National Swedish Centre for Suicide Research and Prevention has (since 1988) been in close collaboration with the Estonian-Swedish Institute of Suicidology regarding the study of violent deaths and suicides in the former USSR [5–9]. This cross-national collaboration has resulted in an interest in investigating whether the suicide trends observed in the former USSR during perestroika (1984–1990) were similar to those which occurred in the rest of Europe during the same time.

The purpose of this study, therefore, is to identify changes in the suicide rates of 22 European countries (see Table 1) between 1984 and 1990, and to compare these to changes in the Baltic and Slavic regions of the former USSR. In the former USSR, 90% of suicides took place in the Slavic and Baltic regions, in which more than 70% of the population lived.

Material and Methods

Suicide mortality for 22 European countries (see Table 1) between 1984 and 1990 was studied using data on certain suicides (E950-E959) from the European Suicide Data Bank [10], collected from WHO statistical year books [3]. For the former USSR from the "Annual report of population change," an unpublished official government document held by the All-Union Statistical Committee in Moscow [11] data were collected. Suicide statistics and population censuses for the Baltic and Slavic regions of the former USSR, published between 1989 and 1990 [12,13] were collected by the responsible organisations in the individual republics: the Slavic republics of Russia, Byelorussia, and Ukraine, and the Baltic republics of Latvia, Lithuania, and Estonia.

Annual suicide rates for each of the individual 22 European countries and for the Slavic and Baltic regions were calculated per 100,000 inhabitants. Pooled suicide rates were calculated for the total of all 22 European countries and for the total of all Slavic and Baltic republics. Data included only people aged 15 years and older, due to the fact that very few suicides were committed by people under 15 years of age, relative to people of other ages, while the population of this group was relatively large.

In order to assess changes in the suicide rates of different European countries, percentage changes in suicide rates between 1984 and the average of 1986, 1987 and 1988 (Tables 1 and 2) were calculated for both men and women in different age groups. The average suicide rate for 1986–1988 was subtracted from the rate for 1984, and the sum was divided by the 1984 rate and multiplied by 100. Similarly, percentage changes were calculated for the difference between the rates of 1986–1988 and 1990. These analyses for the former USSR are published separately [14,15], and are discussed briefly in this article as a means of comparison for the other European countries.

Table 1. Percentage changes in suicide rates of men and women in Europe aged 15 and older, between 1984 and 1986—1988, by age group.

Country	Men								Women							
	15—24	25—34	35—44	45—54	55—64	65—74	75+	All ages	15—24	25—34	35—44	45—54	55—64	65—74	75+	All ages
Austria	−9.1	14.8	−8.9	−8.3	−7.8	−1.1	1.4	−2.6	−5.2	18.8	13.7	−16.2	0.4	8.4	−10.4	0.4
Bulgaria	−6.8	12.8	−9.4	−12.3	−23.0	3.6	−7.8	−6.7	6.8	−9.5	−25.5	−10.1	−3.0	−5.0	14.3	−1.2
Czechoslovakia	−0.8	1.8	−0.5	−3.7	−2.7	−13.0	−6.7	−2.8	−10.1	4.5	8.5	6.2	−11.2	−1.8	−5.0	−1.5
Denmark	1.4	−8.8	−9.2	−4.3	−12.4	2.0	2.5	−5.6	52.9	−1.4	−17.6	−15.6	1.9	−13.5	−9.7	−8.2
Finland	0.2	5.1	9.9	12.7	8.4	6.2	−1.3	7.6	70.7	−7.1	21.2	25.0	−4.5	44.6	−26.4	14.7
France	−9.1	−1.5	4.3	−0.6	−4.0	−14.8	−1.9	−2.5	−3.6	−16.2	−0.5	12.6	5.5	−5.4	−3.3	−0.9
GFRG	−12.2	−13.6	−17.4	−10.5	−5.5	−10.3	−0.2	−9.4	−6.3	−8.6	−25.3	−12.0	−18.3	−9.5	−13.3	−13.0
Greece	9.2	8.7	−8.1	−3.9	−10.0	−11.5	26.6	2.1	−36.0	−53.3	7.5	−10.3	43.2	1.8	163.4	−0.7
Hungary	−18.3	5.5	−13.5	−3.7	−11.3	−3.9	−6.7	−6.6	34.0	11.6	−8.3	12.0	−4.4	−5.5	−12.3	−0.5
Iceland	−48.5	a	a	a	a	a	a	−34.9	a	a	a	a	a	a	a	42.2
Ireland	61.5	24.8	15.9	−18.1	22.7	−5.5	a	20.2	−23.2	40.6	−18.6	−4.1	−13.8	−18.6	a	−4.2
Italy	15.9	6.2	−1.6	−2.9	−9.5	−3.0	−2.0	−0.4	−8.0	−21.9	−11.0	−5.0	−10.6	2.0	10.5	−4.3
Luxembourg	a	−26.8	20.3	−13.9	a	a	a	−7.9	a	a	a	a	a	a	a	−11.3
Malta	a	a	a	a	a	a	a	a	a	a	a	a	a	a	a	a
Netherlands	20.8	−16.4	−19.8	−18.7	−14.0	−14.6	−1.9	−12.0	−12.8	−11.7	−10.9	−13.4	−19.8	−37.0	−15.5	−17.6
Norway	−7.1	25.0	11.9	20.0	−13.1	−26.6	34.2	2.3	−8.8	42.8	34.8	26.2	−17.7	9.6	−7.1	9.9
Poland	−8.8	−18.6	−13.1	−4.7	8.4	2.5	5.6	−8.1	−28.3	−7.1	−9.1	−3.7	−5.6	−5.2	1.3	−7.6
Portugal	−33.7	−21.8	−26.8	−3.0	−13.6	−5.1	58.6	−9.4	−46.9	−17.4	−39.5	−32.9	13.2	−29.9	1.5	−24.2
Sweden	11.1	−18.3	−12.3	−6.3	2.2	1.2	2.2	−3.9	4.4	−29.2	1.3	−7.2	−4.5	−24.6	16.3	−8.7
Switzerland	−18.3	−7.3	−5.1	−7.0	−11.5	−14.3	21.6	−7.4	0.7	−10.6	−17.5	−19.4	−8.8	−1.1	31.8	−5.9
UK	37.4	7.2	85.7	−12.4	−3.3	−3.5	−1.4	17.7	43.9	4.6	−23.4	−25.8	−28.9	−17.8	−16.5	−17.5
Yugoslavia	−6.7	−5.9	11.6	−15.9	−5.9	5.4	−1.8	−3.0	−9.6	−2.2	14.4	−0.9	−0.3	4.7	9.5	3.6
Total	−4.5	−6.2	6.0	−6.6	−5.4	−6.8	−1.2	−2.6	−3.7	−8.7	−10.4	−4.7	−9.4	−7.1	−5.6	−6.7

aFewer than six cases of suicide per year. Suicides in this group were used to calculate percent change for the total of all countries.

Table 2. Percentage changes in suicide rates of men and women in Europe aged 15 and older, between 1986–1988 and 1990, by age group.

Country	Men								Women							
	15–24	25–34	35–44	45–54	55–64	65–74	75+	All ages	15–24	25–34	35–44	45–54	55–64	65–74	75+	All ages
Austria	−14.2	−24.6	−20.3	−8.9	−11.3	0.8	−4.9	−12.5	−27.0	−28.5	−13.3	−7.6	−3.0	−22.9	10.2	−10.3
Bulgaria	15.4	−2.3	−20.0	−6.1	−7.5	−21.4	−17.5	−10.4	−32.4	5.9	22.1	−8.4	−23.1	−2.8	−8.6	−7.0
Czechoslovakia	−12.2	−16.9	−4.4	14.3	−1.3	2.9	−0.7	−2.4	13.5	−12.9	0.7	−12.9	−9.0	−9.4	−1.5	−6.0
Denmark	−13.5	−22.0	−8.0	−2.9	−23.9	−5.0	11.1	−9.0	−36.6	−45.8	−21.1	−21.3	−18.9	−8.3	10.6	−17.2
Finland	35.6	14.5	9.1	−2.3	3.8	−16.0	28.0	10.4	37.2	20.4	20.7	−18.2	19.6	15.2	7.7	8.1
France	−5.4	−7.4	−1.8	−5.7	−13.6	−14.7	−7.6	−6.8	2.2	−5.4	−14.6	−16.8	−6.5	−22.9	−8.2	−11.2
GFRG	−12.1	−11.8	−17.3	−18.6	−15.2	−19.9	−4.9	−13.7	−6.7	−16.3	−24.7	−22.0	−20.7	−22.6	−2.2	−16.1
Greece	6.0	−12.7	2.4	−14.4	−21.7	−21.8	−11.1	−10.4	−16.4	6.0	−47.4	2.4	−46.6	−40.1	−52.3	−30.5
Hungary	−8.1	−12.5	−9.9	−7.6	−3.6	−10.9	7.5	−7.0	−15.0	−36.8	−25.7	−12.7	−18.8	−28.7	0.8	−17.8
Iceland	84.9	a	a	a	a	a	a	36.7	a	a	a	a	a	a	a	a
Ireland	11.4	18.8	47.1	85.7	10.0	−2.0	4.8	23.9	62.2	85.3	14.1	−5.1	3.2	34.0	a	25.7
Italy	17.7	3.3	1.6	−16.4	−13.7	−19.2	4.8	−3.7	39.2	18.9	−4.7	−18.5	−9.3	−24.9	−18.5	−9.4
Luxembourg	a	−20.2	−7.4	−2.6	a	a	a	2.2	a	a	a	a	a	a	a	3.6
Malta	a	a	a	a	a	a	a	a	a	a	a	a	a	a	a	a
Netherlands	−2.9	2.0	6.1	−19.0	−20.9	−36.7	−18.8	−10.1	11.4	−19.2	−12.0	−21.3	−13.0	−29.9	21.3	−11.5
Norway	−6.0	−4.5	10.8	−14.3	6.7	24.8	8.5	1.9	34.9	−20.1	−11.3	−12.9	1.3	5.4	41.8	−0.6
Poland	−2.4	2.9	2.8	3.0	7.1	−6.2	−13.1	1.6	2.4	−19.3	−0.2	94.2	16.0	0.3	14.5	6.4
Portugal	−1.2	41.4	−9.7	−20.7	−11.6	−3.7	−2.6	−2.2	−1.5	−7.0	−4.9	−6.7	−20.9	−12.6	37.8	−1.7
Sweden	−19.3	−13.1	−15.0	−21.6	−4.1	2.4	13.4	−8.9	−18.4	0.8	−16.8	−20.3	19.4	5.0	9.3	−4.1
Switzerland	−10.9	−10.6	−16.8	−4.0	−3.7	2.0	7.8	−5.8	−20.9	−9.6	−6.9	15.1	−16.7	−6.2	−4.2	−5.2
UK	15.4	10.5	5.7	5.8	−14.8	−15.0	−12.1	2.1	−14.6	0.8	−9.5	−23.1	−28.6	−27.0	−26.8	−19.2
Yugoslavia	−18.5	−11.1	−7.4	−1.5	−12.1	−10.9	3.9	−6.9	−30.3	−21.8	9.5	−8.3	−19.1	−10.6	−1.1	−10.0
Total	−2.6	−6.6	−4.3	−7.1	−9.9	−12.1	−3.7	−5.9	−4.7	−12.1	−11.6	−11.7	−13.1	−19.1	−4.8	−11.0

[a] Fewer than six cases of suicide per year. Suicides in this group were used to calculate percentage change for the total of all countries.

Results and Discussion

Suicide rates in Europe

The total mean suicide rate for 22 European countries in 1990 was 18 per 100,000 inhabitants; 15 years and older: 10 per 100,000 females and 27 per 100,000 males. In 1984, the combined rate was 20 per 100,000 inhabitants; 11 per 100,000 females and 30 per 100,000 males.

Suicide trends in Europe 1984—1990

As described by Platt [16], suicide rates for people in Europe aged 15 years and older increased in most countries between 1972 and 1984. Particularly a steep increase has been observed in Ireland and in Norway, where rates rose by approximately 127% for men and 57% for women. Exceptions to this trend were observed in countries such as Czechoslovakia, West Germany, Spain and Sweden, where suicide rates decreased during this period. Other studies also found that suicide rates in most European countries increased during the past several decades [17,18].

Between 1984 and 1990, however, a different trend was seen (Tables 1 and 2). Suicide rates for the total of the 22 European countries studied decreased by 11.1%, with a decrease of 8.4% observed for men and 17.0% for women. This trend was evident between 1984 and 1986—1988, also between 1986—1988 and 1990 in most countries studied. Particularly, large declines of 34.9% in Iceland and 12.0% in The Netherlands were observed between 1984 and 1986—1988 for men, and declines of 24.2% in Portugal, and 17.5% in the UK and The Netherlands were observed for women.

Marked decreases were seen between 1986—1988 and 1990 in Austria (12.5%) and GFRG (13.7%) for men, Denmark (17.2%), Greece (30.5%), Iceland (53.9%), Hungary (17.8%), GFRG (16.1%) and the UK (19.2%) for women.

Comparison with suicide trends in the Baltic and Slavic republics of the former USSR

Changes in suicide rates in 1984 to 1986—1988
In comparison to the 4.3% decrease in suicide rates (2.6% for men and 6.7% for women) in the 22 European countries studied, suicide rates in the Baltic and Slavic republics of the former USSR decreased between 1984 and 1986—1988 by 35.6%, 40.3% for men and 17.8% for women. Changes in suicide rates of men in the other European countries did not reach the dimensions of the decreases observed in the Baltic and Slavic regions between 1984 and 1986—1988, with the exception of females in Portugal.

Changes in suicide rates 1986—1988 to 1990
After the sharp fall in the Baltic and Slavic republics, suicide rates increased

between 1986–1988 and 1990 by 10.8% total (14.5% for men, while rates continued to decrease by 1.6% for women), while in the 22 European countries suicide rates decreased by an additional 7.2%, or 5.9% for men and 11.0% for women. Decreases in individual European countries between 1986–1988 and 1990 were, in most cases, greater than those occurring during the same periods in the Baltic and Slavic regions, where suicide rates were advancing towards their preperestroika heights.

Changes in suicide rates between 1984 and 1990
Still, the overall decline between 1984 and 1990 in the Baltic and Slavic republics was 28.6%, 31.6% for men and 19.1% for women, while suicide rates decreased by only 11.1% total in the 22 European countries studied, or 8.4% for men and 17.0% for women. Decreases for women in the 22 European countries (17.0%) during the whole period studied were similar to those of women in the Baltic and Slavic republics (19.1%).

Age-specific suicide trends in Europe

Platt's observation [16] that suicide rates for European countries tended to increase with age, continued to be the case for the period between 1984 and 1990 (Fig. 1). Also, a bimodal distribution identified by Platt, with peaks in rates for age groups 45–54 and 75 years and older, was seen in several European countries, though not always in the same countries during 1972–1984 and 1984–1990. Only for women in Hungary and Sweden was this pattern found

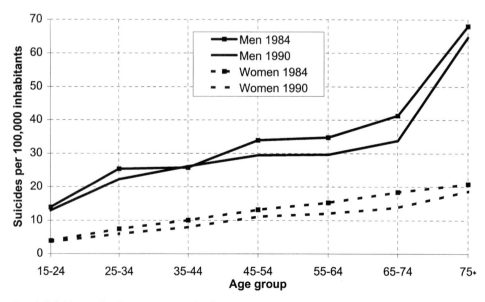

Fig. 1. Suicide rate for European countries for 1984 and 1990.

consistently both before and after 1984.

Between 1972 and 1984 suicide rates increased in the majority of European countries for all age groups, except for women aged 55–64 years. For most age groups the increase was greater for men. The increase was greater among women only for those over the age of 64 years [16].

In contrast, in the current study it has been found that for the combined total of the 22 European countries studied, suicide rates decreased for nearly every age group of both men and women between 1984 and 1986–1988, and between 1986–1988 and 1990 (Tables 1 and 2). The one exception was for men aged 35–44 years, for whom no decrease occurred between 1984 and 1986–1988. Decreases in suicide rates of women were in many, but not all cases, greater than those of men. Decreases observed for the total of all European countries studied were not always seen when individual countries were studied.

In countries such as Ireland and the UK, suicide rates increased between 1984 and 1986–1988, in contrast to the rest of Europe. However, this was not consistent for all age groups. In Ireland, where suicide rates increased overall for men by 20.2% during 1984–1990, a decrease of 18.1% was observed for men aged 45–54 years, and of 5.5% for men aged 65–74 years. Similarly in the UK, where overall suicide rates for men increased between 1984 and 1986–1988 by 17.7%, small decreases were in fact observed for people aged 45 years and older.

Comparison with age-specific suicide trends in the Baltic and Slavic regions

For men in the Slavic and Baltic regions, as in some other European countries, suicide showed a bimodal distribution with peaks at ages 45–54 years and 75 and older. Among women, suicide rates increased directly with age.

In the Baltic and Slavic regions, a sharp decrease in suicide rates was observed between 1984 and 1986–1988, particularly for the age group 25–54 years, where it averaged 45% for men and 33% for women. Decreases for age groups 25–54 years in the 22 European countries averaged 2.3% for men and 7.9% for women. A decrease in suicide rates of comparable size to that which occurred in the Slavic and Baltic regions was observed for this age group in Iceland for men and women but in Greece, Luxembourg and Portugal for women only. However, Luxembourg and Iceland have small populations and Greece a low number of suicides per year which means that the risk of random error is great.

Conclusion

In Europe between 1984 and 1990, a decrease in suicide rates of 8.4% for males and 17.0% for females took place, following the increase in rates that was previously observed for 1972–1984. In the Slavic and Baltic regions a decrease of 40.3% for men and 17.8% for women was observed between 1984 and 1986–1988, followed by an increase of 14.5% for men in 1990. For the period 1984–1990, suicide rates decreased overall in these regions by 31.6% for men and 19.1% for women.

The monitoring of suicide trends is an important measure for the planning and evaluation of suicide preventive programmes.

Acknowledgements

Karolinska Institute grants, Grants from the Swedish National Board of Health and Welfare and the Eastern European Committee.

References

1. Guidelines for the Primary Prevention of Mental, Neurological and Psychosocial Disorders Suicide. Division of Mental Health, World Health Organization, Geneva 1993 (WHO/MNH/MND/93/24).
2. Beskow J, Allebeck P, Wasserman D, Åsberg M. Självmord i Sverige. En epidemiologisk översikt. (Suicide in Sweden. An epidemiological review). Med Res Council 1993;1–140.
3. World Health Statistics Annual. Geneva: World Health Organization, 1984, 1985, 1986, 1987, 1988, 1989, 1990.
4. Cullberg J, Wasserman D, Stefansson C-G. Who commits suicide after a suicide attempt? An 8 to 10 year follow up in a suburban catchment area. Acta Psychiatr Scand 1988;77:598–603.
5. Värnik A. Suicide in Estonia. Acta Psychiatr Scand 1991;84:229–232.
6. Värnik A, Wasserman D. Suicides in the former Soviet republics. Acta Psychiatr Scand 1992;86: 76–78.
7. Wasserman D, Värnik A, Eklund G. Male suicides and alcohol consumption in the former USSR. Acta Psychiatr Scand 1994;89:306–313.
8. Värnik A, Wasserman D, Eklund G. Suicides in the Baltic Countries, 1968–90. Scand J Soc Med 1994;3:166–169.
9. Wasserman D, Värnik A. Increase in suicide among men in the Baltic countries. Lancet 1994; 343(8911):1504–1505.
10. European Suicide Data Bank. National and Stockholm County Council Centre for Suicide Research and Prevention; National Institute for Psychosocial Factors and Health / Karolinska Institute.
11. All-Union Statistical Office of Moscow. Annual reports of population change: Unpublished government document.
12. Demograficzeskij jezjegodnik SSSR 1990 (Demographic Yearbook 1990). Moscow: Goskomstat SSSR, 1990.
13. Demograficheskij jezjegodnik 1991 (Statistical yearbook). Moscow: Statkomitet SNG, 1991.
14. Värnik A, Wasserman D, Dankowicz M, Eklund G. Marked decrease in suicide for men and slight decrease for women in the former USSR during perestroika, 1984–1990, as compared to 22 European countries. (Submitted).
15. Värnik A, Wasserman D, Dankowicz M, Eklund G. Age-specific suicide rates in the Slavic and Baltic regions of the former USSR during perestroika, 1984–1990. (Submitted).
16. Platt S. Suicide trends in 24 European countries, 1972–1984. In: Möller H-J, Schmidtke A, Welz R (eds) Current Issues of Suicidology. Berlin: Springer-Verlag, 1988;3–13.
17. Diekstra RFW. The epidemiology of suicide and parasuicide. Acta Psychiatr Scand 1993;(Suppl 371):9–20.
18. La Vecchia C, Lucchini F, Levi F. Worldwide trends in suicide mortality, 1955–1989. Acta Psychiatr Scand 1994;90:53–64.

The epidemiology of death and suicide symptoms in primary health care

V.G. Mavreas[1] and T.B. Ustun[2]

[1]*Department of Psychiatry, Athens University Medical School, Eginition Hospital, Athens, Greece; and* [2]*World Health Organization, Division of Mental Health and Prevention of Substance Abuse, Geneva, Switzerland*

Abstract. This paper reports preliminary epidemiological data regarding the rates of death (thoughts of death and wishes of death) and suicidal symptoms (suicidal thoughts and attempted suicide) from the large multicentric epidemiological study "Psychological Problems in Primary Health Care" which was carried out in 14 countries. Death symptoms were quite common in patients visiting healthcare settings, especially among patients suffering from mental disorders, or subthreshold conditions. Suicide symptoms were less common, especially suicide attempts. They occurred mainly among patients suffering from mental disorders, usually depression. These symptoms, in most cases were commoner among females as compared to males. Differences between centres were observed in all four symptoms, not always reflecting differences in the rates of mental disorders. These symptoms were found to be related with disability and severity of the disorder, in patients suffering from depression or dysthymia. These findings underline the importance for the early diagnosis of these symptoms in patients visiting primary healthcare services.

Keywords: death symptoms, primary care epidemiology, suicidal symptoms.

Introduction

Primary care is the "gate" of entrance of a patient to the healthcare system in most parts of the world. Primary care physicians are supposed to care for ailments and problems of different kinds, among them psychiatric problems. Suicide and suicide attempt, as a major problem in human societies related to the health, both physical and mental, and care of the individual, is a problem which primary care physicians face quite often [1–3]. It especially accompanies common mental disorders often met in primary care [4–7], although, as it has often been pointed out, it is partly unexplained, as regards its relation to mental or physical health diagnosis [8]. The importance of early detection of suicidal behaviour in primary care has been pointed out, and prevention programmes have been created [9,10].

Cross-cultural differences in the epidemiology of suicidal behaviour have also been found, with great differences between countries and societies in the frequency of suicidal behaviour [11]. From the early studies [12], explanations imply social and cultural factors play a role in these differences.

The present article reports initial epidemiological findings of symptoms related

Address for correspondence: V.G. Mavreas, Athens University Medical School, Department of Psychiatry, Eginition Hospital, 72-74 Vas Sophias Av., Athens 115 28, Greece.

to suicidal behaviour (death and suicide symptoms) from the largest multicentric study in primary healthcare settings of 15 research centres in 14 countries. The study offers the opportunity to estimate the prevalence rates of suicidal symptoms in primary care settings and pinpoint differences across cultures.

Methods

The World Health Organization Collaborative Study on Psychological Problems in General Health Care provides cross-national data on the frequency, correlates, management and outcomes of psychological disorders common among primary care patients. The objectives of this study are:

1. To understand the frequency, comorbidity, and symptom profiles of well-defined psychological disorders, subthreshold disorders and symptoms.
2. To understand how a research diagnosis of psychological disorder relates to the primary care clinician's diagnosis and to functional disability.
3. To develop longitudinal information on the management and outcomes of psychological illness among primary care patients.
4. To understand similarities and differences in psychological illness, its management and outcomes across widely varying cultural settings.

The study took the form of longitudinal morbidity surveys of primary care patients that were undertaken in 15 different centres worldwide. The 15 centres are in alphabetical order: Ankara (Turkey), Athens (Greece), Bangalore (India), Berlin (Germany), Groningen (The Netherlands), Ibadan (Nigeria), Mainz (Germany), Manchester (UK), Nagasaki (Japan), Paris (France), Rio de Janeiro (Brazil), Santiago (Chile), Seattle (USA), Shanghai (China) and Verona (Italy). All questions of the study instruments were translated and backtranslated and reliability was tested at each centre. Across all 15 centres, 25,916 general healthcare patients were screened by use of the GHQ questionnaire (12-item version) [13]. A stratified second-stage sample according to the CHQ-12 scores of 5,438 patients completed a comprehensive baseline interview. A subsample of 3,063 patients was assessed 3 months later, while about 2,703 completed the 12-month follow-up. A multitrait, multimethod assessment strategy was used, so that key study variables were assessed by multiple methods including structured assessment, self-rating and, when possible, physician rating. A primary care version of the CIDI [14] was administered along with the GHQ-28 [13] and questions about pathways to care. Disability was assessed by the work role section of the Groningen Social Disability Schedule [15] and by a brief self-report disability questionnaire (BDQ) with items taken from the MOS short form [16]. The primary care physician completed a brief form rating the severity of physical and of psychological illness. For patients with recognised psychological illness, the physician recorded how the patient was managed. At 3-month follow-up, the GHQ-28, self-report disability, self-related health status, use of health care and use of medications were assessed. At the 1-year follow-up, the baseline assessment was readministered. A detailed description of the methodology of the study is included in the published monograph of the study [17].

As regards symptoms related to death and suicide, the following four items from the CIDI interview, were asked:
— thoughts of death,
— wishes of death,
— suicidal thoughts, and
— suicidal attempts.
To be rated as present, the first two symptoms should have occurred for a period lasting at least 2 weeks.

Descriptive analyses were employed for differences between groups of prevalence rates and frequencies. Prevalence rates are based on weighted data, according to the initial sampling frame.

Results

Table 1 shows the lifetime and past-month prevalence rates of thoughts of death in each sex in all 15 centres of the study. As seen in all of these centres, this symptom is much more common among females as compared to males (lifetime rates for males 25.5 vs. 33.5% for females), although this difference varies, from more than double in Verona to minimal in Groningen, Seattle and Ankara. In two of the centres (Santiago and Seattle), lifetime rates of this symptom are well above 50%. Past-month rates are higher in females than males (15.3 vs. 9.6%). Certain centres reported very low lifetime rates in both sexes, compared to the rest (Bangalore, Ibadan, Nagasaki and Shanghai). In Ankara, Athens and Manchester, lifetime rates are rather low for both sexes, not exceeding 33%. Finally, the two German centres (Berlin and Mainz) and Groningen reported average lifetime rates of the symptom. As regards past-month rates, the highest rates were observed in Santiago for both sexes (17.7 vs. 37.6%, respectively) and the lowest in Nagasaki (3.7 and 2.9%, respectively) and in Verona in males (1.1%). As regards differences between sexes in individual centres, statistically significant differences were found in Berlin, Nagasaki, Rio de Janeiro, Verona and Santiago (rates in females being higher than males).

In Table 2, the lifetime and past-month rates of wishes of death by sex are reported. In all centres, this symptom is reported, for both sexes, less frequently than the previous one, in all cases prevalence not exceeding 50%. Lifetime rates were on average 8.2% in males and 15.9% in females and past-month rates were 2.8 and 5.4%, respectively. In all but one (Manchester) centres of the study, lifetime rates were much higher among females, as compared to males. The highest lifetime rates for both sexes were reported in the centres of Santiago and Paris, while lifetime rates for females were quite high in Rio de Janeiro and Athens. Very low lifetime rates were reported for both sexes in Ibadan, Nagasaki and Shanghai. In eight centres (Athens, Bangalore, Mainz, Nagasaki, Rio de Janeiro, Santiago, Seattle and Shanghai,), lifetime rates were statistically significantly higher in females as compared to males.

Table 1. Prevalence (%) of thoughts of death in the centres of the study.

	ANK	ATH	BAN	BER	GRO	IBA	MAI	MAN	NAG	PAR	RIO	SAN	SEA	SHA	VER	ALL
Males																
In past only	6.7	14.9	3.5	24.2	22.6	1.4	26.7	18.2	1.8	21.5	6.5	39.2	41.8	5.7	13.8	15.9
In past month	19.4	4.5	5.6	6.8	12.4	9.5	11.0	9.1	3.7	15.0	13.9	17.7	13.9	2.8	1.1	9.6
Females																
In past only	3.0	15.6	4.5	28.5	22.8	3.6	29.8	12.9	8.7	25.7	21.6	24.2	46.6	7.2	21.0	18.2
In past month	24.3	15.5	10.4	17.0	14.9	8.2	17.5	13.9	2.9	20.4	25.8	37.6	8.4	4.4	11.1	15.3

Statistically significant differences:
Between centres: Males: $\chi^2 = 307.2$ (df = 28), p<0.000; Females: $\chi^2 = 572.3$, p<0.000.
Males vs. females: $\chi^2 = 47.8$ (df = 2), p<0.000.
Males vs. females by centre: BER: $\chi^2 = 11.7$ (df = 2), p<0.005; NAG: $\chi^2 = 7.8$ (df = 2), p<0.05; RIO: $\chi^2 = 24.6$ (df = 2), p<0.000; SAN: $\chi^2 = 11.7$, p<0.005; VER: $\chi^2 = 12.1$ (df = 2), p<0.005.

Table 2. Prevalence (%) of wishes of death in the centres of the study.

	ANK	ATH	BAN	BER	GRO	IBA	MAI	MAN	NAG	PAR	RIO	SAN	SEA	SHA	VER	ALL
Males																
In past only	5.3	3.0	2.5	11.8	8.8	1.4	2.9	4.5	0.6	11.6	1.9	9.0	8.2	0.5	8.5	5.4
In past month	5.3	1.5	5.6	1.2	2.9	1.4	2.3	6.0	0.0	1.4	4.6	7.7	1.6	0.5	0.0	2.8
Females																
In past only	4.9	20.3	5.1	13.2	13.3	1.5	10.5	5.1	4.6	19.6	13.1	21.2	20.7	3.6	9.3	10.5
In past month	8.0	3.9	11.2	1.3	2.5	2.0	4.4	4.1	0.6	5.3	11.3	21.2	1.6	1.4	4.9	5.4

Statistically significant differences:
Between centres: Males: $\chi^2 = 106.7$ (df = 28), p<0.0000; Females: $\chi^2 = 336.6$ (df = 28), p<0.000.
Males vs. females: $\chi^2 = 69.1$ (df = 2), p<0.000. Past month – $\chi^2 = 3.9$, p<0.05.
Males vs. females by centre: ATH: $\chi^2 = 12.1$ (df = 2), p<0.005; BAN: $\chi^2 = 6.1$ (df = 2), p<0.005. MAI: $\chi^2 = 10.1$ (df = 2), p<0.05. NAG: $\chi^2 = 6.2$ (df = 2), p<0.05; PAR: $\chi^2 = 10.6$ (df = 2), p = 0.005; RIO: $\chi^2 = 16.7$ (df = 2), p<0.000; SAN: $\chi^2 = 16.3$ (df = 2), p<0.000; SEA: $\chi^2 = 9.3$ (df = 2), p = 0.01; SHA: $\chi^2 = 6.6$ (df = 2), p<0.05.

Table 3 shows the lifetime and past-month prevalence rates for each sex of suicidal thoughts. Lifetime rates were on average 13.7% for males and 18.0% for females and past-month rates were 2.5 and 2.9%, respectively. In most centres lifetime rates were higher in females in comparison to males, although, in many instances, these differences were minimal. In Ankara, Santiago and Seattle lifetime rates were higher in males. Lifetime rates above 25% for both sexes, were reported in Santiago, Seattle and Berlin, while in Mainz and Paris rates exceeded 25% in females only. Very low rates for both sexes were reported in Ibadan, Ankara, Bangalore, Nagasaki and Verona. As regards differences between sexes in past-month rates, the highest rates were found in Groningen in males and Bangalore, Santiago and Rio de Janeiro in females. Statistically significant differences between males and females were found in Athens, Groningen, Mainz, Rio de Janeiro, Santiago and Shanghai.

In Table 4 the lifetime and past-month prevalence rates of attempted suicide are reported. In most centres, lifetime rates were much higher in females as compared to males. Lifetime rates ranged from 4.6% in males and 5.8% in females and past-month rates 0.4% in both sexes. In Ankara and Santiago lifetime rates of males were found to be higher than females. High lifetime rates (above 10%) in both sexes were reported in Santiago, while lifetime rates were particularly high for women in Paris and Mainz. Low lifetime rates, below 5%, were reported for both sexes in Ibadan, Groningen, Shanghai and Verona for males only in Athens, Bangalore, Mainz, Rio de Janeiro and Seattle, and for females only in Ankara. The highest past-month rates of attempted suicide, were found for males in Ankara and for females in Bangalore. Statistically significant differences between sexes were found only in Athens, Santiago and Seattle.

As regards the distribution of these symptoms in different age groups, these are included in Table 5, for all centres of the study taken together. As seen, regarding thoughts of death, the lifetime and postmonth rates of the middle and older age groups were higher than in the youngest group. The lifetime rates of wishes of death were higher in the two oldest groups, as were also the past-month rates of this symptom. These differences were not statistically significant. Suicidal thoughts were significantly less common in the older age group, while not statistically significant differences between age groups were found for attempted suicide. Further analyses, not included here, show that thoughts of death and wishes of death, are significantly more common in the middle age group in males and the oldest age group in females, while suicidal thoughts in males are significantly more common in the middle age group as compared to the other two and attempted suicide in the two oldest age groups.

Tables 6−9 show the frequencies of the four symptoms in patients with different diagnostic status during the month prior to the interview. As seen here, all these symptoms are more common in patients with an ICD-10 diagnosis of a mental disorder or alcohol-related problems, but they are also met in patients with subthreshold disorders, or with only a few psychiatric symptoms. They are also found, although less commonly, in patients without other psychiatric symptoms.

Table 3. Prevalence (%) of suicidal thoughts in the centres of the study.

	ANK	ATH	BAN	BER	GRO	IBA	MAI	MAN	NAG	PAR	RIO	SAN	SEA	SHA	VER	ALL
Males																
In past only	6.0	4.3	3.5	25.5	10.9	1.4	11.0	7.5	1.8	17.3	1.9	41.0	38.2	1.4	5.3	11.2
In past month	3.0	1.4	3.5	3.1	8.0	1.4	1.7	4.7	0.6	1.9	2.8	2.6	1.6	0.5	1.1	2.5
Females																
In past only	4.9	21.1	4.5	30.8	17.2	1.0	23.7	7.1	10.4	24.7	15.1	22.8	34.0	6.9	8.6	15.1
In past month	2.6	2.3	8.0	1.7	1.5	0.5	3.9	3.0	0.6	4.2	6.0	6.7	1.6	0.8	1.2	2.9

Statistically significant differences:
Between centres: Males: $\chi^2 = 306.2$ (df = 28), p < 0.000; Females: $\chi^2 = 326.2$ (df = 28), p < 0.000.
Males vs. females: $\chi^2 = 18.2$ (df = 2), p < 0.000.
Males vs. females by centre: ATH: $\chi^2 = 10.2$ (df = 2), p < 0.01; GRO: $\chi^2 = 10.7$ (df = 2), p < 0.005; MAI: $\chi^2 = 12.9$ (df = 2), p < 0.005; NAG: $\chi^2 = 10.6$ (df = 2), p = 0.005; RIO: $\chi^2 = 16.2$ (df = 2), p < 0.000; SAN: $\chi^2 = 10.0$ (df = 2), p = 0.01; SHA: $\chi^2 = 9.0$ (df = 2), p < 0.05.

Table 4. Prevalence (%) of attempted suicide in the centres of the study.

	ANK	ATH	BAN	BER	GRO	IBA	MAI	MAN	NAG	PAR	RIO	SAN	SEA	SHA	VER	ALL
Males																
In past only	3.7	1.5	1.5	6.8	3.6	1.4	4.0	4.5	1.2	6.0	2.8	34.6	1.6	0.5	1.1	4.2
In past month	3.0	0.0	1.0	0.6	0.0	0.0	0.0	0.8	0.0	0.0	0.0	1.3	0.0	0.0	0.0	0.4
Females																
In past only	2.2	8.6	2.5	6.4	3.9	0.5	9.6	6.4	2.3	11.6	5.6	15.0	8.4	0.3	1.9	5.4
In past month	0.4	0.0	3.5	0.0	0.0	0.0	0.4	0.7	0.0	0.5	0.0	1.6	0.0	0.0	0.0	0.4

Statistically significant differences:
Between centres: Males: $\chi^2 = 233.4$ (df = 28), p < 0.000; Females: $\chi^2 = 165.7$ (df = 28), p < 0.000.
Males vs. females by centre: ATH: $\chi^2 = 3.9$ (df = 1), p < 0.05; SAN: $\chi^2 = 13.0$ (df = 2), p = 0.001; SEA: $\chi^2 = 6.4$ (df = 1), p < 0.001.

Table 5. Age-specific prevalence rates (%) of the death and suicidal symptoms.

Symptom	Age		
	18—29 years	30—44 years	45—65 years
Thoughts of death[a]			
In past only	15.6	19.8	16.4
In past month	11.3	13.4	14.2
Wishes of death[b]			
In past only	7.4	9.1	8.8
In past month	4.0	4.5	4.7
Suicidal thoughts[c]			
In past only	14.1	14.7	12.5
In past month	2.8	3.4	2.2
Attempted suicide[d]			
In past only	5.1	5.1	4.8
In past month	0.7	0.5	0.2

[a]$\chi^2 = 20.3$ (df = 4), $p < 0.000$; [b]$\chi^2 = 4.5$ (df = 4), ns; [c]$\chi^2 = 10.2$ (df = 4), $p < 0.05$; [d]$\chi^2 = 5.8$ (df = 4), ns.

The commonest symptom is thoughts of death, followed by wishes of death, suicidal thoughts and attempted suicide.

In Table 10, the frequencies of all four symptoms in the five more common psychiatric diagnoses found in the study are reported. As seen, in all these diagnoses, most of these symptoms are much more frequently found in patients suffering from these disorders. As regards the most serious of these symptoms, the lifetime rates of suicidal thoughts range between 38 and 60% in patients with these disorders, past-month prevalence rates ranging between 12.4 and 23.3%. Lifetime rates of attempted suicide range between 16 and 30%, with past-month rates ranging between 1.7 and 2.7%.

Table 11 reports the relationships between these symptoms and ratings indicating disability and severity of the disorder (Groningen Social Disability Schedule, Brief Disability Questionnaire, number of depressive symptoms) in patients found to suffer from depressive disorder or dysthymia. As seen here, with the exception of ratings of the BDQ in attempted suicide, all these relationships are statistically significant indicating a higher degree of disability or severity of the psychiatric disorder in patients reporting these symptoms, especially during past month.

Table 6. Prevalence (%) of thoughts of death by current diagnostic status (ICD-10).

	Well	Few symptoms	Subthreshold	Alcohol only	ICD-10 disorder	Total sample
In past only	12.8	19.6	16.6	29.4	16.8	17.2
In past month	0.4	9.9	24.7	11.2	43.8	21.9

$\chi^2 = 1096.5$ (df = 8), $p < 0.000$.

Table 7. Prevalence (%) of wishes of death by current diagnostic status (ICD-10).

	Well	Few symptoms	Subthreshold	Alcohol only	ICD-10 disorder	Total sample
In past only	3.1	8.8	14.1	15.5	16.3	11.9
In past month	0.1	1.2	7.8	3.2	21.2	9.0

$\chi^2 = 188.2$ (df = 8), p < 0.0000.

Discussion

The findings reported in this article, show that death symptoms are quite common among patients visiting the primary care services. They are found not only in patients suffering from mental disorders, but also (although less frequently), in patients having subthreshold disorders or only a few psychiatric symptoms. Suicidal symptoms, especially current symptoms, occur less frequently in primary care patients, usually in patients suffering from psychiatric disorders, mainly depression. However, their lifetime occurrence is not so infrequent, taking into account that suicidal thoughts were found in 13.7% of male and 18% of female patients and that a lifetime history of attempted suicide was found in 4.6% of male and 5.8% of female patients.

These findings are in accordance with those of other epidemiological studies in primary care [1—3]. These studies have shown high rates of these symptoms in patients of primary care services, usually in patients suffering from mental disorders.

Differences between sexes in this study are not so clear-cut, although in most cases females had higher rates of these symptoms. Variations between centres in this respect occurred, in some cases males having higher rates of these symptoms than females. These findings may reflect cultural differences. In a previous study, Williams and Skuse [18] found no relationship between sex and these symptoms.

As regards prevalence rates of these four symptoms in the different centres of the study, it must be pointed out that they do not in all cases directly reflect the rates of psychiatric disorders or depression of a particular centre. Ankara, where very high past month rates of thoughts of death and attempted suicide (the latter one only in males) were found, had average rates of psychiatric disorders and

Table 8. Prevalence (%) of suicidal thoughts by current diagnostic status (ICD-10).

	Well	Few symptoms	Subthreshold	Alcohol only	ICD-10 disorder	Total sample
In past only	7.1	12.7	19.3	39.6	24.4	17.2
In past month	0.1	0.9	4.3	3.7	13.3	9.7

$\chi^2 = 598.2$ (df = 8), p < 0.000.

Table 9. Prevalence (%) of attempted suicide by current diagnostic status (ICD-10).

	Well	Few symptoms	Subthreshold	Alcohol only	ICD-10 disorder	Total sample
In past only	1.4	3.5	8.2	9.1	14.5	7.8
In past month	0.0	0.0	0.4	1.1	1.9	0.8

$\chi^2 = 284.0$ (df = 8), $p < 0.000$.

Table 10. Prevalence (%) of death and suicidal symptoms in different psychiatric disorders.

	Depression	Dysthymia	GAD	Agoraphobia	Panic
Thoughts of death					
In past only	13.8	9.9	17.4	18.9	22.4
In past month	52.8	44.8	45.8	59.7	47.4
Wishes of death					
In past only	15.6	14.9	18.1	18.9	21.6
In past month	27.3	28.4	21.9	34.6	31.0
Suicidal thoughts					
In past only	24.1	22.0	25.4	27.0	29.3
In past month	17.4	18.8	12.4	20.8	23.3
Attempted suicide					
In past only	16.1	14.3	14.4	20.8	28.4
In past month	2.5	2.7	1.9	2.5	1.7

Statistically significant differences (vs. primary care patients without the disorder):

Thoughts of death
Depression: $\chi^2 = 849.3$ (df = 2), $p < 0.000$; Dysthymia: $\chi^2 = 76.2$ (df = 2), $p < 0.000$; GAD: $\chi^2 = 293.7$ (df = 2), $p < 0.000$; Agoraphobia: $\chi^2 = 157.7$ (df = 2), $p < 0.000$; Panic disorder: $\chi^2 = 56.5$ (df = 2), $p < 0.000$.

Wishes of death
Depression: $\chi^2 = 683.3$ (df = 2), $p < 0.000$; Dysthymia: $\chi^2 = 122.5$ (df = 2), $p < 0.000$; GAD: $\chi^2 = 228.1$ (df = 2), $p < 0.000$; Agoraphobia: $\chi^2 = 165.3$ (df = 2), $p < 0.000$; Panic disorder: $\chi^2 = 92.6$ (df = 2), $p < 0.000$.

Suicidal thoughts
Depression: $\chi^2 = 475.2$ (df = 2), $p < 0.000$; Dysthymia: $\chi^2 = 88.3$ (df = 2), $p < 0.000$; GAD: $\chi^2 = 119.9$ (df = 2), $p < 0.000$; Agoraphobia: $\chi^2 = 97.6$ (df = 2), $p < 0.000$; Panic disorder: $\chi^2 = 89.9$ (df = 2), $p < 0.000$.

Attempted suicide
Depression: $\chi^2 = 210.9$ (df = 2), $p < 0.000$; Dysthymia: $\chi^2 = 27.3$ (df = 2), $p < 0.000$; GAD: $\chi^2 = 65.7$ (df = 2), $p < 0.000$; Agoraphobia: $\chi^2 = 50.0$ (df = 2), $p < 0.000$; Panic disorder: $\chi^2 = 75.0$ (df = 2), $p < 0.000$.

Table 11. One-way ANOVA between ratings in death and suicidal symptoms and disability and severity ratings in depressed and dysthymic patients (n = 1,287).

	GSDS		BDQ		No. of depressive symptoms	
	x	f	x	f	x	f
Thoughts of death						
Never	1.36 (0.88)	9.94[a]	1.37 (1.11)	17.16[a]	6.28 (3.58)	170.28[a]
In past only	1.46 (0.91)		1.40 (1.09)		7.14 (3.76)	
In past month	1.60 (0.89)		1.73 (1.05)		10.56 (4.25)	
Wishes of death						
Never	1.41 (0.90)	15.93[a]	1.43 (1.07)	17.64[a]	7.01 (3.61)	220.36[a]
In past only	1.43 (0.96)		1.56 (1.10)		8.04 (3.85)	
In past month	1.73 (0.82)		1.84 (1.08)		12.24 (4.30)	
Suicidal thoughts						
Never	1.39 (0.89)	22.20[a]	1.49 (1.08)	6.92[b]	7.46 (3.96)	126.38[a]
In past only	1.52 (0.91)		1.56 (1.10)		8.58 (4.13)	
In past month	1.84 (0.81)		1.80 (1.10)		12.39 (4.36)	
Attempted suicide						
Never	1.45 (0.90)	8.64[a]	1.53 (1.09)	2.42[b]	8.09 (4.22)	45.44[a]
In past only	1.67 (0.89)		1.63 (1.12)		10.27 (4.57)	
In past month	1.91 (0.72)		1.91 (1.01)		13.70 (5.34)	

Note: standard deviations are given in parentheses. [a]$p < 0.0000$; [b]ns ($p = 0.09$).

depression [19]. The same was observed in Seattle [20], but only for males. In Groningen [21], despite the high rates of depression, the past month rates of wishes of death were average. These findings pinpoint cross-cultural differences in rates and reporting of these symptoms.

Our finding that these symptoms occurred quite frequently not only in patients with clear-cut psychiatric disorders, but also in patients with a few psychological symptoms or subthreshold disorders, bears special attention. Other reports from the same study [22–24] have reported high rates of suicidal symptoms among patients with recurrent brief depressive disorder, which belongs to the group of subthreshold disorders.

These symptoms, as expected, occurred more frequently among patients found to suffer from psychiatric disorders, especially depression, dysthymia, and anxiety disorders. The importance of identifying them in primary care patients suffering from these disorders becomes evident by the fact that all of them were found to be related to disability and severity of the disorder. However, data not reported here have shown that the occurrence of these symptoms did not improve the recognition rate of psychiatric disorders by the primary care physicians. Arensman et al. [25] showed that 28% of suicide attempts in The Netherlands were reported exclusively by general practitioners, who are important agents for the early detection of suicidal behaviour, since, as research has shown [26], patients who commit suicide increase their attendance rates in the period before suicide.

The data reported in this paper, are only descriptive and preliminary. More detailed analyses are planned, in order to construct models which take into account different variables (e.g., sociodemographic and clinical) in order to explain these rates and differences found.

Acknowledgements

This paper is based on the data and experience obtained during the participation of the authors in the WHO Project on Psychological Problems in General Health Care, and funded by the World Health Organization and the participating field research centres. The collaborating investigators in this study have been: at Headquarters in WHO, Geneva — Dr N. Sartorius and Dr T.B. Ustun. In the field research centres in: Ankara — Dr O. Ozturk and Dr M. Rezaki; Athens — Dr C. Stefanis and Dr V. Mavreas; Bangalore — Dr S.M. Channabasavanna and Dr T.G. Sriram; Berlin — Dr H. Helmchen and Dr M. Linden; Groningen — Dr W. van den Brink and Dr B. Tiemens; Ibadan — Dr M. Olatawura and Dr O. Gureje; Mainz — Dr O. Benkert and Dr W. Maier; Manchester — Dr D. Goldberg and Dr R. Gater; Nagasaki — Dr Y. Nakane and Dr S. Michitsuji; Paris — Dr Y. Lecrubier and Dr P. Boyer; Rio de Janeiro — Dr J.A. Costa e Silva and Dr L. Villano; Santiago de Chile — Dr R. Florenzano and Dr J. Achene; Seattle — Dr M. von Korff and Dr G. Simon; Shanghai — Dr Yan He-Qin and Dr Xaio Shi Fu; and Verona — Dr M. Tansella and Dr C. Bellantuono.

References

1. Olfson M, Weissman NM, Leon AC, Sheehan DV, Farber L. Suicidal ideation in primary care. J Gen Int Med 1996;11:447—453.
2. Lish JD, Zimmerman M, Farber NJ, Lush DT, Kuzma MA, Plescia G. Suicide screening in a primary care setting at a Veterans Affairs medical center. Psychosomatics 1996;37:413—424.
3. Diekstra RFW. The epidemiology of suicide and parasuicide. Arch Suicide Res 1996;2:1—29.
4. Shepherd M, Cooper B, Brown AC, Kalton G. Psychiatric illness in general practice. Oxford: Oxford University Press, 1966.
5. Goldberg D, Clifford K, Thompson L. Psychiatric morbidity in general practice and the community. Psychol Med 1976;6:665—669.
6. Mari JJ, Williams P. A validity study of a psychiatric screening questionnaire (SRQ-2) in primary care in the city of Sao Paulo. Psychol Med 1986;16:23—26.
7. Bellantuono C, Williams P, Tansella T. Psychiatric morbidity in general practice. In: Tansella M (ed) Psychological Medicine, Monograph No. 19, 1991.
8. Diekstra RFW. Epidemiologie du suicide. Encephale 1996;22(4):15—18.
9. Lin EHB, Von Korff M, Wagner EH. Identifying suicide potential in primary care. J Gen Int Med 1989;4:1—6.
10. Roberts A. Defeating depression: where do we stand? J R Soc Health 1996;116:190—294.
11. La Vechia C, Luchini F, Levi F. Worldwide trends in suicide mortality, 1955—1989. Acta Psychiatr Scand 1994;90:53—64.
12. Durkheim E. Suicide. London: Routledge and Kegan Paul, 1952 (original in French, 1897).
13. Goldberg D, Williams P. A users guide to the General Health Questionnaire. Windsor: NFER-NELSON, 1988.

22

14. Robins LN, Wing JK, Wittchen HU, Helzer JE, Babor TF, Burke JD, Farmer A, Jablenski A, Pickens R, Regier DA, Sartorius N, Towle LH. The Composite International Diagnostic Interview (CIDI). Arch Gen Psychiatr 1988;45:1069–1077.
15. Wiersma D, Jong A, Kraaijkamp H, Ormel J. GSDS-II: The Groningen Social Disabilities Schedule, 2nd edn. Groningen: University of Groningen.
16. Stewart AL, Hays RD, Ware JEJ. The MOS short-form general health survey: reliability and validity in the general population. Med Care 1988;26:724–735.
17. Von Korff M, Ustun TB. Methods of the WHO collaborative study on "Psychological Problems in General Health Care". In: Ustun TB, Sartorius N (eds) Mental Illness in General Health Care. An International Study. Chichester: Wiley, 1995;19–38.
18. Williams P, Skuse D. Depressive thoughts in general practice attenders. Psychol Med 1988;18: 469–475.
19. Yan HW, Xiao SF, Lu YF. Results from the Shanghai centre. In: Ustun TB, Sartorius N (eds) Mental Illness in General Health Care. An International Study. Chichester: Wiley, 1995; 285–300.
20. Picinelli M, Pini S, Bonizzatto P, Paltrinieri E, Saltini A, Scantaburlo L, Bellantuono C, Tansella M. Results from the Verona centre. In: Ustun TB, Sartorius N (eds) Mental Illness in General Health Care. An International Study. Chichester: Willey, 1995;301–321.
21. Simon G, von Korff M. Results from the Seattle centre. In: Ustun TB, Sartorius N (eds) Mental Illness in General Health Care. An International Study. Chichester: Wiley, 1995;265–284.
22. Maier H, Herr R, Ganshike M, Lichtermann D, Houshangpour K, Benkert O. Recurrent brief depression in general practice. Clinical features, comorbidity with other disorders, and need for treatment. Eur Arch Psychiatr Clin Neurosci 1994;244:196–204.
23. Weiller E, Lecrubier Y, Maier W, Ustun TB. The relevance of recurrent brief depression in primary care. A report from the WHO project on psychological problems in general health care conducted in 14 countries. Eur Arch Psychiatr Clin Neurosci 1994;244:182–189.
24. Weiller E, Boyer P, Lepine JP, Lecrubier Y. Prevalence of recurrent brief depression in primary care. Eur Arch Psychiatr Clin Neurosci 1994;244:174–181.
25. Arensman E, Kerkhof AJFM, Hengeveld NW, Mulder JD. Medically treated suicide attempts: A four year monitoring study of the epidemiology in The Netherlands. J Epidemiol Community Health 1995;49:285–289.
26. Power K, Davies C, Swanson V, Gordon D, Carter H. Case-control study of GP attendance rates by suicide cases with or without a psychiatric history. Br J Gen Pract 1997;47:211–215.

1997 Elsevier Science B.V.
Suicide: Biopsychosocial Approaches.
A.J. Botsis, C.R. Soldatos and C.N. Stefanis, editors.

Suicide in the United States military*

Emmanuel G. Cassimatis[1] and Joseph M. Rothberg[1,2]

[1]*Department of Psychiatry, F. Edward Hébert School of Medicine, Uniformed Services University of the Health Sciences, Bethesda, Maryland; and* [2]*Department of Military Psychiatry, Walter Reed Army Institute of Research, Washington, D.C., USA*

Abstract. The authors provide a historical overview of suicide rates within the US military. They report that the US military crude suicide rate (number of suicides divided by the population number) has been stable during the last 15 years at approximately 12 per 100,000. This rate is slightly lower than the crude suicide rate in the USA during the same time period, which has also been stable at approximately 12.25 per 100,000. They compare these data to available international data, and discuss known risk factors and demographics. They then focus on standardized suicide rates (adjusted for age and sex) and report that for the segment of society which provides the predominant source of soldiers (young males), the suicide rate within the military has, in recent years, been significantly lower than in the comparable civilian population.

They speculate that the lower suicide rate may in part be due to the US military's fitness screening enlistment procedures; but that it may also reflect community values and support systems unique to the military community, as illustrated by the US Army's suicide prevention program.

Keywords: army, prevention, rate, standardized.

Introduction

The crude suicide rate (number of suicides divided by the population number) in the USA during the last 15 years has been stable at approximately 12.25 per 100,000. During the same period, the crude suicide rate for the US military has also been stable and slightly lower than the civilian rate at approximately 12 per 100,000. If, however, we focus on the segment of society which provides the predominant source of soldiers (young males), we find that the suicide rate within the military has, in recent years, been significantly lower than in the comparable civilian population. This may in part be due to the US military's fitness screening enlistment procedures; but may also reflect community values and support systems unique to the military community.

In this chapter, we provide a historical overview of suicide rates within the US military, compare these data to available international data and discuss known

---

Address for correspondence: Emmanuel G. Cassimatis MD, COL, MC, USA, Associate Dean for Clinical Affairs, Room A-1008, USUHS-SOM, 4301 Jones Bridge Road, Bethesda, MD 20814-4799, USA.

*The opinions and assertions continued herein are the private views of the authors and are not to be construed as official or representative of the views of the Department of Defense or the Department of the Army.

risk factors and demographics. We then focus on standardized suicide rates (adjusted for age and sex) and discuss various parameters, illustrated by the US Army's Suicide Prevention Program, which we feel may be contributing to the significantly lower rate for young individuals in the military.

Historical overview

The earliest figure available for suicide rates within the US military was provided by Durkheim who reported a rate of 68 per 100,000 for the US Army during the period from 1870 to 1884 [1]. The US Army suicide rate remained high during the first half of the century (20—50 per 100,000) with the exception of the years of the first and second World Wars when the suicide rate dropped to below 15 per 100,000 or less. Throughout the first half of the century, suicides as a cause of death within the US Army were second only to accidents. As noted by Oesterlen, over 100 years ago [2], the military suicide rate decreases during war. In the US Army, the rate decreased significantly during both World Wars. Although the suicide rate dropped somewhat during the Korean War, the effect, perhaps given the already low "baseline", was less dramatic than during the World Wars. As there are no data available for the 1958 through 1975 time frame, it is not possible to comment on the impact of the Vietnam War on the army suicide rate [3].

A comparison of US Army suicide rates with suicide rates in the armies of four other countries is provided in Fig. 1.

As can be seen from the graph, we found data for Italy [4], France [5], Finland [6] and Germany [7] only for a limited, and varying, number of years and,

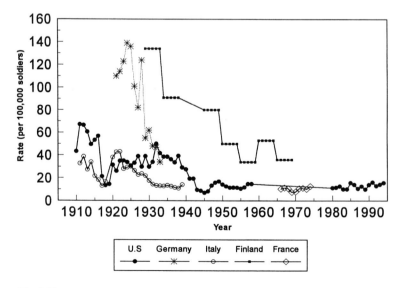

Fig. 1. For source, see text.

accordingly, we are unable to draw any firm conclusions from the comparison. It would appear, however, that suicide rates in the US Army during the 20th century fall somewhere in the middle range. Army suicide rates are somewhat lower in France and Italy and higher in Finland and Germany, perhaps corresponding to similar differences in the overall suicide rate in these countries.

Suicide rates for the USA, the US Department of Defense (DoD) and each of the services, from 1980 to 1994, are displayed in Table 1.

As can be seen from both Table 1 and Fig. 1, the overall DoD suicide rate (per 100,000) has stayed below 15 during the second half of the 20th century and, more significantly, has remained under 12.5 since 1980. Although no significant differences are apparent between the services, the rate for the Army and Marines seems to be, on average, slightly higher than that for the Air Force and the Navy.

Risk factors and demographics

Rank appears to be a significant factor for suicide in the military, although the risk ratio of officers to enlisted appears to have been reversed during the last 25 years. The suicide rate had been significantly higher for officers than for enlisted from 1865 [8] through the first half of the 20th century. Since 1975, the suicide rate, although significantly lower overall, is consistently higher for enlisted members of the military [9,10]. Seniority within the officer or enlisted ranks also appears to be a factor, suicide being very rare among the higher ranks (above E-7 and above O-4) [11]. Age also appears to be a significant factor; the average

Table 1. US active duty worldwide and US civilian suicide death rates.

	US[a]	DoD[b]	Army[c]	Air force[c]	Navy[c]	Marine[c]
1980	11.8	11.5	11.3	10.9	11.6	15.1
1981	12.0	11.6	11.6	10.2	11.9	17.7
1982	12.2	11.5	12.7	10.5	10.4	14.8
1983	12.1	11.1	10.2	10.5	11.9	15.6
1984	12.4	10.1	10.1	8.9	10.5	12.3
1985	12.4	12.7	15.7	11.1	10.1	13.1
1986	12.9	12.1	14.1	9.6	11.7	13.7
1987	12.7	12.1	10.6	13.0	14.2	9.5
1988	12.4	13.6	12.6	16.6	12.2	12.7
1989	12.2	10.4	9.9	10.3	9.8	14.8
1990	12.4	12.2	13.9	10.5	9.4	16.8
1991	12.2	11.7	13.2	11.8	9.0	10.6
1992	11.9	12.1	13.0	10.7	10.9	10.5
1993	12.1	14.0	14.2	13.3	11.5	19.9
1994	12.0	12.7	15.7	13.4	11.3	13.7

[a]US suicide mortality rate from DHHS/CDC "WONDER" by calender year; [b]DoD suicide mortality rate from OSD/WHS/DIOR Military Casualty Tabulation by fiscal year; [c]Army, Navy, Air Force, and Marine suicide mortality rates computed from fiscal year suicide deaths and fiscal year mean "man-years" strength from OSD/WHS/DIOR.

age for completed suicides is consistently under 30, the highest frequency group being soldiers between the ages of 20 to 25 [12]. With respect to sex, it has been reported by the Centers for Disease Control that males accounted for three-quarters of all suicide deaths in the USA between 1970 and 1980. Women are said to attempt suicide much more frequently than men; but men commit suicide 3 times more often than women. Similar data have been reported within the military [13]. With respect to race, the civilian suicide rate is higher for whites than for nonwhites with a ratio of white to black male suicides being 1.6 to 1. Within the military, however, this relationship does not appear to hold. For example, an analysis of 850 US Air Force suicides that took place between 1979 and 1991 gives a ratio of white to black suicides of 8.3 to 1, a figure that is consistent with the proportion of whites to blacks in the Air Force as a whole. It thus appears that black males in the military are at significantly lower risk for suicide than black males in the US population [14].

The most common precipitant in US military suicides is difficulty in personal intimate relationships. For example, the suicide rate for separated or divorced soldiers was 7 times higher than for married soldiers according to a review of suicide rates in the US Army between 1981 and 1982 [15]. Similar findings have been reported in studies of civilian and other military service populations [16]. For example, in the Air Force study mentioned above, of those victims who were married at the time of their death, 32% were separated from their spouses and 87% were having serious marital problems. Of single suicide victims, 62% had recently terminated an intimate relationship or were having serious problems in such a relationship. According to the same study, work problems were also prevalent in about one-half of the victims, being in some cases secondary to personal problems, but in other instances adding to and compounding the severity of the home problems. Financial problems which, when present, can alert command to the individual's need for help were not a frequent suicide precipitent [17].

Prior or concomitant mental illness is a risk factor within the military as well as in the civilian population. A 24-year (1946—1969) mortality follow-up study of US Army veterans with disability separations for psychoneurosis reports a 20% excess mortality rate, although the increased death risk is attributed to alcoholism and homicide as well as suicide [18]. Another study of suicide in war veterans reports that prior psychiatric illness was associated with a 9-fold increase in the suicide rate [19]. Again, this is similar to the civilian population: One study of civilian mental patients between 1960 and 1970 reports that patients who were either hospitalized or within 1 year of discharge were at 5 times greater risk for suicide compared to the general population [20].

Approximately half the soldiers who commit suicide fail to communicate their intent. Of the 850 military suicides reviewed in the Air Force study, approximately 55% communicated no warning of their intent to commit suicide. Of the remainder, some individuals made their intent clear to their spouse or to friends, who in most instances, did not take the victim's warning seriously. In other instances, the communication of intent was vague and difficult to interpret prior to the actual suicide event [21]. In this connection, military suicide prevention programs must and do involve as one of their goals an effort to educate the chain of command, families and military communities to recognize subtle or vague suicidal threats, to take these threats seriously and to ensure appropriate referral and intervention for the at risk individuals.

The most common method for committing suicide in the military involves the use of a firearm (59% of the group of 850 Air Force suicides discussed above). In the same group, hanging accounted for 14% of the suicides and auto exhaust inhalation for 12%. Drug overdose was the method utilized in 5% of the individuals and jumping or leaping from an elevated point was utilized by 2%. Other methods such as asphyxiation, use of an automobile, cutting of ones veins or drowning accounted for 1% or less each [22].

Several authors have attempted to identify periods that represent an increased risk for suicide either during the calendar year or during an individual's military career. It has, for example, been reported that suicide rates are higher during the first few months of service and during the last few years before retirement. These are obviously periods of psychosocial transition and therefore of increased stress [23]. Similarly, one could postulate that moves would constitute transitions and, therefore, stressors, and might lead to an increased suicide rate. In a study by the second author, correlating suicides to reassignments in the US Army from 1980 to 1983, moves did not appear to have been a strong determinant of suicide. More generally, the timing of suicides and moves did not show a statistical correlation for the Army as a whole, although there appears to be a small effect for the youngest third of the Army associated with moves (accounting for 10% of the variance of the suicide rate) [24].

Indirectly standardized suicide mortality ratios

As was mentioned earlier in this chapter, suicide rates in the US military have been comparable to the civilian population for at least the last 20 years. When rates are calculated for a specific subgroup, however, breaking them down by race, sex and 5-year intervals [25], one finds that total deaths and specifically suicide deaths occur much less frequently in the military than in comparable civilian populations. In the Army, for example, both in the mid-1980s and mid-1990s, total deaths occurred at approximately one-half the rate expected from a comparable civilian population, with suicide occurring at approximately two-thirds the civilian rate. Similarly, during the same time periods, suicide in the US Air Force occurred at a rate only slightly more than one-half that of a comparable civilian population. Indirectly standardized suicide mortality ratios for the US Army are displayed in Table 2.

No data are displayed for women because the number of suicides were too small for any reliable statistical analysis. Nevertheless, it may be worth mentioning that there were three female suicides in the US Army during 1994 and the civilian standardization would also have predicted three. Although the female

Table 2. US Army indirectly standardized suicide mortality ratio and 95% confidence limits by sex and race, 1986, 1994.

	Men			Women			Total		
	White	Black	Total[a]	White	Black	Total[a]	White	Black	Total[a]
1986[b]	63	61	65	...	...	...	68	59	69
	[49−77]	[33−89]	[53−78]				[54−83]	[32−87]	[56−82]
1994[c]	61	65	64	...	...	...	62	66	65
	[44−78]	[32−97]	[55−79]				[45−80]	[34−99]	[51−80]

Ellipses indicate expected number of deaths was less than five and standardized mortality ratio was not calculated.

[a]Total includes nonwhite and nonblack; [b]Life and death in the US Army:... in corpore sano. J.M. Rothberg, P.B. Bartone, H.C. Holloway, D.H. Marlowe, JAMA 1990;264(17):2241−2244; [c]Data from DOD/WHS/DIOR and DHHS/CDC "WONDER" and the method of [1] above.

numbers are too small for any reliable conclusions to be drawn, they are consistent with calculations for other years and seem to suggest that females do not enjoy the protective effect of being in the Army or, more generally, in the military. For males, however, being in the military is clearly associated with a significant decrease in suicide risk. An explanation for this phenomenon may be that the military population does not represent a random subgroup of the larger civilian population but rather a "filtered" subgroup, consisting of individuals who have been carefully screened in accordance with preestablished criteria. For example, individuals with a psychosis, or a major depression requiring treatment with antidepressants or repeated hospitalization are deemed unfit for military service [26]. Nevertheless, community factors may also be very significant. An individual in the military benefits from a well-defined social structure which provides a variety of supports and resources including closer supervision by the chain of command, and readily available medical, mental health and spiritual systems. These community factors are highlighted in the Army Suicide Prevention Program which was initiated in 1985 and fully implemented by 1987.

The Army Suicide Prevention Program

The US Department of Defense Health Promotion Program [27], published in March 1986 with the stated purpose "to improve and maintain military readiness and the quality of life of DoD personnel and other beneficiaries", directs each service component to prepare "a plan for the implementation of a comprehensive health promotion program that includes specific objectives (planned accomplishments) with measurable action steps". It specifically requires health promotion plans and programs to address "smoking prevention and cessation, physical fitness, nutrition, stress management, alcohol and drug abuse, and early identification of hypertension" Although it does not explicitly address suicide prevention, it states that "stress management programs should aim to reduce environmental stressors and help target populations cope with stress"; tasks commanders to "develop leadership practices, work policies and procedures, and physical settings that promote productivity and health for military personnel and civilian employees"; encourages health and fitness professionals to "advise target groups and scientifically support stress management techniques"; and asks that the topic of stress management "be considered for integration into the curricula at appropriate professional military education programs" and in DoD dependents and other schools, to "familiarize students with scientifically supported concepts of stress management for day-to-day problems and life crises". The Army's health promotion program published the following year (November 1987) [28] addresses all of the DoD mandated areas but includes several additional components including weight control, spiritual fitness, oral health and suicide prevention. Paragraph 2-8 on suicide prevention states that "suicide prevention is the concern of every leader, commander, supervisor, soldier and Army civilian"; directs that a "coordinated program for suicide prevention be established at every Army installation, community and activity"; and outlines specific policies for the implementation of such a program. At a minimum, the program must involve suicide prevention education awareness training for military and civilian leaders, managers and supervisors as well as family members; and must address both suicide risk identification and procedures for crises intervention and referral. Army community services, ministry and mental health personnel are required to participate in training programs and to coordinate services in support of the suicide prevention program. Following a completed suicide, an in-depth psychological autopsy in accordance with strict protocol must be completed by the community psychiatrist or other senior mental health professional. The results from the in-depth evaluations are then made available to the Department of the Army headquarters, to the Psychiatry Consultant and to the Army Surgeon General; and to the Walter Reed Army Institute of Research for further study. More explicit guidelines on the Suicide Prevention Program are provided in Army Pamphlet 600-24, published in September 1988 [29]. Has the Army's suicide prevention program made a difference? The Army suicide rate decreased dramatically from 1985 (15.7 per 100,000) to 1989 (9.9 per 100,000) and it is tempting to attribute the change to the suicide prevention program. It is of interest, however, as shown in Table 1, that the Army suicide rate had remained largely below 12 from 1980 to 1984 and increased again after 1989 reaching a peak in 1994. One can thus hypothesize that the suicide prevention program had an impact during its early years, when command and helping professionals were highly sensitized to the program; but that, in the long run, the program has not made a significant difference. Alternatively, it may be that the program remains highly effective but that stresses associated with the Army's dramatic reduction in personnel size in recent years have significantly impacted on the suicide rate which might have been still higher were it not for the suicide prevention program.

If, however, we review the indirectly standardized suicide mortality ratios in Table 2, it becomes apparent that the standardized suicide rate in the US Army did not change from 1986 to 1994. It is, moreover, remarkable that this rate is only two-thirds of the suicide rate for comparable civilian populations. (As discussed above, this seems to reflect a difference in the male population, independently of race, and no difference in the female population.) How is this finding to be explained? It is our contention that the military community represents a unique society, within which a multiplicity of factors result in a reduced risk for suicide. Command supervision, early attention to problems (behavioral, psychological and alcohol or drug-related) as well as free and readily available medical and psychological care constitute a significant difference compared to most civilian communities. The extensive integration of chaplains into the community, the availability of community services and the frequent rapid involvement of command when family problems arise are factors that mitigate stress and probably reduce the risk of suicide. Although the military has its own unique stresses, the relative career security (albeit significantly reduced in recent years), the extensive support systems and the military's unique values (which emphasize teamwork and community involvement) probably more than counterbalance the periodic but significant additional stressors. It is our belief that the Army's unique values and support systems have been evolving steadily during the past 50 years and are reflected in the Army's dramatically lower suicide rate during this time. The suicide prevention program recognizes and harnesses many of these values, forces and support systems; and in so doing may have had an additional positive impact on the Army's suicide rate, at least during the first few years of its implementation.

Conclusion

In summary, suicide continues to be a concern in the US military although its prevalence is significantly lower than in corresponding civilian populations. For the US Army specifically, the suicide rate declined somewhat following the institution of the suicide prevention program, but has increased slightly in recent years suggesting that community and chain of command efforts to identify and treat potential victims must continue or even increase.

References

1. Durkheim E. (trans. Spaulding JA, Simpson G.) Suicide: A study in sociology. New York: The Free Press, 1951.
2. Oesterlen, Handbook of Medical Statistics 1865;851. (Cited in Masaryk, TG. Suicide and the Meaning of Civilization (Weist WB, Batson RG (trans.)). Chicago: The University of Chicago Press, 1970 (original, Vienna, 1881).
3. Rothberg JM, Ursano RJ, Holloway HC. Suicide in the United States military. Psychiatr Ann 1987;17:545—548.
4. Pozzi E. Suicide among the military. La Critica sociologica 1971;17:58—85
5. Bazot M, Bertrand M. Suicidal conduct and statistics in a military community. Psychol Med (Paris) 1979;11:63—72.

6. Ponteva M, Kaukinen K, Loikkanen I, Lumio J. Suicides in the Finnish Defense Forces. Sotila-slaak. Aikak (Finland) 1971;46:41–55.

7. Brickenstein R. Prevention of suicide in the (German) Federal Defense Forces. Nervenarzt (West Germany) 1972;43:211–216.

8. Oesterlen, Handbook of d. Medical Statistics 1865;734. (Cited in Masaryk, TG. Suicide and the Meaning of Civilization (Weist WB, Batson RG (trans.)). Chicago: The University of Chicago Press, 1970 (original, Vienna, 1881).

9. Datel WE, Johnson AW. Suicide in United States army personnel. Mil Med 1979;144:239–244.

10. Yessler PG. Suicide in the military. In: Resnik HLP (ed) Suicidal Behaviors. Boston: Little Brown and Co., 1968;241–254.

11. McDowell CP, Rothberg JM, Lande RG. Homicide and suicide in the military. In: Jones FD, Sparacino LR, Wilcox VL, Rothberg JM (eds) Military Psychiatry: Preparing in Peace for War. Textbook of Military Medicine. Washington, D.C.: Office of the Surgeon General, U.S. Department of the Army and Borden Institute, 1994;91–113.

12. Rothberg JM, Ursano RJ, Holloway HC. Suicide in the United States military. Psychiatr Ann 1987;17:546–547.

13. McDowell CP, Rothberg JM, Lande RG. Homicide and suicide in the military. In: Jones FD, Sparacino LR, Wilcox VL, Rothberg JM (eds) Military Psychiatry: Preparing in Peace for War. Textbook of Military Medicine. Washington, D.C.: Office of the Surgeon General, U.S. Department of the Army and Borden Institute, 1994;104–105.

14. McDowell CP, Rothberg JM, Lande RG. Homicide and suicide in the military. In: Jones FD, Sparacino LR, Wilcox VL, Rothberg JM (eds) Military Psychiatry: Preparing in Peace for War. Textbook of Military Medicine. Washington, D.C.: Office of the Surgeon General, U.S. Department of the Army and Borden Institute, 1994;104.

15. Rothberg JM, Rock NL, Jones, FD. Suicide in United States army personnel, 1981–1982. Mil Med 1984;149:537–541.

16. Jacobson GF, Portuges SH. Relation of marital separation and divorce to suicide: A report. Suicide Life-Threat Behav 1973;8:217–224.

17. McDowell CP, Rothberg JM, Lande RG. Homicide and suicide in the military. In: Jones FD, Sparacino LR, Wilcox VL, Rothberg JM (eds) Military Psychiatry: Preparing in Peace for War. Textbook of Military Medicine. Washington, D.C.: Office of the Surgeon General, U.S. Department of the Army and Borden Institute, 1994;105–107.

18. Keehn RJ, Goldberg ID, Beebe GW. Twenty four year mortality follow-up of Army veterans with disability separations for psychoneurosis in 1994. Psychosom Med 1974;36:27–46.

19. Pokorny AD. Suicide in war veterans: Rates and methods. J Nerv Ment Dis 1967;144:224–229.

20. Sletten IW, Brown ML, Evenson RC, Altman, H. Suicide in mental hospital patients. Dis Nerv Sys 1972;33:328–334.

21. McDowell CP, Rothberg JM, Lande RG. Homicide and suicide in the military. In: Jones FD, Sparacino LR, Wilcox VL, Rothberg JM (eds) Military Psychiatry: Preparing in Peace for War. Textbook of Military Medicine. Washington, D.C.: Office of the Surgeon General, U.S. Department of the Army and Borden Institute, 1994;108–112.

22. McDowell CP, Rothberg JM, Lande RG. Homicide and suicide in the military. In: Jones FD, Sparacino LR, Wilcox VL, Rothberg JM (eds) Military Psychiatry: Preparing in Peace for War. Textbook of Military Medicine, table 6-16. Washington, D.C.: Office of the Surgeon General, U.S. Department of the Army and Borden Institute, 1994;105.

23. Rothberg JM, Ursano RJ, Holloway HC. Suicide in the United States military. Psychiatr Ann 1987;17:546.

24. Rothberg JM. Stress and suicide in the U.S. Army: Effect of relocation on service members mental health. Armed forces and society 1991;17:449–458.

25. Rothberg JM, Bartone PT, Holloway HC, and Marlowe DH. Life and death in the U.S. army: in corpore sano. JAMA 1990;264:2241–2244.

26. U.S. Department of Army regulation 40-501: Standards of medical fitness. Washington, D.C.,

July 1987.

27. U.S. Department of Defense directive 1010.10: Health promotion. Washington, D.C., March 1986.

28. U.S. Department of the Army regulation 600-63. Army Health Promotion, Washinton, D.C., November 1987.

29. U.S. Department of the Army pamphlet 600-24: Suicide prevention and psychological autopsy. Washington, D.C., September 1988.

Suicide in mood disorders

Erkki T. Isometsä and Jouko K. Lönnqvist

Department of Mental Health and Alcohol Research, National Public Health Institute, Helsinki, Finland

Abstract. The relationship between mood disorders and completed suicide has been investigated in numerous studies during the last few decades. About one-third of all those who have committed suicide have been found to have suffered from major depressive disorder, which is related to about 20-fold suicide mortality as compared to the general population. The prevalence of other unipolar depressive disorders among suicides has been found variable, but also these disorders are associated with markedly increased suicide mortality. Suicide risk among subjects with bipolar disorder is comparable to that of unipolar major depressive disorder, however, there are somewhat conflicting findings concerning the role of bipolar II disorder in suicide. Based on the findings of studies conducted as a part of the National Suicide Prevention Project in Finland, about one-third (31%) of all suicide victims were found to have suffered from DSM-III-R major depression, 27% from other unipolar nonorganic mood disorders (nonmajor depressions), and about 3% from bipolar disorders. For suicide prevention, the findings related to the adequacy of treatment received for depression before suicide seem a major concern. The implications of the findings for suicide prevention include the need for active recognition, treatment and follow-up of depression and suicidal ideation in all health care settings. A crucial question for suicide prevention is the ability of health care to provide effective treatment for depressed male subjects with comorbid mental and physical disorders.

Keywords: bipolar disorder, depression, mood disorders, suicide.

Introduction

In the present review we will first give a brief review of the current knowledge of the relationship between suicide and mood disorders. Secondly, we will specifically review pertinent findings from the research phase of the National Suicide Prevention Project in Finland.

Suicide mortality in mood disorders

Major depressive disorder

Three lines of evidence have established the strong association between major mood disorders and completed suicide: psychological autopsy studies, cohort studies and lifetime suicide mortality studies.

Address for correspondence: Erkki T. Isometsä MD, PhD, Chief of Research on Mood Disorders and Self-Destructive Behavior, Department of Mental Health and Alcohol Research, National Public Health Institute, Mannerheimintie 166, FIN-00300 Helsinki, Finland. Tel.: +358-0-4744-313. Fax: +358-0-4744-478. E-mail: Erkki.Isometsa@ktl.fi

Altogether, 20 psychological autopsy studies over the past 30 years have shown that 13—86% of all suicide victims have suffered from various forms of depression before suicide [1—20], the median of these estimates being 55%. However, the proportion of depression is highly dependent on differences in diagnostic methodology, particularly on whether comorbid and secondary cases, or milder depressions are included or not. About half of these depressed suicides have been found to have suffered from current unipolar major depression, and the other half mostly from milder depressive syndromes. For example, in the diagnostic study of the National Suicide Prevention Project in Finland, 66% of all suicides had suffered from depressive syndromes, including 31% with major depression [14].

A recent meta-analysis by Harris and Barraclough [21] collated data from 23 cohort studies providing estimates for suicide mortality of subjects with major depressive disorder (Table 1), and estimated standardized mortality ratio (SMR) to be about 20 [21]. There is a considerable sex difference in suicide mortality, as annual mortality figures have varied between $180—500/10^5$ among females but $400—1,100/10^5$ among males [22—25]. In studies providing sex-specific estimates for SMR, these have been 5—29 among males and 10—89 among females [23,24,26—31]; the higher risk ratios among females despite the lower overall risk are due to the lower general suicide mortality among females. Male sex has also been found to be a risk factor for suicide in controlled studies comparing depressive suicides and living depressives [32,33]. Thus, while depression in most countries is more common among females, the risk of completed suicide would seem to be higher among males. It appears that suicide risk is particularly high among depressed psychiatric inpatients recently discharged from a psychiatric hospital [34].

In their classical study Guze and Robins estimated the lifetime suicide mortality in major mood disorders to be about 15% [35]. Goodwin and Jamison [36], summarizing findings from 30 studies providing data on lifetime suicide mortality, including also the studies reported in [35], estimated it at 19%. However, the high prevalence of clinically unrecognized depression in the general population, the tendency of suicidal cases to be overrepresented in clinical populations [37], and the fact that cases with recurrent depressive episodes were probably overrepresented in many of the studies are all likely to bias these estimations and

Table 1. Suicide mortality in different diagnostic groups of mood disorders.

Subgroup	No. of studies	No. of suicides observed	No. of suicides expected	SMR	95% C.I.
Major depression	23	351	17.3	20.35	18.27—22.59
Bipolar disorder	14	93	6.18	15.05	12.25—18.44
Dysthymia	9	1436	118.5	12.12	11.50—12.77
Mood disorder NOS	12	377	23.41	16.10	14.52—17.81

Adopted from from a meta-analysis by Harris and Barraclough [21].

result in high estimates that are true only for a subgroup of patients with major mood disorders. Quite recently, Blair-West et al. [38] have suggested the true life-time suicide mortality for major depression in the general population to be about 3.5%. As already noted by Harris and Barraclough [21], there seems to be a wide variation in the suicide mortality reported from different settings. Future mortality studies should be able to illuminate the mortality differences between clinically relevant subgroups of patients in a better way, as well as treated and untreated populations.

Bipolar disorder

The issue of completed suicide in bipolar disorder is seldom investigated; most of the studies reporting suicides of bipolar cases suffer from methodological prob-lems, including selected patient groups or low numbers of suicide cases [36]. In psychological autopsy studies of unselected suicides, the prevalence of bipolar disorders has usually been found to be less than 10% [1—20], with the exception of Rihmer et al. reporting such high proportions as 46% [39] and 36% [40] of suicides with primary affective disorder in Budapest and Gotland, respectively, as having suffered from bipolar II disorder. The lifetime mortality studies collated by Guze and Robins [35] and Goodwin and Jamison [35] included both unipolar and bipolar populations. In a meta-analysis by Lester [41] comparing lifetime risk of suicide between unipolar and bipolar major affective disorders, no major differences in suicide risk were found. However, on the grounds of 14 cohort studies, Harris and Barraclough [21] estimated the standardized mortality ratio of subjects with bipolar I disorder to be 15 (Table 1). Thus, the latter meta-analy-sis would suggest the suicide risk of subjects with bipolar I disorder to be some-what lower than among unipolar subjects.

Unipolar nonmajor depressions

The suicide risk in depressions not fulfilling the criteria of major depression is a relatively neglected area of research. However, these disorders are very prevalent, and are therefore likely to burden health care institutions quite as much as more severe depressions. The psychological autopsy studies that have used DSM-III, DSM-III-R, or RDC criteria have reported 4—42% cases of depression milder than major depression among suicides [7,8,10—15,17—19]. Mild depression appears to be particularly prevalent among adolescent and young adult suicides [7,11,13,15,17] and comorbidity with other psychiatric disorders and physical ill-ness has been common among these cases. On the grounds of 12 studies, Harris and Barraclough in their meta-analysis [21] estimated the standardized mortality for mood disorders NOS to be 16.10 (95% C.I., 14.52—17.81). However, the validity of this type of risk estimates is limited by the fact that it is usually impos-sible in a cohort study to exclude the possibility that a person with a mild depres-sion would not later suffer from major depression. Similarly, while the standardized mortality ratio for dysthymia is also high, the large overlap with major depressive disorder, i.e., double depression, reduces the validity of this estimate concerning the risk for suicide in dysthymia per se.

Risk factors for suicide among subjects with mood disorders

The diagnosis of mood disorder, as such, suggests highly elevated suicide risk compared with the general population. In addition, some specific characteristics modify this basic risk.

Various clinical features of depression have been found to be associated with suicide, several with relevance to treatment. Some studies have found symptoms of insomnia, impaired memory and self-neglect to be more common, along with a greater overall severity of illness, among suicides than in living depressives [3,33,34]. A large, prospective cohort study found anhedonia, anxiety symptoms, difficulty in concentrating and alcohol abuse to be short-term predictors, while hopelessness, mood cycling and history of previous suicidal behavior were long-term predictors of completed suicide [42]. The role of hopelessness as a risk factor for suicide in depression has been confirmed in two prospective studies [43,44]. A history of previous suicide attempts has been more prevalent among suicides than living controls in severe depressions [3,32,33,45]. The specific role of psychotic symptoms in the suicide risk of such patients is controversial [46—48]. Several studies have raised the possibility that various forms of comorbidity increase the risk of suicide [17,18,42,49,50]. In particular, major depression with concurrent alcohol dependence may be related to higher suicide risk than any other comorbidity pattern [18]. Overall, while knowledge of established risk factors aids clinicians to recognize cases with particularly increased suicide risk, the single most important factor indicating high risk is still a diagnosis of mood disorder [36]. Studies that have attempted to predict suicide among affective patients on the grounds of currently known risk factors have not been successful [51,52].

The effect of treatment on suicide mortality

Previous studies that have reported treatment received before suicide by depressed subjects have generally found only a minority to have had contact with psychiatric care [3,12,39], or to have received antidepressant treatment in the period preceding suicide [3,5,39,53]. Studies of prescription databases also suggest that only a few have been prescribed antidepressants before suicide [54,55]. The efficacy of electroconvulsive therapy in major depression has been well-documented. Several studies suggest reduced suicide mortality among recipients [56]. Also, lithium treatment has been suggested as a potential method for preventing suicides in major mood disorders. Several studies suggest an effect of lithium on the number of completed suicides and suicide attempts, particularly in long-term use, during which suicide mortality of treated patients seems to approach that of the general population [57—59]. In a large prospective multicentre study the overall frequency of suicidal acts was found lower among lithium-treated than carbamazepine-treated patients [60]. These findings support the view that during an ongoing long-term lithium prophylaxis, suicide risk is reduced. However, given the problems concerning rebound episodes after discontinuation; the difficulty of distinguishing a true drug effect from selection factors related to ability and the will to comply with a long-term treatment, the true effectiveness of lithium in suicide prevention is still unclear at present.

Education of primary care doctors in the treatment of depression has been shown to be successful. After such an educational program on Gotland, reduced suicide mortality for several years was found [61]. Although it cannot be excluded that the reduction in suicide rate could have been a result of random fluctuation of the suicide level in a small population [62], the convergence of the changes in utilization of treatments and services [63] suggests that improvements in the treatment of depression were likely to have been the cause of the reduction. Very recently, pharmacoepidemiological data has been suggested to support the value of antidepressant treatment in preventing suicides [64]. Overall, the effectiveness of treatment for depression in preventing suicides is supported by suggestive and convergent evidence, but remains to be definitively proven. Given the statistical rarity of completed suicide even in the high-risk population in short-term follow-up, thus necessitating extremely large study populations in order to show a statistically significant effect, the obvious ethical limitations related to the subject, as well as the other problems involved, the task of providing definitive evidence for the ability of treatment to prevent suicides is very difficult indeed.

Findings from the research phase of the National Suicide Prevention Project in Finland

The National Suicide Prevention Project in Finland

The National Suicide Prevention Project was set up by the Finnish National Board of Health in 1986. Its explicated aim has been to reduce suicide mortality in Finland. During the research phase of the project, all suicides committed in Finland between 1 April 1987 and 31 March 1988 (n = 1,397) were carefully recorded and analyzed using the psychological autopsy method [65—68].

Data concerning victims classified as suicides in forensic examinations were collected via comprehensive interviews of the relatives and attending health care personnel, from psychiatric, medical and social agency records, police investigations and suicide notes. Details of methodology have been reported [13,14,69—71]. The mental disorders of suicide victims in Finland were examined in a diagnostic study of a nonstratified random sample of 229 (16.4%) of the total 1,397 suicides in the research period [14]. The retrospective diagnostic evaluation of the cases according to DSM-III-R criteria [72], weighing and integrating all available information, took place in two phases [14]. First, two pairs of psychiatrists independently made provisional best estimate diagnoses whose reliability was tested; second, all cases involving any diagnostic disagreement were reanalyzed with a third psychiatrist to achieve consensus for the final best estimate diagnoses. The reliability achieved ranged from moderate to excellent [14]. In the diagnostic study, 93% of the suicide victims were found to have suffered from a current DSM-III-R axis I mental disorder. Altogether, 66% had had a depressive syndrome and 43% alcohol dependence or abuse. A diagnosis of axis II personality disorder was received by 31% of the victims. A major finding in the study was that only 12% of the victims had one axis I diagnosis with no comorbidity [14].

In addition to the diagnostic study described above, some specific diagnostic subgroups, e.g., bipolar disorders, were investigated from the whole database of 1,397 suicides. The findings reviewed here come from a series of studies [70,73–80] concerning four study populations:

1. The suicide victims with major depression in the diagnostic study of the random sample (n = 71).
2. The 58 suicide victims with best estimate diagnoses of depressive disorder NOS (n = 48), adjustment disorder with depressed mood (n = 6) and dysthymia (n = 4) in the diagnostic study, i.e., the nonmajor depressive subjects.
3. The suicide victims having suffered from bipolar disorder, identified from all 1,397 suicides by first collecting suspected cases, and then using a diagnostic procedure identical to the diagnostic study (n = 31).
4. The suicide cases having received lithium treatment during the last 3 months (n = 20).

Suicide among subjects with major depression

Overall, about one-third (31%) of all suicides in the random sample representing all suicides in Finland in 1987–1988 were found to have suffered from major depression. Most of these cases (63%) were males, the mean age being 50 years. The vast majority (85%) of them were comorbid cases [14]. The form of comorbidity was found to considerably depend on sex and age, as psychoactive substance-use disorders were almost exclusively male problems, while physical illnesses were very clearly more common among the elderly. Personality disorders may be more common among younger major depressive suicides.

The vast majority had received no specific treatment for depression, and if they had, it seems usually to have been inadequate. Only one-third had received antidepressant therapy, a proportion identical to the 30% of depressives reported by Barraclough et al. [3] and Chynoweth et al. [5]; which was higher than the 11% reported by Rihmer et al. [39] but lower than the 58% in the clinical suicide population described by Modestin [54]. Also, the doses were too low in almost all cases; only 3% had received antidepressants in doses equivalent to 150 mg or more of tricyclic antidepressant (Table 2). One-fourth of the suicides had had the very minimum of psychotherapeutic contact before death, but even a mere 1

Table 2. Suicide in major depression in Finland in 1987–1988. Antidepressant treatment received before death.

Dose level	Males (n = 42)		Females (n = 24)		Total (n = 66)	
	n	(%)	n	(%)	n	(%)
No antidepressant	33	(79)	11	(46)	44	(67)
0–74 mg TCA	3	(7)	6	(25)	9	(14)
75–149 mg TCA	5	(12)	6	(25)	11	(17)
150–300 mg TCA	1	(3)	1	(4)	2	(3)

$p < 0.05$.

month of once-a-week psychotherapy by a trained therapist was received by only 7%. In addition, in a separate analysis of ECT among all the 1,397 suicides, only two cases were found to have received electroconvulsive therapy during the final 3 months [78]. Overall, if strict criteria are used to define adequate treatment, almost all suicides in major depression seem to occur in untreated or undertreated cases [70].

The lack of specific treatment for major depression in our study population was not only due to a lack of contact with psychiatric care. Three-quarters had a history of psychiatric treatment, two-thirds had a psychiatric contact during the last year and 45% at time of death. As many as 39% of victims had visited a health professional in the week preceding their suicide and 39% had been treated in a psychiatric hospital during the final depressive episode. For suicide prevention the need to improve the quality of care and continuous follow-up in the treatment of major depression seems evident. However, this is complicated by the likelihood of comorbidity, a variable period (up to 27 years) between first psychiatric contacts and completed suicide, and the common lack of communication of suicidal intent to health care workers [70].

The issue of suicide methods used by major depressive suicide victims is very important in estimating risks and benefits of treatment. The vast majority of victims were found to have used violent suicide methods, while only a small minority (13%) used an overdose of psychopharmacological agents. Surprisingly, we found the proportion of overdoses not different even if only those with regular psychopharmacological treatment at the time of death are included (14%). Only 8% of the victims committed suicide using an antidepressant overdose [70].

Depression is more common among females, but due to a higher suicide risk, the majority (63%) of suicides in major depression were men. Overall, it seemed to us that the previous studies had not sufficiently recognized the sex differences in suicides of subjects with major depression. The vast majority of females had both a history of psychiatric treatment (88%) as well as current treatment contact (65%), were treated with low doses of antidepressants (54%), often had a psychotherapeutic contact (42%), rarely had psychoactive substance use disorders (8%) and more often communicated suicidal intent to both family members and treatment organizations (26%). The males also had a psychiatric history (67%) but only a minority were receiving psychiatric treatment at the time of death (33%), and many had no contact with health care services at all (22%); almost half were dependent or abused psychoactive substances, usually alcohol (44%), few received antidepressants (21%) and few had psychotherapeutic contacts (16%); suicidal intent was rarely communicated in more than one direction (9%) and few used other than violent suicide methods even if drug-treated (22%). Many of the differences in specific treatments between sexes were due to whether or not psychiatric treatment was received at the time of death; though contrary to our expectations this was not due to differences in comorbidity. For suicide prevention the main problem seems to be how to effectively treat and maintain psychiatric contact, especially with the male depressed patients [70].

While we would have expected to find differences in characteristics between psychotic and nonpsychotic suicides with major depression, there were few. The majority of both psychotic (79%) as well as nonpsychotic (87%) major depressive suicide victims were found to be comorbid cases. The only major difference between the psychotic and nonpsychotic victims was that almost all (88%) psychotic victims had used violent suicide methods [73].

The majority of females (65%) committing suicide in major depression were receiving psychiatric care at the time of death, and females comprised half of the major depressive suicide victims within psychiatric care. In general practice and other medical and surgical settings 74%, and among those not having contact with health care, 83% of the major depressive suicides were men. Thus, outside psychiatric care, three-quarters of suicides in major depression were males. This finding stresses the necessity of studying the sex-specific problem areas of treatment in major depression.

Suicides among subjects with nonmajor depressions

We estimated that altogether 27% of suicide victims in Finland in 1987−1988 had suffered from milder unipolar depressions not fulfilling the criteria of major depression [14,77]. Although the majority of mildly depressed patients in the community and in clinical populations are females, the vast majority (81%) of nonmajor depressive suicide victims were males. In contrast to the marked differences in characteristics between sexes among major depressives suicides [70], among these nonmajor depressive suicides the sexes were strikingly similar. Almost all (95%) of the suicide victims in the nonmajor depression subgroup were comorbid cases. Most commonly the victims had suffered from alcoholism (59%), personality disorder (53%) or physical illness (47%), and having three or more diagnoses was common. In comparison with the suicides in major depression, particularly alcoholism, but also personality disorders were more common among the nonmajor depressives. The proportion of secondary cases was also very significantly higher among the milder depressives (90 vs. 47%). The finding is interesting as some cohort studies [81,82] have suggested higher suicide risk among secondary depressives, although this was not confirmed in a large cohort study [29].

It is obvious from our findings that half of victims even having had contact with health care before death were almost completely untreated as regards their current depression. Even undertreatment, relatively common among major depressive suicide victims both in Finland [70] and elsewhere [3,5,39], was uncommon. If judged by the dose criteria used in major depression, none of these victims had received adequate antidepressant treatment. Neither had anyone received weekly psychotherapy from a properly trained therapist. The lack of treatment for depression could be partly a consequence of the secondary nature of the depression in most cases. For suicide prevention it would seem important to evaluate the applicability of the current treatments for depression in milder secondary depressions, besides improving recognition and access to treatment [77].

Recent stressful life events have been shown to be associated with the onset of depression [83] as well as suicide [84,85]. In our study, suicides in nonmajor depressions seemed more often to be related to life events than suicides in major depression. In particular, there seemed to be a difference concerning the very recent stressors occurring during the final week before suicide. In two-thirds (70%) of the non-major depressives (in 42% of the major depressives) at least one adverse life event during the final week was reported. However, the differences between these two groups were mainly due to a significantly higher proportion of cases with possible dependent events among the victims with nonmajor depressions, and no differences were found if only independent events were included. Thus, many of the recent life events experienced particularly by the nonmajor victims before suicide were likely to be consequences of the victim's own behavior, although probably rarely intentionally inflicted. As discussed by Miller et al. [86], such adverse events may nonetheless have a major impact on the individuals life. As both the small number of adjustment disorder diagnoses and the high proportion of victims with events in the final week implicate, the depression was usually already present when the adverse events occurred. If the adverse life events had a role in the suicide, they seemed to thus usually trigger suicidal behavior in already depressed persons rather than to initiate the final episode [77].

Suicides among subjects with bipolar disorder

Of all suicides in Finland in 1987−1988, 46 (3%) were found to have suffered from a bipolar disorder. Thirty-one of these had definite bipolar I disorder [75]. The sex ratio among the bipolar victims was roughly equal, but the mean age of the males was 11 years, and the time from first treatment contacts 13 years shorter than for the females. Noteworthily, the majority (71%) of the bipolar suicide victims were comorbid cases, and the sexes differed in comorbidity, as more than half of the males but none of the females had become alcohol dependent. Compared with previous studies of suicide in bipolar disorder [20,25−27], the proportion of late suicides seemed to be higher in our suicide population, and the time from first treatment contacts to suicide ranged up to 49 years. Our finding was in accordance with Roy-Byrne et al. [87], who found the most severe suicide attempts to occur later in the course of affective illness.

As expected, the vast majority (79%) of the bipolar victims had a major depressive episode immediately before death. A minority had a mixed state, a syndrome possibly associated with high suicide risk [36]. Contrary to previous reports, some suicides seemed to occur during or immediately after remission in psychotic mania in cases with no reported severe depressive symptoms. However, a last-moment switch process, a moodswing [88] or an unrecognized depressed state can never be entirely ruled out.

Although three-quarters of the victims had received psychiatric care at the time of death, the treatment the bipolar victims had received for the current illness episode was considered adequate for only some cases. Despite all having had the indication, only one-third (32%) were on lithium, half with suboptimal serum levels, and all but three with poor compliance were reported. Of the depressed, about one-half were receiving antidepressants, but only a small minority (11%) at probably adequate doses. None of the bipolar victims had received electroconvulsive therapy during the final 3 months [75]. Our study showed more undertreatment among bipolar suicide victims than in Denmark, as described by Schou and Weeke [89]. For suicide prevention the major finding was that most suicides in bipolar disorder seem to occur in cases not receiving adequate treatment for the current illness episode [72].

When psychopharmacological treatments are used in suicidal populations there is increased access to a potentially lethal method of suicide. However, although almost all of the victims had received prescriptions during the last months, only about one-third used drugs as a suicide method. Nevertheless, this proportion is significantly higher than among the unipolars (13%). The drugs most often used in fatal overdoses were high-dose neuroleptics [75].

Only two out of all the 1,397 suicide victims were found to have died of lithium intoxication [80]. Eight of the victims (40%) fulfilled the criteria of recent adequate lithium prophylaxis, while the rest had lower serum levels, shorter duration of treatment or the treatment was discontinued before death. Most importantly, in the majority of cases (85%), compliance problems during the final 2 years were reported [80].

Conclusions

Findings from the research phase of the National Suicide Prevention Project in Finland suggest that completed suicides in mood disorders occur commonly among subjects with comorbid mental and physical disorders, and more often among males. While a high proportion of these subjects have received psychiatric treatment during their lifetime, not all of them have been receiving current treatment. In particular, very few have received specific, adequate treatment for the mood disorder. The most important implications for suicide prevention include the need for active recognition, treatment and follow-up of depression and suicidal ideation in all health care settings. A crucial question for suicide prevention is the ability of health care to provide effective treatment for depressed male subjects with comorbid mental and physical disorders.

References

1. Robins E, Gassner S, Kayes J, Wilkinson RH, Murphy GE. The communication of suicidal intent: a study of 134 consecutive cases of successful (completed) suicide. Am J Psychiat 1959; 115:724—733.
2. Dorpat TL, Ripley HS. A study of suicide in the Seattle area. Compr Psychiat 1960;1:349—359.
3. Barraclough BM, Bunch J, Nelson B, Sainsbury P. A hundred cases of suicide: clinical aspects. Br J Psychiat 1974;125:355—373.
4. Beskow J. Suicide and mental disorder in Swedish men. Acta Psychiat Scand 1979;277(Suppl): 1—138.
5. Chynoweth R, Tonge JI, Armstrong J. Suicide in Brisbane: a retrospective psychosocial study. Aust NZ J Psychiat 1980;14:37—45.
6. Mitterauer B. Mehrdimensionale Diagnostik von 121 Suiziden im Bundesland Salzburg im Jahre 1978. Wien Med Wochenschr 1981;131:229—234.
7. Shafii M, Steltz-Lenarsky J, Derrick AM, Beckner C, Whittinghill JR. Comorbidity of mental disorders in the post-mortem diagnosis of completed suicide in children and adolescents. J Affect Disord 1988;15:227—233.
8. Rich CL, Young D, Fowler RC. San Diego Suicide Study I: young vs. old subjects. Arch Gen Psychiat 1986;43:577—582.
9. Arato M, Demeter E, Rihmer Z, Somogyi E. Retrospective psychiatric assessment of 200 suicides in Budapest. Acta Psychiat Scand 1988;77:454—456.
10. Brent DA, Perper JA, Goldstein CE, Kolko DJ, Allan MJ, Allman CJ, Zelenak JP. Risk factors for adolescent suicide: a comparison of adolescent suicide victims with suicidal inpatients. Arch Gen Psychiat 1988;45:581—588.
11. Runeson B. Mental disorders in youth suicide: DSM-III-R axes I and II. Acta Psychiat Scand 1989;79:490—497.
12. Åsgård U. A psychiatric study of suicide among urban Swedish women. Acta Psychiat Scand 1990;82:115—124.
13. Marttunen MJ, Aro HM, Henriksson MM, Lönnqvist JK. Mental disorder in adolescent suicide. DSM-III-R Axes I and II among 13 to 19 year olds in Finland. Arch Gen Psychiat 1991; 48:834—839.
14. Henriksson MM, Aro HM, Marttunen MJ, Heikkinen ME, Isometsä ET, Kuoppasalmi KI, Lönnqvist JK. Mental disorders and comorbidity in suicide. Am J Psychiat 1993;150:935—940.
15. Brent DA, Perper JA, Moritz G, Allman C, Friend A, Roth C, Schweers J, Balach L, Baugher M. Psychiatric risk factors for adolescent suicide: a case-control study. J Am Acad Child Adolesc Psychiat 1993;32(3):521—529.
16. Apter A, Bleich A, King RA, Kron S, Fluch A, Kotler M, Cohen DJ. Death without warning? A clinical postmortem study of suicide in 43 Israeli adolescent males. Arch Gen Psychiat 1993; 50:138—142.
17. Lesage AD, Boyer R, Grunberg F, Vanier C, Morissette R, Ménard-Buteau C, Loyer M. Suicide and mental disorders: a case-control study of young men. Am J Psychiat 1994;151:1063—1068.
18. Cheng AT. Mental illness and suicide. Arch Gen Psychiat 1995;52:594—603.
19. Conwell Y, Duberstein P, Cox C, Herrmann JH, Forbes NT, Caine ED. Relationships of age- and axis I diagnoses in victims of completed suicide: A psychological autopsy study. Am J Psy-

chiat 1996;153:1001—1008.

20. Foster T, Gillespie K, McClelland R. Mental disorders and suicide in Northern Irelend. Br J Psychiat 1997;170:447—452.

21. Harris EC, Barraclough B. Suicide as an outcome for mental disorders. A meta-analysis. Br J Psychiat 1997;170:205—228.

22. Weeke A. Causes of death in manic-depressives. In: Schou M, Strömgren E (eds) Origin, Prevention and Treatment of Affective Disorders. London: Academic Press, 1979;289—299.

23. Hagnell O, Lanke J, Rorsman B. Suicide rates in the Lundby study: Mental illness as a risk factor for suicide. Neuropsychobiology 1981;7:248—253.

24. Evenson RC, Wood JB, Nuttall EA, Cho DW. Suicide rates among public mental health patients. Acta Psychiat Scand 1982;66:254—264.

25. Pokorny AD. Prediction of suicide in psychiatric patients. Report of a prospective study. Arch Gen Psychiat 1983;40:249—257.

26. Tsuang MT, Woolson RF. Excess mortality in schizophrenia and affective disorders. Do suicides and accidental deaths solely account for this excess? Arch Gen Psychiat 1978;35:1181—1185.

27. Black DW, Warrack, Winokur G. The Iowa Record-Linkage Study. I. Suicides and accidental deaths among psychiatric patients. Arch Gen Psychiat 1985;42:71—75.

28. Weeke A, Vaeth M. Excess mortality in bipolar and unipolar manic-depressive patients. J Affect Disord 1986;11:227—234.

29. Black DW, Winokur G, Nasrallah A. Suicide in subtypes of affective disorder. A comparison with general population suicide mortality. Arch Gen Psychiat 1987;44:878—880.

30. Newman SC, Bland RC. Suicide risk varies by subtype of affective disorder. Acta Psychiat Scand 1991;83:420—426.

31. Buchholtz-Hansen PE, Wang AG, Kragh-Sörensen P and the Danish University Antidepressant Group. Mortality in major affective disorder: relationship to subtype of depression. Acta Psychiat Scand 1993;87:329—335.

32. Barraclough BM, Pallis DJ. Depression followed by suicide: a comparison of depressed suicides with living depressives. Psychol Med 1975;5:55—61.

33. Modestin J, Kopp W. Study on suicide in depressed inpatients. J Affect Disord 1988;15:157—162.

34. Goldacre M, Seagrott V, Hawton K. Suicide after discharge from psychiatric inpatient care. Lancet 1993;342:283—286.

35. Guze SB, Robibs E. Suicide and primary affective disorder. Br J Psychiat 1970;117:437—438.

36. Goodwin FK, Jamison KR. Manic-depressive illness. New York: Oxford University Press, 1990.

37. Brown GW, Craig TKJ, Harris TO. Depression: distress or disease? Some epidemiological consideration. Br J Psychiat 1985;147:612—622.

38. Blair-West GW, Mellsop GW, Eyeson-Annan ML. Down-rating lifetime suicide risk in major depression. Acta Psychiat Scand 1997;95:259—263.

39. Rihmer Z, Barsi J, Arato M, Demeter E. Suicides in subtypes of primary major depression. J Affective Disord 1990;18:221—225.

40. Rihmer Z, Rutz W, Pihlgren H. Depression and suicide on Gotland. An intensive study of all suicides before and after a depression-training programme for general practitioners. J Affect Disord 1995;35:147—152.

41. Lester D. Suicidal behavior in bipolar and unipolar affective disorders: a meta-analysis. J Affect Disord 1993;27:117—121.

42. Fawcett J, Scheftner WA, Fogg L, Clark DC, Young MA, Hedeker D, Gibbons R. Time-related predictors of suicide in major affective disorders. Am J Psychiat 1990;147:1189—1194.

43. Beck AT, Steer RA, Kovacs M, Garrison B. Hopelessness and eventual suicide: A 10-year prospective study of patients hospitalized with suicidal ideation. Am J Psychiat 1985;142:559—563.

44. Beck AT, Brown G, Berchick RJ, Stewart BL, Steer RA. Relationship between hopelessness and ultimate suicide: A replication with psychiatric outpatients. Am J Psychiat 1990;147:190—195.

45. Roy A. Suicide in depressives. Compr Psychiat 1983;24(5):487—491.

46. Roose SP, Glassman AH, Walsh BT, Woodring S, Vital-Herne J. Depression, delusions and suicide. Am J Psychiat 1983;140:1159–1162.
47. Coryell W, Tsuang MT. Primary unipolar depression and the prognostic importance of delusions. Arch Gen Psychiat 1982;39:1181–1184.
48. Black DW, Winokur G, Nasrallah A. Effect of psychosis on suicide risk in 1,593 patients with unipolar and bipolar affective disorders. Am J Psychiat 1988;145:849–852.
49. Murphy GE, Wetzel RD, Robins E, McEvoy L. Multiple risk factors predict suicide in alcoholism. Arch Gen Psychiat 1992;49:459–463.
50. Murphy GE, Wetzel RD. The lifetime risk of suicide in alcoholism. Arch Gen Psychiat 1990;47:383–392.
51. Goldstein RB, Black DW, Nasrallah A, Winokur G. The prediction of suicide. Sensitivity, specificity, and predictive value of a multivariate model applied to suicide among 1906 patients with affective disorders. Arch Gen Psychiat 1991;48:418–422.
52. Pokorny AD. Prediction of suicide in psychiatric patients: report of a prospective study. In: Maris RW, Berman AL, Maltsberger JT, Yufit RI (eds) Assessment and Prediction of Suicide. New York: Guilford Press, 1992:105–129.
53. Modestin J. Antidepressive therapy in depressed clinical suicides. Acta Psychiat Scand 1985;71:111–116.
54. Isacsson G, Boëthius G, Bergman U. Low level of antidepressant prescription for people who later commit suicide: 15 years of experience from a population-based drug database in Sweden. Acta Psychiat Scand 1992;85:444–448.
55. Isacsson G, Holmgren P, Wasserman D, Bergman U. Use of antidepressants among people committing suicide in Sweden. Br Med J 1994;308:506–509.
56. Tanney BL. Electroconvulsive therapy and suicide. Suicide Life-Threat Behav 1986;16(2):198–221.
57. Coppen A, Standish-Barry H, Bailey J, Houston G, Silcocks P, Hermon C. Does lithium reduce the mortality of recurrent mood disorders? J Affect Disord 1991;23:1–7.
58. Müller-Oerlinghausen B, Ahrens B, Grof E, Grof P, Lenz G, Schou M, Simhandl C, Thau K, Volk J, Wolf R, Wolf T. The effect of long-term lithium treatment on the mortality of patients with manic-depressive and schizoaffective illness. Acta Psychiat Scand 1992;86:218–222.
59. Ahrens B, Müller-Oerlinghausen B, Grof P. Length of lithium treatment needed to eliminate the high mortality of affective disorders. Br J Psychiat 1993;163(Suppl 21):27–29.
60. Thies-Fletcher K, Müller-Oerlinghausen B, Seibert W, Walther A, Greil W. Effect of prophylactic treatment on suicide risk in patients with major affective disorders. Pharmacopsychiatry 1996;29:103–107.
61. Rutz W, von Knorring L, Wålinder J. Frequency of suicide on Gotland after systematic postgraduate education of general practitioners. Acta Psychiat Scand 1989;80:151–154.
62. Gunnel D, Frankel S. Prevention of suicide: aspirations and evidence. Br Med J 1994;308:1227–1233.
63. Rutz W, von Knorring L, Wålinder J, Wistedt B. Effect of an educational program for general practitioners on Gotland on the pattern of prescription of psychotropic drugs. Acta Psychiat Scand 1990;82:399–403.
64. Isacsson G, Rich CL. Depression, antidepressants, and suicide. Pharmacoepidemiological evidence for suicide prevention. In: Maris RW, Silverman MM, Canetto SS (eds) Review of Suicidology. New York: Guilford Press, 1997.
65. Litman RE, Curphey T, Shneidman ES, Farberow NL, Tabachnik N. Investigations of equivocal suicides. JAMA 1963;184:924–929.
66. Shneidman ES. The psychological autopsy. Suicide Life-Threat Behav 1981;11:325–340.
67. Clark DC, Horton-Deutsch SL. Assessment in absentia: The value of the psychological autopsy method for studying antecedents of suicide and predicting future suicides. In: Maris RW, Berman AL, Maltsberger JT, Yufit RI (eds) Assessment and Prediction of Suicide. New York: Guilford Press, 1992:144–182.

46

68. Lönnqvist J, Aro H, Marttunen M, editors. Itsemurhat Suomessa 1987-projekti. Toteutus, aineisto ja tutkimustuloksia. Gummerus: Jyväskylä, STAKESin tutkimuksia 25, 1993.
69. Lönnqvist J. National Suicide Prevention Project in Finland: a research phase of the project. Psychiat Fenn 1988;19:125—132.
70. Isometsä ET, Henriksson MM, Aro HM, Heikkinen ME, Kuoppasalmi KI, Lönnqvist JK. Suicide in major depression. Am J Psychiat 1994;151:530—536.
71. Heikkinen ME, Aro HM, Henriksson MM, Isometsä ET, Sarna SJ, Kuoppasalmi KI, Lönnqvist JK. Differences in recent life events between alcoholic and nonalcoholic depressive suicides. Alcohol Clin Exp Res 1994;18:1143—1149.
72. American Psychiatric Association (APA). Diagnostic and Statistical Manual of Mental Disorders DSM-III-R, 3rd edn (revised). Washington, DC: American Psychiatric Association, 1987.
73. Isometsä E, Henriksson M, Aro H, Heikkinen M, Kuoppasalmi K, Lönnqvist J. Suicide in psychotic major depression. J Affect Disord 1994;31:187—191.
74. Isometsä ET, Aro HM, Henriksson MM, Heikkinen ME, Lönnqvist JK. Suicide in major depression in different treatment settings. J Clin Psychiat 1994;55:523—527.
75. Isometsä ET, Henriksson MM, Aro HM, Lönnqvist JK. Suicide in bipolar disorder. Am J Psychiat 1994;151:1020—1024.
76. Isometsä E, Heikkinen M, Henriksson M, Aro H, Lönnqvist J. Recent life events and completed suicide in bipolar affective disorder. A comparison with major depressive suicides. J Affect Disord 1995;33:99—106.
77. Isometsä ET, Heikkinen ME, Henriksson MM, Aro HM, Marttunen MJ, Kuoppasalmi KI, Lönnqvist JK. Suicide in non-major depressions. J Affect Disord 1996;36:117—127.
78. Isometsä ET, Henriksson MM, Heikkinen ME, Lönnqvist JK. Completed suicide and recent electroconvulsive therapy in Finland. Convul Ther 1996:12:152—155.
79. Isometsä ET, Henriksson MM, Heikkinen ME, Aro HM, Marttunen MJ, Lönnqvist JK. Differences between urban and rural suicides. Acta Psychiat Scand 1997:95:297—305.
80. Isometsä E, Henriksson M, Lönnqvist J. Completed suicide and recent lithium treatment. J Affect Disord 1992;26:101—104.
81. Martin RL, Cloninger CR, Guze SB, Clayton PJ. Mortality in a follow-up of 500 psychiatric outpatients, II: Cause-specific mortality. Arch Gen Psychiat 1985;42:58—66.
82. Akiskal HS, Bitar AH, Puzantian VR, Rosenthal TL, Walker PW. The nosological status of neurotic depression. A prospective three- to four-year follow-up examination in light of primary-secondary and unipolar-bipolar dichotomies. Arch Gen Psychiat 1978;35:756—766.
83. Paykel ES, Cooper Z. Life events and social stress. In: Paykel ES (ed) Handbook of Affective Disorders. Edinburgh: Churchill Livingstone, 1992:149—170.
84. Paykel ES, Dowlatshahi D. Life events and mental disorder. In: Fisher S, Reason J, (eds) Handbook of Life Stress, Cognition and Health. Chichester: John Wiley & Sons, 1988;241—263.
85. Heikkinen M, Aro H, Lönnqvist J. Life events and social support in suicide. Suic Life-Threat Behav 1993;23:343—358.
86. Miller McC, Dean P, Ingham JG, Kreitman NB, Sashidharan SP, Surtees PG. The epidemiology of life events and difficulties, with some reflections on the concept of independence. Br J Psychiat 1986;148:686—696.
87. Roy-Byrne PP, Post RM, Hambrick DD, Leverick GS, Rosoff AS. Suicide and course of illness in major affective disorder. J Affect Disord 1988;15:1—8.
88. Schweizer E, Dever A, Clary C. Suicide upon recovery from depression. A clinical note. J Nerv Ment Dis 1988;176:633—636.
89. Schou M, Weeke A. Did manic-depressive patients who committed suicide receive prophylactic or continuation treatment at the time? Br J Psychiat 1988;153:324—327.

1997 Elsevier Science B.V.
Suicide: Biopsychosocial Approaches.
A.J. Botsis, C.R. Soldatos and C.N. Stefanis, editors.

Suicide in schizophrenia

Alec Roy

Department of Veterans Affairs, New Jersey Healthcare Systems, East Orange, New Jersey, USA

Abstract. Suicidal behavior among schizophrenics is a major public health problem.

Methods. The literature about the social, psychiatric and biologic risk factors for suicide among schizophrenics is reviewed.

Conclusion. The schizophrenic at risk to commit suicide is young, male, in the first few years of illness, has a relapsing disorder, has reduced central serotonin, has been depressed in the past and recently, has changed from in to outpatient care and is socially isolated.

Keywords: risk-factors, schizophrenia, suicide.

Introduction

Suicidal behavior among schizophrenics is a major problem. This is because approximately 10% of schizophrenics end their lives by committing suicide and up to 50% attempt suicide at some time [1—3]. This paper will review the social, psychiatric and biologic risk factors for suicide as they pertain to schizophrenia [4].

Age and sex

Schizophrenics who commit suicide tend to be male and young. Since 1980 12 studies have reported on chronic schizophrenic patient suicide victims (reviewed in [5]). Among the total 449 suicide victims, 66.4% were male and the mean age at suicide was 33.9 years.

Previous suicide attempt

There are 15 studies that report whether or not schizophrenic patient suicides have previously attempted suicide (reviewed in [5]). Among the total 535 suicide victims 281 (52.5%) had previously attempted suicide.

Depression

Depressive symptoms have been noted in the last period of psychiatric contact in a substantial percentage of schizophrenic patient suicide victims. There have

Address for correspondence: Alec Roy MD, Department of Veterans Affairs, New Jersey Healthcare Systems, 385 Tremont Avenue/Psychiatry 116A, East Orange, NJ 07018, USA.

been nine studies reporting on the presence or absence of associated affective symptoms [5]. Among the total of 280 schizophrenic patient suicide victims in these studies, in approximately 60% of them affective symptoms were noted during the last period of contact before the patient committed suicide.

That the schizophrenic patient who commits suicide is vulnerable to develop depression is illustrated by the study of Roy [6]. Thirty chronic schizophrenic suicide victims were matched for age and sex with 30 living chronic schizophrenic control patients. Seventeen of the 30 suicides (56.6%) had a past depressive episode and 14 (46.6%) had been treated with antidepressants or ECT (for depression) (Table 1). Similarly, in their last period of psychiatric contract, 16 of the 30 suicides (53.5%) were diagnosed as suffering from a depressive episode compared with only four controls (13.3%) (Table 1).

Drake and Cotton [7] have further examined the relationship between depression and suicide in schizophrenics. They compared 15 schizophrenic suicide victims with 89 schizophrenic patients who did not commit suicide. The suicides were much more likely to manifest persistent depressed mood as well as many of the other features of depression during their index hospital admission.

They were not, however, significantly more likely to meet criteria for a major depressive episode. Breaking down the depressive symptoms into somatic and psychological symptoms revealed the reason for this. The suicides clearly demonstrated the psychological features of depression, including hopelessness, but not the somatic symptoms that are usually needed to make the diagnosis of a major depressive episode.

Reasons for admission

Roy [6] compared schizophrenic suicide victims and living schizophrenic controls for the reasons for all their admissions to the psychiatric hospital where they received most of their treatment. Significantly more of the admissions of the eventual schizophrenic suicide victims were for a mental state consisting of a mixture of schizophrenic and affective symptoms (Table 2).

Similar results were obtained when the reason for the last psychiatric hospital

Table 1. Schizophrenic suicide victims and living schizophrenic controls compared for history of depression. (From Roy [6].)

	Schizophrenic suicides n = 30	Schizophrenic control n = 30	Significance
Psychiatric history			
Past depressive episode	17	5	0.001
Past treatment for depression	14	7	0.05
Last episode			
Depressed in last episode	16	4	0.001
Treated for depression in last episode	9	6	ns

Table 2. Schizophrenic suicide victims (n = 27) and controls (n = 25) compared for reason for all their psychiatric admissions. (From Roy [6].)

	Schizophrenic suicides		Schizophrenic controls		Significance
	Number of admissions	%	Number of admissions	%	
Schizophrenic symptoms plus depressive episode	15	17.4	4	6.7	0.05
Schizophrenic symptoms plus suicide	18	20.9	7	11.7	ns
Depressive episode or situational crisis	8	9.3	2	3.4	ns
Schizophrenic symptoms	45	52.3	47	78.3	0.01

admission was examined. Significantly more of the eventual suicide victims had their last admission because of associated suicidal impulses or depressive symptoms (Table 3).

Time of suicide

The first few years of schizophrenic illness are a period of increased risk of suicide. Schizophrenic patients tend to commit suicide in relationship to their last psychiatric hospitalization. There are 10 studies reporting when schizophrenic patients commit suicide [5]. Among the total 259 suicide victims, 81 (31.2%) committed suicide while inpatients. Among schizophrenic outpatients, the first few weeks and months after discharge from a hospitalization are a period of increased suicide risk.

Psychodynamics

Drake and Cotton [8] noted that their schizophrenic suicide victims had shown high premorbid achievement, high self-expectations of performance, and high awareness of their pathology. For example, 73% of the suicide victims were college-educated compared with 29% of the controls. They made the important

Table 3. Schizophrenic suicide victims and controls compared for reason for last hospitalization. (From Roy [6].)

	Schizophrenic suicides n = 29	Schizophrenic controls n = 29	Significance
Schizophrenic symptoms plus suicidal/depressed	16	7	0.02
Situational crisis	3	2	ns
Schizophrenic symptoms only	10	19	0.01

point that in such patients: "Given their inability to achieve major life goals, they felt inadequate, feared further deterioration of their mental abilities, and decided to end their lives rather than continue living with chronic mental illness. To the extent that their decisions represented realistic estimations of current and future functioning in relation to goals, rather than mood-distorted perceptions of the future, perhaps these patients should be considered to suffer from despair rather than depression". Drake and Cotton concluded that such patients: "are likely to experience hopelessness defined as negative expectancies about the future and other psychological features of depression".

Prediction by clinical variables

Among 100 chronic schizophrenics seen at the National Institute of Mental Health, six committed suicide over a 4.5-year follow-up period [9]. Seven combinations of the sociodemographic and clinical variables discussed earlier were used to try to identify these six suicide victims. However, five of the seven strategies used identified only one of the six patients who eventually committed suicide; one strategy identified none and another identified only two of the six suicides.

Schizophrenic suicide among psychiatric hospital inpatients

Schizophrenia is the most common diagnosis in state hospital inpatient suicides. For example, 28 of 37 inpatient suicides (75.7%) from an Ontario Provincial Psychiatric Hospital suffered from schizophrenia [10] (Table 4).

When the schizophrenic inpatient suicides were compared with living schizophrenic inpatient controls, significantly more of the schizophrenic suicide victims than schizophrenic controls had made a past suicide attempt ($p < 0.007$) and more had made two or more past attempts (eight of 28, 28.6% vs. 0 of 13, 0%, $p < 0.05$). There was a trend for more of the schizophrenic suicide victims to be living alone before their last admission ($p < 0.12$) (Table 5). Only two of the 28

Table 4. Comparison of psychiatric hospital inpatient suicide victims and age- and sex-matched inpatient controls for psychiatric diagnosis. (From Roy and Draper [10].)

Psychiatric	No. of suicides (n = 37)	No. of controls (n = 37)	Significance
Schizophrenia	28	12	$p < 0.0005$
Affective disorder	5	7	ns
Personality disorder	1	10	$p < 0.003$
Epilepsy	3	0	$p < 0.077$
Alcoholism	0	4	$p < 0.04$
Adjustment disorder	0	1	ns
Mental retardation	0	2	ns

schizophrenics committed suicide within the first 2 months of admission compared with five of the nine patients with other diagnoses (7.1 vs. 55.6%, $p < 0.005$).

It is also noteworthy that 10 of 12 (83.3%) inpatients who committed suicide after having been in hospital over 1 year were schizophrenic. A proximal factor to the suicide in several of these long-stay patients was discharge planning which had led to the painful realization that they were losing the hospital and staff and/or that their family was not prepared to have them home.

Positive and negative symptoms and schizophrenic suicide

Fenton et al. [11] followed up, for an average of 19 years, schizophrenic patients who had been admitted to Chestnut Lodge in Maryland. They found that schizophrenic patients who had died as a result of suicide had significantly lower negative symptom severity at index admission than patients without suicidal behaviors (Table 6). Two positive symptoms (suspiciousness and delusions), however, were more severe among successful suicides. The paranoid schizophrenia subtype was associated with an elevated suicide risk (12%) and the deficit subtype was associated with a reduced risk (1.5%) of suicide. They concluded that these findings suggest that prominent negative symptoms, such as diminished drive, blunted affect, and social and emotional withdrawal, counter the emergence of suicidality in patients with schizophrenia spectrum disorders and that the deficit syndrome defines a group at relatively low risk for suicide. Prominent suspiciousness in the absence of negative symptoms defines a relatively high risk group.

Table 5. Comparison of schizophrenic suicide victims and schizophrenic controls. (From Roy and Draper [10].)

	Schizophrenic suicide victims (n = 28)	Schizophrenic controls (n = 13)	Significance
Past suicide attempt	17	2	x = 7.3
Involuntary at last admission	19	6	p < 0.007
Live alone	20	6	ns
Age (years)	39.0 ± 14.1	37.2 ± 10.1	x = 2.45
Male	20	9	p < 0.12
Female	8	4	ns
Single	20	8	ns
Separated/divorced/widowed	5	3	ns
No psychiatric admissions	6.7 ± 14.1	7.3 ± 6.3	ns
Length of last inpatient stay (days)	588.1 ± 973.6	170.4 ± 196.2	ns
Unemployed	27	11	ns
Alcohol and/or drug abuse	12	3	ns
Received antidepressants	9	5	ns
Received lithium	4	2	ns
Received ECT	11	6	ns

Table 6. Severity of positive and negative symptoms at index admission among 295 patients with schizophrenia or schizophrenia spectrum disorders who did or did not commit suicide during long-term follow-up. (From Fenton et al. [11].)

System	Committed suicide (n = 19)		Did not commit suicide (n = 276)		Analysis		
	Mean	SD	Mean	SD	t	df	p
Negative symptoms							
Blunted affect	1.6	1.1	2.3	1.4	2.26	293.00	0.02
Emotional withdrawal	2.1	1.1	2.8	1.6	2.67	23.59	0.01
Poor rapport	2.6	1.5	2.9	1.7	0.72	293.00	ns
Social withdrawal	2.0	1.0	2.9	1.7	3.57	26.02	0.001
Abstract thinking	1.6	1.1	2.2	1.5	1.77	293.00	ns
Poverty of speech	1.6	1.0	2.2	1.7	2.25	26.05	0.02
Stereotyped thinking	1.3	0.6	1.8	1.3	3.60	32.27	0.001
Global negative	12.8	3.5	17.2	7.8	4.67	32.06	0.0001
Positive symptoms							
Delusions	4.3	1.7	3.5	1.8	− 1.96	293.00	0.05
Conceptual disorganization	1.9	1.0	2.4	1.4	1.90	23.45	ns
Hallucinations	3.2	1.8	2.5	1.8	− 1.70	293.00	ns
Excitement	3.3	1.9	2.9	1.6	− 1.16	293.00	ns
Grandiosity	2.8	2.0	2.1	1.4	− 1.66	19.28	ns
Suspiciousness	3.6	1.4	2.7	1.4	− 2.63	293.00	0.009
Hostility	3.1	2.1	2.8	1.6	− 0.52	19.37	ns
Global positive	22.3	8.1	18.9	6.5	− 2.19	293.00	0.03

CSF 5-HIAA and suicidal behavior in schizophrenia

Reduced central serotonin has been implicated in suicidal behavior [12]. Schizophrenic patients who attempt suicide have been found in some, but not all, studies to have low concentrations of the serotonin metabolite 5-hydroxyindoleacetic acid (5-HIAA) in the cerebrospinal fluid (CSF) [13–17]. Follow-up studies have shown that low CSF 5-HIAA predicts suicidal behavior in schizophrenia [18–20].

Conclusion

Studies have suggested that the risk factors for suicide in schizophrenia include being young and male, having reduced central serotonin, having a relapsing illness with positive symptoms, having been depressed in the past, being currently depressed, having been admitted in the last period of psychiatric contact with depressive symptoms or suicidal ideas, having recently changed from in to outpatient care and from being socially isolated.

References

1. Roy A. Depression, attempted suicide and suicide in patients with chronic schizophrenia. Psychiatr Clin North Am 1986;9:193–206.
2. Roy A. Suicide in schizophrenia. In: Roy A (ed) Suicide. Baltimore: Williams & Wilkins, 1986; 97–112.
3. Roy A, Mazonson A, Pickar D. Attempted suicide in chronic schizophrenia. Br J Psychiat 1984; 144:303–306.
4. Roy A. Risk factors for suicide in psychiatric patients. Arch Gen Psychiat 1982;1089–1095.
5. Roy A. Suicide in schizophrenia. Int Rev Psychiat 1992;4:205–209.
6. Roy A. Suicide in chronic schizophrenia. Br J Psychiat 1982;141:171–177.
7. Drake R, Cotton P. Depression, hopelessness and suicide in chronic schizophrenia. Br J Psychiat 1986;148:554–559.
8. Drake R, Gates C, Cotton P. Suicide among schizophrenics: a comparison of attempters and completed suicides. Br J Psychiat 1986;149:784–787.
9. Roy A, Schreiber J, Mazonson A, Pickar D. Suicidal behavior in schizophrenic patients: a follow-up study. Can J Psychiat 1986;31:737–740.
10. Roy A, Draper R. Suicide among psychiatric hospital inpatients. Psychol Med 1995;52: 199–202.
11. Fenton W, McGlashan T, Victor B, Blyler C. Symptoms, subtype, and suicidality in patients with schizophrenia spectrum disorders. Am J Psychiat 1997;154:199–204.
12. Roy A, DeJong J, Linnoila M et al. Cerebrospinal fluid monoamine metabolites and suicidal behaviour in depressed patients. Arch Gen Psychiat 1989;46:609–612.
13. van Praag H. CSF 5-HIAA and suicide in non-depressed schizophrenics. Lancet 1983;ii: 977–978.
14. Banki C, Arato M, Papp Z, Kurez M. Biochemical markers in suicidal patients. J Affect Disord 1984;6:341.
15. Ninan P, van Kammen D, Scheinen M et al. CSF 5-hydroxyindoleacetic acid levels in suicidal schizophrenic patients. Am J Psychiat 1984;141:566–569.
16. Roy A, Ninan P, Mazonson A et al. CSF monoamine metabolites in chronic schizophrenic patients who attempt suicide. Psychol Med 1985;15:335–340.
17. Lemus C, Lieberman L, Johns C et al. CSF 5-hydroxyindoleacetic acid levels and suicide attempts in schizophrenia. Biol Psychiat 1990;27:923–926.
18. Roy A. Serotonin, suicide and schizophrenia. Can J Psychiat 1993;38:369.
19. Faustman W, Ringo D, Faul K. An association between low levels of 5-HIAA and HVA in cerebrospinal fluid and early mortality in a diagnostically mixed psychiatry sample. Br J Psychiat 1993;163:519–521.
20. Cooper S, Kelly C, King D. 5-hydroxyindoleacetic acid in cerebrospinal fluid and prediction of suicidal behaviour in schizophrenia. Lancet 1992;340:940–941.

The relationship of suicide attempts to licit and illicit drug use

A. Kokkevi, K. Politikou and C. Stefanis

University Mental Health Research Institute and Department of Psychiatry, Athens University Medical School, Athens, Greece

Abstract. A strong association seems to exist between substance use and suicidal attempts. Data supporting the above association derive from several studies carried out in Greece by the Department of Psychiatry and the University Mental Health Research Institute of the Athens University:
1. A nationwide survey on adolescent students aged 14–18 years.
2. A general population survey of the greater Athens area.
3. Studies on samples of drug-dependent individuals.
In the student adolescent population the odds of suicidal attempts in drug users were about 7 times higher for boys and 5 times higher for girls compared to nonusers. In the general population the odds of suicide attempts in drug users were 19 times higher than nonusers for men and 5 times for women. Finally, in the sample of drug addicts (mainly opioid dependents) self-reported suicide attempts were reported by a much higher percentage (27%) than the control group drawn from the general population (0.5%) with an odds ratio of 54. Findings from both surveys show a linear trend between the frequency of substance consumption and suicide attempts. The association of suicide attempts to substance use is further discussed in conjunction with mood and behavioral-impulsivity disorders.

Keywords: drug abuse, substance use, suicidality.

Introduction

Suicide and substance abuse constitute major problems amongst the youth of our societies. Epidemiologic data demonstrate a parallel spread of both conditions in the last 30 years. While drug abuse has developed into one of the most alarming epidemics among young people, the number of suicides has increased almost 3-fold in the 15–24 age group. Moreover, a growing number of studies in the recent years show that strong associations exist between drug and alcohol addiction on the one hand and suicide or parasuicide on the other. More than half (53%) of young suicides were found to have a principal diagnosis of addictive disorder in a San Diego suicide study [1], while studies of substance-abusing populations show that up to 61% are suicide attempters [2–6].

A causal relationship has been postulated between substance abuse and suicide, and drug usage has been claimed to be the most important factor in the increasing suicide rate amongst the youth of the USA [7,8]. However, research findings are not conclusive on whether drug abuse itself or a comorbid psychopathology

Address for correspondence: Dr Anna Kokkevi, Associate Professor, University Mental Health Research Institute, Athens University Medical School, 72-74 Vas. Sofias Avenue, 115 28 Athens, Greece.

(e.g., depression) is the main contributing cause of suicidal behaviour, nor on the temporal sequence of drug abuse and psychopathology.

This paper presents our findings derived from surveys we carried out in Greece on the relationship between suicide and substance use. The study focused on self-reported suicide attempts by respondents at different stages of their involvement with illicit drug use: firstly, young students in the phase of experimenting with illicit drugs; secondly, respondents from the general population with a history of occasional use; and thirdly, drug addicts, mainly opioid dependent, with a long history of drug dependence.

Methods

School population survey

The survey was conducted during Spring 1993, on a nationwide stratified clustered probability sample, consisting of 10,543 high-school students aged 14—18 years old (43.5% boys and 52.5% girls). Students answered a self-completed anonymous questionnaire in their classrooms under the supervision of two research staff in the absence of their teacher.

The questionnaire was mainly focused on licit and illicit drug use but also covered a wide range of questions including sociodemographic characteristics, lifestyles, attitudes, physical and psychosocial health. A question was included on whether the respondents had attempted suicide and how many times. Rates of self-reported suicide attempts were calculated separately for boys and girls. Odds ratios were calculated to measure the effect of illicit substance use on the risk of suicide attempts. Mantel-Haenzel χ^2 tests were performed in order to reveal possible trends in the odds ratios with increasing involvement in licit and illicit substance use.

General population survey

The survey was conducted in Spring 1993 on a clustered probability sample, comprising 2,103 residents of Greater Athens aged 12—65 years (43.2% males, 56.8% females). Results given in the present paper use data only from the 1,559 respondents aged 18 years and above. Respondents were interviewed within their own homes using a prestructured questionnaire by specially trained interviewers who were graduates in the health and social sciences. The duration of the interview was 70—90 min. Great care was taken to ensure confidentiality and anonymity of the respondents.

The questionnaire comprised a wide range of questions mainly focused on licit and illicit drug use, but extending also to other topics such as lifestyles, attitudes, physical and psychosocial health. A question on whether the respondent had ever attempted suicide, and how many times, was included.

Odds ratios were calculated to measure the effect of substance use on the risk of suicide attempts separately for each sex. Exact methods were used to calculate p values and confidence intervals when the data were sparse.

Survey on drug dependents

The sample consisted of 176 drug-dependent men, diagnosed according to DSM-III criteria. Almost half of the subjects (44.9%) were consecutive admissions to all existing treatment services in Athens. The remainder were randomly recruited from the main prison in Athens. Their mean age was 28.9 years (±7.1 SD).

This study was part of a larger project assessing psychosocial aspects of drug abuse in Greece and psychiatric comorbidity carried out in 1988. Respondents were interviewed by appropriately trained social scientists with the aid of a pre-structured questionnaire focusing on drug abuse but covering also sociodemographic, psychosocial and health aspects. A question about having attempted suicide and how many times was included.

A control group of the same age range as the drug-dependent population was drawn from the nationwide survey. Odds ratios were calculated to measure the effect of drug dependence on suicide attempts (Table 1).

Results

The nationwide prevalence for illicit drug use[1] in the adolescent school population was 6.1% (6.4% of boys and 2.9% of girls) while a much higher percentage of 30% (26% of boys and 36% of girls) reported unprescribed use of prescription type psychoactive drugs[2]. The great majority of students who had experience with illicit drugs reported using marijuana, whereas no other illicit substance had been used by more than 1.5% of the sample. Tobacco smoking in the last 30 days was reported by 28.7% (29.0% of boys and 28.3% of girls) and three-quarters (80.3% of boys and 71.8% of girls) reported use of alcohol in the past month.

Lifetime prevalence of illicit drug use[3] among 18–65 year olds in the Athenian general population was 11.9%, while 3.8% reported use in the last year and 1.7% in the last month. Marijuana was the most prevalent drug used. Almost one-quarter (21.3%) reported lifetime unprescribed use of prescription type psychoactive drugs[4], whereas prevalence in the last year was 8.1% and in the last month 3.0%.

---

[1]Illicit drug use was defined as the use of any of the following at least once: cannabis, cocaine, crack, opium, hallucinogens, heroin.
[2]Unprescribed use of prescription type psychoactive drugs was defined as the use of any of the following without a doctor's prescription at least once: amphetamines, painkillers, codeine, barbiturates, hypnotics, tranquillizers, anticholinergics and antidepressants.
[3]Illicit drug use was defined as above but excluding opium.
[4]Compared to the above definition, barbiturates were excluded but opium and anabolics were included.

Table 1. Population samples studied.

Type of survey	Sample	n	Age (years)
High school	Stratified clustered probability	10543	14–18
General population	Clustered probability	1559	18–65
Drug dependent	Random sample of males from treatment services and prison	176	28.9 ± 7.1

The majority of the drug-dependent sample were polydrug users, with heroin being the primary substance of dependence for 94.3%. They had been using drugs for an average of 12.4 years (±6.1 SD) and heroin for 6.9 years (±4.7 SD).

As shown in Table 2, the prevalence of self-reported suicide attempts was much higher among those reporting drug use compared to nonusers in all three samples of adolescent students, general population adults and drug dependents.

The odds ratios indicate a highly significant increase of suicide risk among users compared to nonusers for both genders, but more so for males. The odds of suicide attempts were 7.4 times higher for boys and 5.1 higher for girls who reported drug use than nonusers in the same population. In the general population the odds of suicide attempts were 19.3 times higher for men who reported drug use and 5.1 for women compared to those who denied such use. Finally, the odds of suicide attempts in male drug dependents were 54 times higher than in a non-drug-using control group from the general population.

To study further the relationship between self-reported suicide attempts and substance use, students in the school survey were divided into eight subgroups according to their experience with licit and illicit substances:

1. No regular use of any licit substance and no use whatsoever of any illicit substance (36.5%).
2. Smoking five or more cigarettes a day (2.2%).
3. Drinking alcohol regularly but not smoking five or more cigarettes a day (11.0%).
4. Smoking five or more cigarettes a day and drinking alcohol regularly (4.7%).

Table 2. Lifetime prevalence of self-reported suicide attempts in illicit drug users and nonusers.

	Males			Females		
	Users (%)	Nonusers (%)	O.R.	Users (%)	Nonusers (%)	O.R.
High school students	19.1	3.1	7.42 ($p<0.001$)	34.2	9.3	5.1 ($p<0.001$)
General population	3.7	0.2	19.3 ($p<0.002$)	10.0	2.1	5.1 ($p = 0.007$)
Drug dependents	27.4	0.5[a]	54 ($p<0.001$)	—	—	—

[a]Refers to the control group of nonusers of the same age range as the drug dependents drawn from the nationwide general population survey.

5. Use of one to two types of licit psychoactive drugs without prescription (34.7%).
6. Use of three or more types of psychoactive drugs without prescription (5.0%).
7. Use of illicit drugs excluding heroin (5.3%).
8. Use of heroin (0.7%).

The close relationship between self-reported suicide attempts and substance use (both licit and illicit) is shown in Fig. 1.

The risk for suicide attempts compared to nonusers was much higher for those students who have been involved with harder illicit drugs (heroin) than those who reported use of illicit drugs other than heroin (25.2 and 5.5 times higher risk, respectively) (Table 3).

Furthermore, as shown in Figs. 2—4, a linear trend appeared to exist between self-reported suicide attempts and the frequency of use of licit drugs such as tobacco and alcohol.

Discussion

The findings of this study demonstrate the close association not only between self-reported suicide attempts and illicit drug use but also between suicide attempts and licit drug use. Moreover, the findings show that the stage of involvement in the use of licit and illicit substances is highly correlated with self-

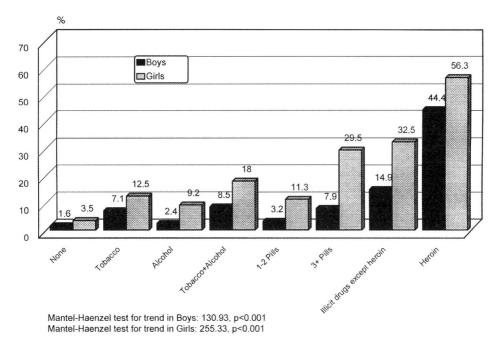

Mantel-Haenzel test for trend in Boys: 130.93, p<0.001
Mantel-Haenzel test for trend in Girls: 255.33, p<0.001

Fig. 1. Self-reported attempts and involvement with licit and illicit substance use in the school population.

Table 3. Suicide attempts and stage of involvement with illicit drug use among high-school students.

Lifetime drug use	Boys					Girls				
	n	%	O.R.	95% C.I.	p	n	%	O.R.	95% C.I.	p
None	4477	3.1	1.0	—	—	5195	9.3	1.0	—	—
Illicit drugs other than heroin	323	14.9	5.5	(3.8,7.9)	<0.001	209	32.5	4.7	(3.5,6.5)	<0.001
Heroin	54	44.4	25.2	(21.6,71.6)	<0.001	16	56.3	7.6	(2.6,22.4)	<0.001

reported suicide attempts. The significant associations found with the frequency of use of licit substances such as tobacco and alcohol, and alcohol-related problems such as drunkenness, further collaborates reports that the two phenomena of suicide and substance use are closely linked.

A question to be answered is whether the strong association between drug use and suicide attempts is a primary association or if it is mediated by other factors

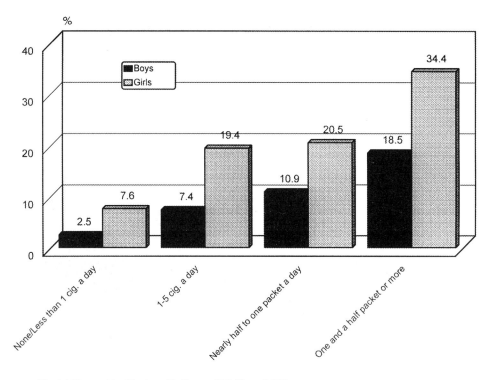

Mantel-Haenzel test for trend in Boys : 182,57, p<0.001
Mantel-Haenzel test for trend in Girls: 191,37, p<0.001

Fig. 2. Frequency of tobacco smoking and self-reported suicide attempts in the school population.

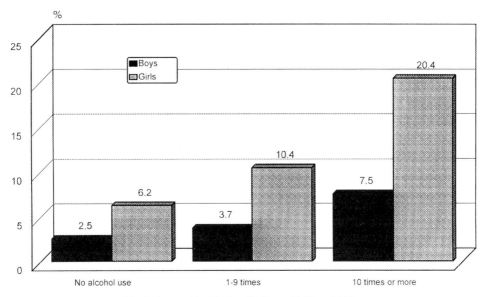

Mantel-Haenzel test for trend in Boys: 30.73, p<0.001
Mantel-Haenzel test for trend in Girls: 81.88, p<0.001

Fig. 3. Alcohol use and self-reported suicide attempts in the school population.

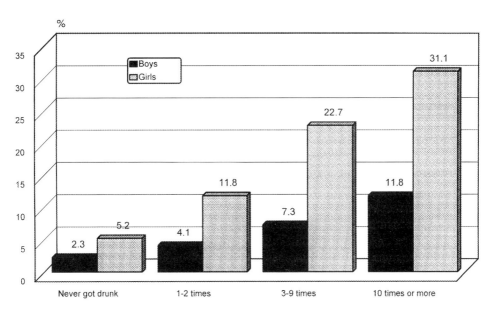

Mantel-Haenzel test for trend in Boys: 83.09, p<0.001
Mantel-Haenzel test for trend in Girls: 269.33, p<0.001

Fig. 4. Drunkenness and self-reported suicide attempts in the school population.

such as psychiatric disorders or psychopathological symptoms coexisting with drug abuse.

Psychiatric comorbidity in substance use has been found in recent studies to be highly prevalent [3,9—11]. Research has also shown that not only full-blown psychiatric disorders such as depression and personality disorders but also certain symptoms related to these diagnoses may increase the risk for suicide [12].

Findings from all three surveys reported in this paper as well as from previous surveys conducted in Greece show that among the most prevalent psychiatric disorders in substance abuse are psychopathic personality, mood and anxiety disorders [2,3,13]. Moreover, as shown by findings from previous published data on school population surveys in this country, the association between the stage of a student's involvement with licit and illicit substance use and antisocial personality, depressive symptoms, and with other psychological characteristics such as tension-impulsivity, feelings of loneliness and low self-esteem all follow the same pattern (linear trend) as the association between substance use and suicide attempts [14].

Our study on psychiatric comorbidity on drug addicts shows that dependence is associated with more than one psychiatric disorder. It has been shown that the presence of antisocial personality disorder increases the odds of occurrence of anxiety disorders by 5.6. [3].

It may thus be assumed that substance use and psychiatric morbidity, including suicide attempts, are interdependent variables and that common personality and psychopathology factors might constitute predisposing factors to both substance use and suicide attempts. The interaction of psychopathology and substance use, in conjunction with other risk factors, might act as a triggering mechanism for the suicidal act. This is borne out by the findings in our school survey which have shown that polydrug use and the type of substance used (heroin in combination with other drugs) increase by 25 times the risk of suicide attempts.

The findings reported in this paper, in addition to providing further evidence on the close association between suicidality, psychopathology and substance use, may contribute to implement more insightful strategies in the field of suicide prevention particularly among the youth.

References

1. Fowler RC, Rich CL, Young D. San Diego suicide study: II. Substance abuse in young cases. Arch Gen Psychiat 1986;43:962—965.
2. Kokkevi A, Stefanis C. Depression and drug use. Psychopathology 1986;19:124—131.
3. Kokkevi A, Stefanis C. Drug abuse and psychiatric comorbidity. Compr Psychiat 1995;36: 329—337.
4. Bukstein OG et al. Risk factors for completed suicide among adolescents with a lifetime history of substance abuse: a case control study. Acta Psychiat Scand 1993;88:403—408.
5. Deykin EY, Buka SL. Suicidal ideation and attempts among chemically dependent adolescents. Am J Publ Health 1994;84:634—639.
6. Madianos M, Gefou-Madianou D, Stefanis C. Symptoms of depression, suicidal behavior and

use of substances in Greece: a nation-wide general population survey. Acta Psychiat Scand 1994;89:159—166.

7. Miles CP. Conditions predisposing to suicide: A review. J Nerv Ment Dis 1977;164:231—246.

8. Levy JC, Deykin EY. Suicidality, depression, and substance abuse in adolescence. Am J Psychiat 1989;146:1462—1467.

9. Mirin SM, Weissman MM, Michael J et al. Psychopathology in drug abusers and their families. Compr Psychiat 1991;32:36—51.

10. Regier DA, Farmer ME, Rae DS et al. Comorbidity of mental disorders with alcohol and other drug abuse. Results from the Epidemiologic Catchment Area (ECA) Study. JAMA 1990;264: 2511—2518.

11. Hendriks VM, Steer RA, Platt JS et al. Psychopathology in Dutch and American heroin addicts. Int J Addict 1990;25:1051—1063.

12. Kokkevi A, Stefanis C. Psychiatric Comorbidity in Substance Abuse. In: Stefanis C, Hippius H (eds) Research in Addiction: An Update. Seattle, Toronto, Bern, Goettingen: Hogrefe & Huber Publishers, 1993.

13. Sternberg DE. Suicide in Drug and Alcohol Addiction. In: Miller N (ed) 1991 Comprehensive Handbook of Drug and Alcohol Addiction. New York: Marcel Dekker, Inc., 1991.

14. Kokkevi A, Madianou D, Stefanis C. Drug Abuse in Greece: Substance use in the School Population. Biblioteca Psychiatrica, Athens, 1992. (In Greek with extended summary in English.)

Physical illness and suicide: the facts

Constantin R. Soldatos

Department of Psychiatry, University of Athens, Eginition Hospital, Athens, Greece

Abstract. Recent research data show that suicide risk is only definitely increased for patients suffering from AIDS, various malignancies, Huntington's disease, multiple sclerosis, peptic ulcer, renal diseases, spinal cord injury and systemic lupus erythematosus. Since this cluster of illnesses includes a rather benign condition such as peptic ulcer, while it does not include many other chronic and debilitating conditions, it appears that a host of various illness-specific clinical characteristics and/ or psychosocial consequences underlies the suicidal process, which should be expected to vary extensively from one physical illness to another as well as from patient to patient. In cancer patients, for example, it seems that it is not the cancer diagnosis itself but the progression and severity of the disease process, the intensity of pain and discomfort, the degree of physical disability, the level of social impairment and the consequent losses that cause emotional distress and depression, which in turn lead to suicidal ideation and eventual attempts or completed suicides. Yet, in spite of all of the above factors being present in many cancer patients, the excess mortality among them is only about 2-fold that of the general population. Obviously, a balance of countervailing forces towards continuing life operates in the vast majority of suicide patients, in accordance with the model for suicide risk proposed by Plutchik and his associates. Such a balance may be operating to a varying extent in patients with many other chronic and debilitating physical illnesses as well. Nonetheless, until now suicide research in patients with physical illnesses appears to be flawed with certain methodological problems, which could interfere with reliable results. Some of these problems are detailed in this paper.

Keywords: AIDS, cancer, physical illness, suicide.

Introduction

The relation of suicide to physical illness has attracted relatively less attention than its respective relationship to psychiatric disorders [1,2]. Based on their clinical experience, physicians tend to believe that patients suffering from any serious physical illness are at high risk for suicide. However, research data indicate that this assumption has not entirely proven to be true [2]. The main purpose of this paper is to examine the overall relationship of suicide to poor physical health. Subsequently, a detailed description of the various factors influencing the development of suicidality will be provided by focusing on suicides in cancer patients. Finally, reference will be made to the methodological problems that may confound relevant research to suicide among the physically ill.

Address for correspondence: C.R. Soldatos MD, Department of Psychiatry, University of Athens, Eginition Hospital, 74, Vas. Sophias Ave., Athens, Greece.

Suicidality and poor physical health

Although various medical illnesses have been associated with a high risk for suicide [1], until a few years ago [2] the exact relationship between poor physical health and suicide was not documented. This relationship has now been established to a certain degree.

An investigation of the potential role of recent life events in 400 suicide victims [3] has shown that somatic illness was rated by their spouses as the second most critical precipitating factor (in 57% of the cases). A recent statistical overview of 63 medical conditions, which might be associated with an altered suicide risk, showed that there is definitely an increased risk ($p < 0.05$ when comparing observed suicide numbers to the expected ones) for patients suffering from: AIDS, malignant neoplasms, Huntington's disease, multiple sclerosis, peptic ulcer, renal disease, spinal cord injury and systemic lupus erythematosus [2]. Also, some inconclusive evidence (N.S.) for increased suicide risk was shown for amputation, heart valve replacement and surgery, disorders of the intestine (Crohn disease, ileostomy, ulcerative colitis), hormone replacement therapy, alcoholic liver disease, neurofibromatosis, systemic sclerosis and Parkinsons's disease [2]. Pregnancy and the puerperium were found to have decreased suicide risks ($p < 0.05$), whereas there was no evidence of either increased or decreased risk for any of the remaining 44 medical conditions, which have been previously considered to have an altered suicide risk [2]. As far as the actual relative risks are concerned, only the observed rate of suicide for AIDS is quite high (7-fold higher than expected), while that for cancer has been found to be only 2-fold higher than expected [4—6].

Based on the above data, physical illness is a frequent precipitant among suicide victims (i.e., in more than half of the cases), while among physically ill patients an increased suicide risk is definitively found only for those suffering from AIDS, malignancies, Huntington's, multiple sclerosis, peptic ulcer, renal disease, spinal cord injury and systemic lupus erythematosus [2,3]. As expected, this cluster of illnesses does include certain chronic, debilitating and life-threatening medical conditions. However, it does not include many other similarly chronic and/or debilitating ones, such as epilepsy or ankylosing spondylitis, which have been previously considered to have a high suicide risk [7,8]. More surprisingly, it includes peptic ulcer [2], which by no means is a debilitating condition. Therefore, the only factor for an increased suicide risk may not be the chronic clinical course and/or the unfavourable outcome of a physical illness. It may rather be that a host of illness-specific clinical characteristics and/or psychosocial consequences underlies the suicidal process which is expected to vary extensively from one physical illness to another and, therefore, it deserves special consideration for each separate nosological entity. Because of space limitations, a detailed description will be provided by focusing only on cancer, e.g., the medical condition best studied in terms of its relationship to suicidality.

Suicidality and cancer

There is about a 2-fold excess mortality among cancer patients compared to the general population [5,6]. Yet, the absolute number of suicides associated with a cancer diagnosis is quite low, amounting to less than 1% of all deaths in cancer patients [6].

Cancer patients committing suicide when compared to other persons committing suicide are found to be significantly older and more often male, as well as being found to suffer more pain and physical disability [9]. It should also be noted that among cancer suicides cancer itself is found to be the main underlying factor in the suicide process in 62% of the patients and a contributing factor in 23% [9].

In terms of the site of the tumour, a particularly high excess mortality in suicide was found for cancer of the respiratory organs and the gastrointestinal system [5,6], as well as the nervous system and the kidney [10]. It has also been shown that nonlocalized cancer has a higher suicide risk compared to localized cancer [10]. These findings suggest that rapidly progressing tumours, such as lung cancer, are more likely to be associated with suicidality. Another indication of the severity of the cancer playing a major role in the development of suicidality is the finding that the relative risk for suicide is increased only during the first 2 years after diagnosis [6,10], i.e., in the cases surviving for 3 or more years the suicide risk is not increased any more. Consistent with this finding is the fact that cancer patients who commit suicide during the first year after diagnosis are more often found to have advanced or rapidly progressing disease [11].

No major differences are found regarding the method of committing or attempting suicide between cancer and noncancer suicides [6,12]. Yet, although cancer patients compared to other individuals committing suicide are not at relatively higher risk for taking an overdose of analgesics or other lethal drugs, caution is required when prescribing such medications to these as well as to any other patients.

Another important issue relates to the prevalence and role of mental disorders in cancer suicides. The overall prevalence of clinical depression among any cancer patients has been estimated to be about 25% [13]. This compares to an 80% prevalence of depressive syndromes among cancer suicides, which does not differ from that found among noncancer suicides (82%) [14]. Major depression and substance abuse are more common among suicide victims with cancer in remission than in terminal cases. Only a small minority of cancer suicides occur in the absence of mental disorders [14]. These findings underline the role of mental disorders, particularly that of depression, in the development of suicidal risk among cancer patients.

For obvious reasons, it is of interest to know what are the chances for the development of suicidality in the newly diagnosed patients with a serious malignancy of relatively unfavourable prognosis. A recent study [15] showed that 31% of lung cancer patients had recurring thoughts of death, while 13% considered suicide. It is remarkable that, in that study, the prevalence of diagnosable psychiatric disorders was quite low (e.g., affective disorder in 4% and adjustment disorder in 12%). However, there was a rather high prevalence of symptoms indicative of psychopathology and/or psychosocial concerns (i.e., insomnia in 52%, loss of libido in 48%, reduced ability to work or loss of interest in 33%, concern about family in 29%). Yet 38% of these newly diagnosed lung cancer patients were accepting their diagnosis and 10% expressed optimism.

Taking into account all the information presented in this part of the paper we may conclude that it is not the cancer diagnosis itself, but the progression and severity of the disease, the intensity of pain and discomfort, the degree of physical disability, the level of social impairment and the consequent losses that cause emotional distress and depression, which in turn lead to suicidal ideation and eventual attempts or even completed suicides. Of course, in each individual case of a cancer patient various opposing factors are expected to operate either favouring or preventing suicidality and, thus, determining the outcome. In this respect, a plausible model for suicide risk should be that of the countervailing forces as proposed by Plutchik et al. [16,17]. Obviously, a balance of the countervailing forces towards continuing life operates effectively in the vast majority of cancer patients. Thus, the absolute number of suicides in these patients is kept quite low.

Methodological considerations

As detailed above, a relatively small number of physical illnesses is clearly associated to an increased suicide risk [2]. Even in most cases of these illnesses the numbers of patients committing suicide are quite low, e.g., in cancer patients the observed rate of suicides is only 2-fold compared to the expected [5,6]. However, suicide research in patients with various medical conditions may present with certain methodological problems which could interfere with reliable results.

The authors of a statistical overview of previously published studies have required three criteria for inclusion of a study in their analysis:
1. Availability of reliably observed and expected suicide rates.
2. A 2-year follow-up to establish mortality due to suicide.
3. A small percentage of subjects lost, i.e., less than 10% [2].
Yet, because of their rapid fatal course, many serious illnesses do not allow for adequate follow-up to establish survival including that related to suicide. Moreover, for most serious physical illnesses it is practically impossible to estimate the rates of assisted suicide or hastened death, i.e., events which directly affect suicide rates. Also, appropriate control samples are not easily employed because it may be extremely difficult to control across study groups for certain disease-specific relevant factors such as pain, depressive mood, quality of life, etc.

Guidelines to overcome methodological difficulties in suicide research with the medically ill cannot be easily formulated at this point. Nonetheless, the following methodological issues should be taken into account when considering suicide in physical illness:
1. Establishment of a reliably observed suicide rate depends upon:

(a) the rapidity of the clinical course of the illness allowing for adequate follow-up;

(b) the presence of a serious physical and/or mental impairment limiting or preventing the suicidal acts;

(c) the availability or unavailability of suicidal means which influence completion of suicide; and

(d) the interference of obvious, yet occult, sources of bias such as assisted suicides or hastened deaths as well as violent and apparently accidental deaths of all kinds.

2. Establishment of a reliable expected suicide rate may be influenced by the selection of the control group. The assumption that an adequate control group is that of the general population can be erroneous, because crucial factors which are not controlled for are consequently being neglected. Such factors include:

(a) degree of pain and physical disability;

(b) severity of distress and depressive mood;

(c) level of social impairment; and

(d) estimation of quality of life, etc.

References

1. Lester D. Why people kill themselves. A 1990's summary of research findings on suicidal behavior. Springfield, IL: Charles C. Thomas, 1992.
2. Harris EC, Barraclough BM, McHugh PR. Suicide as an outcome for medical disorders. Medicine 1994;73:281—298.
3. Heikkinen M, Aro H, Lonnqvist J. Recent life events and their role in suicide as seen by the spouses. Acta Psychiatr Scand 1992;86:489—494.
4. Cote TR, Biggar RJ, Dannenberg AL. Risk of suicide among persons with AIDS: A national assessment. J Am Med Assoc 1992;268:2066—2068.
5. Louhivuori KA, Hakama M. Risk of suicide among cancer patients. Am J Epidemiol 1979;109: 59—65.
6. Allebeck P, Bolund C. Suicides and suicide attempts in cancer patients. Psychol Med 1991;21: 979—984.
7. Barraclough BM. The suicide rate in epilepsy. Acta Psychiatr Scand 1987;76:339—345.
8. Radford E, Doll R, Smith P. Mortality among patients with ankylosing spondylitis not given x-ray therapy. N Engl J Med 1977;297:572—576.
9. Hietanen P, Lonnqvist J, Henriksson M, Jallinoja P. Do cancer suicides differ from others? Psycho-Oncol 1994;3:189—195.
10. Storm HH, Christensen N, Jensen OM. Suicides among Danish patients with cancer: 1971 to 1986. Cancer 1992;69:1507—1512.
11. Bolund C. Suicide and cancer. II. Medical and care factors in suicides by cancer patients in Sweden, 1973—1976. J Psycho-Oncol 1985;3:31—52.
12. Allebeck P, Bolund C, Ringback G. Increased suicide rate in cancer patients: a cohort study based on the Swedish Cancer-Environment Register. J Clin Epidemiol 1989;42:611—616.
13. McDaniel JS, Musselman DL, Porter MR, Reed DA, Nemeroff CB. Depression in patients with cancer: diagnosis, biology and treatment. Arch Gen Psychiat 1995;52:89—99.
14. Henriksson MM, Isometsa ET, Hietanen PS, Aro HM, Lonnqvist JK. Mental disorders in cancer suicides. J Affect Dis 1995;36:11—20.

15. Ginsburg ML, Quirt C, Ginsburg AD, MacKillop WJ. Psychiatric illness and psychosocial concerns of patients with newly diagnosed lung cancer. Can Med Assoc J 1995;152:701—708.
16. Plutchik R, van Praag HM, Conte HR. Correlates of suicide and violence risk: III. A two-stage model of countervailing forces. Psychiat Res 1989;28:215—225.
17. Plutchik R, Botsis AJ, Weiner MB, Kennedy GJ. Clinical measurement of suicidality and coping in late life. A theory of countervailing forces. In: Kennedy GJ (ed) Suicide and Depression in Late Life. Critical Issues in Treatment, Research, and Public Policy. New York: John Wiley & Sons, 1996;83—102.

Etiopathogenetic considerations

Some biological and psychological aspects of suicidal behavior: An attempt to bridge the gap

H.M. van Praag

Department of Psychiatry & Neuropsychology, Maastricht University, Maastricht, The Netherlands

Abstract. The 5-HT-ergic impairment in certain types of depression is a trait phenomenon. This disturbance makes the individual susceptible for perturbation of anxiety and aggression regulation. Anxiety (overt or suppressed) and anger are core constituents of the stress syndrome. Thus, the 5-HT-ergic disturbance will induce a heightened sensitivity to stressful events (i.e., the latter will induce more readily than normal stress phenomena), among which anxiety and anger. The latter psychological features induce lowering of mood and thus "drive" the patient into a full-blown depression. Patients with the hypothesized depression type show increased stressor susceptibility and labile anxiety and aggression regulation. For those reasons, it is assumed that they run an increased suicide risk.

Keywords: aggression, anxiety, depression, serotonin, suicide.

Introduction

The most studied variable in biological suicide research is cerebrospinal fluid (CSF) 5-hydroxyindoleacetic acid (5-HIAA), an indicator of 5-hydroxytryptamine (serotonin, 5-HT) metabolism in (certain parts of) the brain. The relationship between lowered CSF 5-HIAA and suicidal behavior is a robust one [1] and tentative evidence suggests that not only 5-HT metabolism but likewise 5-HT-receptor function is downregulated in depressed and suicidal patients [2—4].

Psychologically and psychopathologically, however, suicide is such a complex behavior that simply relating it to perturbations in one neurobiological system seems reductionistically undue. Rather than to discuss biological data in isolation, I will submit to you a hypothesis in which they blend together with psychological and psychopathological variables in one coherent framework.

The hypothesis relates primarily to a new depression type that we have recently proposed and named 5-HT-related, anxiety/aggression-driven, stressor-precipitated depression [5]. I will characterize this depression subtype biologically, psychopathologically and in terms of personality dysfunctions, and subsequently point out its relatedness with suicidal behavior.

Address for correspondence: H.M. van Praag, Department of Psychiatry & Neuropsychology, Maastricht University, P.O. Box 616, 6200 MD Maastricht, The Netherlands. Tel.: +31-43-3877440. Fax: +31-43-3875444.

Hypothesis

The hypothesis I will submit in this paper is composed of three components. First, a subgroup of depression exists in which 5-HT-ergic dysfunctions play a pathogenetic role. Second, in those so-called 5-HT-related depressions, dysregulation of anxiety and/or aggression are the primary symptoms while mood lowering is a derivative phenomenon. Third, the 5-HT related, anxiety/aggression-driven depressions are precipitated by stressors in individuals who are susceptible to the psychologically disrupting effects of (certain types) of psychotraumatic events. I will discuss the evidence in favor of these three components separately.

5-HT-related depression

Disturbances in 5-HT metabolism and 5-HT receptor function

In a subgroup of depression disturbances in central 5-HT-ergic systems have been ascertained. The most significant of them being lowering of baseline and post-probenecid levels of 5-hydroxyindole-acetic acid (5-HIAA), the major metabolite of 5-HT (Fig. 1). These phenomena can be considered as an indication of diminished metabolism of 5-HT in (certain parts of) the central nervous system (CNS) [6—9].

Moreover, challenge tests, with the indirect 5-HT agonists L-tryptophan and fenfluramine [10—15], the partial 5-HT$_{1A}$ agonists buspirone [14] and ipsapirone [16], and the full 5-HT$_{1A}$ agonist flesinoxan [17], generated results suggestive of (certain) 5-HT receptors hyposensitivity. The diagnostic specificity of those tests, has hardly been studied, neither is it known whether they are nosologically or functionally specific, i.e., related to a particular categorical diagnostic construct or to a particular dysfunctioning psychological domain, irrespective of diagnosis.

Interestingly, the 5-HT$_2$ receptor system might be upregulated. SPECT studies revealed an increase of 5-HT$_2$ receptor density in the frontal cortex of some depressed patients [18]. Increased numbers of 5-HT$_2$ receptors have also been found in the frontal cortex of suicide victims [19] and in blood platelets in depression [20], in particular suicidal depressions [21].

5-HT$_2$ receptor upregulation could be a phenomenon secondary to downregulation of 5-HT$_{1A}$ receptors, or a compensatory response to diminished 5-HT metabolism. Alternatively, the changes in 5-HT$_2$ receptor density could be primary and the diminution of 5-HT metabolism secondary, i.e., compensatory. This latter hypothesis seems at present unlikely [22].

Other 5-HT disturbances

Several, though not all [23], authors have reported that plasma L-tryptophan, and the ratio plasma L-tryptophan vs. competing amino acids is lowered in

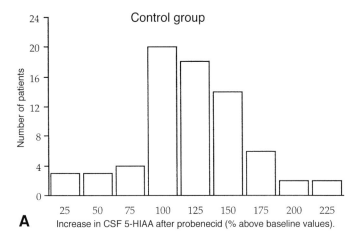

A

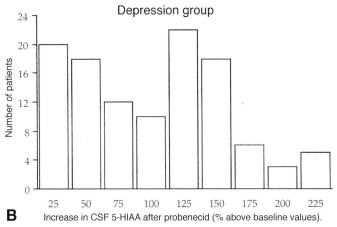

B

Fig. 1. Increase of CSF 5-HIAA concentration after probenecid in patients suffering from major depression, melancholic type (vital depression; endogenous depression) (**B**) and in a nonpsychiatric control group (**A**). The columns indicate the number of patients showing the increase in concentration given at the bottom of the column. The distribution in the depression group is bimodal. The depression group shows a significant increase in individuals with low CSF 5-HIAA [96].

patients with major depression [24]. Diminished tryptophan availability would limit 5-HT synthesis in the brain. This phenomenon, too, has not been studied as to categorical or functional specificity.

Another indication of the involvement of diminished 5-HT-ergic activity in mood disorders is the fact that most antidepressants augment 5-HT-ergic activity, albeit via different mechanisms [25], while tryptophan depletion has a depressogenic effect. Tryptophan depletion is induced with a mixture of amino acids devoid of tryptophan. Being the mother substance of 5-HT, as well as an essential amino acid, tryptophan depletion will rapidly lead to a 5-HT shortage in the brain and elsewhere. In depressed patients who had been successfully treated

76

with selective 5-HT uptake inhibitors (SSRIs) tryptophan depletion led to a rapid recurrence of depressive symptoms [26] and to mood lowering in normal subjects [27], in particular those with a genetic risk for major affective disorder [28]. Tryptophan-depleted normal subjects showed also higher anxiety levels, while aggression scores did not change [28]. On the other hand, it has been shown that acute tryptophan depletion aggravates the premenstrual syndrome and particularly the irritability component [29]. In addition, in an adult autistic patient, tryptophan depletion led to a marked exacerbation not only of depression but also of anxiety, anger, irritability and agitation [30].

These findings seem to suggest that tryptophan depletion influences mood, anxiety and aggression regulation, in a sequence that is unclear and in a diagnostically nonspecific fashion.

The mutual relation between the various indices of 5-HT-ergic dysfunction in depression is insufficiently studied and thus unknown. In the rest of this dissertation I will focus predominantly on one particular sign of 5-HT-ergic dysfunction, i.e., lowering of CSF 5-HIAA.

Specificity

Lowering of CSF 5-HIAA appeared not to be correlated with the type of depressive syndrome, mood disorder or severity of depression [37]. The changes in 5-HT metabolism were, instead, linked to components of the depression, in particular with heightened anxiety (Fig. 2) and aggression dysregulation both inwardly and outwardly directed (Fig. 3) [32—36]. Interestingly, no correlation could be established between lowering of CSF 5-HIAA and mood lowering [31] (Fig. 4).

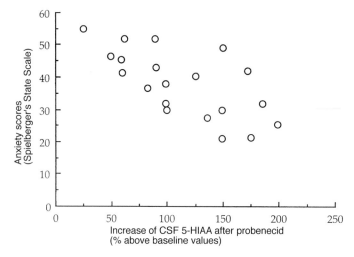

Fig. 2. Concentration of 5-HIAA in CSF in relation to the degree of trait anxiety in patients with major depression, melancholic type (endogenous depression; vital depression) [78].

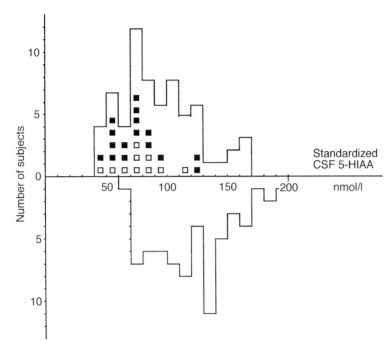

Fig. 3. Standardized concentration of CSF 5-HIAA in patients who have attempted suicide (upward) and healthy volunteer control subjects (downward). ■, Suicide attempts by a violent method (any method other than drug overdose, taken by mouth, or a single wrist cut). □, A subject who subsequently died from suicide, in all cases but one within 1 year after the lumbar puncture [34].

The correlation between 5-HT disturbances on the one hand, and anxiety and aggression dysregulation on the other, is not restricted to depression, but was found in nondepressive psychiatric disorders as well [38–49]. Thus, 5-HT disturbances in depression appear to be, what I have called functionally specific (i.e., coupled to specific psychological dysfunctions), rather than syndromic or nosologically specific. They occur across diagnoses [38,39].

Pathophysiological relevance

In most depressed patients the 5-HT disturbances, as manifested in the lowering of CSF 5-HIAA, persist in times of remission [31,35,50,51]. Maintenance treatment of recurrent unipolar depression with 5-hydroxytryptophan (5-HTP), in combination with a peripheral decarboxylase inhibitor, normalizes the CSF 5HIAA level and reduces the relapse frequency of depression [52–54]. 5-HTP is a 5-HT precursor that is centrally and readily transformed into 5-HT. Thus it could be expected to eliminate the alleged deficit in 5-HT synthesis in certain forms of depression.

We considered the observation that an additional supply of 5-HT exercises a prophylactic effect in recurrent unipolar depression to be an indication that the

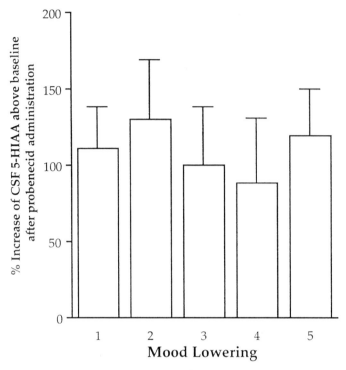

Fig. 4. Concentration of 5-HIAA in CSF in relation to the degree of mood lowering as assessed by the treating physician on a 5-point scale in untreated patients with major depression, melancholic type [37].

5-HT disturbances in certain types of depression are part of the pathophysiology of those conditions and not just secondary phenomena, marginal with respect to the pathogenetic process.

Anxiety- and/or aggression-driven depression

In a subgroup of depressed patients, a depressive episode is heralded by increased anxiety and/or signs of dysregulated outward directed aggression (e.g., irritability, eccentricity, bursts of anger). Mood lowering in those cases comes later [31,55,56] (Table 1).

In addition, in some depressed patients, the first symptoms to respond to anti-depressants are anxiety and aggression, while mood elevation appears to have a later outcome [57].

The two subgroups, the first in which anxiety/aggression heralds the depression and the second in which anxiety/aggression are first to respond to antidepressants, coincide to a large extent. Fifty-nine percent of depressed patients in whom anxiety/aggression appeared as precursor symptoms, showed an early response of anxiety and aggression to antidepressants. In the group of patients

Table 1. First manifestation of the depression in 50 patients with major depression and 50 with dysthymia and the occurrence of those features in a normal control group [56].

	Major depression		Dysthymic depression		Controls (n = 50)
	Symptoms pronounced	Symptoms mild or absent	Symptoms pronounced	Symptoms mild or absent	
Low spirits	11	39	42	8	2
Anxiety	41	9	24	26	3
Irritability	38	12	21	29	4
Inability to enjoy	16	34	7	43	1
Lack of drive	18	32	11	39	2
Diminished concentration	21	29	17	33	2
Difficulties thinking through	12	38	8	42	1
Fatigue	9	41	29	21	6
Disturbed sleep	24	26	24	26	3
Diminished appetite	14	36	6	44	2

with early symptoms of a different nature it was 29%.

Finally, anxiety and aggression are not independent phenomena but occurred highly intercorrelated in all the diagnostic categories we studied, i.e., schizophrenia, major depression and personality disorder. Thus this relationship is demonstrable across diagnoses [58–60] (Table 2). Based on these data, we formulated the hypothesis of an anxiety-/aggression-driven depression, i.e., a subtype of depression in which dysregulated aggression and/or anxiety are the primordial symptoms and in which mood lowering is the derivative.

Do the subgroups of 5-HT-related depression and anxiety-/aggression-driven depression coincide?

The link between 5-HT disturbances and anxiety/aggression

The decreased CSF 5-HIAA level observed in a subgroup of depression (suggestive of lowered 5-HT metabolism in certain parts of the central nervous system), supposedly carries pathogenetic significance. Moreover, this disturbance is strongly linked to the anxiety and aggression dimensions of the depressive syn-

Table 2. Correlation between anxiety and aggression in acute psychiatric inpatients from different diagnostic categories [58].

Suicide risk	Violence risk	Impulsivity	State anxiety	Trait anxiety
Suicide risk	0.53[a]	0.50[a]	0.47[a]	0.67[a]
Violent risk		0.39[b]	0.33[b]	0.48[a]
Impulsivity			0.33[b]	0.48[a]

[a]$p < 0.001$; [b]$p < 0.01$.

drome.

If a subgroup of anxiety/aggression-driven depression does indeed exist, one would expect patients with anxiety/aggression, as precursor symptoms of depression, to be overrepresented in the group of 5-HT-related depression, i.e., the patients with lowered CSF 5-HIAA. This could indeed be shown. In the low CSF 5-HIAA group, 62% of patients mentioned anxiety/aggression, not mood lowering, as the first manifestations of depression. In the normoserotonergic group this was 30% (unpublished observations).

In other words, signs of decreased 5-HT metabolism and the occurrence of anxiety/aggression as early symptoms of depression are clearly coupled. Anxiety and aggression dysregulation are the first symptoms to occur and hence are probably primordial and "driving", i.e., driving the patient into a full-blown state of depression. Moreover in patients with decreased 5-HT metabolism a successful treatment with antidepressants is often inaugurated by amelioration of anxiety and aggression dysregulation. Mood elevation occurs later, supposedly because the driving mechanisms have first to be switched off.

Parkinson's disease is frequently accompanied by depression [61], a complication possibly related to destruction of 5-HT-ergic neurons [62]. Interestingly, anxiety is a prominent feature of psychopathology in Parkinson's that frequently precedes the onset of depression [63]. Parkinson depression possibly belongs to the group of 5-HT-related, anxiety-/aggression-driven depressions [5].

Therapeutic expectations

If a 5-HT-related subgroup of depression in which anxiety and aggression are the driving forces does indeed exist, one would expect that those depressions would preferentially respond to compounds that diminish anxiety and/or aggression via regulation of the 5-HT-ergic system [64]. To date, some findings suggest that at least part of this prediction is being fulfilled.

Members of the azapirone class of compounds have been successfully used as anxiolytics. These compounds are partial agonists of 5-HT_{1A} receptors (e.g., buspirone and ipsapirone). Anxiolytic activity has also been reported of flesinoxan, a nonazapirone, full 5-HT_{1A} agonist. The anxiolytic potential of these compounds is contingent on regulation of 5-HT-ergic circuits [36,65,66]. Initially, they activate both the presynaptic — somatodendritic and terminal — and the postsynaptic 5-HT_{1A} receptors. Presynaptic activation leads to a decrement in the firing rate and of synaptic 5-HT release, superseding the effect of postsynaptic 5-HT_{1A} receptor activation [67,68]. Gradually, however, the presynaptic 5-HT_{1A} receptors become desensitized and the effect of postsynaptic 5-HT_{1A}-receptor activation becomes manifest [25,69]. The anxiolytic effect of these drugs, too, develops gradually and hence is probably contingent on activation of postsynaptic 5-HT_{1A} receptors.

Increasing evidence indicates that 5-HT_{1A} agonists, in addition to being anxiolytics, possess antidepressant properties [17,66,70–72]. It is unknown whether the group of 5-HT-related, anxiety- and/or aggression-driven depressions respond preferentially.

Eltoprazine is a rather selective agonist of 5-HT$_{1b}$ receptors and exhibits in animals a strong and selective aggression-reducing action. Human data, though very scarce, show a similar action [73]. In addition, some, admittedly very preliminary findings suggest an additional antidepressive component. Data on a possible preferential effect in 5-HT-related, anxiety- and/or aggression-driven depression are not available.

Life events and 5-HT-related, anxiety-/aggression-driven depression

Life events and 5-HT-related depression

The 5-HT disturbances in depression, at least the lowering of the CSF 5-HIAA level, carry a trait character. Depression frequently takes a recurrent, rather than a chronic course. Assuming that the 5-HT disturbances have pathogenetic significance, we hypothesised that they could possibly be conceived as vulnerability factors, decreasing coping ability and increasing the risk of depression in case of mounting stress [54].

In order to get an impression of the stress level prior to the onset of depression, we used the life event scale developed by Paykel et al. [74]. Based on data obtained from 213 psychiatric patients and 160 relatives of psychiatric patients, these authors rank-ordered 61 life events according to their psychotraumatic weight. We extended the "top five" events a score of 12, the subsequent five a score of 11, and so on, so that the last six events received a score of 1. If a patient mentioned more than one event the scores were averaged.

From a cohort of 203 patients with depression in whom CSF 5-HIAA had been measured, we contrasted those 25 with the lowest CSF 5-HIAA concentrations, with those with the highest CSF 5-HIAA values in terms of the seriousness, i.e., the "weight" of the life events that had occurred in the 3 months prior to the onset of the depression. As far as age and gender go, the two groups were comparable. They were not and could not be matched as to social support and socioeconomic status.

The average "weight" of life events that had occurred in that period was significantly less in the low CSF 5-HIAA group (5.1 ± 0.9) than in the high CSF 5-HIAA group (7.8 ± 1.1). This observation permits two explanations. First, 5-HT-related depression arises in large measures autonomously, i.e., independent of psychotraumatic events. Second, in 5-HT-related depression the susceptibility for (certain) psychotraumatic events is increased. Probably, this is the reason why ostensibly minor events exercise a powerful decompensating effect [74]. The probability of the second hypothesis is greater than that of the first, a conclusion which is based on considerations discussed in the next section.

Personality and 5-HT-related depression

In the group of low CSF 5-HIAA depressives, manifestations of personality disorder were more prevalent than in the group of high CSF 5-HIAA depressives. In this study, we focussed on ego-syntonic, as opposed to ego-dystonic symptoms. Ego-dystonic symptoms of a personality disorder are experienced by the patient as pathological. Examples are excessive fears, outspoken moodiness and perfectionism with difficulties to terminate, to a degree that task completion is interfered with. Ego-syntonic symptoms, on the other hand, are experienced as part of one's self — "it is just the way I am, doctor" — though they may profoundly compromise the quality of and the satisfaction with one's life. Ego-syntonic personality disorder corresponds with Freud's concept of character neurosis. The transition from an ego-syntonic to an ego-dystonic personality disorder is gradual, but yet the distinction is important, because these "character neuroses" (mild forms of personality disorder, one could say) largely escape the instruments used for the assessment of personality disorders and thus, remains a "stepchild" of experimental psychiatry.

To trace symptoms of an ego-syntonic personality disorder we did not rely on available questionnaires because they are largely geared towards the ego-dystonic counterparts. Instead, we used structured interview techniques focussing on Jaspers' [75] phenomenological phenomena, i.e., we concentrated on the individual's own experiences [31,76.77]. In this case we tried to explore whether the patient experienced his or her personality make-up as being neurotic, i.e., as a source of dissatisfaction and displeasure. We qualified a personality as (character) neurotically disturbed if, in a structured interview, the following experiential qualities were thought to be present by at least two clinicians' independent evaluation:

1. Basic feelings of discontent with one's life situation and one's own psychological make-up. Feelings that life has treated one unfairly, in that it had blessed most others with more pleasure and satisfaction than oneself.
2. Unhappiness with one's personal relations, ranging from parental relations and school and work experiences, to marital relations and relations with one's children. The other is felt to be not forthcoming, distant, threatening, cold, abrasive or in any other way not meeting the individual's expectations and needs. As a consequence, a chronic feeling of loneliness and solitude has developed.
3. Emotional instability, in that the basic discontent ignites a range of emotions varying from mood lowering to guilt, anger, despair and anxiety. These emotions are generally intense, vary abruptly and frequently, sometimes ignited by traceable events in the life situation, sometimes not clearly so.

We scored each of the three factors on a five-point scale ranging from 4 to 0 so that a maximum score of 12 and a minimum score of 0 could be obtained. Interviews were done when patients were in remission [78]. The average score on the three items was 9.8 in the group of low 5-HIAA depressives and 6.1 in that of high 5-HIAA depressives. The former group thus held a larger proportion of (ostensibly) "asymptomatic" or "minor" personality disorder, than the group of high 5-HIAA depressives.

Moreover, we explored in detailed free interviews the character of the life events occurring in the 3-month period prior to the onset of the depression. In the low 5-HIAA group the majority ranked rather low on the more or less objective Paykel's scale. Rating them on a global impact scale ranging from 0 (unimportant) to 4 (severely disrupting) the patients themselves, however, considered them to be severe (mean rating 3.1), i.e., as serious blows to an already meager sense of independence and self-appreciation. Examples are a derogatory remark of one's superior at work, a disappointing date, an expected invitation that had not been forthcoming. Due to personality imperfections these individuals were vulnerable to psychotraumatic events, particularly those that reinforced feelings of insecurity, loneliness, nonacceptance, and dependence.

In conclusion, in 5-HT-related depression the susceptibility for (certain) life events is increased, and this is the reason why seemingly insignificant events may exercise, psychologically, a powerful decompensating effect. This conclusion is phrased with caution. Concepts like "character neurosis" and "stressor vulnerability" are hard to assess reliably and have been largely neglected in experimental psychiatry. This study was a first attempt to approach subjective components of the psychopathological specimen in an experimental fashion [31].

5-HT-related, anxiety-/aggression-driven, stressor-precipitated depression

A mental state an individual cannot adequately cope with generates, initially, feelings of discomfort and thereupon a conglomerate of physical and psychological symptoms carrying the name of the stress syndrome. The stress-phenomena generating conditions are called stressors [79]. The composition of the stress syndrome varies considerably among individuals, but two elements are almost universally present, i.e., anxiety and anger. Anger might be overt or suppressed and directed towards the instigators of the stress, or towards oneself for being unable to handle the stressful situation adequately. Stress-syndrome-prone individuals, i.e., stress-prone individuals, develop stress symptoms under burdensome conditions more readily than normals.

Patients with 5-HT-related depression can be considered to be stress prone. First, because of a biological impairment, i.e., a trait-related 5-HT disturbance, linked to an instability of anxiety and aggression regulation. That is why these individuals will readily respond with anxiety and/or anger in taxing conditions. Stress proneness is further conditioned by debilitating personality traits and corresponding oversensitiveness for the unsettling effects of (particular) psychotraumatic life events.

The biological and psychological impairments converge, in making patients with 5-HT-related depression susceptible for the stress syndrome, the anxiety/ aggression components of which serve as pacemakers for mood lowering, driving

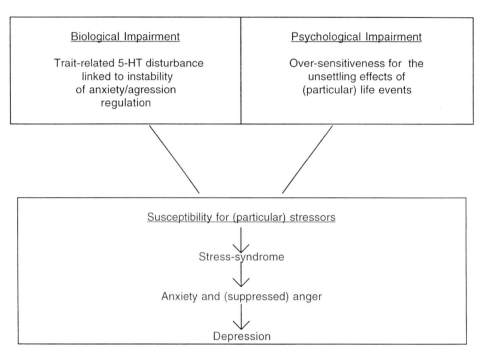

Fig. 5. Schematic representation of the relation between 5-HT disturbances, depression and psycho-traumatic events.

the patient into a full-blown depression (Fig. 5).

Thus, a 5-HT-related, anxiety-/aggression-driven, stressor-precipitated depression has been conceptualized, an as yet hypothetical construct that I shall set out to define and to support.

Discussion

Inevitably, the proposed hypothesis leaves many questions unanswered. The exact nature of 5-HT disturbances in depression is unknown. They could be related to metabolism, receptor function, uptake mechanism and second messenger systems. They could be genetically determined, the consequence of acquired brain damage, induced by sustained stress or by combinations of these variables. It is possible that all 5-HT disturbances in depression are anxiety/aggression driven, but it is equally conceivable that the 5-HT system can be disturbed in various ways in different groups of depressed patients and that not all disturbances are stress driven. These questions should be addressed in subsequent research.

Another intriguing question is whether 5-HT dysfunction and hypercortisol-aemia are interrelated. In many depressives the hypothalamo-pituitary-adrenal (HPA) axis is activated, a cascade ultimately leading to increased secretion of cortisol by the adrenal cortex [80,81]. This phenomenon could be linked to the depression per se or, rather, to the increased stress level preceding and/or accompanying the depressive state. The latter hypothesis seems more likely than the former [82,83].

A sustained rise in the cortisol level could influence the 5-HT system function in several ways. First, by induction of the enzyme tryptophan pyrolase in the liver, a mechanism through which tryptophan is shunted into the kynurenine-nicotinamide pathway and thus away from 5-HT synthesis [84,85]. Furthermore, cortisol influences 5-HT receptor sensitivity, in downregulating the 5-HT$_{1A}$ receptor [86—88] and upregulating the 5-HT$_2$ receptor [89]. Both effects probably contribute to destabilisation of anxiety regulation [90—92].

It is thus conceivable that sustained stress, by causing a prolonged increase in cortisol secretion, contributes to a disruption of the 5-HT system, particularly in those individuals in which that system is marginally functioning to begin with [52,53,56]. Cortisol hypersecretion could thus initiate the cascade of events hypothesized in this paper, leading from stressor exposure, via destabilisation of anxiety and aggression regulation to, ultimately, a state of depression.

The hypothesis proposed here implies that serotonergically acting anxiolytics (and serenics), such as the 5-HT$_{1A}$ agonists, will be the treatment of choice in 5-HT-related, anxiety- and/or aggression-driven depression. This hypothesis agrees well with Deakin's proposal that the 5-HT$_{1A}$ system promotes resistance to stress in situations of adversity [93]. Benzodiazepines, the classical anxiolytics, have in no subgroup of depression been shown to be effective antidepressants. The reason for this could be that these compounds act not serotonergically but via the GABA/benzodiazepine receptor system. The fact that no evidence today suggests that the current antidepressants are ineffective in the alleged subgroup of anxiety-/aggression-driven depression, is also not incompatible with the expectation that serotonergic anxiolytics (and serenics) will be the most specific treatment of anxiety-/aggression-driven depression. Most of today's antidepressants increase, via different mechanisms, 5-HT-ergic activity [25]. Accordingly, in humans these drugs augment the prolactine response to L-tryptophan. This augmentation is indicative of increased 5-HT receptor responsiveness, in particular of the 5-HT$_{1A}$ receptor [14]. This could explain the efficacy of these drugs in anxiety-/aggression-driven depression.

Finally, one may raise the issue whether 5-HT disturbances in depression could justifiably be called nosologically nonspecific, or rather related to a diagnostic concept, i.e., that of "mixed anxiety depression disorder". That diagnosis, however, seems to me [56] and others [94] to be a would-be diagnosis. If two sets of pathological phenomena, in this case anxious and depressive phenomena, frequently occur together, logic dictates to question and to study the validity of the diagnostic demarcation between mood and anxiety disorders, rather than to create a new "disorder", such as mixed anxiety depression disorder.

Apart from its confirmation or repudiation, one cannot deny this hypothesis' centripetal quality. It provides a framework for a set of, so far, disconnected stress-related, biological and psychopathological data. Psychiatry needs this type of bridging hypotheses, lest it ultimately falls apart in a series of largely independently operating subdisciplines.

Furthermore the hypothesis demonstrates the importance of what I have called "functionalisation" [38,95] and "verticalisation" [56,76] of psychiatric diagnosis. Psychiatric diagnoses are generally limited to a characterisation of the disorder, e.g., major depression and of the predominant symptomatology (e.g., major depression, melancholic type). The third or functional tier of diagnosing is disregarded. At that diagnostic level the psychopathological syndrome is dissected in its component parts, i.e., the psychological dysfunctions, such as, in the case of depression, disturbances in mood, anxiety and aggression regulation, in hedonic functions, in memory, concentration and information processing, in motoricity, and level of initiative. The present research demonstrates the importance of including this third tier in the diagnostic process, if the goal is to increase insight in brain and behavior relationships.

In present day psychiatry, moreover, we tend to group symptoms horizontally as if they were all of equal diagnostic weight. The group of mood disorders is no exception to this rule. Symptoms are not being weighed as to their diagnostic importance. It is a priori unlikely, however, that they are equal in this respect. Some, supposedly, are primary, i.e., the immediate consequence of the pathogenetic process, while others are derivatives. The present studies are a case in point. They suggest that in a subtype of depressions anxiety and aggression are the primary symptoms and that mood lowering is a secondary phenomenon. This observation has, as I have discussed, important consequence for treatment and for the development of novel treatment strategies.

The significance of the proposed hypothesis, thus, reaches beyond its actual contents.

The psychobiological bridge to suicidal behavior

Patients with the hypothesized depression type show three distinguishing features, with relevance to suicidal behavior. Firstly, stressors susceptibility is increased and secondly, anxiety regulation is easily perturbed. Like depression [96], we

Table 3. Anxiety (attacks) in the 2 weeks preceding a suicide attempt in 100 consecutive patients hospitalized after a suicide attempt and in two control groups [97].

	No.	Number of patients	
		Chronic anxiety	"Bursts" of anxiety
Suicide attempters	100	38	33
Depression (anxiety in 2 weeks before hospitalization)	79	41	5
Normals (anxiety in 2 weeks before interview)	54	2	—

found anxiety — often in panic outbursts — to frequently precede suicide attempts [97] (Table 3). Thirdly, aggression regulation is likewise labile and aggressive impulses are a prerequisite for suicidal behaviour [98].

Those are the reasons that I predict that 5-HT-related, anxiety-/aggression-driven depression represents a group of depressions with greatly increased suicide risk. In this manner a provisional bridge is conceptualized between psychological and biological determinants of suicidal behavior; presumably one of many.

Summary

The concept of a 5-HT-related, anxiety- and/or aggression-driven, stressor-precipitated depression is formulated and discussed. It comprises the following elements.

The 5-HT-ergic disturbances found in some depressed individuals — and in those who presented with a particularly lowered CSF 5-HIAA — are linked to the anxiety and the aggression components of the depressive syndrome.

In this type of depression — called 5-HT-related depression — dysregulation of anxiety and/or aggression is primordial and mood-lowering is a derivative phenomenon. In other words, this is the group of anxiety-/aggression-driven depression.

The 5-HT-ergic impairment in certain types of depression is a trait phenomenon, i.e., it persists during remission. This disturbance makes the individual susceptible for perturbation of anxiety and aggression regulation. Anxiety and (overt or suppressed) anger, are core constituents of the stress syndrome. Thus, the 5-HT-ergic disturbance will induce a heightened sensitivity for stressful events (i.e., the latter will induce more readily than normal, stress phenomena), among which anxiety and anger. The latter psychological features induce lowering of mood and thus "drive" the patient into a full-blown depression.

Furthermore, it is predicted that anxiolytics and serenics (i.e., antiaggressive drugs) that act via normalisation of 5-HT-ergic circuits, will exert an antidepressant effect in 5-HT-related depression, in addition to their therapeutic actions in anxiety disorders and states of increased aggressiveness, respectively.

Patients with the hypothesized depression type show increased stressor susceptibility and labile anxiety and aggression regulation. For those reasons it is assumed that they run an increased suicide risk.

References

1. Lester D. The concentration of neurotransmitter metabolites in the cerebrospinal fluid of suicidal individuals: a meta-analysis. Pharmacopsychiatrist 1995;28:45–50.
2. Mann JJ, McBride PA, Malone KM, DeMeo M, Keilp J. Blunted serotonergic responsivity in depressed inpatients. Neuropsychopharmacy 1995;13:53–64.
3. Coccaro EF, Siever LJ, Klar HM, Maurer G, Cochrane K, Cooper FB, Mohs RC, Davis KL. Serotonergic studies in patients with affective and personality disorders. Arch Gen Psychiat 1989;46:587–599.

4. Lopez-Ibor JJ, Lana F, Saiz-Ruiz J. Impulsive suicidal behavior and serotonin. Actas Luso Esp Neurol Psiquiatr 1990;18:316–325.

5. Van Praag HM. Serotonin and affective psychopathology in Parkinson's disease. A psychobiological hypothesis with therapeutic consequences. In: Wolters EC, Scheltens P (eds) Mental Dysfunction in Parkinson's Disease. Amsterdam: Vrije Universiteit, 1993;325–348.

6. Van Praag HM, Korf J, Puite J. 5-Hydroxyindoleacetic acid levels in the cerosbrospinal fluid of depressive patients treated with probenecid. Nature 1970;225:1259–1260.

7. Van Praag HM, Korf J. Endogenous depressions with and without disturbances in the 5-hydroxytryptamine metabolism: a biochemical classification? Psychopharmacology 1971;19:148–152.

8. Meltzer HJ, Lowy MT. The serotonin hypothesis of depression. In: Meltzer HJ (ed) Psychopharmacology. The Third Generation of Progress. New York: Raven Press, 1987;513–526.

9. Westenberg HGM, Verhoeven WMA. CSF monoamine metabolites in patients and controls: support for a bimodal distribution in major affective disorders. Acta Psychiatr Scand 1988; 478:541–749.

10. Caldecott-Hazard S, Guze BH, Kling MA, Kling A, Baxter LR. Clinical and biochemical aspects of depressive disorders: I. introduction, classification, and research techniques. Synapse 1991;8:185–211.

11. Siever LJ, Kahn RS, Lawlor BA, Trestman RL, Lawrence TLL, Coccaro EF. II. Critical issues in defining the role of serotonin in psychiatric disorders. Pharmacol Rev 1991;43:509–525.

12. Deakin JWF, Pennell I, Upadhyaya AJ and Lofthouse R. A neuroendocrine study of 5-HT function in depression: evidence for biological mechanisms of endogenous and psychosocial causation. Psychopharmacology 1990;101:85–92.

13. O'Keane V, Dinan TG. Prolactin and cortisol responses to d-fenfluramine in major depression: evidence for diminished responsivity of central serotonergic function. Am J Psychiat 1991;148:1009–1015.

14. Cowen PJ. The effect of tryptophan on brain 5-HT function: a review. Hum Psychopharmacol 1994;9:371–376.

15. Cowen PJ, Power AC, Ware CJ, Anderson IM. 5-HT$_{1a}$ receptor sensitivity in major depression. A neuroendocrine study with buspirone. Br J Psychiat 1994;164:372–379.

16. Lesch KP, Mayer S, Disselkamp-Tietze J, Hoh A, Wiesmann M, Osterheider M, Schulte HM. 5-HT$_{1a}$ receptor responsivity in unipolar depression evaluation of ipsapirone-induced ACTH and cortisol secretion in patients and controls. Biol Psychiat 1990;28:620–628.

17. Ansseau M, Pitchot W, Gonzalez Moreno A, Wauthy J, Papart P. Pilot study of flesinoxan, a 5-HT$_{1a}$ agonist, in major depression: effects on sleep REM latency and body temperature. Hum Psychopharmacol 1993;8:279–283.

18. D'Haenen H, Bossuyt A, Mertens J, Bossuyt-Piron C, Gijsemans M, Kaufman L. SPECT imaging of serotonin$_2$ receptors in depression. Psychiat Res 1992;45:227–237.

19. Arango V, Ernsberger P, Marzuk PM, Chen J-S, Tierney H, Stanley M, Reis DJ, Mann J. Autoradiographic demonstration of increased serotonin 5-HT$_2$ and β-adrenergic receptor binding sites in the brain of suicide victims. Arch Gen Psychiat 1990;47:1038–1047.

20. Arora RC, Meltzer HY. Increase Serotonin$_2$ (5-HT$_2$) receptor binding as measured by ^{3}H-lysergic acid diethylamide (^{3}H-LSD) in the blood platelets of depressed patients. Life Sci 1989;44:725–734.

21. Pandey GN, Pandey SC, Janicak PG, Marks RC, Davis JM. Platelet serotonin-2 receptor binding sites in depression and suicide. Biol Psychiat 1990;28:215–222.

22. Cowen PJ. Serotonin receptor subtypes in depression: evidence from studies in neuroendocrine regulation. Clin Neuropharm 1993;16(Suppl 3):S6–S18.

23. Taracha E, Szukalsi B. Serum tryptophan levels in patients with endogenous depression. I. Differences between unipolar and bipolar forms of affective disorder. New Trends Exp Clin Psychiat 1994;10:9–13.

24. Maes M, Meltzer H. The serotonin hypothesis of major depression. In: Bloom FE, Kupfer DJ

(eds) Psychopharmacology: The Fourth Generation of Progress. New York: Raven Press, 1995; 1–11.

25. Blier P, de Montigny C. Current advances and trends in the treatment of depresssion. TIPS 1994;15:220–226.

26. Delgado PL, Charney DS, Price LH, Aghajanian GK, Landis H, Heninger GR. Serotonin function and the mechanism of antidepressant action. Arch Gen Psychiat 1990;47:411–418.

27. Young SN, Smith SE, Pihl RO, Erving FR. Tryptophan depletion causes a rapid lowering of mood in normal males. Psychopharmacology 1985;87:173–177.

28. Benkelfat C, Ellenbogen MA, Dean P, Palmour RM, Young SN. Moodlowering effect of tryptophan depletion. Enhanced susceptibility in young men at genetic risk for major effective disorders. Arch Gen Psychiat 1994;51:687–697.

29. Menkes DB, Coates DC, Fawcett JP. Acute tryptophan depletion aggravates premenstrual syndrome. J Affec Disord 1994;32:37–44.

30. McDougle CJ, Naylor ST, Goodman WK, Volkmar FR, Cohen DJ, Price LH. Acute tryptophan depletion in autistic disorder: a controlled case study. Biol Psychiat 1993;33:547–550.

31. Van Praag HM. Reconquest of the subjective. Against the waning of psychiatric diagnosing. Br J Psychiat 1992;160:266–271.

32. Kahn RS, Wetzler S, Van Praag HM, Asnis GM. Behavioral indications for serotonin receptor hypersensitivity in panic disorder. Psych Res 1988;25:101–104.

33. Kahn RS, Wetzler S, Van Praag HM, Asnis GM. Neuroendocrine evidence for 5-HT receptor hypersensitivity in patients with panic disorder. Psychopharmacology 1988;96:360–364.

34. Asberg M, Norstrom P, Traskman-Bendz L. Biological factors in suicide. In: Roy A, (ed) Suicide. Baltimore, MD: Williams & Wilkins, 1986.

35. Asberg M, Schalling D, Traskman-Bendz L, Wagner A. Psychobiology of suicide, impulsivity, and related phenomena. In: Meltzer HJ (ed) Psychopharmacology: The Third Generation of Progress. New York: Raven Press, 1987;655–668.

36. Eison AS, Eison MS. Serotonergic mechanisms in anxiety. Prog Neurol Psychopharmacol Biol Psychiat 1994;18:47–62.

37. Van Praag HM. About the centrality of mood lowering in mood disorders. Eur Neuropsychopharmacol 1992;2:393–404.

38. Van Praag HM, Kahn RS, Asnis GM, Wetzler S, Brown S, Bleich A, Korn M. Denosologization of biological psychiatry or the specifity of 5-HT disturbances in psychiatric disorders. J Affec Disord 1987;13:1–8.

39. Van Praag HM, Asnis GM, Kahn RS, Brown SL, Korn M, Harkavy Friedman, JM, Wetzler S. Monoamines and abnormal behavior. A multi-aminergic perspective. Br J Psychiat 1990;157: 723–734.

40. Traskman-Bendz L, Alling C, Alsén M, Regnéll G, Simonsson P, Ohman R. The role of monoamines in suicidal behavior. Acta Psychiat Scand 1993;(Suppl 371):45–47.

41. Winchel RM, Stanley M. Self-injurious behavior; a review of the behavior and biology of self-mutilation. Am J Psychiat 1991;148:306–317.

42. Deakin JF, Graeff FG. Critique, 5-HT and mechanisms of defence. J Psychopharmacol 1991; 5:303–341.

43. Brain PF, Haug M. Hormonal and neurochemical correlates of various forms of animal "aggression". Psychoneuroendocrinology 1992;17:537–551.

44. Coccaro EF. Impulsive aggression and central serotonergic system function in humans; an example of a dimensional brain-behavior relationship. Int Clin Psychopharmacol 1992;7:3–12.

45. Nutt D, Lawson C. Panic attacks: a neurochemical overview of models and mechanisms. Br J Psychiat 1992;160:165–178.

46. Simeon D, Stanley B, Frances A, Mann JJ, Winchel R, Stanley M. Selfmutilation in personality disorders: psychological and biological correlates. Am J Psychiat 1992;149:221–226.

47. Pratt JA. The neuroanatomical basis of anxiety. Pharmacol Ther 1992;55:149–181.

48. Handley SL, McBlane. 5HT drugs in animal models of anxiety. Psychopharmacology 1993;112:

13–20.

49. Benkert O, Wetzel H, Szegedi A. Serotonin dysfunctions syndromes: a functional common denominator for classification of depression, anxiety, and obsessive-compulsive disorder. Int Clin Psychopharmacol 1993;8(Suppl 1):3–14.

50. Van Praag HM. Significance of biochemical parameters in the diagnosis, treatment and prevention of depressive disorders. Biol Psychiat 1977;12:101–131.

51. Traskman L, Asberg M, Bertilsson L, Sjostrand L. Monoamine metabolites in CSF and suicidal behavior. Arch Gen Psychiat 1981;38:633–636.

52. Van Praag HM, De Haan S. Central serotonin metabolism and frequency of depression. Psych Res 1979;1:219–224.

53. Van Praag HM, De Haan S. Depression vulnerability and 5-hydroxytryptophan prophylaxis. Psych Res 1980;3:75–83.

54. Van Praag HM, De Haan S. Central serotonin deficiency. A factor which increases depression vulnerability? Acta Psychiat Scand 1980;(Suppl 61):89–95.

55. Fava GA, Kellner R. Prodromal symptoms in affective disorders. Am J Psychiat 1991;148:823–830.

56. Van Praag HM. Make Believes in Psychiatry or the Perils of Progress. New York: Brunner Mazel, 1992.

57. Katz MM, Koslow S, Maas J, Frazer A, Kocsis J, Secuna S, Boden C, Casper R. Identifying the specific clinical actions of amitriptyline: inter-relationships of behavior, affect, and plasma levels in depression. Psychol Med 1991;21:599–611.

58. Apter A, Praag HM, Plutchik R, Sevy S, Korn M, Brown SL. Inter-relationships among anxiety, aggression, impulsivity, and mood: a serotoninergically linked cluster. Psych Res 1990;32:191–199.

59. Katon W, Roy-Byrne PP. Mixed anxiety and depression. J Abnorm Psychol 1991;100:337–345.

60. Coryell W, Endicott J, Winokur G. Anxiety syndromes as epiphenomena of primary major depression: outcome and familial psychopathology. Am J Psychiat 1992;149:100–107.

61. Gotham A, Brown RG, Marsen CD. Depression in Parkinson's disease: a quantitative analysis. J Neurol Neurosurg Psychiat 1986;49:381–389.

62. Mayeux R, Stern Y, Sano M, Williams JBW, Côté LJ. The relationship of serotonin to depression in Parkinson's disease. Move Disord 1988;3:237–244.

63. Henderson R, Jurlan R, Kersun JM, Como P. Preliminary examination of the comborbidity of anxiety and depression in Parkinson's disease. J Neuropsychiat 1992;4:257–264.

64. Van Praag HM, Kahn R, Asnis GM, Lemus CZ, Brown SL. Therapeutic indications for serotonin potentiating compounds. A hypothesis. Biol Psychiat 1987;22:205–212.

65. Deakin JF. A review of clinical efficacy of 5-HT$_{1a}$ agonists in anxiety and depression. J Psychopharmacol 1993;7:283–289.

66. Hjorth S, Auerbach S. Futher evidence for the importance of 5-HT$_{1a}$ autoreceptors in the action of selective serotonin reuptake inhibitors. Eur J Pharmacol 1994;260:251–255.

67. Invernizzi R, Bramante M, Samanin R. Chronic treatment with citalopram facilitates the effect of a challenge dose on cortical serotonin output: role of presynaptic 5-HT$_{1a}$ receptors. Eur J Pharmacol 1994;260:243–246.

68. Chaput Y, De Montigny C, Blier P. Effects of a selective 5-HT reuptake blocker, citalopram, on the sensitivity of 5-HT autoreceptors: Electrophysiological studies in the rat brain. Naunyn-Schmied Arch Pharmacol 1986;333:342–348.

69. Rickels K, Amsterdam J, Clary C, Hassman J, London J, Purruoli G, Schweizer E. Buspirone in depressed outpatients: A controlled study. Psychopharmacol Bull 1990;26:163–167.

70. Heller AH, Beneke M, Kuemmel B, Spencer D, Kurtz NM. Ipsapirone: evidence for efficacy in depression. Psychopharmacol Bull 1990;26:219–222.

71. Stahl SM, Gastpar M, Keppel Hesselink JM, Traber J. Serotonin 1A Receptors. New York: Raven Press, 1992.

72. Verhoeven WMA, Tuinier S, Sijben NAS, Van den Berg Y WHM, De Witte, EPPM, Pepplinkhui-

zen L, Van Nieuwenhuizen O. Eltoprazine in mentally retarded self-injuring patients. Lancet 1992;340:1037—1038.

73. Paykel EG, Prusoff BA, Uhlenhuth EH. Scaling of life events. Arch Gen Psychiat 1971;24: 340—347.

74. Van Praag HM. Serotonin-related, anxiety/aggression-driven, stressor-precipitated depression. A psychobiological hypothesis. Eur Psychiat 1996;(In press).

75. Jaspers K. Allgemeine Psychopathologie. Berlin/Heidelberg: Springer, 1948.

76. Van Praag HM. Diagnosis, the rate limiting factor of biological depression research. Neuropsychobiology 1993;28:197—206.

77. Van Praag HM. Diagnosing depression — looking backward into the future. Psychiat Devel 1989;7:375—394.

78. Hirschfeld R, Klerman GL, Clayton PJ, Keller MB, McDonald-Scott P, Larkin BH. Assessing personality: effects of the depressive state on trait measurement. Am J Psychiat 1983;140: 695—699.

79. Selye H. Selye's Guide to Stress Research, vol 1. New York: Van Nostrand Reinhold, 1980.

80. Checkley S. Neuroendocrine mechanisms and the precipitation of depression by life events. Br J Psychiat 1992;160:7—17.

81. Dinan TG. Glucocorticoids and the genesis of depressive illness. A psychobiological model. Br J Psychiat 1994;164:365—371.

82. Ceulemans DLS, Westenberg HGM, Van Praag HM. The effect of stress on dexamethasone suppression test. Psych Res 1985;14:189—195.

83. Van Eck MM, Nicolson NA. Perceived stress and salivary cortisol in daily life. Ann Behav Med 1994;16:221—226.

84. Morgan CJ, Badaway AAB. Effects of a suppression test dose of dexamethasone on tryptophan metabolism and disposition in the rat. Biol Psychiat 1989;25:359—362.

85. Maes M, De Ruyter M, Suy E. The renal excretion of xanthurenic acid following l-tryptophan loading in depressed patients. Hum Psychopharmacol 1987;2;231—235.

86. Young AH, MacDonald LM, John HST, Dick H, Goodwin GM. The effects of corticosterone on 5-HT receptor function in rodents. Neuropharmacology 1992;31:433—438.

87. Watanabe Y, Sakai RR, McEwen BS, Mendelson S. Stress and antidepressant effects on hippocampal and cortical 5-HT$_{1a}$ and 5-HT$_2$ receptors and transport sites for serotonin. Brain Res 1993;615:87—94.

88. Meijer OC, De Kloet ER. Corticosterone suppresses the expression of 5-HT$_{1a}$ receptor mRNA in rat dentate gyrus. Eur J Pharmacol 1994;266:255—261.

89. Kuroda Y, Mikuni M, Ogawa MT, Takahashi K. Effect of ACTH, adrenalectomy and the combination treatment on the density of 5-HT$_2$ receptor binding sites in neocortex of rat forebrain and 5-HT$_2$ receptor-mediated wet-dog shake behaviors. Psychopharmacology 1992;108:27—32.

90. Kenneth GA, Curzon G. Evidence that mCPP may have behavioural effects mediated by central 5-HT$_{1c}$ receptors. Br J Pharmacol 1988;94:137—147.

91. Kenneth GA, Pittaway K, Blackburn TP. Evidence that 5-HT$_{2c}$ receptor antagonists are anxiolytic in the rat Geller-Seifter model of anxiety. Psychopharmacology 1994;114:90—96.

92. Przegalinski E, Chojnacka-Wojcik E, Flip M. Stimulation of Postsynaptic 5-HT$_{1a}$ receptors is responsible for the anticonflict effect of ipsapirone in rats. J Pharm Pharmacol 1992;44: 780—782.

93. Deakin JF. Serotonin subtypes and affective disorders. In: Idzikowski C, Cowen PJ (eds) Serotonin, Sleep and Mental Disorder. Petersfield: Wrightson Biomedical Publishing, 1991;161—178.

94. Preskorn SH, Fast GA. Beyond signs and symptoms: The case against a mixed anxiety and depression category. J Clin Psychiat 1993;54(Suppl):24—32.

95. Van Praag HM. Two-tier diagnosing in psychiatry. Psych Res 1990;34:1—11.

96. Van Praag HM. Depression, suicide and the metabolism of serotonin in the brain. J Affec Disord 1982;4:275—290.

97. Van Praag HM. Serotonergic mechanisms and suicidal behavior. Psychiat Psychobiol 1988;3:

335—346.

98. Plutchik, R, Van Praag HM, Conte HR. Correlates of suicide and violence risk, III. A two-stage model of countervailing forces. Psychiat Res 1989:215—225.

Neurobiological insights into the pathogenesis of self-mutilation and suicidal behavior

J. John Mann, Kevin M. Malone, Barbara Stanley, Mark D. Underwood and Victoria Arango

Department of Psychiatry, Columbia University and Department of Neuroscience, New York State Psychiatric Institute, New York, New York, USA

Abstract. There have been great advances in the study of suicidal behavior in terms of its underlying neurobiology. As an initial step, the distinction between self-destructive behaviors, self-mutilation, and suicide attempt behavior is critical. We discuss the important clinical differences between these three categories of behavior. Making these distinctions is crucial because these behaviors may often occur in the same patient. Studies of brainstem nuclei, such as the locus coeruleus have revealed important morphological alterations that may have major biochemical and behavioral consequences. Promising new research strategies include functional brain imaging and molecular genetics.

Keywords: locus coeruleus, molecular genetics, neurochemistry, positron emission tomography, suicide.

The range of self-destructive behaviors is so broad that precise definition is essential in order to guide a meaningful scientific research effort. Self-destructive behaviors include activities such as alcohol abuse, smoking, use of illicit drugs such as extacy or heroin and noncompliance with medical treatment. For example, patients with severe chronic illnesses, such as renal failure or advanced malignancy, are known to worsen their condition by not complying with dialysis regimes and chemotherapy programs. Noncompliance with medical treatment in the situation of irreversible, severe medical illness is often understandable in terms of the suffering that is associated with the treatment and the absence of guaranteed benefit.

There is another range of behaviors that involve self-mutilation; these are somewhat distinct from active suicide attempts. Self-mutilatory behavior involves a self-inflicted injury without clear suicidal intent. Self-injury often has a ritualistic quality and is repetitive. It may be associated with the inflicting of some physical pain that actually results in the relief of emotional tension. There is often a compulsive quality to the behavior where the individual resists but finally injures themselves in order to relieve the build up of tension or psychic pain. Methods of self-injury include burning and cutting as the most common examples.

Address for correspondence: J. John Mann MD, Chief, Department of Neuroscience, New York State Psychiatric Institute, 722 West 168th Street, Box 28, New York, NY 10032, USA. Tel.: +1-212-543-5571. Fax: +1-212-543-6017.

In contrast to self-mutilation, suicide attempts are generally less frequent and accompanied by some intent to die. The individual may well be ambivalent about this intent, but at least some component is present as the motive for the suicide attempt.

Neurobiological correlates of self-mutilation in personality disorders

Although there have been a number of studies looking at psychopathological correlates of self-mutilation, there have been very few studies looking at neurobiological correlates. Characteristics such as borderline personality disorder, obsessionality, dissociative states, outwardly directed hostility, introversion, and neuroticism have all been reported in association with self-mutilation. In terms of neurobiology, higher levels of plasma met-enkephalin have been found in self-mutilators compared to control subjects. Gardner et al. [1] found no difference in cerebrospinal fluid 5-hydroxy-indoleacetic acid (CSF 5-HIAA) levels between 12 self-mutilators and five nonmutilators in a group of patients with borderline personality disorder. The study was somewhat confounded by the high rate of suicide attempts in the two groups.

We conducted a study in self-mutilators that was reported in detail elsewhere [2]. In that study, 26 self-mutilators with personality disorders and 26 control subjects with personality disorders and no history of self-mutilation, were compared in terms of psychopathology and several indices of neurochemical function, including CSF 5-HIAA and platelet imipramine binding. In terms of psychopathology, the two groups did not differ in terms of depression and hopelessness as has been reported by others. However, the self-mutilators were characterized by greater anxiety, somatization and cognitive disturbance. They also had more severe borderline personality disorder measures and a greater level of externally directed aggression. The severity of self-mutilation correlated with chronic anger and somatic anxiety, suggesting that externally directed aggression was related to self-directed aggression. There was also a negative correlation between degree of self-mutilation and hopelessness as well as a trend for a correlation between self-mutilation and severity of lifetime aggression. Hopelessness may be a state of mind that directs aggression towards the self, whereas anger would otherwise direct aggression externally. Biological measures identified no differences in CSF 5-HIAA in the self-mutilator group compared to the control group. Similarly, the number of imipramine binding sites and their affinity did not differ between the two groups. Thus, this study did not find evidence of serotonergic abnormalities in the self-mutilator group. Further studies need to be conducted controlling for the possible significance of a history of suicide attempts. Presumably, the presence or absence of a history of suicide attempts, in addition to self-mutilation, may be significant in terms of interpreting the biological findings.

Although CSF 5-HIAA levels have been found to be related to externally directed impulsive aggression and serious suicidal behavior, and appear to predict future completed suicide as well as recidivism in impulsive murderers, we were not able to find a relationship of CSF 5-HIAA to self-mutilation. Platelet serotonin transporter binding has been found to be altered in individuals with a history of assaultive behavior [3] as well as in children with conduct disorder. Nevertheless, we did not find any relationship of imipramine binding to self-mutilation. As indicated above, other investigators have implicated the opiate system in self-mutilation; investigation of the dopaminergic and noradrenergic systems would also be of interest in this condition. Investigations of other neurotransmitter systems should also take into account the possible impact of the primary psychiatric diagnosis as well as a history of externally directed aggression or suicide attempts in order to interpret the findings.

Noradrenergic function and the locus coeruleus in suicide victims

Studies suggest abnormalities in brainstem noradrenergic neurons in suicide. After a series of brainstem studies beginning nearly 30 years ago [4], the main body of research into the neurobiology shifted to neurotransmitter receptors in the cerebral cortex. Only recently have investigators begun to study the monoaminergic neurons whose cell bodies are in the brainstem. The advent of molecular biology methodologies amenable to postmortem human brain and unbiased techniques for the quantification of neuron morphometry offer additional methods to obtain objective, quantitative measures of neuron function compared to neuropathologic methods in the past that generated mostly qualitative data.

Changes in neurotransmitter measures in postmortem brain tissue and comparable findings in vivo suggest altered noradrenergic neurotransmission in suicide. Noradrenergic innervation of the mammalian cerebral cortex arises from pigmented neurons of the locus coeruleus (LC) [5—9]. These norepinephrine synthesizing neurons have been demonstrated to provide widespread innervation throughout the entire brain in animals and, presumably, humans.

Evidence from neurotransmitter or metabolite concentrations in the cerebrospinal fluid (CSF) of suicide attempters is unconvincing in terms of demonstrating a relationship between suicidal acts and the noradrenergic system. Only a minority [10,11] of studies [12—17] have found reduced concentrations of the norepinephrine metabolite 3-methoxy, 4-hydroxyphenyl glycol (MHPG). Reduced excretion of the metabolite MHPG in the urine of suicide attempters is further, albeit indirect, evidence of reduced noradrenergic function [11]. β-adrenergic receptor binding is increased in the cerebral cortex of suicide victims [18—20]. Altered α_1-adrenergic and/or α_2-adrenergic receptor binding in the cerebral cortices of suicide victims are also reported [21—23].

The primary source of norepinephrine in the forebrain arises by way of a noradrenergic innervation from neurons in the LC. In humans, LC noradrenergic neurons are naturally pigmented. LC neurons are located bilaterally and symmetrically in the dorsomedial pons, ventral and lateral to the central gray. Detailed discussion of the distribution and morphology of LC neurons in humans can be found elsewhere [24,25].

We reported a marked reduction in the number of noradrenergic locus coeruleus neurons in the brain of completed suicides compared to controls [26]. We found that suicides have 23% fewer LC neurons and a 38% lower density of LC neurons than controls [26]. The reduction in neuron number was localized to the rostral two-thirds of the LC. Every suicide case we studied had fewer neurons in the left than the right LC, whereas no left-right difference was present in the control group. Neither the LC length nor the LC volume in suicide victims differs from controls. Interestingly, Ordway et al. found increased binding to α_2-adrenergic receptors [27] and an increased amount of the norepinephrine biosynthetic enzyme tyrosine hydroxylase [28] in the LC of suicide victims; but no difference in the number of LC neurons [28] or the concentration of norepinephrine in the LC [27]. We have sought evidence of neuropathology in these neurons using computer-assisted morphometry. Measures of size (area, perimeter) and shape (form factor) were made at three rostrocaudal levels of the LC. Rostrocaudal differences in the anatomical distribution of neuron size and shape were found within the LC of both suicides and controls, but there were no significant differences in either the size or shape of neurons between groups in any region of the LC. Interestingly, females and males differed in neuron morphometry. Females had greater neuron area and perimeter on the left side compared to the right side of the LC, whereas there was no significant difference between the two sides in males. Similar sex differences were found in neuron shape.

We also examined noradrenergic neurons in alcoholics [29] and alcoholics who died by suicide [30]. LC neuron counts were obtained from a total of 32 subjects. In all groups, the number of neurons decreased with age, and by age 40 years, the number of LC neurons among the suicide and/or alcoholic groups was less than among controls. The age-related decline of LC neuron number was significantly greater in suicides than in controls, whereas in alcoholics the age-related decline in neuron number was the same as for the controls. The number of LC neurons in alcoholic-suicides was statistically indistinguishable from those of suicides. The age-related changes in LC neuron number may reflect duration of alcoholism. In any case, there was a reduction in LC neurons in suicide victims, independent of the effects of alcoholism.

Further studies are needed to determine the mechanisms of noradrenergic neuron loss and whether it is associated with an underlying major depression in suicide victims, or acquired after a period of excessive alcohol consumption.

New biological methods for detection of high-risk suicidal patients

The studies of the serotonergic system over the last 15 years have yielded a number of possible methods for developing tests that will detect high-risk patients. Clinically, there appears to be little difference, in terms of objective severity of depression, between patients who have made suicide attempts compared to patients with no history of suicide attempts. This suggests that other indicators are necessary in order to detect high-risk suicidal patients. The observation by

Asberg et al. [31] that CSF 5-HIAA was low in individuals who have a history of serious suicide attempts in the context of major depression has led to an enormous amount of research that has largely confirmed the original findings. More recently, it has been reported that CSF 5-HIAA may predict future suicide and suicide attempts in depressed patients and schizophrenics [31−34]. Low levels of CSF 5-HIAA are associated with a 4- to 6-fold increased risk of suicide within 1 year of discharge from hospital [33]. The potential of CSF 5-HIAA to distinguish individuals with a past history of a suicide attempt is actually less than the ability of CSF 5-HIAA to predict future suicide. These results indicate that CSF 5-HIAA should be evaluated further as a potential clinical tool in the prediction of patients who are at risk for suicide in the period following discharge from hospital.

Other tests that have shown some promise in terms of distinguishing individuals with a history of a suicide attempt are platelet 5-HT$_{2A}$ receptor binding [35,36] and the prolactin response to the serotonin-releasing drug, fenfluramine [37−39]. However, neither of these measures has been adequately tested in a prospective study in order to determine whether they can predict the risk of future suicide attempts or completed suicide. Clearly, such studies would be of great interest, as the potential for prediction may not necessarily be the same as the ability to distinguish individuals with a past history of a suicide attempt.

Another approach is to take advantage of the observation that there are genetic factors that contribute to suicide risk. The evidence indicating a role for genetic factors in determining suicide risk comes from twin studies that have demonstrated a high rate of concordance for suicidal behavior in monozygotic vs. dizygotic twins, evidence of a familial association of suicidal behavior, and adoption studies that indicate the biological transmission of the risk for suicidal behavior [40]. Recently, two groups [41,42] have reported an association of a polymorphism in intron 7 of the gene for tryptophan hydroxylase, the rate-limiting biosynthetic enzyme for serotonin. Although there is a negative report in the literature [43], the presence of these two positive studies indicates that a strategy of examining candidate genes, such as those associated with the serotonergic system, may be informative.

Reports from postmortem studies [44] that the ventral prefrontal cortex of suicide victims is characterized by changes in serotonin receptor binding, raises the possibility that this area of the brain is abnormal in individuals who are at risk for suicide. At this stage, there are a number of structural studies of the prefrontal cortex in individuals subject to major depression that have reported abnormalities [45]. Complementary similar findings of disturbed blood flow, and glucose metabolism or uptake in the prefrontal cortex of patients with major depression have also been reported [46]. Although many studies have been carried out in individuals with major depression, there are almost no data dividing these individuals into suicide attempters and nonattempters. Similarly, there is a paucity of data from prospective studies. Examination of the prefrontal cortex of individuals thought to be at risk for suicidal behavior should be of great interest. Thus,

98

initiatives in neurochemistry, molecular genetics and functional brain imaging, offer new possibilities in terms of detection of high-risk patients, thereby extending the hope of better treatment.

Acknowledgements

This paper was expertly typed by Ms Nancy Geibel. This work was supported by grants MH46745, MH40210, MH48514, AA09004 and MH41847 from the National Institutes of Health.

References

1. Gardner DL, Lucas PB, Cowdry RW. CSF metabolites in borderline personality disorder compared with normal controls. Biol Psychiat 1990;28:247–254.
2. Simeon D, Stanley B, Frances A, Mann JJ, Winchel R, Stanley M. Self-mutilation in personality disorders: Psychological and biological correlates. Am J Psychiat 1992;149:221–226.
3. Stoff DM, Ieni J, Friedman E, Bridger WH, Pollock L, Vitiello B. Platelet ^{3}H-imipramine binding, serotonin uptake, and plasma α_1 acid glycoprotein in disruptive behavior disorders. Biol Psychiat 1991;29:494–498.
4. Shaw DM, Camps FE, Eccleston EG. 5-Hydroxytryptamine in the hind-brain of depressive suicides. Br J Psychiat 1967;113:1407–1411.
5. Dahlström A, Fuxe K. Evidence for the existence of monoamine-containing neurons in the central nervous system. I. Demonstration of monoamines in the cell bodies of brain stem neurons. Acta Physiol Scand 1964;62:232:1–55.
6. Levitt P, Moore RY. Noradrenaline neuron innervation of the neocortex in the rat. Brain Res 1978;139:219–231.
7. Freedman R, Foote SL, Bloom FE. Histochemical characterization of a neocortical projection of the nucleus locus coeruleus in the squirrel monkey. J Comp Neurol 1975;164:209–232.
8. Jones BE, Moore RY. Ascending projections of the locus coeruleus in the rat. II. Autoradiographic study. Brain Res 1977;127:23–53.
9. Porrino LJ, Goldman-Rakic PS. Brainstem innervation of prefrontal and anterior cingulate cortex in the rhesus monkey revealed by retrograde transport of HRP. J Comp Neurol 1982;205: 63–76.
10. Ågren H. Symptom patterns in unipolar and bipolar depression correlating with monoamine metabolites in the cerebrospinal fluid. II. Suicide. Psychiat Res 1980;3:225–236.
11. Ågren H. Depressive symptom patterns and urinary MHPG excretion. Psychiat Res 1982;6: 185–196.
12. Roy A, Pickar D, De Jong J, Karoum F, Linnoila M. Suicidal behavior in depression: Relationship to noradrenergic function. Biol Psychiat 1989;25:341–350.
13. Brown GL, Ebert MH, Goyer PF, Jimersom DC, Klein WJ, Bunney WE Jr, Goodwin FK. Aggression, suicide and serotonin: Relationships to CSF amine metabolites. Am J Psychiat 1982;139:741–746.
14. Pickar D, Roy A, Breier A, Doran A, Wolkowitz O, Colison J, Ågren H. Suicide and aggression in schizophrenia. Neurobiologic correlates. Ann NY Acad Sci 1986;487:189–196.
15. Roy A, Ninan PT, Mazonson A, Pickar D, van Kammen DP, Linnoila M, Paul SM. CSF monoamine metabolites in chronic schizophrenic patients who attempt suicide. Psychol Med 1985; 15:335–340.
16. Secunda SK, Cross CK, Koslow S, Katz MM, Kocsis J, Maas JW, Landis H. Biochemistry and suicidal behavior in depressed patients. Biol Psychiat 1986;21:756–767.
17. Träskman L, Åsberg M, Bertilsson L, Sjöstrand L. Monoamine metabolites in CSF and suicidal

behavior. Arch Gen Psychiat 1981;38:631—636.

18. Mann JJ, Stanley M, McBride PA, McEwen BS. Increased serotonin$_2$ and β-adrenergic receptor binding in the frontal cortices of suicide victims. Arch Gen Psychiat 1986;43:954—959.

19. Arango V, Ernsberger P, Marzuk PM, Chen J-S, Tierney H, Stanley M, Reis DJ, Mann JJ. Autoradiographic demonstration of increased serotonin 5-HT$_2$ and β-adrenergic receptor binding sites in the brain of suicide victims. Arch Gen Psychiat 1990;47:1038—1047.

20. Biegon A, Israeli M. Regionally selective increases in β-adrenergic receptor density in the brains of suicide victims. Brain Res 1988;442:199—203.

21. Arango V, Ernsberger P, Sved AF, Mann JJ. Quantitative autoradiography of α$_1$- and α$_2$-adrenergic receptors in the cerebral cortex of controls and suicide victims. Brain Res 1993;630: 271—282.

22. Meana JJ, García-Sevilla JA. Increased α$_2$-adrenoceptor density in the frontal cortex of depressed suicide victims. J Neural Transm 1987;70:377—381.

23. González AM, Pascual J, Meana JJ, Barturen F, Del Arco C, Pazos A, García-Sevilla JA. Autoradiographic demonstration of increased α$_2$-adrenoceptor agonist binding sites in the hippocampus and frontal cortex of depressed suicide victims. J Neurochem 1994;63:256—265.

24. German DC, Manaye KF, White CL III, Woodward DJ, McIntire DD, Smith WK, Kalaria RN, Mann DMA. Disease-specific patterns of locus coeruleus cell loss. Ann Neurol 1992;32: 667—676.

25. Baker KG, Törk I, Hornung J-P, Halasz P. The human locus coeruleus complex: An immunohistochemical and three dimensional reconstruction study. Exp Brain Res 1989;77:257—270.

26. Arango V, Underwood MD, Mann JJ. Fewer pigmented locus coeruleus neurons in suicide victims: Preliminary results. Biol Psychiat 1996;39:112—120.

27. Ordway GA, Widdowson PS, Smith KS, Halaris A. Agonist binding to α$_2$-adrenoceptors is elevated in the locus coeruleus from victims of suicide. J Neurochem 1994;63:617—624.

28. Ordway GA, Smith KS, Haycock JW. Elevated tyrosine hydroxylase in the locus coeruleus of suicide victims. J Neurochem 1994;62:680—685.

29. Arango V, Underwood MD, Mann JJ. Fewer pigmented neurons in the locus coeruleus of uncomplicated alcoholics. Brain Res 1994;650:1—8.

30. Arango V, Underwood MD, Pauler DK, Kass RE, Mann JJ. Differential age-related loss of pigmented locus coeruleus neurons in suicides, alcoholics and alcoholic suicides. Alcohol Clin Exp Res 1996;20:1141—1147.

31. Åsberg M, Träskman L, Thorén P. 5-HIAA in the cerebrospinal fluid. A biochemical suicide predictor? Arch Gen Psychiat 1976;33:1193—1197.

32. Cooper SJ, Kelly CB, King DJ. 5-Hydroxyindoleacetic acid in cerebrospinal fluid and prediction of suicidal behaviour in schizophrenia. Lancet 1992;340:940—941.

33. Nordström P, Samuelsson M, Asberg M, Träskman-Bendz L, Aberg-Wistedt A, Nordin C, Bertilsson L. CSF 5-HIAA predicts suicide risk after attempted suicide. Suicide Life Threat Behav 1994;24:1—9.

34. Roy A, De Jong J, Linnoila M. Cerebrospinal fluid monoamine metabolites and suicidal behavior in depressed patients. A 5-year follow-up study. Arch Gen Psychiat 1989;46:609—612.

35. Pandey GN, Pandey SC, Janicak PG, Marks RC, Davis JM. Platelet serotonin-2 receptor binding sites in depression and suicide. Biol Psychiat 1990;28:215—222.

36. Pandey GN, Pandey SC, Dwivedi Y, Sharma RP, Janicak PG, Davis JM. Platelet Serotonin-2A receptors: A potential biological marker for suicidal behavior. Am J Psychiat 1995;152: 850—855.

37. Mann JJ, McBride PA, Malone KM, DeMeo MD, Keilp J. Blunted serotonergic responsivity in depressed patients. Neuro Psycho Pharmacol 1995;13:53—64.

38. Malone KM, Corbitt EM, Li S, Mann JJ. Prolactin response to fenfluramine and suicide attempt lethality in major depression. Br J Psychiat 1996;168:324—329.

39. Coccaro EF, Siever LJ, Klar HM, Maurer G, Cochrane K, Cooper TB, Mohs RC, Davis KL. Serotonergic studies in patients with affective and personality disorders. Arch Gen Psychiat

1989;46:587—599.

40. Roy A, Segal NL, Centerwall BS, Robinette CD. Suicide in twins. Arch Gen Psychiat 1991;48: 29—32.

41. Nielsen DA, Goldman D, Virkkunen M, Tokola R, Rawlings R, Linnoila M. Suicidality and 5-hydroxyindoleacetic acid concentration associated with a tryptophan hydroxylase polymorphism. Arch Gen Psychiat 1994;51:34—38.

42. Mann JJ, Malone KM, Nielsen DA, Goldman D, Erdos J, Gelernter J. A polymorphism of the tryptophan hydroxylase gene appears associated with suicidal behavior in depressed patients. Am J Psychiat 1997;(In press).

43. Abbar M, Courtet P, Amadéo S, Caer Y, Mallet J, Baldy-Moulinier M, Castelnau D, Malafosse A. Suicidal behaviors and the tryptophan hydroxylase gene. Arch Gen Psychiat 1995;52: 846—849.

44. Arango V, Underwood MD, Gubbi AV, Mann JJ. Localized alterations in pre- and postsynaptic serotonin binding sites in the ventrolateral prefrontal cortex of suicide victims. Brain Res 1995; 688:121—133.

45. Soares JC, Mann JJ. The anatomy of mood disorders — Review of structural neuroimaging studies. Biol Psychiat 1997;41:86—106.

46. Soares JC, Mann JJ. The functional neuroanatomy of mood disorders. J Psychiat Res 1997;(In press).

Heredity and suicidality

George N. Papadimitriou

Athens University Medical School, Department of Psychiatry, Clinical and Molecular Neurogenetics Unit, University Mental Health Research Institute, Eginition Hospital, Athens, Greece

Abstract. The results from genetic epidemiology on family, twin and adoption studies support the hypothesis of genetic contribution in the familial expression of suicidal behavior. The presence of positive family history of suicide as well as history of previous suicide attempts significantly increase the suicidal risk and thus can be considered as prognostic vulnerability factors of suicidality. Disturbances of biogenic amines activity, mainly of serotonin, seem to be implicated in the manifestation of suicidal behavior, but specific factors of suicidality were not identified and the existent biological markers are associated mainly with major depression. The search for molecular, in addition to other neurobiological and clinical variables, may contribute to the sorting out of specific vulnerability factors for suicidality. Genetic factors related to suicide may largely represent a genetic predisposition for psychiatric disorders,, particularly affective disorder, associated with suicide. Additionally, there is evidence for an independent genetic component for suicide, perhaps additive to psychiatric disorder transmission, and possibly related to the control of impulsive behavior. However, the question concerning the behavioral trait that is genetically transmitted is still left open.

Keywords: adoption, family, genetic factors, molecular studies, suicide, twin.

Introduction

Durkheim with his excellent work on suicide, 100 years ago [1], opened new horizons for the investigation of this characteristic example of disturbed human behavior. Suicide is a multidetermined act resulting from an interaction between state- and trait-related effects; it is difficult among the different biological, psychological, as well as socioenvironmental factors to single out any particular one as a major determinant.

Mental illness has been associated with suicidal behavior, since the majority of attempters suffer from psychiatric disorders at the time of the attempt [2,3] and suicide is sometimes the earliest sociably recognized manifestation. A close pathogenetic and/or causal relationship exists between suicidality and affective disorder, and since Kraepelin, depression has been associated with suicidal behavior in the sense that suicidality comprised part of its symptom profile [4]. Depressed patients present a risk of suicide 30 times greater than the risk of the

Address for correspondence: George N. Papadimitriou MD, Associate Professor of Psychiatry, Athens University Medical School, Department of Psychiatry, Clinical and Molecular Neurogenetics Unit, Eginition Hospital, 74 Vas. Sophias Ave., 115 28 Athens, Greece. Tel.: +30-1-7217-763. Fax: +30-1-7243-905.

general population. About 80% of suicide attempts are expressed during depression, or depression does, in most cases, precede suicidal behavior [2,3]. It is worth noting that about 15% of patients with primary major affective illness die by committing suicide [2]. More recent findings also support the view that suicidal behavior is a frequent manifestation of major depression [5—8].

In spite of the important progress in the field of investigation of the pathogenesis of affective disorder, little is known concerning the clinical and phenomenological elements of suicidal behavior in depressed patients and it remains unclear why some depressed patients attempt suicide and others not.

Alcohol and other drug use, personality disorder and traits such as impulsivity, aggressivity, as well as schizophrenia are also implicated as causes in the manifestation of suicidal behavior [3,9,10]. Patients with increased levels of psychiatric comorbidity had markedly high risks of serious suicidal attempts [11]. Incidence and seasonal variations of suicide mortality have been observed with a peak in June [12]. Suicidal patients, in comparison with nonsuicidal, tend to use coping styles less frequently and may have inadequate mental resources to deal with life problems [13].

There appears to be a familial loading or genetic vulnerability in the expression of suicidal behavior [14—21]. It has been postulated that among all individuals exposed to some stressful life event, those who commit suicide may have a genetic predisposition.

The role of genetic factors in the manifestation of suicidal behavior has been systematically investigated over the last decades. On the other hand, recent studies also emphasize the important role of genetic factors in affective disorders [22,23].

In the present chapter an effort will be made for the current aspects about the role of heredity in suicidality to be presented. Genetic epidemiology research for suicide, as for other psychopathological conditions [24], is mainly based on family, twin and adoption studies that provide the best evidence for the heritability of this condition, while molecular and neurobiological investigation seems also to play an important role.

Family studies

Family studies on suicide aim to investigate the incidence of suicidal behavior in the relatives of individuals who attempted or committed suicide in comparison with the relatives of normal subjects. In addition, the risk of suicidal behavior in the families of depressed patients, since it has been suggested that affective disorders, which are known to run in families [22], are associated with suicidality [5—8].

Families with multiple individuals in several generations who committed suicide with different means have been reported in the literature and in the majority of them suicide was made during a depressive episode [25—27]. In the Lykouras et al. study [27], in the family of a suicidal attempter, the familial loading of aggressive behavior was expressed either as suicide in four members or homicide committed by one member, while another person in the same family was murdered. In the expression of aggressive behavior, genetic, as well as environmental factors, have been reported to contribute significantly [28].

Psychopathology in parents can be considered among the most potent risk factors for adolescent suicidality [29]. Parents of adolescents who committed suicide more frequently have depression and substance abuse, in comparison to the parents of adolescents without suicidal behavior [30]. Regarding suicide attempts, an increased morbidity for these acts has been found in the first and second degree relatives of adolescent suicidal attempters, compared with first and second degree relatives of normal control adolescents [31].

Parental loss and the age of a child at the moment of this event seem to play an important role in the later manifestation of suicidal behavior. Early parental loss through death or suicide is a significant psychosocial stressor associated with depression later in life and also suicidality [32]. In Roy's study [14], children younger than 11 years of age at the time of parental suicide have a rate of 75% to later attempt suicide themselves. For children between 11 and 20 years of age, the risk to attempt suicide in the future was 62%, while children older than 20 years of age with the same experience later attempted suicide at a rate of 47%, a difference statistically significant. The author concluded that early parental loss by suicide is followed by increased risk of suicide attempt later in the life of the individual [14]. Recently, it has been demonstrated that suicide attempters who were 18 years of age were more likely than nonattempters to have lost at least one parent through death before the age of 11 [7]. In the same study, the parents of suicidal attempters had attempted suicide more frequently, than those of nonattempters, despite similar rates of major depression in both parents groups [7]. Although not statistically significant, twice as many suicidal attempters had siblings who had attempted but not completed suicide [7].

The Amish population study is very informative. For a period of 100 years (1880—1980), 26 completed suicides have been reported clustering only in four families. Among them, 92% of the persons who committed suicide suffered from affective disorder [16]. It is worth emphasizing that in other Amish families, in spite of a strong genetic component for affective disorder, suicidality was not manifested [16].

In the Iowa study of the long-term follow-up of 500 psychiatric patients, the risk of suicidal behavior was observed to be nearly eight times higher in the relatives of the patients (5.5%), than in the relatives of control subjects (0.6%) [15]. The relatives of the patients who committed suicide were exposed to 8% suicidal risk, which was almost four times greater than the risk of 2% in the relatives of patients who did not commit suicide [15]. In the relatives of schizophrenic patients a suicidal risk of 1.2% was observed, which was very similar to the risk of 1.5% in the relatives of patients with mania. Both these risks were significantly lower than the risk of 3.4% in the relatives of patients suffering from depression. In the relatives of manics who committed suicide, the suicidal risk increased to

9.4% which was not significantly different from the risk of 10.2% for the relatives of depressives who committed suicide [15].

Regarding gender, it has been reported that females who attempted suicide were more likely to have a relative who committed or attempted suicide, than male attempters [33].

Genetic implication in suicidality seems to be further supported by the observations that suicidal behavior rates in migrants, independently of the duration of their stay in the new country, were the same as in their country of origin [34].

Suicidal behavior was classified as violent or nonviolent according to the criteria by Paykel and Rassaby [35]. All other means were considered as violent, while drug overdoses and superficial wrist cuts were considered as nonviolent methods. The rates of violent and nonviolent suicidal attempts in depressed patients in relation to the manifestation of suicidality in the first and second degree relatives of the family were investigated by Linkowski et al. [17,36], who have found that suicidal behavior, mainly violent, aggregates in families of probands with major depression. The authors suggest that a violent, rather than a nonviolent, suicide attempt of a family member may be related to more frequent suicidal behavior in the family [17].

In conclusion, we can assume that family studies have demonstrated a significantly greater risk for suicidal behavior in the relatives of psychiatric patients than among the relatives of normal subjects, and in the families of patients who committed suicide than in the families of those who have not committed suicide [14,15,17].

The role of personal and family history of suicidality in suicidal behavior

Family studies have shown that personal and family history of suicidality play an important role in the manifestation of suicidal behavior.

In adolescent attempters, a family history of suicide can be considered among the most potent risk factors [29].

Individuals with a major affective disorder and a positive family history of suicide more often attempt suicide [14,15,17].

A history of prior attempts may be associated with greater suicidal risk in patients with primary affective disorders. Clinical studies have shown that patients with affective disorder who have attempted suicide had their first depressive episode at a significantly early age. In the course of their illness they presented more severe episodes, schizotypal features, psychomotor activity with agitation or retardation, also the majority of them suffered from bipolar affective disorder [6,36,37]. Other studies have demonstrated that patients with a past history of suicide attempts cannot be distinguished on the basis of severity of current depression, past course of illness, or on the presence of current or past psychosis, although they do have more severe suicidal ideation [38].

The proportion of depressed patients with a past history of suicidal behavior either of a violent or nonviolent nature, ranges between 32 and 44%, while history of previous suicide attempts has been suggested as a predictor of eventual suicide in psychiatric patients [17]. The results of the studies have shown that a positive family history of suicide, mainly of the violent type, was more frequent in patients who had made a violent suicidal attempt [6]. Also, that it significantly increased the probability of finding a suicide attempt, especially a violent one, in depressed bipolar female probands and in males not affected by the polarity [17,36]. Thus, a positive family history for violent suicide should be carefully considered as a major risk factor in the assessment of potentially suicidal patients and in the clinical management and suicidal prevention of patients with affective disorder [15,17,36].

It has been suggested that the use of family history of affective disorders is not a clinically meaningful indicator of a potential suicidal risk factor in depressed patients [39]. A familial loading for affective disorder is not in itself a predictor of suicidal behavior and possibly there is a type of suicide which is not necessarily associated with mental illness, since we observed large pedigrees with heavy loading for affective disorders but without suicidal behavior. This hypothesis of familial loading or genetic vulnerability for suicidal behavior is supported in the studies by Mitterauer et al. [40,41], who have demonstrated that in the population of the Salzburg area of Germany, suicidal behavior with positive family history of suicide was observed as a different genetic expression and not exclusively in patients suffering from endogenous depression. This suggests that suicidal behavior may arise from a vulnerability which operates independently of major depressive disorder severity and duration.

A systematic investigation of the family history of suicidal behavior combined with clinical diagnosis should prove useful in identifying individuals at high risk of suicide and could strengthen reliability and validity of psychiatric genetic counseling [42].

Twin and adoption studies

In the investigation of the interaction of genetic and environmental factors in suicidal behavior, the contribution of twin and adoption studies is very important. The twin strategy may also help to address the question of whether a predisposition for suicidal behavior may be genetically transmitted independently of psychiatric disorder. The observation of higher concordance rates in monozygotic (MZ), in comparison to dizygotic (DZ) twins, is compatible with the genetic contribution in psychopathology, since the majority of studies support the validity of the equal environment assumption in MZ and in DZ twin pairs [43].

Suicidality in twins has been reported since the past century with cases from single pairs of twins who committed suicide [44,45]. In the 1940s, Kallman et al. [46] showed higher concordance rates in MZ, than in DZ twin pairs, of manic-depressive illness, but no concordance at all for suicide. The authors concluded that genetic factors did not operate significantly in suicidal behavior [46,47]. Haberlandt, in 1967 [48], presented all reports on suicide since 1830.

Among the 149 reported cases, concordance for completed suicide was observed in nine out of 51 MZ pairs (18%), while no DZ twin pairs (0%) were found in which both twins had committed suicide. It is worth noting that out of the nine concordant for suicide MZ twin pairs, only four pairs were found to be concordant for major psychiatric diagnosis (three pairs suffered from affective and one pair from schizophrenic disorder) [48].

Concordance for suicide has also been observed in four out of 19 MZ twin pairs (22.2%); in none of 58 DZ pairs (0%) [49]; in seven out of 62 MZ (11.3%) and in two out of 114 DZ twin pairs (1.8%) [20,50]. Finally, in a recent study concerning all the reports in the literature, a concordance rate of 13.2% in MZ twins (17 out of 129 MZ pairs) and of 0.7% in DZ twin pairs (two out of 270 DZ pairs) has been reported [20].

Twin strategies provide convincing evidence that genetic factors play an important role in suicidal behavior by the fact that significantly higher concordance rates for suicide have been observed in MZ, compared to DZ twin pairs.

On the other hand, the role of environmental factors and the interaction with genetic liability must also be taken into consideration [10,51], since if the trait was exclusively genetic and dominant, a 100% concordance rate would have been expected in MZ twins who have all their genes in common. Psychosocial factors, either enhancing or attenuating the risk of suicide, cannot easily be controlled [52]. It has been suggested that an environmental stressor which is a necessary contributing factor to suicide in one twin is not present in the other and that suicide in one twin actually diminishes the possibility of suicide in the remaining twin through psychological mechanisms [52]. Recently, Roy et al. [53] have demonstrated in a sample of surviving co-twins of MZ and DZ twins who committed suicide, that 10 of 26 surviving MZ co-twins, but none of the nine DZ co-twins, had themselves attempted suicide. Among MZ twins, eight of the 10 pairs were females. According to these results, living MZ twins whose co-twin committed suicide may be at greater risk for suicidal behavior. The authors concluded that, although MZ and DZ twins may have some differing developmental experiences, their findings suggest that genetic factors play a role in suicidal behavior [53].

The possible role of genetic and environmental factors in suicidality is better evaluated in adoption studies aiming at the comparison of the expression of suicidal behavior between the biological and adoptive relatives of adoptees who committed suicide and the relatives of control subjects.

The most informative adoption study was carried out in Denmark in collaboration with American investigators. In this excellent work, out of 5,483 adoptees in the Copenhagen greater area between 1924 and 1947, the 57 who had committed suicide were studied [9,21,52,54]. These cases were matched according to age and sex with 57 nonsuicidal adoptee controls. Regarding suicidality in the biological relatives of adoptees, significantly more biological relatives of suicidal adoptees had committed suicide (12/269, 4.5%), in comparison to the biological relatives of nonsuicidal adoptees (2/269, 0.7%), while none of the adopting relatives had committed suicide (0/148 and 0/150, respectively) [9,21,52,54].

In the same study, the relationship of suicidality between affectively ill probands and suicidal behavior among their biological relatives was investigated in 71 adoptees suffering from affective disorder in comparison with 71 age- and sex-matched adopted controls. A significantly greater number of biological relatives of depressed adoptees was found to have committed suicide (15/ 407, 3.7%) in comparison to the biological relatives of the controls (1/360, 0.3%) [9]. In the adopted relatives of patients and controls, the investigators found 1/187 (0.5%) and 2/171 (1.2%) completed suicides, respectively [52].

In conclusion, the genetic contribution in suicidal behavior is strongly supported by the adoption studies which have demonstrated a significantly increased incidence of suicidal behavior among the biological relatives of adopted individuals who had committed suicide or who had suffered from depression, in comparison with the adopted relatives or with the biological relatives of adopted control individuals [21,52].

Neurobiological and molecular studies

There is substantial evidence that serotonin is implicated in the expression of suicidal behavior, since deficiency of this amine has been found within the brain of depressed suicidal patients [55,56]. A reduction in CSF 5-HIAA (the metabolite of serotonin) in suicidal attempters with major depression and in completed suicide, mainly in those using violent means, compared to patients who have a major depression but no life time history of suicidal attempts has been found [57]. In schizophrenia the findings are similar. More significant are the findings in personality disorders [57]. Individuals with low CSF 5-HIAA concentrations may have alterations in the control of serotonin synthesis and metabolism [58]. This metabolite, being a biological marker, has been suggested to be a trait with high heritability [59] and predictive of susceptibility to suicidal behavior [60].

An hypothesis of a serotonin deficiency in suicidal behavior has been proposed [61]. Recent studies have shown no evidence of a reduced 5-HT, NA or DA turnover in either cortical or subcortical regions from suicide victims as compared to matched controls [62]. Regarding the number of 5-HT 1A binding sites, no significant differences have been observed between suicide victims and controls [63,64]. However, when only the violent subgroup was considered, a 70–80% increase in DOPAC (metabolite of dopamine) concentrations was found [62].

Many of the genes potentially involved in the control of serotonin metabolism have been cloned, such as tryptophan hydroxylase (TPH) [65], serotonin receptors [66] and transporters [67], and monoamine oxidases A and B type [68].

A polymorphism in the human gene of TPH was identified [69] and by using this polymorphism, TPH was genetically mapped to the short arm of chromosome 11, in close proximity to the tyrosine hydroxylase gene (TH), that takes part in the biosynthesis of catecholamines [69].

A significant association between the TPH genotype and CSF 5-HIAA concentrations has been reported in a sample of alcoholic violent offenders [58]. No association of TPH genotype with impulsive behavior was detected. The polymorphism of TPH was also associated with a history of suicide attempts, independent of impulsivity status and cerebrospinal fluid 5-HIAA concentrations [58]. One of the TPH alleles was found to be strongly associated with suicide attempts in a group of impulsive alcoholic violent offenders [59]. It has been suggested that in some individuals a genetic variant of the TPH gene may influence the concentrations of 5-HIAA in the CSF and predispose to suicidal behavior [58].

In other studies no association between two unspecified TPH polymorphisms and suicidal behavior in psychiatric patients was observed [60]. Recently, Abbar et al. [70] revealed genotyping and allelic frequencies at a polymorphic Ava ii restriction site with the use of the complementary DNA tryptophan hydroxylase probe C2-38 in 62 suicidal attempters. No association between TPH and suicidal behavior was detected. The authors concluded that the TPH gene was not a susceptibility factor for suicidal behavior and postulated that the decreased levels of 5-HIAA in the CSF of subjects with a history of suicidal behavior may be associated with TPH-independent mechanisms and possibly with abnormalities in other serotonergic candidate genes such as MAO genes [70].

Serotonin transporter (5-HTT) has been found to be altered in postmortem brain samples from persons committing suicide [71]. This finding defines the 5-HTT gene, physically mapped to chromosome 17 [72], as a candidate gene [71]. Recently, it has been demonstrated that 5-HTT mRNA levels in dorsal and median raphe nuclei were not different between depressed persons committing suicide and control subjects [64].

Hypotheses of genetic implication in suicidal behavior

A possible answer to the question of the genetic implication in suicidal behavior could be that genetic factors may be attributable to the genetic transmission of mental disorders, mainly affective disorder, since a high incidence of suicidality is observed in depressed patients. A threshold and vulnerability for suicidal behavior is hypothesized, whereby onset of depression may precipitate suicidality in predisposed individuals [7].

Depression and other mental disorders are, indeed, associated with suicidality in relatives. Since, although in approximately 50% of relatives who committed suicide no history of these disorders was found, it has been suggested that there is a type of suicide not necessarily associated with mental disorder.

According to the hypothesis by Kety [52], the inability to control impulsive behavior is a possible genetic factor of suicide, while depression and other mental disorders as well as environmental stress serve as potentiating mechanisms which foster or trigger the impulsive behavior directing it towards a suicidal act. Another possibility is the genetic transmission of psychological or personality traits or reactions that may predispose the individual to attempt suicide under frustrating circumstances [9].

The notion that there may be an independent genetic factor for suicide in relation to the genetic transmission of a psychiatric disorder is a possible confounding factor in the examination of twin data [20]. The fact that discordance for a specific psychiatric disorder has been observed in twins concordant for suicide [48] might suggest some independence of genetic factors in suicidality.

A genetically determined transmission of suicidal behavior, possibly independent of depression or other mental disorders, has thus been proposed and suicidal behavior may then be expressed on the basis of an inherited biological deviation [9].

Specific vulnerability factors of suicidality have been proposed. In this line, serotonergic activity may be a biochemical trait that is associated with certain behavioral traits, including a lower threshold for self-directed and externally directed aggression [7]. The levels of 5-HIAA in the CSF may be a biochemical trait that is predictive of susceptibility to suicidal behavior [70].

It has also been suggested that a family member who had committed suicide may serve as a role model for a disturbed individual [73].

Regarding the possible mode of transmission of suicidal behavior, we have applied the computational model of Slater [74], based on the analysis of ancestral secondary cases on the paternal and maternal sides of the probands in a sample of depressed patients with a lifetime history of violent and nonviolent suicidal attempts [18,75]. This model requires that each proband should have at least two ancestral secondary cases who committed suicide. In the pattern of a single gene dominant transmission the number of unilateral pairs of secondary cases of paternal and maternal sides should be significantly greater than the number of bilateral pairs (from both sides). In a polygenic inheritance the proportion should appear as one bilateral to two unilateral pairs [74].

The results of the study were compatible with polygenic inheritance of suicidal behavior since a significantly greater number of unilateral pairs of secondary cases, as would be expected in single gene dominant transmission, was not found [18,75].

In the same study an interesting finding was the fact that suicidal attempters-probands using violent methods, in comparison with nonviolent ones, had a greater percentage of two or more ancestral secondary cases who committed suicide and most of them were on the maternal side. On the other hand, in the non-violent group most secondary cases were on the paternal side. According to these results, it seems that the choice of violent or nonviolent methods from the attempters is associated with different paternal and maternal loading of suicide in the family [75].

In conclusion, heredity seems to be implicated in the manifestation of suicidal behavior, but specific genetic mechanisms underlying suicidal behavior have not as yet been identified. Suicidality seems to be more likely to occur when an individual had genetic vulnerability to both suicide and affective disorder. The question of what is actually transmitted and to what extent genetic predisposition together with sociocultural factors help determine suicide remains unanswered.

References

1. Durkheim E. Suicide. Paris: Free Press of Glencoe. New York: McMillan, 1897.
2. Guze S, Robins E. Suicide and primary affective disorders. Br J Psychiat 1970;117:437–438.
3. Roy A. Risk factors for suicide in psychiatric patients. Arch Gen Psychiat 1982;39:1089–1095.
4. Kraepelin E. Manic-depressive insanity and paranoia. In: Robertson GM (ed) Edinburgh: Churchill Livingstone, 1921.
5. Newman SC, Bland RC. Suicide risk varies by subtype of affective disorder. Acta Psychiat Scand 1991;83:420–426.
6. Roy A. Features associated with suicide attempts in depression: A partial replication. J Affect Dis 1993;27:35–38.
7. Malone KM, Haas GL, Sweeney JA, Mann JJ. Major depression and the risk of attempted suicide. J Affect Dis 1995;34:173–185.
8. Bronisch T. The relationship between suicidality and depression. Arch Suicide Res 1996;2: 235–254.
9. Schulsinger F, Kety SS, Rosenthal D. A family study of suicide. In: Schou M, Stromgren E (eds) Origin, Prevention and Treatment of Affective Disorders. New York: Academic Press, 1979; 277–287.
10. Dimitriou EC, Giouzepas J, Beratis S. Self-destructive behaviour: Risk factors and preventive principles. In: Christodoulou GN, Kontaxakis VR (eds) Topics in Preventive Psychiatry. Basel: Karger, Bibliothca Psychiat 1994;No.165:56–62.
11. Beautrais AL, Joyce PR, Mulder RT, Fergusson DM, Deavoll BJ, Nightingale SK. Prevalence and co-morbidity of mental disorders in persons making serious suicide attempts: a case-control study. Am J Psychiat 1996;153:1009–1014.
12. Bazas T, Jemos J, Stefanis C, Trichopoulos D. Incidence and seasonal variation of suicide mortality in Greece. Compr Psychiat 1979;20:15–20.
13. Botsis AJ, Soldatos CR, Liossi A, Kokkevi A, Stefanis CN. Suicide and violence risk. Relationship to coping styles. Acta Psychiat Scand 1994;89:92–96.
14. Roy A. A family history of suicide. Arch Gen Psychiat 1983;40:971–974.
15. Tsuang MT. Risk of suicide in the relatives of schizophrenics, manics, depressives and controls. J Clin Psychiat 1983;44:396–400.
16. Egeland JA, Sussex JN. Suicide and family loading for affective disorders. JAMA 1985;254: 915–918.
17. Linkowski P, De Maertelaer V, Delarbre C, Papadimitriou GN, Mendlewicz J. Familial factors in suicidal behaviour. Int J Fam Psychiat 1988;9:123–133.
18. Papadimitriou GN, Linkowski P, Mendlewicz J. Genetic aspects of suicidal behaviour. In: Stefanis CN, Soldatos CR, Rabavilas AD (eds) Psychiatry: A World Perspective. Amsterdam: Elsevier, 1990;2:530–533.
19. Papadimitriou GN, Linkowski P, Souery D, Mendlewicz J. Genetic factors in suicidal behavior. In: Papadimitriou GN, Mendlewicz J (eds) Genetics of Mental Disorders, Part II: Clinical Issues. Bailliere's Clinical Psychiatry, International Practice and Research. London: Bailliere Tindall, 1996;71–82.
20. Roy A, Segal NL, Centerwall BS, Robinette D. Suicide in twins. Arch Gen Psychiat 1991;48: 29–32.
21. Schulsinger F. US-Denmark adoption studies. In: Mendlewicz J, Papadimitriou GN (eds) Genetics of Mental Disorders. Part I: Theoretical Aspects. Bailliere's Clinical Psychiatry, International Practice and Research. London: Bailliere Tindall, 1995;63–75.
22. McGuffin P, Katz R. The genetics of depression and manic-depressive disorder. Br J Psychiat

1989;155:294—301.
23. Mendlewicz J. New molecular genetic studies in affective disorders. Pharmacopsychiatry 1992; 25:29—32.
24. Stefanis CN, Dikeos DG, Papadimitriou GN. Clinical strategies in genetic research. In: Mendlewicz J, Papadimitriou GN (eds) Genetics of Mental Disorders. Part I: Theoretical Aspects. Bailliere's Clinical Psychiatry, International Practice and Research. London: Bailliere Tindall, 1995;1—18.
25. Dabbagh F. Family suicide. Br J Psychiat 1977;130:159—161.
26. Zaw KM. A suicidal family. Br J Psychiat 1981;139:68—69.
27. Lykouras L, Papadimitriou GN, Kontea M, Stefanis C. A family with suicidal and homicidal members. Eur J Psychiat 1992;6:69—73.
28. Palmour RM. Genetic models for the study of aggressive behaviour. Prog Neuro-Psychopharmacol Biol Psychiat 1983;7:513—517.
29. Brendt DA, Kolko DJ, Goldstein CE, Allan MJ, Brown RV. Suicidality in affectively disordered adolescent inpatients. J Am Acad Child Adolesc Psychiat 1990;29:586—593.
30. Brendt DA, Perper JA, Moritz G, Liotus L, Schweers J, Balach L, Roth C. Familial risk factors for adolescent suicide: a case-control study. Acta Psychiat Scand 1994;89:52—58.
31. Pfeffer CR, Normandin L, Kakuma T. Suicidal children grow up: suicidal behavior and psychiatric disorders among relatives. J Am Acad Child Adolesc Psychiat 1994;8:1087—1097.
32. Adam KS, Bouckoms A, Streiner D. Parental loss and family stability in attempted suicide. Arch Gen Psychiat 1982;39:1081—1085.
33. Johnson GF, Hunt G. Suicidal behavior in bipolar manic-depressive patients and their families. Compr Psychiat 1979;20:159—164.
34. Sainsbury P, Barraclough B. Differences between suicide rates. Nature 1983;220:1252—1253.
35. Paykel ES, Rassaby E. Classification of suicide attempters by cluster analysis. Br J Psychiat 1978;133:45—52.
36. Linkowski P, De Maertelaer V, Mendlewicz J. Suicidal behaviour in major depressive illness. Acta Psychiat Scand 1985;72:233—238.
37. Bulik CM, Carpenter LL, Kupfer DJ, Frank E. Features associated with suicide attempts in recurrent major depression. J Affect Dis 1990;18:29—37.
38. Roy-Byrne PP, Post RM, Hambrick DD, Leverich GS, Rosoff AS. Suicide and course of illness in major affective disorder. J Affect Dis 1988;15:1—8.
39. Scheftner WA, Young MA, Endicott J, Coryell W, Fogg L, Clark DC, Fawcett J. Family history and five year suicide risk. Br J Psychiat 1988;153:805—809.
40. Mitterauer B, Leibetseder M, Pritz WF, Sorgo G. Comparisons of psychopathological phenomena of 422 manic-depressive patients with suicide-positive and suicide-negative family history. Acta Psychiat Scand 1988;77:438—442.
41. Mitterauer B. A contribution on the discussion of the role of the genetic factor in suicide, based on five studies in an epidemiological defined area (province of Salzburg, Austria). Compr Psychiat 1990;31:557—565.
42. Papadimitriou GN. Genetic counseling for major psychiatric disorders. In: Christodoulou GN, Kontaxakis VP (eds) Topics in Preventive Psychiatry. Basel: Karger, Bibliothca Psychiat, 1994; No.165:8—13.
43. Kringlen E. Twin studies in mental disorders. In: Mendlewicz J, Papadimitriou GN (eds) Genetics of Mental Disorders, Part I: Theoretical Aspects. Bailliere's Clinical Psychiatry, International Practice and Research. London: Bailliere Tindall, 1995;47—62.
44. Williams SW. (Cit. Loewenberg 1941), 1812.
45. Baume A. Singulier cas de suicide chez deux freres jumeaux, coincidence bizarre. Ann Medicopsychol (Paris) 1863;312—313.
46. Kallman FJ, Anastasio MM. Twin studies on the psychopathology of suicide. J Nerv Ment Dis 1947;105:40—55.
47. Kallman FJ, De Porte J, De Porte E, Feinhold L. Suicide in twins and only children. Am J Hum

Genet 1949;2:113−126.

48. Haberlandt WF. Apportacion a la genetica del suicidio. Folia Clin Int 1967;17:319−322.

49. Juel-Nielsen N, Videbech TV. A twin study of suicide. Acta Gen Med Gemellol (Roma) 1970; 19;307−310.

50. Roy A, Segal NL, Sarchipone M, Williams J, Solt V. Suicidal behaviour among twins. Neuro Psycho Pharmacol 1994;35:243.

51. Kendler K, Eaves L. Models for the joint effect of genotype and environment on liability to psychiatric illness. Am J Psychiat 1986;143:279−289.

52. Kety SS. Genetic factors in suicide. In: Roy A (ed) Suicide. Baltimore: Williams & Wilkins, 1986;41−45.

53. Roy A, Segal NL, Sarchiapone M. Attempted suicide among living co-twins of twin suicide victims. Am J Psychiat 1995;152:1075−1076.

54. Wender PH, Kety SS, Rosenthal D, Schulsinger F, Ortman J, Lunde I. Psychiatric disorders in the biological and adoptive families of adopted individuals with affective disorders. Arch Gen Psychiat 1986;43:923−929.

55. van Praag HM. Depression, suicide and the metabolism of serotonin in the brain. J Affect Dis 1982;4:275−290.

56. Roy A, De Jong J, Linnoila M. Cerebrospinal fluid monoamine metabolites and suicidal behaviour in depressed patients. A 5-year follow-up study. Arch Gen Psychiat 1989;46:609−612.

57. Mann J, Malone KM, Underwood MD, Arango V. Clinical and neurobiological risk factors for suicidal behavior. In: Judd LL, Saletu B, Filip V (eds) Basic and Clinical Science of Mental and Addictive Disorders. Basel: Karger, Bibliothca Psychiat, 1997;No.167:168−170.

58. Nielsen DA, Goldman D, Vinkunen M, Tokola R, Rawlings, Linnoila M. Suicidality and 5-hydroxyindoleacetic acid concentration associated with a tryptophan hydroxylase polymorphism. Arch Gen Psychiat 1994;51:34−38.

59. Linnoila M, Virkkunen M, Dee Higley J, George DT, Nielsen D, Goldman D. Serotonin and impulse control: from clinic to genes. Neuro Psycho Pharmacol 1994;10:728.

60. Abbar M, Amadeo S, Malafosse A, Shenk L, Mallet J, Castelnau D. An association study between suicidal behaviour and tryptophan hydroxylase markers. Clin Neuro Pharmacol 1992;15(Suppl 1):299.

61. Mann J, Arango V. Integration of neurobiology and psychopathology in a unified model of suicidal behavior. J Clin Psycho Pharmacol 1992;12:2−7.

62. Arranz B, Blennow K, Eriksson A, Mansson JE, Marcusson J. Serotonergic, noradrenergic, and dopaminergic measures in suicide brains. Biol Psychiat 1997;41:1000−1009.

63. Lowther S, De Paermentier F, Cheethan SC, Crompton MR, Katona CLE, Horton RW. 5-HT 1A receptor binding sites in post-mortem brain samples from depressed suicides and controls. J Affect Dis 1997;42:199−207.

64. Little KY, McLauglin DP, Ranc J, Gilmore J, Lopez JF, Watson SJ, Carroll I, Butts JD. Serotonin transporter binding sites and mRNA levels in depressed persons committing suicide. Biol Psychiat 1997;41:1156−1164.

65. Boularand S, Darmon MC, Ganem Y, Launey J-M, Mallet J. Complete coding sequence of human tryptophan hydroxylase. Nucl Acid Res 1990;18:42−57.

66. Julius D. Molecular biology of serotonin receptors. Ann Rev Neurosci 1991;14:335−360.

67. Hoffman BJ, Mezey E, Browmstein MJ. Cloning of the serotonin transporter affected by antidepressants. Science 1991;254:579−580.

68. Bach AW, Lan NC, Johnson DL, Abell CW, Bemenek ME, Kwan S-W, Seeburg PH, Shih JC. cDNA cloning of human liver monoamine oxidase A and B: molecular basis of differences in enzymatic properties. Proc Natl Acad Sci USA 1988;85:4934−4938.

69. Nielsen DA, Dean M, Goldman D. Genetic mapping of the human tryptophan hydroxylase gene on chromosome 11 using an intronic conformational polymorphism. Am J Hum Genet 1992; 51:1366−1371.

70. Abbar M, Courtet P, Amadeo S, Caer Y, Mallet J, Baldy-Moulinier M, Castelnau D, Malafosse

A. Suicidal behaviors and the tryptophan hydroxylase gene. Arch Gen Psychiat 1995;52: 846—849.

71. Arango V, Underwood MD, Perper JL, Mann J. Localized alterations in pre- and postsynaptic serotonin binding sites in the lateral prefrontal cortex of suicide victims. Brain Res 1995;688: 121—133.

72. Lesch KP, Wolozin BL, Murphy DL, Riederer P. Isolation of a cDNA encoding the human brain serotonin transporter. J Neurol Transm 1993;91:67—73.

73. Roy A. Genetic factors in suicide. Psycho Pharmacol Bull 1986;22:666—668.

74. Slater E. Expectation of abnormality on paternal and maternal sides: a computational model. J Med Genet 1966;3:159—161.

75. Papadimitriou GN, Linkowski P, Delarbre C, Mendlewicz J. Suicide on the paternal and maternal sides of depressed patients with a lifetime history of attempted suicide. Acta Psychiat Scand 1991;83:417—419.

Suicide and violence: the two-stage model of countervailing forces

Robert Plutchik

Albert Einstein Medical Center, Bronx, New York and University of South Florida, Sarasota, Florida, USA

Abstract. The thesis of the present paper is that suicide can be best understood as an aspect of the generation and management of aggression and violence. Within this framework, a number of studies have been carried out based upon a model which has been called a two-stage model of countervailing forces. This model assumes that the strength of the aggressive impulsive is controlled by the interaction of different classes of variables called amplifiers and attenuators. These variables also determine the direction of expression of the aggressive impulse (that is, toward self or others) when a behavioral threshold has been exceeded. Examples of amplifiers of the aggressive impulse that have been empirically identified are: depression, impulsivity, number of life problems, recent psychiatric symptoms, rejection by one's father, and use of displacement as a defense mechanism. Examples of attenuators are: social supports, high ego strength, sociability in one's father and mother, and use of denial as a defense mechanism. The vectorial interaction of amplifiers and attenuators creates an unstable equilibrium that makes detailed prediction of suicide and violence extremely difficult. Implication of the model for research and for integrating suicide and aggression as an aspect of the general domain of emotions will be suggested.

Keywords: aggression, prediction of suicide, prediction of violence, protective factors, risk factors.

For many years the study of suicide was largely concerned with the identification of social variables that were correlated with the frequency of suicide in a large population or subgroup. Such factors as sex, religion, marital status, age and race were among the first kinds of risk factors that were identified. However, it gradually became evident that certain kinds of personal or psychological variables were also associated with the risk of suicide. They included depression, loneliness, anomia, and mental illness. By 1985, a review summarized nine classes of variables that have been identified by research studies as predictors of suicide risk. These are: demographic data (age, sex, race), evidence of mental illness, evidence of antisocial behavior, previous suicidal behavior, presence of psychopathological symptoms, poor physical health, social isolation, recent loss and severity of a current suicidal attempt [1].

What was often puzzling about such reports was the great variation in rates that were found in different countries and periods. For example, a review of 10 community surveys of high school adolescents published since 1986 showed estimates of reported suicide attempts to vary from 2.4 to 20% [2]. Suicide rates in

Address for correspondence: Dr Robert Plutchik, 4505 Deer Creek Blvd., Sarasota, FL 34238, USA. Tel.: +1-941-925-7409. Fax: +1-941-912-0221. E-mail: Proban@aol.com

different countries have varied from highs of 38/100,000/year in Hungary to lows of 3/100,000/year in Greece and Mexico [3]. Over the past 35-year period, dramatic increases in adolescent suicides have been reported in Ireland (up to 847% for males and 720% for females) and Norway (up to 439% for males and 530% for females), while the rate has decreased around 85% in Japan. The fact that there are no compelling explanations of these data emphasizes the descriptive nature of much research on suicide.

An issue that arises in traditional research on suicide concerns the question of what should be an appropriate definition of a suicidal act. Although it would seem that the ideal answer to the question is to study people who are known to have killed themselves, this is not as simple a matter as it may seem. For one thing, not all people who kill themselves are identified as suicides by family members or by coroners. There are many ambiguous deaths related to motor vehicle and other accidents that may in fact be suicides. Secondly, since suicide is a relatively rare event, there are relatively few cases to study; the result is that investigations often take long periods of time and are comparatively expensive. Thirdly, retrospective data obtained about suicides from family members or hospital records are often incomplete, unreliable and inaccurate. Family members are affected by feelings of shame, guilt, defensiveness and faulty memories. Fourthly is the fact that the identification of a suicidal patient usually initiates efforts to prevent the suicide. If such efforts are successful, this weakens the degree of relation between predictor variables and outcome.

One solution to the problems cited above is to use suicide attempts as the criterion for suicidal acts, rather than actual suicides. This sometimes enables the researcher to study certain populations both before and after the suicide attempt. It enables the use of standardized measures of risk variables as well as of seriousness of the attempt, also it greatly increases the size of the potential population of relevant subjects, since suicide attempts occur 10—20 times more frequently than actual suicides [2].

The relation between suicides and suicide attempts

Such a strategy, of course, depends upon the belief that suicide attempts are on a linear continuum with actual suicides, and that what we learn from studying attempts generalizes to suicides. Some people have questioned this assumption, pointing out that in most countries, although women tend to make three or four times as many suicide attempts as men, men actually kill themselves three or four times more frequently than do women.

These observations simply reflect the empirical data. In and of themselves, they throw no light on underlying mechanisms of action of variables that in fact determine the presence of suicidal acts. Such data may be totally consistent with the statement that the dynamics of suicide (its theoretical basis and modes of interaction of variables) are precisely the same in men and women, in people of different countries and races, and in people of different ages. At present, the issue is still undecided since few investigators have looked at the problems of understanding suicide in this way.

However, even at a purely descriptive level, there is reasonably good evidence that what we learn from suicide attempters does generalize to actual suicides. The reasons for this statement stem from various sources of evidence. For example, the distribution of diagnosis of those who attempt suicide and those who actually suicide are quite similar [3]. Pokorny concluded from his study of nearly 5,000 patients that "in most respects suicide attempters and suicide completers are similar, that is, they were mostly related to the same predictors and generally in the same direction" [4].

In St. Louis, Sletten [5] also reported that actual suicides generally resembled suicide attempters on a variety of diagnostic, demographic and family variables, more than they resembled patients who were nonattempters. They concluded that completed suicides are mostly drawn from a population of suicide attempters. In 1988, Brent and his group [6] published a comparison between 27 adolescent suicide completers and 56 suicide attempters. No differences were found between the two groups on previous psychiatric history, age of onset of first psychiatric disorder, past frequencies of suicide threats, gestures, and attempts, environmental precipitants and previous exposure to suicide in the family or elsewhere.

A number of recent studies support these earlier observations. Krarup and his colleagues in Denmark [7] followed for 5 years, 99 patients who had been admitted following a suicide attempt. Three-quarters of the patients attempted suicide more than once and 14% killed themselves. In Budapest, Zonda [8] followed up 583 cases of attempted suicide over a 6- to 16-year period. He found that in Hungary, as elsewhere, persons who have already attempted suicide are at a higher risk of committing suicide later. In a review of 69 studies, Appleby [9], in England, concluded that a major factor that increases the risk of suicide is a previous suicide attempt. In Denmark, Nordentoft et. al. [10] studied 974 patients aged 15 years and over, referred to a poisoning treatment center after deliberate self-poisoning. During a 10-year follow-up period, 103 had died by suicide. These authors concluded that more than one previous suicide attempt was a high-risk factor for subsequent suicide. Also in Denmark, Barner-Rasmussen [11] reported that 20—40% of suicides (depending on diagnoses) had made a previous suicide attempt. Pfeffer, Klerman and their associates [12] followed 133 children for 6—8 years. Suicide attempters in the prepubertal years were 6 times more likely than nonpatients to attempt suicide during follow-up.

In Israel, Sheiban [13] followed 1,307 suicide attempters over a 10-year period. He found that 18% of multiple suicide attempters completed suicide. In Finland, Taiminan and Kujari [14] compared 28 schizophrenic patients who had committed suicide with an equivalent matched control group of patients. They found that the schizophrenic group had made significantly more suicide attempts.

These studies all concur in concluding that people who complete suicides are similar to those who attempt suicide. It is, therefore, reasonable to assume that the study of attempted suicide will reveal risk factors that are relevant to actual suicides.

Problems of a risk factor approach to suicide

There are, however, problems with a purely risk factor approach to suicide. This is true for a number of reasons:

1. It often focuses on broad sociological variables such as sex and race that have little value for prediction of individual behavior.
2. It tends to assume that some variables such as depression, because they are found commonly in a suicidal population, are somehow more important in predicting outcome.
3. It has no way of dealing with the fact that large numbers of people have many risk factors and show no signs of suicidal thinking or behavior.

In a recent review of the literature, I identified 55 risk factors that have been reported as correlated with suicide attempts or with actual suicides [15]. The most frequently found variable is the presence of previous suicide attempts. Other risk factors relate to states of distress, psychiatric history, personality disorders, current life events, historical life events, personality traits, coping styles, ego defenses and current environment. It is thus evident that large numbers of risk factors interact or perhaps summate to contribute to a suicidal act. Since it is impossible for clinicians to have information available about all these variables, it is not surprising that the possibilities of prediction are so limited.

A second point concerns the issue of how to judge the importance of a variable in contributing to suicide. Although it is often implied in the literature that depression and psychiatric diagnoses, and perhaps a few other variables, are the really important ones for understanding suicide, this is an invalid conclusion in a multicausal system. Even though depression may occur very frequently in a large group of suicidal patients as compared to a control group, depression alone does not produce suicide. Suicides result from the interaction of multiple causes. In such settings, typical of chaos systems, even a very small, minor, perhaps unique event, may trigger a suicidal act [16]. The relative importance of variables in a multicausal system do not add up to 100%.

The discovery of protective factors

These various observations have gradually led to the idea that the reason people with many risk factors do not commit suicide is that they also possess other special qualities or have had other special experiences which act as "protective factors". The assumption is made that the protective factors somehow cancel or inhibit the risk factors. An example of a protective factor would be strong social support from family members in the presence of stress.

Although the concept of protective factors is evidently an important one, little effort has been made to go beyond purely descriptive statements, and few protective factors have been identified. There remains a need to develop a theory of the interaction of risk and protective factors and to show how this concept has value in the scientific study of suicide. Ideally, a theory of suicide should incorporate both risk and protective factors, discuss their interactions, and use the model for guidance in research and for the generation of some new ideas.

A theory of suicide: the two-stage model of countervailing forces

Clinicians have long recognized a relationship between aggression and suicide and the statement has often been made that suicide is an expression of anger turned inward. Empirical evidence supports this belief in an intimate connection between aggression, violence and suicidal behavior. For example, a number of studies have reported that about 30% of violent individuals have a history of self-destructive behavior, while 10—20% of suicidal persons have a history of violent behavior [17,18]. Both male and female assaultive patients were 3—4 times more likely to have attempted suicide than nonassaultive patients [19]. Evidence of antisocial behavior toward others has been found to be a risk factor for suicide [1,20], just as a history of suicide attempts has frequently been identified among particularly violent prisoners [21—23]. Data on the effects of crowding in prisons [24] indicates that population increases in prisons are associated with increased rates of suicide, disciplinary infractions (violence), psychiatric commitment, and death. Decreases in prison populations are associated with decreases in assaults, suicide attempts, and death rates. Among one sample of serious juvenile delinquents, six out of 10 had made suicide attempts in the past [25]. Among hospitalized, psychotic adolescents, 28% of the group had been both violent and suicidal [26]. There is thus abundant evidence that suicide and aggression are positively correlated and tend to occur together.

What is the most useful way to interpret such observations? They may be placed within the context of a broad ethological-evolutionary view that looks for general principals and common elements across species. One example of such general principles is the universality of aggression (which refers to complex patterns of behavior connected with fight and defense in all species). The ethologists have pointed out that aggressive behavior serves to increase the probability of access to resources, helps deal with conflicts among individuals, and increases the chance of successful courtship and mating. The overall function of aggression is that it increases the chance of individual survival as well as inclusive fitness, i.e., the likelihood of gene representation in future generations.

In addition, neurophysiological research over many decades has established the existence of brain structures that organize patterns of aggressive behavior (e.g., lateral hypothalamus, ventral segmental areas, midbrain central gray area, and the central and anterior portions of the septum). Recent research has also shown that various neurotransmitter systems are involved in the expression of aggression. For example, animals fed a tryptophan-free diet become increasingly aggressive, implying that low serotonin levels are associated with a risk of violent behavior [27].

Finally, the recent literature on behavioral genetics has revealed that many, if not most, emotional characteristics are hereditary. Aggressivity has been shown to be hereditary in mice and dogs [28], and human studies of personality and temperament have also indicated significant genetic components in assertiveness, extroversion and dominance [29—31].

A recent review of the literature on predation within species (i.e., cannibalism) has demonstrated that the killing and eating of an individual of one's own species is very widespread. It has been observed in about 1,300 species, including humans [32]. It appears to have a strong genetic component, although its frequency can be affected by the availability of food supplies. In some species, cannibalism has a major influence on population size. It has been observed in at least 14 species of carnivorous mammals; lion, tiger, leopard, cougar, lynx, spotted hyena, golden jackal, wolf, coyote, dingo, red fox, arctic fox, brown bear, and grasshopper mice. In most cases, adults preyed on immature animals and cubs. Cannibalism has also been reported in 60 human cultures [33].

This brief overview suggests that aggressive behavior has fundamental importance for survival and for regulation of populations in humans and lower animals. The evidence clearly indicates that there are neurological structures and biochemical processes that are intimately connected with aggressive behavior, and that there are genetic contributions to the individual differences seen in aggressive traits.

It is, therefore, a reasonable conclusion that aggression and violence are fundamental processes of evolution and that suicide is a derived condition that applies only to humans under states of great stress or disequilibrium. In other words, we need to understand suicide as derived from aggression under certain specific conditions rather than focus on suicide in isolation. One attempt to do this is what my colleagues and I have described as the two-stage model of countervailing forces.

The theory

The theory is based upon the following ideas.
1. Aggressive impulses are defined as impulses (inner states, tendencies, dispositions, or motivations) to injure or destroy an object or person. An individual may have aggressive impulses without showing violent behavior. In our terminology, aggression refers to a theoretical inner state and violence refers to an overt act.
2. There are various kinds of life events that tend to increase aggressive impulses. These include threats, challenges, changes in hierarchical status, and loss of social attachments [34]. It also includes: physical pain, loss of power or respect, insults and things not working out as expected [35].
3. Whether or not the aggressive impulse is expressed in overt behavior depends on the presence of a large number of variables, some of which act as ampli-

fiers of the aggressive impulse and some act as attenuators of the aggressive impulse. The balance and vectorial interaction of these factors or forces at any given moment determines whether the aggressive impulse exceeds a threshold and is then expressed in overt behavior. We refer to these amplifiers and attenuators as stage I countervailing forces.

4. Overt action, however, requires a goal object toward which it is directed. The model assumes that some variables determine whether the violent behavior will be directed at oneself in a suicidal act, and that different variables determine whether the violent behavior will be directed toward other people.

5. An important idea that is part of the model is that the overt behavior of violence towards others or violence towards oneself serves a negative feedback function in terms of interpersonal interactions. For example, the violent behavior towards others may act as an intimidation that reduces threat or violence from others. The suicidal act may function as a call for help, or as a desire to create guilt, both of which may help the suicidal person deal with a crisis or with an unsatisfactory relationship by reducing the level of stress. The violent behavior thus functions as a feedback system designed to keep social interactions within certain limits. This process is exactly the same as occurs in emotional reactions [36—38]. The study of suicide may thus be thought of as an aspect of the general study of emotion.

Implementing the theory

In order to use the theory in a practical way a number of strategic decisions were made. They concerned the selection of outcome measures of suicide or suicide risk, and of violence or violence risk. They also concerned the selection of test measures of variables that seemed to be of some interest based on previous research or clinical insights.

With regard to measures of suicide and violence we developed indices of risk. We define risk basically in terms of the similarity of any given patient to a special kind of group profile. To obtain this profile, we have identified items (or descriptors) that are more typical of people who are known to have made suicide attempts in the past than they are to other patients without such a history. The sum of all these descriptions forms a scale we call the Suicide Risk Scale [39]. We know from much previous research that patients who have made a suicide attempt are at greater risk of subsequent suicide than other patients. In fact, the more risk factors that apply to a patient, the greater the risk of subsequent suicidal behavior [40—42]. This is exactly the way that medical epidemiologists consider risk factors. People with high blood pressure, high cholesterol, a history of heart disease in a first degree relative, and who smoke are at greater risk of coronary heart disease than people who have none or only one of these risk factors. One of our findings is that scores on the Suicide Risk Scale increase linearly with the number of previous suicide attempts in a patient's history. A parallel scale for the measurement of Violence Risk [23] was also developed. For both,

122

information was obtained on internal reliability, validity, sensitivity and specificity, all of which were adequate.

With regard to the measurement of possible relevant variables, we chose self-
report instruments, because they are easy to administer and to score, and
because there is now considerable evidence to show that patients often provide
more valid information to a test or to a computer than to an interviewer [43].

Initially, we did not attempt to select any particular diagnostic subgroup of
patients. Our experience, and those of others, has indicated that in different samples, anywhere from 20 to 50% of more-or-less randomly selected inpatients
have a history of one or more suicide attempts, about the same number have a
history of violent acts toward others, and about 25% have a history of both suicidal and violent acts [39,44].

The basic model is represented in Fig. 1 in schematic form. It shows that various life events such as threats and challenges influence the strength of the aggressive impulse. Whether or not the impulse becomes expressed in overt action
depends on the presence or absence of a large number of variables which interact
to determine the precise strength of the aggressive impulse at a moment in time.
Amplifiers of the aggressive impulse include a history of poor school performance, the personality trait of distrust, and easy access to weapons (to name a
few). Attenuators of the aggressive impulse include good social supports, the personality trait of timidity, and parents who were high on acceptance (to name a
few). These are the stage I countervailing forces.

This system may be considered to be a vectorial system with the different variables contributing their vector weights in an additive fashion. If the amplifiers
outweigh the attenuators (vectorially), the aggressive impulse may exceed a
threshold value and become expressed in overt behavior. However, overt behavior

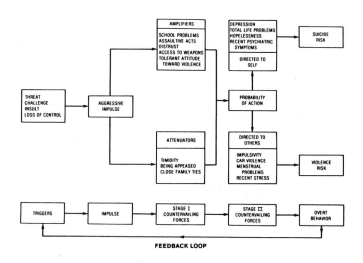

Fig. 1. Two-stage model of suicide and violence.

requires an object, which in this case may be either another person or oneself. The model assumes that different variables determine the direction of expression of the aggression once a threshold has been exceeded. These variables are the stage II countervailing forces. It is important to note that the complexity of the system implies that both suicide and violence be measured in terms of a probability or risk function.

An example of a study based on the theory

In this study, 79 psychiatric inpatients were administered a battery of psycho-metric scales designed to measure depression, ego strength, self-esteem, poor reality testing, sexual desire, sexual inhibition, impulsivity, suicide risk and violence risk [45]. Correlations of each variable with the two outcome measures of suicide and violent risk showed that depression, impulsivity and poor reality testing correlated very highly with both suicide risk and with violence risk and are thus considered to be amplifiers of the aggressive impulse. Both ego strength and self-esteem correlate negatively and significantly with suicide risk and are thus attenuators of the aggressive impulse. The strength of one's sexual drive has no relation to suicide risk but is significantly correlated with violence risk and may thus be considered to be a stage II variable that influences the direction of expression of violent behavior.

Based on this and many other studies a list of 32 amplifiers and 11 attenuators of the aggressive impulse has been compiled [46]. Examples of amplifiers are: depression, previous suicide attempts, recent psychiatric symptoms, impulsivity, use of displacement and projection as defense mechanisms, aggressive behavior in one's mother, feelings of isolation, early loss of mother or father, alcohol abuse, and easy access to weapons. Examples of attenuators are: presence of a large social network and social supports, use of denial and repression as defense mechanisms, ego strength, sociability in father and mother, and timidity as a personality trait. The fact that so many more amplifiers than attenuators have been identified may reflect some basic underlying process, or it may simply reflect the tendencies of researchers to focus primarily on psychopathology.

Some implications of the two-stage model of countervailing forces

In my preceding remarks I have tried to provide a brief overview of the theory. But if a theory is to be considered useful, it should help us to see old data in a new light, it should stimulate fresh ways of doing research, and it should suggest connections between observations that may not seem obviously related. In my final remarks I should like to consider these issues. I shall make eight points.

1. Although much contemporary research on suicide focuses exclusively on suicide and some of its correlates, the present view emphasizes the idea that suicide is part of a suicide-aggression system. All studies of suicide are, therefore, as much about aggression and violence as they are about suicide. Many of

the studies carried out by my colleagues and myself have demonstrated the important insights gained by incorporating measures of violence risk along with measures of suicide risk.

2. It is important to emphasize that the study of amplifiers and attenuators in the context of the theory is different from the study of risk and protective factors. The latter are simply descriptive statements of positive or negative correlations of variables with a suicide measure. In contrast, amplifiers and attenuators are theoretical terms which are imbedded in a broader, evolutionary-based theory of the functioning of aggression and violence in the regulation of inter-personal relations.

3. It is by now evident that there is a potentially very large number of variables that influence both suicidal behavior and violent behavior. Future research should begin to measure and study these many variables and not be limited to traditional sociological, demographic and diagnostic variables. To illustrate the potential value of expanding the range of variables studied, we may note that a number of variables have been identified that correlate with suicide risk as high as or higher than does depression. These variables are: number of life problems; MMPI schizophrenia scale scores; dyscontrol scores; recent psychiatric symptoms; passivity; total number of family problems; impulsivity; and poor reality testing. Such observations suggest that we may have placed too much attention on only a few variables in our research.

4. At the present time we believe that there are at least 32 amplifiers of the aggressive impulse and 55 risk factors for suicide. So far only about 11 attenuators have been identified and relatively few protective factors. Future research should be concerned to an increasing degree with the positive side of life. We assume that large numbers of attenuators must exist in view of the comparatively low frequency in most societies of suicide and violence.

5. The model, which is fundamentally a vectorial one, helps us understand why both suicidal and violent acts are so difficult to predict. It is evident that many of the interacting variables may change from day to day or even moment to moment, so that the dynamic equilibrium between countervailing forces is generally unstable. This is why an apparently trivial event to an outside observer may sometimes appear to trigger a suicide attempt or a violent outburst. This is also why it is impossible to describe the relative importance of each variable as if its effects were forever fixed, and why precise prediction will always be impossible. This notion is similar to some basic concepts of chaos theory where two important principles operate: a) trivial events can have major consequences; and b) variables that are important in a large population may be of little or no importance for an individual case.

6. Because of the emphasis on the interaction of multiple variables in a complex causal system, we suggest that research that attempts to distinguish between "violent" and "nonviolent" suicides is probably too limited. From the point of view of the present model, all suicides are violent acts, and it is only the presence or absence of certain attenuators that determines the precise form of

the violence.

7. Many drug studies have looked at antidepressants as a method of treatment partly because depression is known to be a very common correlate of suicide. However, if the theory is correct that suicide is primarily an aspect of the study of aggression, then medications designed to inhibit aggression should work as well as do antidepressants. It seems likely that the new class of drugs called "serenics" should be at least as effective in reducing suicidal behavior as are antidepressants.

8. Finally, the theory sensitizes clinicians to the multiple variables that are inter-acting to produce suicidal acts. This fact should lead to clinical interventions on the part of the clinician that attempts to decrease the amplifiers of aggression and increase the strength and number of attenuators.

References

1. Burk F, Kurz A, Moller HJ. Suicide risk scales: Do they help to predict suicidal behavior? Eur Arch Psychiat Neurol Sci 1985;235:153−157.
2. Diekstra RFW, Gulbinat W. The epidemiology of suicidal behavior: a review of three continents. World Health Stat Quart 1993;46:52−68.
3. Hendin MH. Suicide: A review of new directions in research. Hosp Commun Psychiat 1986; 37:148−154.
4. Pokorny AD. Prediction of suicide in psychiatric patients. Arch Gen Psychiat 1983;40:249−257.
5. Sletten IW, Everson RC, Brown ML. Some results from an automated statewide comparison among attempted, committed, and non-suicidal patients. Suicide Life-Threat Behav 1973;3: 191−197.
6. Brent DA, Perper JA, Goldstein CE, Kolko DJ, Allan MJ, Allman CJ, Zelenak JP. Risk factors for adolescent suicide: A comparison of adolescent suicide victims with suicidal inpatients. Arch Gen Psychiat 1988;45:581−588.
7. Krarup G, Nielsen B, Rask P, Petersen P. Childhood experiences and repeated suicidal behavior. Acta Psychiatr Scand 1991;83:16−19.
8. Zonda T. A longitudinal follow-up study of 683 attempted suicides, based on Hungarian material. Crisis 1991;12:48−57.
9. Appleby L. Suicide in psychiatric patients: risk and prevention. Br J Psychiat 1992;161: 749−758.
10. Nordentoft M, Breum L, Munck LK, Nordestgaard AG, Hunding A, Laursen L, Bjieldager PA. High mortality by natural and unnatural causes: a 10-year follow-up study of patients admitted to a poisoning treatment centre after suicide attempts. Br Med J 1993;306:1637−1641.
11. Barner-Rasmussen P. Suicide in psychiatric patients in Denmark, 1971−1981. II: Hospital utilization and risk groups. Acta Psychiatr Scand 1986;73:449−455.
12. Pfeffer CR, Klerman GL, Hurt SW, Kakuma T, Peskin JR, Seifker CA. Suicidal children grow up: rates and psychosocial risk factors for suicide attempts during follow-up. J Am Acad Child Adolesc Psychiat 1993;32:1106−1113.
13. Sheiban BK. Mental illness and suicide in Israel. Med Law 1993;12:445−465.
14. Taiminan TJ, Kujari H. Antipsychotic medication and suicide risk among schizophrenic and paranoid inpatients. A controlled retrospective study. Acta Psychiatr Scand 1994;90:52−58.
15. Plutchik R. Outward and inward directed aggressiveness: The interaction between violence and suicidality. Pharmacopsychiatry 1995;28:47−57.
16. O'Carroll PW. Suicide causation: Pies, paths, and pointless polemics. Suicide Life-Threat Behav 1993;12:27−36.

17. Bach-Y, Rita G, Veno A. Habitual violence: A profile of 82 men. Am J Psychiat 1974;131: 1015—1017.
18. Skodal AE, Karasu TK. Emergency psychiatry and the assaultive patient. Am J Psychiat 1978; 145:202—205.
19. Tardiff K, Sweillam A. Assaultive behavior among chronic inpatients. Am J Psychiat 1982; 159:212—215.
20. Shaffii M, Carrigan S,Whillinghil L, Derrick A. Psychological autopsy of completed suicide in children and adolescents. Am J Psychiat 1985;42:1061—1064.
21. Climent CE, Rollins A Ervin FR, Plutchik R. Epidemiological studies of women prisoners I: Medical and psychiatric variables related to violent behavior. Am J Psychiat 1973;130:985—990.
22. Climent CE, Raynes A, Rollins A, Plutchik R. Epidemiological studies of female prisoners II: Biological, psychological and social correlates of drug addition. Int J Addict 1974;9:345—350.
23. Plutchik R, van Praag HM. A self-report measure of violence risk, II. Comprehen Psychiat 1990;31:450—456.
24. Cox VC, Paulus PB, McCain G. Prison crowding research: The relevance for prison housing standards and a general approach regarding crowding phenomena. Am Psychol 1984;39: 1148—1160.
25. Alessi NE, McManus M, Brickman A, Grapentine L. Suicide behavior among serious juvenile offenders. Am J Psychiat 1984;141:286—287.
26. Inamdar SC, Lewis DO, Siomopoulous G, Shanok SS, Lamela M. Violent and suicidal behavior in psychotic adolescents. Am J Psychiat 1982;139:932—935.
27. Gibbons JL, Barr GA, Bridger WH, Liebowitz SF. Manipulation of dietary tryptophan: Effects on mouse killing and brain serotonin in the rat. Brain Res 1979;169:139—153.
28. Fuller JL. Genetics and emotions. In: Plutchik R, Kellerman H (eds) Biol Found Emotions. New York: Academic Press, 1986.
29. Loehlin JC, Horn JM,Willerman L. Personality resemblance in adoptive families. Behav Genet 1981;11:309—330.
30. Loehlin JC, Nichols BC. Heredity, Environment and Personality: A Study of 850 Twins. Austin: University of Austin Press, 1976.
31. Wimer RE, Wimer CC. Animal behavior genetics: A search for the biological foundation of behavior. Ann Rev Psychol 1985;36:171—218.
32. Polis GA. The evolution and dynamics of intraspecific predation. Rev Ecol Systemat 1981;12: 225—252.
33. Schankman P. Le roti et le bouilli: Levi-Strauss' theory of cannibalism. Am Anthropolog 1969; 71:54—69.
34. Blanchard DC, Blanchard RJ. Affect and aggression: An animal model applied to human behavior. In: Blanchard RJ, Blanchard DC (eds) Advances in the Study of Aggression, vol 1. New York: Academic Press, 1984.
35. Shaver R, Schwartz J, Kirson D, O'Connor C. Emotion knowledge: further explorations of a prototype approach. J Personal Soc Psychol 1987;52:1061—1086.
36. Plutchik R. Emotion: A Psychoevolutionary Synthesis. New York: Harper & Row, 1980.
37. Plutchik R. Emotions and their vicissitudes: Emotions and psychopathology. In: Lewis M, Haviland IM (eds) Handbook of Emotions. New York: Guilford, 1993;53—66.
38. Plutchik R. The Psychology and Biology of Emotions. New York: Harper-Collins, 1994.
39. Plutchik R, van Praag HM, Conte HR, Picard S. Correlates of suicide and violence risk I: The suicide risk measure. Comprehen Psychiat 1989;30:1—7.
40. Murphy GE,Wetzel RD, Robins E, MvEvoy L. Multiple risk factors predict suicide in alcoholism. Arch Gen Psychiat 1992;49:459—463.
41. Kotler M, Finkelstein G, Molcho A, Botsis AJ, Plutchik R, Brown SL, van Praag HM. Correlates of suicide and violence risk in an inpatient population: coping styles and social support. Psychiat Res 1993;47:281—290.
42. Vega WA, Gil AG, Zimmerman RS,Warheit GJ. Risk factors for suicidal behavior among Hispa-

nic, African-American, and non-Hispanic white boys in early adolescence. Ethn Dis 1993;3: 229—241.

43. Plutchik R, Karasu TB. Computers in psychotherapy: An overview. Comput Human Behav 1991;7:33—44.

44. Plutchik R, van Praag HM, Conte HR. Correlates of suicide and violence risk: III. A two-stage model of countervailing forces. Psychiat Res 1989;28:215—225.

45. Plutchik R, Botsis A, van Praag HM. Psychopathology, self-esteem, sexual and ego functions as correlates of suicide and violence risk. Arch Suicide Res 1995;1:1—12.

46. Plutchik R, van Praag HM. Suicide risk: amplifiers and attenuators. J Offender Rehabil 1994; 21:173—186.

Suicidal behavior: risk and protective factors

Alexander J. Botsis

Department of Psychiatry, Athens Army Hospital, Pendeli, Athens, Greece

Abstract. Suicide is a relatively rare event and as such it is inherently difficult to predict. Research on suicidology has dealt with the problem of detecting those who are at high risk for attempting or committing suicide. Considering the multifaceted nature of human behavior one should search for a variety of variables that affect it and thus relate to different disciplines. The fact that suicide has multiple determinants, each of which may contribute only slightly to the likelihood of suicidal behavior, complicates the matter of prediction even further. Several variables have been found to increase the probability of a suicidal act (risk factors), while others decrease this probability (protective factors). Both classes of variables are mainly referred either to the individual himself (biological and psychological) or to his environment (sociological, cultural, family).

The more risk factors an individual is confronted with at any given time the more the probability of his/her acting in a suicidal way. On the contrary, the more protective factors he/she possesses, the less the probability of being suicidal. Thus, it seems that the summation of each factor's contribution impels the specific individual toward suicide at a given point in time.

Keywords: attempted suicide, protective factors, risk factors, suicide.

A great part of all physicians training concerns the identification of signs and symptoms that are critical to understanding when, why and to what degree an individual's life is threatened by a physical condition or illness, and subsequently to confront these physical conditions in the best possible way. While this is the case in the training of a physician, how prepared are mental health workers in identifying individuals at high risk for suicide — the most common cause of death in our everyday practice — and how prepared are they to deal with a patient who is in a suicidal crisis? How much of our training is devoted to this issue? Moreover, if we consider that a large proportion of suicide-prone individuals have visited their doctor 1 month prior to their death, then the necessity of focusing on this problem and helping clinicians estimate suicide risk for every single individual who seeks professional help becomes a matter of great importance and priority.

Although suicide has been highly connected to mental illness, or to the presence of psychiatric symptoms, this fact alone cannot give a sensible explanation to why some psychiatric patients commit suicide and others do not. Indeed, according to methodologically well-designed studies around 95% of individuals who commit suicide suffer from at least one mental illness [1,2]. For example, it

Address for correspondence: Alexander J. Botsis MD, Department of Psychiatry, 414 Athens Army Hospital, 6 Gen Veliou St., Pendeli, Athens 15236, Greece.

is estimated that around 18–20% of unipolar or bipolar depressives and around 10–12% of schizophrenics will be lost by suicide. A very logical question, which crosses one's mind from the outcome of these studies is what happens with the rest, i.e., 80% depressives and 90% schizophrenics? What could be the reasons that actually lead this proportion of patients to a natural death? What differentiates the former group of psychiatric patients from the latter? Another important methodological question is, since it is very difficult for obvious reasons to study patients who have committed suicide, can we study instead, people who have attempted suicide and then draw conclusions from these studies about people who commit suicide?

It is a fact that suicide is a somewhat rare event and as such, it is very difficult to predict with accuracy. Research may report rates, frequencies, incidents and correlations but when we turn to, and have to deal with, the specific individual, we ought to assess the extent to which this person is close to the manifestation of suicidal behavior. Over the last 30 years research on suicidology has tried to give answers to the above questions by detecting variables that are positively (risk factors) and others that are negatively (protective factors) related to suicidal behavior. This research data stems mainly from sociological and less from psychological and biological studies of suicidal individuals; it refers to the three basic dimensions of human behavior: the biological, the psychological, and the sociological, considering the individual as a bio-psycho-social entity.

Regarding the second main point, different views have been expressed, which are sometimes controversial, but it is true that most of them converge to the same conclusion and the study results that continuously appear in the literature end up, more or less, with the same conclusion. This common view has been expressed by Pokorny [3]: "In most respects, suicide attempters and suicide completers are similar, that is, they are mostly related to the same predictors and generally in the same direction". In addition, Plutchik et al. [4] have pointed out that "...most studies conclude that completed suicides are quite similar to attempted suicides in most respects and that a continuous spectrum exists ranging from suicidal ideas, to gestures, to mild attempts, to serious attempts and finally to suicide. What is not yet known are all the important variables that influence an individual's progression along this spectrum of suicidality." Another study of young adults [5] who had gone through a detailed medical examination and a general psychological screening showed that the individuals who developed, as they reported, moderate or severe suicidal ideation during their first 10 days in the military service were different from the nonsuicidal ideators, in relation to the same variables that differentiate suicide attempters from those individuals or patients without any history of suicidal behavior. The outcome of this study further supports the existence of the suicidal continuum mentioned above. Another approach in the same direction used by both Hendin [6] and Beautrais et al. [7] has pointed out that the distribution of psychiatric diagnoses among patients who committed suicide and those who attempted suicide is quite similar.

This chapter is an attempt to provide information and assistance to the clinician in order to understand the kind of forces, events, motivations and parameters that predispose and precipitate an individual to become suicidal; and thus to help him in his difficult job to estimate suicide risk of this specific individual with as much accuracy as possible. Moreover, it underlines the factors that protect each individual by decreasing the probability of his acting-out in a suicidal way. Finally and most important, it tries to gather and integrate study results from the three different scientific domains that refer to human nature and behavior in order to offer more understanding and insight to the very common question, that is, why an individual reaches a point where he deliberately harms or kills himself.

Risk factors

Social risk factors

We could divide social factors into those which are related to the individual's broader environment (i.e., country, community) and those related to his immediate environment such as neighborhood, peer group (particularly as concerns adolescents), and family.

Social, cultural and environmental factors

Research on the sociology of suicide is very extensive and concerns itself with data from different countries, communities and their existing cultural aspects that are associated with increases or decreases in the suicide rates at different periods of their development. Sociology of suicide is very important, since nobody lives in a vacuum, but it cannot provide us with reasonable information and it does not give us enough insight and understanding as to why an individual is led to the decision to try to kill him/herself.

Sociological studies have pointed to the strong association between indices of social disorganization and suicidal behavior [8]. For example, Diekstra [9], considering the great increase in suicide rates observed in 1910 in most European countries and the USA, tried to make speculations regarding this phenomenon since research data was missing. At that time, many political and social changes were taking place in these countries. There was World War I and then the Russian Revolution, that had a great impact on these societies. Societal changes such as the rapid development of urban centers, their industrialization, women's involvement in social activities as a consequence of the recognition and legitimization of their rights, changes in the educational system and the consequent changes in the status and societal norms which had existed until then. Indeed, changes in customs and habits, traditions, new relations with the church and ties with religion were the result of the coming new social and cultural status. The transition to the new social status created the so-called political and cultural destabilization which was the origin of many stressful events for societies and individuals as well. It was assumed that the observed increase in suicide rates was related to these stressful events as well as to the increase in production and consumption of alcoholic drinks and other psychoactive substances. The latter probably formed a coping mechanism for suicide-prone individuals to deal with these events by suppressing their negative emotions.

It is evident that social stressful events are more prevalent among adolescents and young adults and that on the other hand their impact on this population is more severe than on older adults [10]. Literature has revealed that social factors such as divorce rates, unemployment, high percentage of young population and female employment are positively related to suicidal behavior. Consistent results were found by Diekstra et al. [11] in an analysis of WHO data regarding increased suicide rates in the 15- to 29-year-old age group, which were observed for the European countries mentioned above over the periods 1960−61 and 1984−85. Moreover, social phenomena like violence, criminality, substance and alcohol abuse were also found to be associated with high suicide rates in this age group.

Immigration and its relation to suicide mortality has also been studied by sociologists. It is obvious that immigration represents a significant change in all aspects of an individual's life, therefore accumulated psychological distress is very prevalent among immigrants during the process of their adaptation to the lifestyle of their new country. Trovato's studies [12,13] of Canadian immigrants, of different ethnic and cultural backgrounds, gave some very interesting results in relation to suicide. Assimilation, as measured by the immigrants propensity to speak English, as well as their satisfactory employment status − indirect indication of their social assimilation into the host country − was positively related to suicidal behavior. In other words, the greater one's integration into the new reality, the greater his tendency to be exposed to, and absorb the values and ideals of the new larger society. The fact that the immigrant assimilates to the host country often implies that his bond with his ethnic community is not strong; even though assimilation may have a variety of positive impacts for the immigrant, it seems that its process entails a great psychological cost for him/her and as a consequence, he/she experiences a greater suicide risk than immigrants who are less assimilated to the dominant culture.

While the above risk factors are related to the individual's broader environment, some study outcomes refer to relationships with his/her peer group and neighborhood. In fact, it has been reported that an individual's early exposure to violent and suicidal incidents in the peer group and neighborhood is associated with an increased suicide risk during his adulthood [14]. Related to the above expressed opinion is the fact that after a prominent display of a suicidal incident in the media there is often an increase in deaths by suicide, particularly among youths [15].

Demographic factors
It is evident that adolescents and young adults form a high risk group as do individuals over 50 years old, particularly the elderly. White people commit suicide

almost 3 times more frequently than black people do. Males commit suicide 3 or 4 times more frequently than females, while females attempt suicide more often. Among the elderly, men make less suicide attempts but with high rates of completed suicides using violent methods. As the age increases, suicide rates between men and women are 12 to 1. People who are single, divorced or separated and widowed, people who are unemployed and live in poverty and individuals who have an easy access to weapons present higher suicide rates. Easy access to weapons seems to be an important suicide risk factor. This happens particularly among adolescents and young adults aged 18–30 years who tend to be more impulsive. We found that in the Greek Army around 85% of the soldiers who committed suicide used their service guns to do so, while in the community only 15% of the same age group used firearms to kill themselves and self-poisoning was the method used more often (Botsis, unpublished data).

Family factors and life events

In the literature on suicide and attempted suicide, it is well-documented that the early social environment of suicidal individuals is often markedly disorganized. Clinical as well as epidemiological studies looking at the early social environment have mainly focused on the family. Dysfunctional family cohesion and adaptability, rigid and hostile family system, rejection by the father, lack of affectionate relationships, overprotective parents and early parental loss, especially the loss of the mother due to death, divorce or separation have been reported as important risk factors predisposing an individual to suicidal behavior [16–19]. Variables such as parental substance abuse, family history of alcoholism, depression or other mental disorders, very few close friends with whom the adolescent enjoys sharing his spare time, school failure and adolescent substance abuse are also highly associated with suicide attempts and suicide in adulthood [2,20].

Although early loss experiences and particularly parental loss have been reported as a high suicide risk factor, studies have mainly focused on the event itself rather than the quality of parental relationships. Our clinical observations converge to the point that the so-called emotional divorce between the parents in families, which have not experienced loss, also predisposes a child or adolescent to future behavioral problems such as emotional instability, affect dysregulation, poor coping styles, impulsive, suicidal and delinquent behaviors. In support of our clinical observations there is a study outcome [21] which reported that an intact home does not necessarily guarantee a stable family environment, nor does a broken home invariably mean instability.

Goldney [22] comparing female suicide attempters to normal controls, found that the former group had suffered more often the loss of one or both parents due to death, separation or divorce. He also found that suicide attempters were more likely to have come from a broken home, and/or with frequent parental quarrels and disagreements as well as to have perceived their parents personality and behavior in a more negative way than normal controls. The above findings indicate that perhaps family instability in childhood rather than early loss may be associated with suicidal behavior in adulthood. A similar finding was reported very early by Farberow [23] in his study on psychiatric patients who had attempted suicide. He found no significant difference in the incidence of loss but he did find more "family strife" due to marital conflicts. It seems that the fact of loss in suicidal individuals plays a crucial negative role when superimposed on a family system which is in the long run unstable, chaotic and disorganized. Thus, this family system is unable to cope with the crisis arising because of the loss, in a productive and constructive way; this is mainly what leads the more disrupted member of the chaotic family to suicidal behavior.

The association between child and adolescent physical abuse and suicide, has been noted by a number of investigators [24,25]. In a very recent study of youths aged 13−24 years who had a history of serious suicide attempts compared to randomly selected community, age-matched controls [26], it was found that childhood experiences such as the ones mentioned previously as well as childhood sexual and physical abuse, were risk factors for serious suicide attempts. Following further statistical analysis, it was found that serious suicide attempts could mainly be predicted on the basis of the childhood experiences of low maternal and paternal care, childhood sexual abuse, and poor parental relationships. Childhood sexual abuse, family instability and lack of affectionate relationships were also reported to be significant suicide risk factors in a Swiss study [18] of suicide attempters interviewed four consecutive times between the ages of 20 and 30 years.

Our research group examined the relation of an individual's exposure to family violence and his behavioral problems with behavioral problems among his first degree relatives during his childhood, to suicide risk in his adulthood [19]. For this reason, a group of suicidal psychiatric inpatients was compared to a control group consisting of psychiatric inpatients who had never manifested suicidal behavior. Suicide risk at the time of the study was positively correlated to family violence to which the individuals had been exposed during their childhood, their early behavioral problems, and the behavioral problems among their first degree relatives, as the patients perceived them.

It has been a consistent finding that suicidal subjects have not only experienced many losses during their early childhood but have also tended to experience significantly more stressful life events during the time period (6−12 months) preceding the suicide attempt or suicide in comparison with nonsuicidal subjects. Several object losses, change of residence and economical status, humiliation in the work environment and physical illness are some of these stressful life events with acute psychiatric illness being the most prominent [27]. In a study of our group [28] of randomly selected conscripts, we found that those conscripts who reported moderate or severe suicidal ideation during their first 10 days in the military had experienced significantly more stressful life events in the year prior to their examination than those individuals who reported no suicidal ideation.

Mental illness and psychopathology

It has been estimated that 95% of the individuals who commit suicide are suffering, as mentioned above, from at least one psychiatric disorder [1,2], while people who attempt suicide are also suffering from either a psychiatric disorder or at least from some kind of psychopathology just before the parasuicide occurs. Moreover, it has been pointed out that the distribution of the diagnoses among those who commit and those who attempt suicide is quite similar between the two groups [6,7]. More specifically, research data show that 15−18% of the patients with any kind of affective disorders [29,30], 10−12% of patients with schizophrenic disorder [31,32], 5% of patients with personality disorders [17], and 15% of the alcoholics [33] will commit suicide at some point in their lives. Mood disorders in general, greatly contribute to the likelihood of suicide attempts and suicide, while the vast majority of suicides are due to affective disorders. What has been observed with regard to depression is the fact that when depression is chronic, recurrent, periodical and especially when accompanied by psychotic features, then suicide risk is 30 times greater than in normal controls [3].

Anxiety disorders have also been reported as an important risk factor for suicidal behavior particularly among children and adolescents. Thus, Shafii et al. [34] in a psychological autopsy study of children and adolescents, found that anxiety psychopathology was related to suicide while Brent et al. [35] in another study found that anxiety disorders were very common among the same age group individuals with suicidal ideation or suicide attempts. Later on, Weissman et al. [36], examining the prevalence of suicidal behavior among a large community sample, found that panic attacks and disorder were associated with an increased risk for suicidal ideation and suicide attempts; while in a study of psychiatric inpatients suicide risk was correlated with trait anxiety as well as with other factors [37]. Recently, we reported [38] four cases of psychiatric inpatients who manifested suicidal and/or violent behavior during the panic state. In a study of patients with panic attacks or disorder, our group found that during the panic episode a significant proportion made suicide attempts. Suicide risk was found to be positively associated with trait but also, and most important, with the state anxiety that patients were experiencing during the panic attack [39]. These patients tended to have an additional personality disorder, particularly of cluster B, according to DSM-III-R criteria [40].

It becomes clear that psychiatric disorder is a very important predisposing factor, but not the only contributor to suicide attempts or suicides. The fact of comorbidity of mental disorders either on only axis I or on both axes I and II form an additional factor that increases the probability for suicidal behavior. The comorbidity with a personality disorder seems to increase the probability for suicidal behavior further. It also plays a crucial role in terms of patient's compliance with the therapy. Some have reported that comorbidity of an affective disorder with a cluster B (aggression dysregulation) personality disorder greatly increases the probability for suicide and attempted suicide [41]. Personality disorders with a higher probability for manifesting suicidal behavior are conduct disorder, antisocial personality, borderline, histrionic, and passive-aggressive personality disorders [42].

Cowell and Brent [43] in a review of psychological autopsies of suicide victims in a community-based sample found that affective disorders, substance abuse, alcoholism and their comorbidity were common in all the individuals who committed suicide independently of their age. The only difference they found was that among the elderly suicide victims depression was more common and substance abuse less frequent compared to the suicide victims of the other two age groups. Similar findings have been reported regarding the relationship of comorbidity to the manifestation of serious suicide attempts in studies of adolescent populations. More specifically, adolescent patients with comorbidity of affective disorders, substance abuse and antisocial personality tended to make more serious suicide attempts [20,26,44]. Furthermore, they found that among suicide attempters, those with personality disorder tended to make more lethal attempts and were more likely to be repeaters [7].

The comorbidity of mental disorders with regard to the increased probability and seriousness of suicidal behavior was studied more thoroughly in an inpatient population, trying to identify factors that are correlates of the higher suicide risk [42]. For this reason, 79 adult psychiatric inpatients were included in the study. They were divided into two groups, those with at least an axis I diagnosis according to DSM-III-R criteria [40] and those who had an additional axis II diagnosis, particularly of cluster B. We found that the latter group was more disturbed in terms of ego functions and psychopathology. They were significantly more impulsive, and more likely for suicidal and violent behavior. The reason for frequent violent behavior was that they tended to perceive their environment as hostile and critical, and they also scored very high on the paranoid ideation subscale of the SCL-90-R (Botsis et al., unpublished data). Disturbed ego functions distinguished patients with only axis I diagnosis from those with an additional personality disorder.

All these data indicate that the presence of mental disorders or psychopathological dimensions are great contributors to suicidal behavior, however, it seems that their presence is not adequate on its own to lead the patient to a suicidal process.

Psychological factors

Many study outcomes on psychology of suicide have reported several factors to be associated with suicide risk. One of the main determinants is the history of suicidal behavior of the individual himself. Indeed, patients who have made a suicide attempt are at greater risk for a subsequent suicide attempt or completed suicide than other patients are [2,3], especially if the individual has recurrent suicidal behavior, then suicide is very close to him or her. Feelings of depression, anxiety, dysphoria, anger, hopelessness, helplessness [45,46], impaired social adjustment, impulsivity [4,19], aggression dysregulation [47,48], delinquent behavior during adolescence, history of violent behavior, lifetime history of aggression, truancy from school or no attendance and problems with the law [14] have been found to be suicide risk factors.

It has been reported that hopelessness is the link between depression and suicide among patients with suicidal behavior [49]. Moreover, in a follow-up study of depressive individuals who had been hospitalized because of suicidal ideation and with a history of suicide attempts, those who committed suicide during a 5- to 10-year follow-up period had scored higher on the Beck Hopelessness Scale and on the item of pessimism in Beck Depression Inventory during their hospitalization [50]. Another study of 1,306 patients with mood disorders showed that hopelessness was 1.3 times more important than depression in explaining the development of suicidal ideation [51]. In a study of our group [28,52], a randomly selected sample of 500 conscripts aged 18−26 years who had previously gone through a detailed medical examination and a general psychological screening was administered a battery of psychometric instruments including MMPI − group format. Only individuals who had reliably filled out the MMPI were included in the study. Results showed that individuals who developed moderate or severe suicidal ideation during their first 10 days in the army reported feelings of hopelessness and depression which were highly correlated. Hopelessness and introverted hostility were the best predictive variables for suicidal ideation and depression measured using Beck Depression Inventory. The same group also scored significantly higher on introverted and extroverted hostility and tended to feel self and social alienation in comparison to those conscripts who did not report suicidal ideation.

It was reported early that feelings of helplessness were associated with the development of suicidal crisis and consequential suicidal behavior [45,53]. It seems that the accumulation of stress in early childhood, facing several stressful events particularly in the family, may be the leading cause of learned helplessness. Under certain circumstances, these individuals during their adulthood are very prone to experiencing feelings of depression, loneliness, helplessness and hopelessness which often characterize the suicidal crisis process. This opinion is supported by some experimental studies in mice as well as by a few clinical studies in man. For example, in a study of individuals aged 20−30 years with a history of suicidal behavior after sequential evaluation during a 10-year period, it was found that those individuals with multiple suicide attempts persistently reported feelings of helplessness [18]. Another study among elderly individuals showed that the most significant factors related to the development of depression, which is highly connected with passive (inanition) or active modes of suicide in this age group, were the loss of mastering personal and environmental problems as well as feelings of helplessness [54,55].

Besides feelings of hopelessness and helplessness, a specific cognitive state is also very often experienced by suicidal subjects. This cognitive state consists of ambivalence, constriction of thinking and the so-called perturbation [45,53]. The individual in suicidal crisis, thinks in an "all or nothing" way. He is not able to think about, or find alternative solutions to his problems. This sort of cognitive disturbance is also known as dichotomous, narrowed or "tunnel vision" thinking. It is supposed to be an acute, probably transient psychological state, characterized by an inflexibility of both the individual's intellectual and emotional functions. As a result, the suicidal individual has no more than two options which probably form the cause of the concomitant ambivalence. The combination of constriction of thinking and perturbation usually leads the person to a strong suicidal intention. There are also many individuals who think in a linear way in their everyday life. These individuals when under stress are prone to develop depressive states which lead them to dichotomous thinking.

Other psychological suicide risk factors have been detected; they mainly stem from the psychoanalytic approach referring to ego defense mechanisms and coping styles. More specifically, ego defense mechanisms are used, unconsciously, by each individual in order to resolve conflicts between instincts and drives, wishes, emotions, personal needs and external reality, as well as, to help keeping an equilibrium in his mental apparatus [56]. The transformation of unconscious ego defenses into conscious ways of interacting with himself, as well as with others, in order to deal with problems and stresses defines coping style as an additional derivative of emotion [57].

Research on those two issues in relation to suicide is very limited. In a study examining the ego defense mechanisms, mainly used by suicidal children [24,58] it was found that suicidal children use introjection as a defense mechanism significantly more frequently compared to nonsuicidal ones. The authors made the speculation that this is due to the severe separation-individuation problems suicidal children experience, given the fact that they have faced more losses compared to nonsuicidal children. Apter et al. [59], in their study of hospitalized suicidal patients, found that suicidal patients tended to use the defense mechanism of regression more frequently compared to the patients without any history of suicidal behavior. In addition, they found that repression was positively correlated with suicide risk. The former finding was explained as a tendency of the suicidal individuals to act-out in a more infantile way than nonsuicidal patients, while the latter as a common mechanism by which aggressive impulses are turned towards themselves. One may also speculate that this finding gives an explanation to the fact that alcohol and drug abuse are very common among suicidal adolescents and young adults. This constellation of behaviors frequently reported among these individuals may form a maladaptive coping pattern in an effort to deal with the aggressive impulses and painful emotions experienced by suppressing them.

As previously mentioned, suicidal subjects tend to experience many stressful life events during their childhood as well as during the period preceding the suicide attempt or suicide. It makes sense that events themselves cannot be considered crucial for the manifestation of suicidal behavior. This underlines the uniqueness of the human being. There are many individuals who experience many and severe losses during their lifetime and operate in a very productive way for themselves and their environment. It seems that it is the interaction between life events and the manner in which an individual deals with them, that is very important in determining the kind of behavior manifestation, rather than the nature and severity of the event itself.

There is only limited empirical work in this direction, i.e., the way of coping with problems in relation to suicide. It has been reported that suicide attempters have more difficulties in coping with interpersonal problems [60], are less able to consider alternatives and think flexibly [61], and they also employ poor problem-solving skills [62,63] in comparison to individuals without any history of suicidal behavior. In a study of our group [47] examining the relation of coping styles to suicidal behavior, psychiatric inpatients admitted to the hospital because of a suicide attempt were compared to psychiatric inpatients who had never been suicidal. It was found that suicidal patients tended to use all coping styles, except suppression, significantly less frequently than the nonsuicidal patients. Moreover, suicide risk in the first group was negatively correlated with coping styles of minimization, replacement (dealing with problems by finding alternative solutions) and blaming others. The former finding indicates that suicidal patients not only experience more life problems than nonsuicidal ones usually, but they probably have less inner energy and resources to deal with them in an active and effective way. The inadequate use of minimization is evidence of their exaggerated reaction to stressful life events, which may be related to suicide attempts. The negative correlation found with the coping style of blaming others is consistent with the psychoanalytic notion. A result of great significance is that even though it is a constant finding that suicidal individuals have experienced many losses, they are not able or have not learned to use the coping style of replacement, which is the specific coping style an individual must possess in order to deal with such kinds of experiences.

Another issue our group focused on, in clinical research on the psychology of suicide, was a study examining the relation of ego functions and sexual drive and conflict to suicide risk in psychiatric inpatients [64]. For this reason, psychiatric inpatients were examined and administered a battery of psychometric instruments related to the variables which were studied. Results showed that suicide risk was positively correlated with disturbed reality testing and sexual conflict. If we consider that ego functions are mental regulatory mechanisms that mediate between an individual's self and external world the association found between poor reality testing and suicide risk implies that disruptions in this particular ego function place an individual at very high risk for suicide. This finding is very similar to and consistent with the well-established fact that psychotic patients run more than 30 times greater risk for suicide than normal controls [3]. Sexual inhibition is often characteristic of neurotic conflicts which in turn is frequently associated with self-blame and development of feelings of guilt. Thus, the finding of the positive relation of sexual inhibition to suicide risk was interpreted as an indication of the presence of neurotic conflicts in our sample, that consequently developed feelings of self-blame and guilt, factors highly associated with suicide risk.

Biological factors

Biological research on suicide has employed two different approaches. The first approach attempts to identify neurotransmitters and their receptors in brains of suicide victims, while the second one involves measurement of biological markers in patients who have made suicide attempts. This indirect approach seems to provide a window to central monoamine function as well as to evaluation of neurotransmitter receptor function. Early research on biology of suicide dealt with measurements of urinary 17-hydroxycorticosteroids in suicidal, vs. nonsuicidal depressed patients, with contradictory results. Other studies in the past decade used measurements of the main metabolites of dopamine (DA), norepinephrine (NE), and serotonin (5HT) in the cerebrospinal fluid (CSF) of suicide attempters, as an index of the metabolism of these neurotransmitters in the CNS. From all these biological studies the most constant finding was that the major serotonin metabolite, 5-hydroxyindoleacetic acid (5-HIAA), was found to be significantly lower in the CSF of patients with a history of suicidal behavior, particularly those who used violent means, than in patients without, irrespective of the psychiatric diagnosis [65—68]. In addition, several groups have reported that individuals committing violent acts, including violent criminal offenders, have decreased CSF 5-HIAA, and that among them, those individuals with an additional history of suicidal behavior have a particularly low CSF 5-HIAA [69]. These findings have demonstrated that decreased central serotonin metabolism is not only related to the underlying psychopathological dimension of suicidality but that it also might in fact reflect aggression dysregulation, in general.

Recently, neuroendocrine challenge studies, utilizing selective 5HTergic agonists such as d-fenfluramine or m-chlorophenylpiperazine (MCPP), with subsequent ongoing measurements of pituitary hormones, thought to be under the specific control of serotonin, in suicidal and/or violent individuals, were conducted. The purpose of these studies was to find out whether decreased central 5HT metabolism reflects either a postsynaptic 5HT receptor hyposensitivity or hypersensitivity (primary or secondary) [48].

Protective factors

Relatively limited research has dealt with variables that may decrease the probability of a suicidal act, or in other words variables that may attenuate aggressive impulses and painful emotions an individual experiences when he confronts with difficult life situations. Each of these attenuators contribute to a different degree, in protecting an individual from developing a suicidal crisis. The protective variables already detected are mainly related to social and family environment, however, they also concern several personality traits and psychological components.

Social protective factors include keeping to society norms, holding to traditions, customs and habits, religious attachment and social integration [10]. Trovato's studies [12,13] with Canadian immigrants gave some interesting results in relation to suicide. It was found that immigrants who keep close ties with the ethnic-immigrant community and their own traditions, run a lower suicide risk than those who are absorbed and assimilated by their host country. The essential function of the ethnic-immigrant community is to provide the individual with a sense of belonging somewhere, and with a supportive network, helping him to cope with the psychosocial distress associated with life in his new social milieu, more effectively and with lower psychological cost. In other words, the greater the degree of an immigrant's ethnic community cohesion and integration, the lower the suicide risk, at least at the first stages of the adaptation process.

Healthy family structure, emotional involvement, support and open communication among the members, close family ties but not overprotection, caring mother and father, assertive parents who are characterized by acceptance and sociability [25] with an extensive network of friends and relatives as well as close peer relations are some very important factors that act as a buffer to any difficulty, help the growing individual to deal with life problems and support and direct him towards a normal psychological development.

Adam et al. [21] prospectively studying parental loss and family stability in a group of suicide attempters and controls from the general practice, found that in the first group parental loss was significantly higher than in normal subjects. They evaluated family stability at different stages: prior to the loss, 12 months after, and finally in the long run. Among controls with a history of loss, it was found that family life prior to the loss was more likely to be stable; parents were available and caring, and regardless of how they had been affected in the period after the event, in the long run family life returned to its normal function.

In one of our studies examining, among other variables, social support in relation to suicide risk, a group of suicidal psychiatric inpatients was compared to a group of psychiatric inpatients without a history of suicidal behavior [46]. A negative correlation was found between social support and suicide risk. In other words, our results indicated that the greater the social support network an individual has, the less the risk for suicide. The specific finding makes clinical sense and is consistent with other study outcomes and opinions expressed.

Personality traits that have been proved to be protective factors for suicidal behavior, include assertiveness, self-control, emotional stability and affect regulation [70]. An individual with these personality traits tends to appraise his life problems in a rather benign way and use his inner energy and resources by involving an action system or behavioral scheme, in order to change and reduce heightened arousal states.

Psychological components that have proved to be protective factors are positive body and self image, particularly among adolescents, possession of problem-solving skills, and use of all basic coping styles. It has been reported that the more coping styles an individual uses in order to deal with difficult life experiences, the more effective the outcome of his confrontation with these situations is. Moreover, there are indications that when a subject tends to use the coping styles of minimization, mapping, replacement, substitution, and improving shortcomings (particularly for elderly people) more frequently, the closer he is in dealing with problems and interacting with himself and his environment in an assertive way [47,55].

Finally, in a study of our group mentioned before, examining the relation of the ego functions to suicide risk [64], we found that ego functions of self-esteem and ego strength were negative correlates to suicide risk. This negative association in combination with other findings of the same study, imply that the more an individual is characterized by intact ego functions (reality testing, self-esteem, and ego strength), the more positive his relationship with himself and the external world is.

Comments

Suicidal behavior is manifested at all ages from childhood and adolescence through to old age. The epidemiological data and patterns of this behavior have been studied extensively. Suicide cuts across many diagnostic categories and is related positively or negatively to many social, psychological and biological variables. The more risk factors a specific individual presents at any given time, the greater the risk for expressing suicidal behavior, and on the other hand, the more protective factors he possesses, at the same time, the less the risk for suicide. The sum total of the contrasting contribution of protective and risk factors determines the degree of the specific individual's proximity to overact in a suicidal way. The fact that each factor's weight differs from individual to individual indicates the way in which all these factors interact with each other, and in particular the aggregated picture that is developed by their interaction in this specific individual is of greater importance than the factors themselves. In other words, it is very important to take into account that every factor somehow acts through the final common pathway which is the individual per se with his own personality traits, his own history, his own needs and expectations from his life, and the like.

In addition, we have to consider that the increase of suicide rates, particularly among youths, is not the only maladaptive behavior with increased rates. There is an obvious increase in delinquency, violence and criminality, drug abuse and dependence. This constellation of behaviors forms a direct index of social stress and pressure, particularly among adolescents and young adults. Beyond the prevalence data, these behaviors seem to be interconnected. Although some of these relationships themselves have been documented, the mediating factors underlying these interrelationships are unclear. In order to understand and prevent suicide we think that we have to understand violence and vice versa. All these behaviors, even though maladaptive, come up in order to master and influence the environment. They form coping patterns which intend to help the individual's adaptation to his changing needs, motivations, expectations and meanings in relation to the needs and demands of his environment. Clinical and epidemiological studies show that there is a great proportion of individuals who have a history of suicidal behavior as well as violent behavior. In all of our studies we have found a significant association between suicide risk and violence risk. Shneidman [53] expressed all these speculations in the following phrase "no one kills himself except as he has fantasized the death of another", while Hendin [6] expressed the same point of view in different words "suicide can be a form of control of violent impulses by people who feel torn apart by them".

Social, environmental and family factors, including early loss and unstable family environment in early childhood, appear to be predisposing factors for suicidal behavior or to increase the vulnerability to suicidal behavior when the individual is faced with stressful life events in his adulthood. However, it is evident that no psychosocial factor per se is either necessary or sufficient to lead the individual to the suicidal act. Many suicides have been attempted or committed by individuals who have not experienced any, recognizable at least, special negative life event. In addition, there are many individuals who have experienced many traumatic events during their lifetime but do not manifest suicidal or other related behaviors. The most appropriate way to approach suicidal behavior is to provide information concerning the interaction of psychosocial factors with the specific individual's psychological and biological profiles; how all these three domains interact, how the specific psychosocial events are perceived and experienced by the specific individual, and how this individual copes with psychosocial factors. In order to have a better understanding of and to acquire more insight in suicidal and other interrelated behaviors as mentioned above, a theoretical concept which will incorporate, gather and integrate already existing research data, as well as future study outcomes, becomes a matter of great necessity. Such a theoretical model is that proposed by Plutchik et al. [71], the so-called "two-stages model of countervailing forces", thoroughly described elsewhere.

Finally, from a clinical point of view, we should always bear in mind, that past behavior of a specific individual forms the best guide for us in terms of predicting his future behavior. In other words, the way an individual has dealt with difficult life situations and life stressors throughout his life can give us valuable information about his behavior in the future.

References

1. Barraclough BM, Bunch J, Nelson B, Sainsbury P. A hundred cases of suicide: clinical aspects. Br J Psychiat 1974;125:355–373.
2. Shaffer D, Garland A, Gould M, Fisher P, Trautman P. Preventing teenage suicide: a critical review. J Am Acad Child Adolesc Psychiat 1988;27(6):675–687.
3. Pokorny AD. Prediction of suicide in psychiatric patients. Arch Gen Psychiat 1983;40:249–257.
4. Plutchik R, van Praag HM. The measurement of suicidality, aggressivity, and impulsivity. Progr Neuropsychopharmacol Biol Psychiat 1989;13:S23–S34.

5. Botsis AJ, Soldatos CR, Kokkevi A, Liossi A, Lyrintzis S, Stefanis CN. Suicidality in Greek military draftees. New Orleans: 144th Annual Meeting of the American Psychiatric Association, Symposium on Assessment of Suicide and Violence, 1991.

6. Hendin MH. Suicide: a review of new directions in research. Hosp Comm Psychiat 1986;37: 148–154.

7. Beautrais AL, Joyce PR, Mulder RT, Fergusson DM, Deavoll BJ, Nightingale SK. Prevalence and comorbidity of mental disorders in persons making serious suicide attempts: a case-control study. Am J Psychiat 1996;153:1009–1014.

8. Maris R. Pathways to Suicide: A Survey of Self-Destructive Behaviors. Baltimore: John Hopkins University Press, 1981.

9. Diekstra RFW. Suicide and the attempted suicide: an international perspective. Acta Psychiatr Scand 1989;80(Suppl 354):1–24.

10. Diekstra RFW. Suicide and suicide attempts in the European Economic Community: an analysis of trends, with special emphasis upon trends among youth. Suicide & Life-Threat Behav 1985;15(1):27–42.

11. WHO. Correlates of Youth Suicide. Geneva: World Health Organization, Division of Mental Health, Technical Document, 1988.

12. Trovato F. A time series analysis of international immigration and suicide mortality in Canada. Int J Soc Psychiat 1986;32(2):38–46.

13. Trovato F. Suicide and ethnic factors in Canada. Int J Soc Psychiat 1986;32(3):55–64.

14. Kom M, Botsis AJ, Kotler M, Plutchik R, Conte HR, Finkelstein G, Grosz D, Kay S, Brown SL, van Praag HM. The suicide and aggression survey: a semistructured instrument for the measurement of suicidality and aggression. Compr Psychiat 1992;33(6):359–365.

15. Gould MS, Shaffer D. The impact of suicide in television movies: evidence of imitation. N Engl J Med 1986;315:690–694.

16. Miles P. Conditions predisposing to suicide. A review. J Nerv Ment Dis 1977;164:231–246.

17. Benjaminsen S, Kraup G, Lauritsen R. Personality, parental rearing behavior and parental loss in attempted suicide: a comparative study. Acta Psychiatr Scand 1990;82:389–397.

18. Angst J, Degonda M, Ernst C. The Zurich study: XV. Suicide attempts in a cohort from age 20 to 30. Eur Arch Psychiat Clin Neurosci 1992;242:135–141.

19. Botsis AJ, Plutchik R, Kotler M, van Praag HM. Parental loss and family violence in relation to suicide and violence risk. Suicide & Life-Threat Behav 1995;25(2):253–260.

20. Allebeck P, Allgulander C. Suicide among young men: psychiatric illness, deviant behavior and substance abuse. Acta Psychiatr Scand 1990;81:565–570.

21. Adam KS, Bouckoms A, Streiner D. Parental loss and family stability in attempted suicide. Arch Gen Psychiat 1982;39:1081–1085.

22. Goldney RD. Parental loss and reported childhood stress in young women who attempt suicide. Acta Psychiatr Scand 1981;64:34–59.

23. Farberow N. Personality patterns of suicidal mental hospital patients. Genet Psychol Monogr 1950;42:3–79.

24. Pfeffer CR, Newcorn J, Kaplan G, Mizruchi MS, Plutchik R. Suicidal behavior in adolescents. J Am Acad Child & Adolesc Psychiat 1988;27:357–361.

25. Kaplan SJ, Pelcovitz D, Salzinger S, Mandel F, Weiner M. Adolescent physical abuse and suicide attempts. J Am Acad Child Adolesc Psychiat 1997;36(6):799–808.

26. Beautrais AL, Joyce PR, Mulder RT. Risk factors for serious suicide attempts among youths aged 13 through 24 years. J Am Acad Child Adolesc Psychiat 1996;35(9):1174–1182.

27. Hagnell O, Lanke J, Rorsman B. Suicide rates in the Lundby study: mental illness as a risk factor for suicide. Neuropsychopharm 1981;7:74–79.

28. Botsis AJ, Soldatos CR, Kokkevi A, Lyrintzis S. Suicidal ideation in military draftees. In: Lester D (ed) Suicide 90: Proceedings of the 23rd Annual Meeting of the American Association of Suicidology. Denver: Am Assoc Suicidol, 1990;294–296.

29. Roy A. Suicide in recurrent affective disorder patients. Can J Psychiat 1984;29:319–322.

30. Guze SB, Robins E. Suicide and primary affective disorders. Br J Psychiat 1970;17:437—438.

31. Roy A. Suicide and psychiatric patients. Psychiatr Clin North Am 1985;8:227—241.

32. Roy A. Suicide in schizophrenia. In: Roy A (ed) Suicide. Baltimore: Williams & Wilkins, 1986; 73—88.

33. Murphy GE. Suicide in alcoholism. In: Roy A (ed) Suicide. Baltimore: Williams & Wilkins, 1986;89—96.

34. Shaffi M, Carrigan S,Whitinghill JR, Derrick A. Psychological autopsy of completed suicides in children and adolescents. Am J Psychiat 1985;142:1061—1064.

35. Brent D, Kalas R, Edelbrock C. Psychopathology and its relationship to suicidal ideation in childhood and adolescence. J Am Acad Child Adolesc Psychiat 1986;25:666—673.

36. Weissman MM, Klerman GL, Markowitz JS, Quelette R. Suicidal ideation and suicide attempts in panic disorder and attacks. N Engl J Med 1989;321:1209—1214.

37. Apter A, van Praag HM, Plutchik R, Sevy S, Korn M, Brown SL. Interrelationships among anxiety, aggression, impulsivity, and mood: a serotonergically linked cluster? Psychiat Res 1990;32:191—199.

38. Korn M, Kotler M, Molcho A, Botsis AJ, Grosz, D, Chen C, Plutchik R, Brown SL, van Praag HM. Suicide and violence associated with panic attacks. Biol Psychiat 1992;31:607—612.

39. Botsis AJ, Soldatos CR, Giotakos O, Polychroni G, Petrovas G, Vrekos S, Stefanis CN. Panic Attacks: Relation to Suicidal and Violent Behavior. Venice, Italy: XVIIIth International Conference of the International Association for Suicide Prevention, 1995.

40. American Psychiatric Association. Diagnostic and Statistical Manual of Mental Disorders: 3rd edn (revised). Washington, DC: APA, 1987.

41. Blumenthal SJ, Kupfer DJ. Generalizable treatment strategies for suicidal behavior. Ann NY Acad Sci 1986;487:327—340.

42. Botsis AJ, Plutchik R, van Praag HM. Ego functions and psychopathology in patients with personality disorders: relation to suicide and violence risk. Suicide & Life-Threat Behav (In press).

43. Cowell Y, Brent D. Suicide and aging. I: Patterns of psychiatric diagnosis. Int Psychogeriatr 1995;7(2):149—164.

44. Brent DA, Perper JA, Moritz G, Allman C, Friend A, Roth C, Schweers J, Balach L, Baugher M. Psychiatric risk factors for adolescent suicide: a case-control study. J Am Acad Child Adolesc Psychiat 1993;32:521—529.

45. Leenaars AA, Balance WDG, Wenckstern S, Rudzinski DJ. An empirical investigation of Shneidman's formulations regarding suicide. Suicide & Life-Threat Behav 1985;15(3):184—195.

46. Kotler M, Finkelstein G, Molcho A, Botsis AJ, Plutchik R, Brown SL, van Praag HM. Correlates of suicide and violence in psychiatric inpatients: coping styles and social support. Psychiat Res 1993;47:281—290.

47. Botsis AJ, Soldatos CR, Liossi A, Kokkevi A, Stefanis CN. Suicide and violence risk: I. Relation to coping styles. Acta Psychiatr Scand 1994;9:91—94.

48. Botsis AJ. Aggression and suicidal behavior: a common biological substrate? Psychiatriki 1995;6(3):260—269.

49. Beck A, Kovacs M, Weissman A. Hopelessness and suicidal behavior. JAMA 1975;234: 1146—1149.

50. Beck AT, Steer RA, Kovacs M, Garrison B. Hopelessness and eventual suicide: a 10-year prospective study of patients hospitalized with suicidal ideation. Am J Psychiat 1985;142:559—563.

51. Beck AT, Steer RA, Beck JS, Newman CF. Hopelessness, depression, suicidal ideation, and clinical diagnosis of depression. Suicide & Life-Threat Behav 1993;23(2):139—145.

52. Botsis AJ, Soldatos CR, Kokkevi A, Lyrintzis S, Brown SL, Stefanis CN. Feelings of hopelessness in young adults. In: Lester D (ed) Suicide 91: Proceedings of the 24th Meeting of the American Association of Suicidology. Denver: Am Assoc Suicidol, 1991:203—205.

53. Shneidman ES. Some essentials of suicide and some implications for response. In: Roy A (ed) Suicide. Baltimore: Williams & Wilkins, 1986;1—16.

54. Solomon K. The depressed patient: Social antecedents of psychopathologic changes in the

elderly. J Am Geriatr Soc 1981;29(1):14—18.

55. Plutchik R, Botsis AJ, Bakur-Weiner M, Kennedy G. Clinical measurement of suicidality and coping in late life: a theory of countervailing forces. In: Kennedy G (ed) Suicide and Depression in Late Life: Critical Issues in Treatment, Research and Public Policy. New York: John Wiley & Sons Inc., 1996;83—102.

56. Vaillant GE. Theoretical hierarchy of adaptive ego mechanisms. Arch Gen Psychiat 1973;24:107—118.

57. Plutchik R. Emotion: A Psychoevolutionary Synthesis. New York: Harper & Row, 1980.

58. Pfeffer C, Plutchik R, Mizruchi M, Lipkin R. Suicidal behavior in child psychiatric inpatients, outpatients and nonpatients. Am J Psychiat 1986;143:733—738.

59. Apter A, Plutchik R, Sevy S, Korn M, Brown SL, van Praag HM. Defense mechanisms in risk of suicide and risk of violence. Am J Psychiat 1989;146:1027—1031.

60. Linehan MM, Chiles JA, Egan KJ. Presenting problems of parasuicides versus suicide ideators and nonsuicidal psychiatric inpatients. J Consult Clin Psychol 1986;54:880—881.

61. Chiles JA, Stroshal KP, McMurtray I. Modeling effects on suicidal behavior. J Nerv Ment Dis 1985;173(8):477—481.

62. Levenson M, Neuringer C. Problem-solving behavior in suicidal adolescents. J Consult Clin Psychol 1971;37:433—436.

63. Weishaar ME, Beck AT. Hopelessness and suicide. Int Rev Psychiat 1992;4(2):177—184.

64. Plutchik R, Botsis AJ, van Praag HM. Psychopathology, self-esteem, sexual and ego functions as correlates of suicide and violence risk. Arch Suicide Res 1995;1:1—12.

65. Asberg M, Traskman L, Thoren P. 5HIAA in cerebrospinal fluid: a biochemical suicide predictor? Arch Gen Psychiat 1976;33:1193—1197.

66. Brown GL, Ebert MH, Goyer PF, Jimerson DF, Klein WJ, Bunney WE, Goodwin F. Aggression, suicide and serotonin: relationships to CSF amine metabolites. Am J Psychiat 1982;139:741—746.

67. van Praag HM. Neurotransmitters and CNS disease: depression. Lancet 1982;2:1259—1264.

68. van Praag HM. CSF 5-HIAA and suicide in non-depressed schizophrenics. Lancet 1983;2:977—978.

69. Brown SL, Botsis AJ, van Praag HM. Suicide: CSF and neuroendocrine challenge studies. Int Rev Psychiat 1992;4:141—148.

70. Zlotnick C, Donaldson D, Spirito A, Pearlstein T. Affect regulation and suicide attempts in adolescent inpatients. J Am Acad Child & Adolesc Psychiat 1997;36(6):793—798.

71. Plutchik R, van Praag HM, Conte HR. Correlates of suicide and violence risk: III. A two stage model of countervailing forces. Psychiat Res 1989;28:215—225.

The psychology of suicide: past and present

Norman L. Farberow

Los Angeles Suicide Prevention Center, Los Angeles, California, USA

Abstract. The continuing search for factors significant in the etiology of suicide has focused on the experiences crucial to the development of self, with some theorists emphasizing the structural and functional aspects of the self and others noting its development in relationships with others. The search for contributing elements has led researchers to a broader conception of the possible sources of influence, arising from all the major domains of human function: psychosocial, psychiatric disorders, biological vulnerabilities, personality, familial and genetic. Counterbalancing this trend has been the search for commonalities among the many different kinds of self-destruction, to the point of designating a single factor, psychache, as the basis of all suicidal behavior.

While able to assess suicidal potential and status, experience has led us finally to set aside the goal of prediction of individual suicides. We seem to be on the brink of a comprehensive classification system that will encompass and differentiate among the wide range of suicidal behaviors, a significant achievement for our field.

A new model of treatment has focused on primary prevention, suggesting the development of coordinated programs with planned intervention aimed at the early multidimensional risk factors already identified. Future directions will probably see community programs that will include suicide prevention as part of programs developed for many other problems, such as reduction of family violence, prevention of psychopathology, and control of substance abuse. Meanwhile our efforts should be to use all the information we have to reduce risk for known at-risk populations in specific settings.

Suicide prevention has had a productive psychological past; its active present points to an even fuller gratifying future of lives saved and suffering reduced.

Keywords: intervention, personality, prevention programs, psychology, suicide.

Introduction

This paper discusses only the psychological aspects of suicide. As a result, references to the many other aspects of suicide, e.g., biological, sociological, medical, economic, etc., are sparse, although their absence does not in any way deny their significance for our common goal, the understanding and prevention of suicide. However, these areas are effectively covered by other chapters in this volume. Further, this paper presents an overview of the past and present of the psychology of suicide focused on three basic aspects: 1) theory and psychodynamics, 2) assessment and prediction, and 3) treatment and prevention.

Address for correspondence: Norman L. Faberow PhD, 1068 Casiano Road, Los Angeles, CA 90049, USA. Tel.: +1-310-476-9204.

Theory and psychodynamics

Early 20th century concepts

The major early writings about the theory and psychodynamics of suicide were by psychoanalysts. In general, their theories were about the development of the self and how it was involved in suicide, with two major emphases: 1) the self and how its structure and functions were affected; and 2) the self as it developed in response to the impact of influence of others upon it.

Freud's two theories exemplify both approaches. In his 1917 theory [1], he extended his conceptualization of what occurred in the self in depression and melancholia to suicide, with the self-destructive behavior representing the aggression directed against a part of the self that had incorporated a loss or rejection of love object. The primary affects experienced were rage, depression and anxiety, affects resulting from the loss and consequent changes in the relationship (Table 1).

Freud's [2] later theory of suicide was more psychobiological with the conceptualization of a death instinct. In a sense, Freud was forced to develop the construction of a death instinct because he found himself continually faced with the evidence of self-destructive behaviors with no dynamics to account for them; Eros could not. The behavior could then be more readily explained by the dual instincts, one of Eros as a life-enhancing life-sustaining drive that was always seeking new experiences and at the same time was in constant interaction with Thanatos, the aggressive death instinct, as it pushed towards conservatism and the past.

The self, in Jung's concept [3], contained the life-preserving forces of the individual which allowed him to achieve personal meaning in his life. Positive and negative values were individually determined rather than directed by instincts. There might even be a preference for death in selected situations, such as the exaltation of martyrdom, or freedom from intractable pain, or unbearable mental anguish. Suicide might also reflect a longing for spiritual rebirth, in which the attraction of increased self-realization permitted risking one's life in a gamble with death.

Adler's [4] concept of "social interest" was a reflection of the basic interrelatedness between the individual, his fellow men, the social world and the universe. Where social interest was defective or deficient, feelings of inferiority appeared. Suicide was a way of attaining a feeling of mastery over life and death and thus overcoming feelings of inferiority. Suicide might also be "veiled aggression", a way of expressing reproach or revenge against others.

Menningers's [5] adoption of Freud's construction of the death instinct led him to the psychodynamic triad of the "wish to kill", "the wish to be killed", and "the wish to die". Similar to Freud's concept, all three wishes were assumed to be interacting with each other and with Eros in varying degrees and changing patterns to form a continuum of self-destructive behavior from indirect or covert self-destructive behavior to overt, nonambivalent, completed suicide.

Zilboorg [6] viewed suicide as a way of thwarting outside forces that were making living feel impossible. Suicide was a paradoxical way of living in which killing oneself was a way of exercising control over one's life and thus maintaining the self rather than destroying it.

Sullivan [7] and Horney's [8] theories were also developed primarily from interpersonal relations, with suicide viewed as either the individual's hostile attitude toward other people redirected against the self (Sullivan), or as a "performance death" resulting from a sense of failure in meeting the standards expected by society (Horney).

Midcentury concepts

Psychoanalytic thinking on suicide continued to focus on either the features and functions of the self or on the self in relation to others, or both. Melanie Klein's [9] theory of object relations considered suicidal behavior to be an aggressive attack against the "bad part" of an internalized love object; Margaret Mahler [10] and others [11,12], focused on developmental aspects of the self in which failure of the necessary separation-individuation transition phase resulted in symbiotic object choices. Significant others were then treated as parts of the self rather than as separate others.

Hendin [13] added fantasies and wishes to the basic affect of depression, such as expiation, self-punishment for delusions of guilt or sin, and forcing of affection and spite. Hendin also emphasized the role of cultural factors, especially in child-rearing practices, also in attitudes toward death and dying.

Litman and Tabachnick [14] summarized their psychoanalytic approach to suicide as essentially a failure to achieve adaptation arising from situations of confusion and growing feelings of loss of control. They also identified a number of unconscious fantasy wishes that contribute in variable proportions to every suicide: e.g., such as a tired wish to escape, a guilty wish for expiation, a discouraged wish for punishment for inadequacies; a hostile, aggressive wish for revenge, power and control; an erotized wish for masochistic surrender, possibly reunion with a dead loved one; and a hopeful wish for rebirth and renewal.

Kohut [15] felt that self-destructiveness occurred as an expression of narcissistic rage and an inability to tolerate self-condemnatory feelings of shame. Kernberg [16] described suicide as being motivated by a number of dynamics: the result of efforts to re-establish control over a chaotic inner world; a way to claim superiority over death; or a reaction to bizarre fantasies and/or auditory hallucinations. Buie and Maltsberger's [17] concept of suicide emphasizes the frustrated dependency aspects of the patient. The dynamics presume psychological vulnerability, stemming from an inability to tolerate intense feelings of aloneness and overwhelming negative feelings of the self. Suicidal acts are motivated by a need to regain feelings of self-esteem which can only occur by merging with a lost loved object through death.

Other theories

Other theories of suicide reflect the multifaceted complexity of suicide, and have drawn from all areas of human functioning that have been identified as predis-

Table 1. Suicide: theorists, psychodynamics, affects, sources, causes.

Theorists	Psychodynamics	Affects
Psychoanalytic (early)		
Freud (1917)	Loss of or rejection by incorporated love object	Rage, depression
Freud (1922)	Death instinct interacting with life instinct	Aggression split: self-destructive part directed inward; aggressive part directed outward
Jung (1933)	Constant search for meaning of self; longing for spiritual rebirth	Emptiness, confusion, depression, meaninglessness
Adler (1958)	Inferiority feelings: incompletely developed "social interest", revenge drive for mastery	Dependency "veiled aggression", depression, rage, reproach
Menninger (1938)	Death instinct: wish to kill, wish to be killed; wish to die	Depression, aggression
Zilboorg (1936)	Thwarting outside forces; living by killing oneself	Need for control; aggression aimed at external controls
PSA (midcentury)		
Melanie Klein (1968)	Aggressive attack against "bad" part of an internalized love object	Self-contempt; aggression
Mahler (1968)	Failed separation-individuation; poor love-object selection	Dependency, depression, anxiety
Hendin (1963)	Expiation; way to force affection; spite; retaliatory abandonment, punishment	Depression resulting from loss; guilt; shame; feeling worthless
Litman/Tabachnick (1968)	Failure in adaptation; wishes: escape, expiation, punishment, revenge, power, reunion with loved one	Crises lead to confusion; loss of control; attachment to ideas of dying; symbiotic destructive dependency; rage; guilt; anxiety; ego-splitting
Baechler (1979)	Escape; aggression; sacrifice; proving worth through ordeal	Intolerable pain; hostility; revenge; anger; ambivalence
Kohut (1978)	Destruction of unacceptable parts of self	Narcissistic rage; oppressive feelings of shame
Kernberg (1984)	Efforts to re-establish control over chaotic inner world; responses to fantasies/hallucinations	Depression; severe anxiety; confusion; rage; fear
Buie/Maltsberger (1989)	Rage against lost self-object; need to regain source of self-esteem by merging after death; escape from psychological pain	Frustrated dependency; intense feelings of loneliness; worthlessness; vulnerabilities; rage

(cont.)

Table 1. Continued.

Theorists	Psychodynamics	Affects
Other — developmental		
Noam/Borst (1994)	Developmental phases	Failures; disruptions
Pfeffer (1994)	Developmental phases	Transitions; source of identity continuity; self esteem; ego-development
Adam	Causal matrix	Predisposing, precipitating and contributory factors, especially psychological stress
Blumenthal/Kupfer/ Vaillant(1990)	Multiaxial causes from five domains: psychosocial; personality, psychiatric disorder, family, biological	Patterns of vulnerability; identification of protective defensive mechanisms
Other — unifying		
Shneidman (1985)	Commonalities: motivations	Seeking: solution; way out; cessation of consciousness; communication
	Emotions	Unbearable psychological pain; hopeless-helpless; frustration of needs; ambivalence
	Character	Life-long patterns; constriction
Shneidman (1993)	Intense psychological pain	Thwarting psychological needs

posing a person to a state of vulnerability for suicide. These provide a state of readiness for suicidal behavior when precipitating factors occur.

Pfeffer [18] and Noam and Borst [19] have focused on the developmental processes in childhood and youth for the indications of such experiences. Pfeffer, for example, urges special attention to the subtle causal links within the transition between developmental phases that may become significant because of additive elements and cumulative influence. She suggests areas of investigation such as the complex factors that contribute to feelings of continuity and identity, the foundation of self-esteem and other processes in ego development.

Adam's [20] causal matrix model classifies suicidal factors into three groups: predisposing, precipitating, and contributory. Psychosocial stressors especially, such as family disturbances, or separations and/or losses contribute to vulnerability and play a primary role, especially in association with related personality variables, like low self-esteem, poor impulse control, and interpersonal hostility. Adam also urges that we examine how the individual's coping and support systems best serve the individual.

Vaillant and Blumenthal [21] conceptualize a multiaxial causation of suicide resulting from a convergence of predisposing and precipitating risk factors from five domains (psychosocial, personality, psychiatric disorder, family disorders and biologic factors) that overlap with each other. People move in and out of suicidal crises at different points in their lifetime depending on the disruptions, stressors and contributing conditions that occur along with the presence or absence of protective elements.

While most of the current theories have been characterized by an expanding search for dynamics and contributing factors, Shneidman's contributions have been in the opposite direction, essentially looking for common ground and unifying aspects. In a 1985 proposal Shneidman [22] described 10 commonalities allegedly underlying all suicidal behavior, regardless of kind. Four commonalities are motivational: seeking a solution and a way out, moving toward cessation of consciousness and communication; two are emotional: emotional/helpless, frustration of psychological pain, ambivalence; and two are characterological: constriction, consistent with life-long coping patterns.

More recently, Shneidman [23] has proposed an even more unifying position stating that psychological pain lies at the core of all suicidal behaviors. The psychological pain results from the frustration of one or more of Murray's [24] 20 basic psychological needs, such as affiliation, aggression, autonomy, play, order, nurturance, etc. The ensuing emotional turmoil, described in terms of perturbation, stress, and pain, results in a suicidal state. Suicide occurs when the individual can no longer endure the pain.

Summary

In summary, early theories focused on concepts of the self, with suicide appearing on the one hand as features of its own function and structure, but on the other hand as an emphasis on its interaction and relationship to significant others. Failures in the developmental and adaptational processes are reflected in negative self-images and extreme fantasies or wishes, also the preponderance of such feelings as depression, shame, anger (rage), guilt, worthlessness, anxiety and many other feelings. More recent theories on the etiology of suicide have focused on identifying contributing factors from all domains of human experiences. In another approach, a unifying effort has appeared in the indication of common elements found in all suicidal behavior within the proposal of a single psychological factor, unbearable psychological pain, as the underlying factor in all suicidal behavior.

Assessment and prediction

Early problems

An early chapter on assessment and prediction of suicidal behavior by Farberow [25] described scales of clinical signs and patterns and assessment procedures then in use for evaluating suicide potential in a wide variety of populations, such as adolescents, SPC callers, psychiatric hospital patients, repeaters and other subgroups. The major problems of assessment at that time were seen as evaluation of suicide potential for short-term clinical use, i.e., for immediate intervention and/or treatment; and the longer term assessment for the purpose of screening of groups or large population subgroups. A prominent concern was the high numbers of false positives and negatives. A strong recommendation was that assessment scales should be constructed of risk factors identified for selected subgroups as well as for both short- and long-term needs.

There were also questions about the nature of suicide, such as: How was suicidal behavior distributed in the general population? Was it symmetrical? And, if so: What did the center of the curve represent? Where did "normal" suicidal behavior fall? Definitions of suicide made for considerable confusion, with some categories determined by outcome, as on a continuum from noninjury on suicide ideation, to injury, as in suicide attempts, to committed suicide or deaths; others determined by kinds of behavior, such as ideation, verbal, preparatory, action; and still others determined by types, such as gestures, communication, serious, etc. Methodological problems were noted, as in achieving accuracy of predictions in a field where the results of the measurements might require initiating treatment and thus invalidate the prediction; of choosing adequate control groups or subjects for appropriate comparison and the identification of positive as well as negative factors which play different roles at different times depending on age, sex, culture, support, past experiences, etc.

Progress

A few of the early questions have been answered. For example, a strong approach toward acceptable definitions has been made with Diekstra's [26] proposals to WHO of the kinds of behavior to be considered suicide, suicide attempts, suicide ideation and parasuicide. There have been a number of efforts to establish order in our field, i.e., to develop a commonly accepted classification of the phenomena with which we are concerned. Maris [27] has pointed out that our scientific study of suicide could be greatly facilitated if there was a simple standardized classification system, similar to the DSM-IV or the ID-9, allowing the researcher, clinical, epidemiologist or theoretician to communicate with each other using mutually understood terms (Table 2).

Most of the psychological (psychiatric) classifications are based on outcome. Beck et al. [28] adopted the familiar classifications of committal (death), nonfatal attempts (injury or harm), and ideation (noninjury), but with ratings of intention, lethality, mitigating circumstances, method and certainty added.

Baechler [29] proposed four major types (and 11 subtypes) of escapist, aggressive, oblational (sacrifice), and ludic (gamble).

Jobes et al. [30] have proposed a classification system for committed suicide only, based on two conditions, that the death be self-inflicted and that there be evidence, whether direct or indirect, of intent to die.

Ellis [31] proposed a scheme for rating the "dimensions" of suicide that classified the major types as descriptive (using behavior like committal, parasuicide, ideation, method, lethality, and communication); situational (loss, conflict); psy-

Table 2. Classification schemes in suicide.

Classifiers	Types	Components
Beck (1973)	Outcome — commit, attempt, ideation	Ratings of intention to die; certainty of rater; lethality (medical); mitigating circumstances; method
Baechler (1979)	Purpose: (1) escapist, (2) aggressive, (3) oblational (sacrifice), (4) ludic (gamble)	(1) Flight, grief, punishment; (2) vengeance, crime, blackmail, appeal; (3) sacrifice, transfiguration; (4) ordeal, game
Jobes, Berman and Josselson (1987)	Outcome – completed	Requires: (1) self-inflicted, (2) evidence of intention
Ellis (1988)	Dimensions – (1) dimensions, (2) situational, (3) psychological/ behavioural, (4) teleological	(1) Suicide, parasuicide, ideation, indirect; (2) loss, conflict; (3) diagnostic, cognitive, skill-deficit; (4) instrumental, cessation, impulse
Maris (1992)	Behaviors — (1) completed, (2) nonfatal attempts, (3) suicidal ideation, (4) mixed, (5) Indirect self-destructive behavior	(1—3) Escape, revenge, altruistic, risk-taking; (4) modes — natural, accident, homicide, suicide, mixed; (5) substance abuse, medical non-compliance. Also ratings of certainty, lethality, intention, mitigating circumstances, method, demography

chological/behavioral (diagnosis, cognition); and teleological (instrumental and cessation).

Maris [32] multiaxial scheme classified all suicidal behavior on three major axes, the type of suicide, the characteristics, and indirect self-destructive behavior (ISDB). The type of suicidal behavior is categorized into five groups: completed, nonfatal suicide attempts, ideation, mixed and indirect, with each of the three behavioral groups (completed, attempts and ideation) further divided into five subtypes in terms of purpose: escape, revenge, altruistic, risk-taking and mixed. In addition, the classifier rates certainty, lethality, intention and mitigating circumstances (e.g., psychotic, impulsive, intoxicated, confused, etc.). Indirect self-destructive behaviors are listed as copresent features or are used to describe the particular mode.

Scales and tests

Most new assessment scales and schedules published in the last two or three decades have aimed at estimating suicide risk within specific populations using already identified risk factors from areas associated with suicidal behavior, such as psychopathology, substance abuse, familial, situational, etc. In general, note has been of Motto's [33] caution that it was impossible to "predict" individual suicides, that there are too many elements of uniqueness in each individual in terms of personal characteristics, threshold for pain tolerance and current pain level, which are in constant flux.

One area continues to be significantly underexplored, the identification of significant protective factors and an evaluation of their characteristics. The first scale to address this question was the Reasons for Living Inventory by Linehan et al. [34] with 48 true-false statements developed from a population of college students, workers and senior citizens. The scale has been found useful in differentiating suicide ideators, parasuicides and nonsuicides, and has been reported valid for adolescents. Since the appearance of this scale a similar scale has been developed by Westefeld et al. [35] focusing on the specific subpopulation of college students, called the Reasons for Living Inventory for College Students.

Another recent scale, still under construction, is the Life Attitudes Scale by Lewinsohn et al. [36] that is aimed at assessing the degree of suicide proneness in the general population, where it is hypothesized to be distributed normally, with only a small percentage identified as extremely high or extremely low on the dimension. It is measured on the basis of responses to items asking about action, thoughts and feelings in relation to death, health, injury and the self. The authors postulate a single domain of behaviors to which all life-threatening and life-enhancing behaviors belong, existing on a continuum extending from negative to positive. In their early results, the authors found support for their assumption of a bipolar continuum, learning that it was important to identify individuals who were not engaging in positive behaviors even if they were not engaged in negative behaviors.

Assessment vs. prediction

The question whether it is possible to predict individual suicides at a practical level was definitively answered by a study reported by Pokorny [37,38]. While the study examined this question in a long-term follow-up of a group of hospitalized psychiatric patients, a group already known to be at higher risk for suicide than the general population, the results are applicable to the broader question of prediction in general.

Briefly, the study followed, for a mean of 5 years after discharge, 4,800 patients (veterans) admitted for the first time to an inpatient psychiatric service. A subgroup of this population (about 15%) was composed of patients who were identified as high risk on the basis of 21 literature-derived indicators. Annual suicide rates confirmed the high-risk status of this population, they were: 1) study population, n = 279, about 12 times the expected rates of 23 for all vets; 2) high-risk population, n = 747, about 32 times the expected rate; and 3) another subgroup, patients with prior suicide attempts, n = 1,702, or about 2% of the group each year.

Diagnostically, the highest suicide rates were among patients with diagnoses of affective disorder (n = 695), schizophrenia (n = 456) and substance abuse (n = 190). The risk factors used to identify the patients judged to be high-risk were substantiated, with 10 of the 21 items being significant. Eight of them related to past or current suicidal behavior. A number of significant differences between the compared subgroups were found.

Pokorny then tried to determine whether it was possible to predict which individual would commit suicide, using two of the more powerful statistical tools available today, stepwise discrimination analysis and logistic regression. The results were disappointing. While sensitivity and specificity were high, the predictive value was low. It was possible to identify correctly only 2.8% of those with positive predictions, at a cost of an inordinate number of false positives, 97.2%. Even with manipulation of the base rate (by artificially changing the actual number of suicides to an increasingly large proportion of the sample) the predictive value did not change enough to provide a "predictive instrument" that was feasible and cost-effective.

Personality tests

Early exploration of assessment and prediction with the most familiar personality scales and projective tests have shown them to be of relatively little use in suicide prediction. Eyman and Eyman [39], reviewing the efforts over the past two decades, indicate no new advances. At best, the Eymans conclude, the most common test, such as the TAT, Rorschach and MMPI, may be useful only tangentially in assessing characterological and personality features that may differentiate seriously suicidal individuals from mild attempters. In general, personality and projective tests may be helpful in providing information about other self-other views, coping and defense mechanisms and the kind of circumstances that may lead a person to consider suicide as a possible choice of action.

It is clear that there are major differences between the tasks of assessment and prediction. Basically, the assessment's task is to evaluate the current risk, the potential, or the degree of intention for suicide; prediction is aimed at foretelling whether a specific individual will kill himself within a certain period of time, usually short, within a week or month. Clinically, we may be asked to make both such predictions, so it is important to know that our lists of risk factors can provide only an estimate of the degree of risk for suicide and that the presence or absence of the factors cannot predict whether that individual will kill himself.

Risk assessment

A number of scales and lists indicative of suicide potential have been proposed. The items have come from a wide variety of sources, e.g., demographic items, previous and/or current suicidal behaviors, depression scales, scales measuring cognition, feelings, anxiety, tension, fears, impulses, diagnoses, social adjustment, familial history and others. It is of interest to note that among all the scales that have been proposed, there are factors than seem to appear over and over. For example, Maris et al. [27] listed 15 factors most commonly identified as significant predictors in all the chapters making up their book, "Assessment of Suicide".

The list makes a generally useful set of single-variable assessment items for suicide risk (Table 3).

The items listed first — depression, affective disorder, mental disorder — were the most common ones for both fatal and nonfatal suicidal behavior. Tanney [40], reviewing the diagnoses of suicide among psychiatric patients, found affective disorders to be the most frequent in committed suicides, followed by schizophrenia and substance abuse disorders. Among the nonfatal suicides the most frequently found disorders were affective disorder, antisocial personality disorder, and borderline personality disorders. These were followed by adjustment disorders, substance abuse, eating disorders, suicide ideation, talk and preparation, parasuicide attempts, lethal methods, isolation, living alone and/or loss of support. Some personality items appear along with items on family life events, medical status and comorbid features. Tanney [40] estimated the likelihood of suicide for emotionally disturbed patients to be approximately 5 times that of the general population. In terms of discriminative power, however, prior suicidal behavior continued to rank highest. He cautions that the diagnosis of mental disorder is not a sufficient explanation for suicidal behavior. The problem is too complex and most likely there are multiple explanations operating simultaneously.

Summary

Progress has been made in bringing order to our field, with workable definitions of terms and classifications of our subject phenomena. We are beginning to recognize the need to specify and assess protective factors as well as vulnerability factors. We have also, albeit somewhat reluctantly, come to accept that we cannot efficiently predict a suicide, but we have compensated for that by increasing our

Table 3. Frequent single-item predictors of suicide.

Depressive illness, mental disorder
Alcoholism/drug abuse
Suicide ideation, talk, preparation; religious ideas
Prior suicide attempts
Lethal methods
Isolation, living alone, loss of support
Hopelessness, cognitive rigidity
Being an older white male
Modelling, suicide in the family, genetics
Work problems, economics, occupation
Marital problems, family pathology
Stress, life events
Anger, aggression, irritability, 5-HIAA
Physical illness
Repetition and co-morbidity of factors above; suicidal careers

From [27].

ability to assess the risk of suicide by identifying risk factors for groups with specific characteristics such as age, sex, race, in particular places at specific times.

Treatment

Suicide prevention centers/crisis intervention centers

The early years of clinical work with suicidal persons were filled with the excitement of developing clinical responses to crisis situations in unusual places, using unfamiliar procedures for critical problems. An early hurdle was learning to use the telephone to provide treatment instead of the traditional face-to-face contact, an inherent requirement if we were to adapt to the demands of the suicide emergency. We also had to be accessible at all times, which could only be by telephone and we also had to be available at all hours, day and night. This led to a 24-h service, which was feasible only by using trained volunteers, carefully selected non- or semiprofessional people, necessary because getting professional people to service a 24-h response was prohibitively expensive.

Since those early days in the 1960s the Suicide Prevention Center and Crisis Center model has spread throughout the world with modifications and adaptations to accommodate the needs of the localities and populations they served. The changes in this area of treatment today are mainly in expansion of services and refinement of therapeutic techniques and client management. Efficient training has been developed to meet the need for skilled counselors and both professional and nonprofessional volunteers. Services in many of the agencies have broadened from crisis telephone response to include walk-in services, outreach, follow-up, individual therapy, group, family, age-focused groups and survivors of suicide programs, to mention only a few. This kind of external expansion of additional services directed to the community has been paralleled by intensive internal examination aimed at improving quality along with the increased quality of services.

Standards for Suicide Prevention Centers and Crisis Intervention Centers

Standards for agency operation and individual performance, reflected in the criteria for certification, have been adopted in the USA, Canada, and other countries [41]. The standards define criteria for desired levels of operation not only in performance with client callers in terms of effectiveness, assessment of lethality, follow-up, rescue capability, etc., but also in many other aspects of optimal mental-health agency functioning such as in training, administration, accountability, ethical issues, community, integration and self-evaluation.

Individual psychotherapy

Descriptions of the psychotherapy process for the individual suicidal patient conducted in an outpatient office have been relatively few. Some specific treatment approaches have been described, such as empathy therapy by Jacobs [42]; a system or architectural model focused on the feeling of self-worth by Mack [43]; the need to replace a punitive superego and build an internal ally by Havens [44]; helping the patient to acquire "self-soothing" introjects by Buie and Maltsberger [17]; fostering of interconnectedness by Kahn [45] etc., Lester's [46] concise book: "Psychotherapy for Suicidal Clients", describes 10 different approaches, some familiar, others less so, such as Freudian psychoanalytic, Jungian analysis, Rogers' person-centered approach, Glasser's reality therapy, Beck's cognitive therapy, Perls' Gestalt psychotherapy, Berne's transactional analysis, Yalom's existential analysis and Janov's primal scream approach. A brief description of each system introduces the theory and indicates how psychotherapy in general is conducted in each one; then gives examples of how it has been applied to the psychotherapy of the suicidal person.

Other books describing treatment include a very complete description of cognitive therapy with suicidal people by Freeman and Reinecke [47]; family therapy as a means of focusing on those suicidal situations that are embedded in familial problems by Richman [48]; and the special aspects and concerns of suicide survivors by Dunne et al. [49].

Standards of care for outpatient and inpatient treatment

Concern about the treatment and care of suicidal outpatients in individual therapy with mental health professionals and of suicidal patients in inpatient facilities, has led to efforts to establish acceptable standards of care for such treatment [50–52]. It is a fact that the most common legal action involving psychiatric care in the USA is the failure to reasonably protect patients from harming themselves. The standards in outpatient treatment indicate the most common errors: failure to evaluate suicidal risk at intake and management transitions; to establish an adequate treatment plan; to document judgement properly and to provide rationale for actions taken; to get supervision and consultation; to specify criteria for and implement hospitalization.

Courts have imposed much stricter standards of care on inpatient than on outpatient care. When a hospital is on notice that a patient has suicidal tendencies, the hospital also assumes the duty of safeguarding the patient from self-inflicted injury or death [53]. The factor of foreseeability puts the hospital on notice, not in terms of being able to predict a suicide, but rather as an indication that the suicide potential has been adequately assessed. Some of the most common failures for the outpatient clinician occur in: the use of appropriate treatment modalities; medication, prescription and management and adequate documentation. For the hospital and its inpatient staff, major problems are: appropriate communication of suicidal risk to each other; assessment of changes in suicidal risk and providing a protective environment.

Prevention vs. treatment

Possibly the most significant change in treatment approaches in recent years has been the proposal that attention has been shifted from treatment per se, to prevention of suicide. Pointing to the fact that our ability to predict suicide has been poor and that our efforts at prevention developed thus far have been very expensive and cost-ineffective (except for the suicide prevention centers and the crisis centers), new ways to address the problem have been proposed [54]. One major suggestion has been to change our emphasis on treatment in the secondary and tertiary phases of our public health model to prevention in the primary phase, i.e., to focus more on the antecedent conditions and developmental concerns that contribute to suicide rather than concentrate so exclusively on the treatment of behaviors when they appear [55].

Stressing that suicide is multidetermined, the model describes suicide, like many other pathological behaviors, as the end result of a wide range of psychological, biological, genetic, sociological experiences with no specific etiologic factor. Suicidal behaviors are thus the culmination of multiple factors derived from many experiences that appear long before the suicide itself occurs, with these contributing toward a cumulative risk potential. Special terms emerge. The early experiences are seen as predisposing factors and distal to the suicide, contributing to a pattern of vulnerabilities, depending on the concomitant development of protective factors and coping experiences. Proximal circumstances are precipitating conditions that contribute more directly to a suicide, usually much closer temporally, if not immediately preceding the event. The model suggests that when the (proximal) precipitating conditions interact with the general state of vulnerability formed by the (distal) predisposing circumstances the probability that suicidal behavior will occur increases. The model illustrates both the fact that there are many sequences or pathways that eventually end in suicidal behavior, and at the same time points out that there are a great many additional opportunities for intervention and prevention. Examples might be interventions to mitigate predisposing or precipitating conditions in major areas of experience, such as familial (violence), educational (school), social (delinquency), or economic (unemployment).

The focus moves beyond the treatment of the individual as the familiar focus of enquiry, and supports an intervention program in areas that would correct or mitigate those deviations and conditions that have often been found to be comorbid with suicide. In effect, the model suggests that prevention activities be directed toward the morbidity associated with suicidal behavior as well as the mortality of completed suicide.

Litman [56] proposes a program that also involves a marked change in the strategy of treatment. His review of the literature and his clinical experience has convinced him that psychiatric hospitalization, which accounts for the greatest expense in treatment of seriously suicidal patients, has not been shown to be a necessity, or even always helpful, therapeutic intervention. Hospital treatment does not seem to prevent suicides of patients after they are discharged, whether voluntary or involuntary, as seen in rates similar to the suicide rate reported in follow-up studies of outpatients treated for depression [57,58]. Litman suggests that we turn away from the focus on high-risk subgroups for prevention to a focus on screening and case finding in the general population, with the aim of bringing several million more low and medium suicide risk patients into treatment with persons who are trained and educated to treat "suicidality" as one component of the need for help. This would require increasing the number of primary care/family doctors and their assistants and improving their sensitivity in treatment of patients with suicidal behavior in outpatient practice. Litman suggests that computer technology can be used to educate and train both primary care providers and outpatient mental health workers as well as to establish communication networks for maintaining continuity of care and consultation. It would mean changing our focus from the relatively few high-risk suicide patients (where the suicide rate continues despite inpatient treatment) to the much larger number of low- and moderate-risk suicide patients, with the goal of preventing them from becoming high-risk patients.

Summary

Suicide prevention and crisis centers continue to service their communities with expanded services and improved skills. Standards have been developed for clinical and agency performance as well as for treatment of suicidal outpatients and inpatients. A variety of psychotherapy techniques have been developed for treatment of the individual suicidal patient. The most significant change may well be in proposals that we shift from an emphasis on treatment to one of prevention, focusing on programs aimed at mitigating the predisposing and precipitating vulnerabilities of co-morbid as well as identified life-damaging experiences, and on programs supporting the development of life-enhancing, protective and coping mechanisms. Another suggestion has been to shift our focus from the treatment of high-risk patients in psychiatric hospitals to treatment of low- and moderate-risk patients with adequately trained outpatient services.

References

1. Freud S. Mourning and Melancholia (1917). In: Collected Papers, vol IV. London: Hogarth Press, 1950.
2. Freud S. Beyond the Pleasure Principle (1922). London: Hogarth Press, 1950.
3. Jung CF. The soul and death. (Translated by Hull RPC, from Wirklichkeit der Seele, 1934.) In: Feifel H (ed) The Meaning of Death. New York: McGraw-Hill, 1959.
4. Adler A. Suicide. J Ind Psychol 1958;14:57–61. (Translated from Selbstmord. Int Zeitschr Individ Psychol 1937;15:49–52.)
5. Menninger KA. Man Against Himself. New York: Harcourt Brace, 1938.
6. Zilboorg G. Differential diagnostic types of suicide. Arch Neurol Psychiat 1936;35:270–291.
7. Sullivan HS. Clinical Studies in Psychiatry. New York: Norton, 1956.
8. Horney K. Neurosis and Human Growth. New York: W.W. Norton, 1950.

162

9. Klein M. A contribution to the psychogenesis of manic-depressive status (1935). In: Klein M (ed) Contributions to Pschyoanalysis, 1921–1945. London: Hogarth Press, 1968.

10. Mahler M. On Human Symbiosis and the Vicissitudes of Individuation, vol I: Infatile Psychosis. New York: International Universities Press, 1968.

11. Asch S. Suicide and the hidden executioner. Int Rev Psychoanal 1980;7:51–60.

12. Masterson JF. Abandonment depression in borderline adolescents. In: Golombeck H, Garfinkel B, Madison CT (eds) The Adolescent and Mood Disturbance. New York: International Universities Press, 1989.

13. Hendin H. The psychodynamics of suicide. J Nerv Mental Dis 1963;136:236–244.

14. Litman RE, Tabachnick ND. Psychoanalytic theories of suicide. In: Resnik HLP (ed) Suicidal Behaviors. New York: Little Brown & Co, 1968.

15. Kohut H. In: Orstein PH (ed) The Search for the Self: Selected Writings of Heinz Kohut. New York: International Universities Press, 1978.

16. Kernberg O. Severe Personality Disorders: Psychotherapeutic Strategies. New Haven, CT: Yale University Press, 1984.

17. Buie DH, Maltsberger JT. The psychological vulnerability to suicide. In: Jacobs D, Brown HN, Madison CT (eds) Suicide: Understanding and Responding. Madison, CT: International Universities Press, 1989.

18. Pfeffer CR. Development issues in child and adolescent suicide: a discussion. In: Noam GG, Borst S (eds) Children, Youth and Suicide: Developmental Perspective. San Francisco: Jossey-Bass, 1994.

19. Noam GG, Borst S. Children, Youth and Suicide: Developmental Perspectives. San Francisco: Jossey-Bass, 1994.

20. Adam KS. Loss, suicide and attachment. In: Parkes CM, Stevenson-Hinde J (eds) The Place of Attachment in Human Behavior. New York: Basic Books, 1982.

21. Vaillant GE, Blumenthal SJ. Introduction. In: Blumenthal SJ, Kupfer DJ (eds) Suicide Over the Life Cycle. Washington, DC: American Psychiatric Press, 1990.

22. Shneidman ES. Definition of Suicide. New York: Wiley, 1985.

23. Shneidman ES. Suicide as Psychache. Northvale, NJ: Jason Aronson, 1993.

24. Murray H. Explorations in Personality. New York: Oxford University Press, 1938.

25. Farberow NL. Assessment of suicide. In: McReynolds P (ed) Advances In Psychological Assessment. San Francisco: Jossey-Bass, 1981.

26. Diekstra RFW. Definitions and category systems for suicide. Draft ICD-10. Geneva: World Health Organization, Division of Mental Health, 1988.

27. Maris RW. Overview of the study of suicide assessment and prediction. In: Maris RW, Berman AL, Maltsberger JT, Yuffit RI (eds) Assessment and Prediction of Suicide. New York: Guilford, 1992.

28. Beck AT, Dans JH, Frederick CJ, Perlin S, Pokorny AD, Schulman RE, Seiden RH, Wittlin BJ. Classification and nomenclature. In: Resnik HLP, Hathorne BC (eds) Suicide Prevention in the 70's. Washington, DC: US Government Printing Office, 1973.

29. Baechler J. Suicides. (Translated by Cooper B.) New York: Basic Books. Originally published in 1975.

30. Jobes DA, Perman AL, Josselson AR. Improving the validity and reliability of medical-legal certifications of suicide. Suicide Life-Threat Behav 1987;17:310–325.

31. Ellis TE. Classification of suicidal behavior: a review and step toward integration. Suicide Life-Threat Behav 1988;18:358–371.

32. Maris RW. How are suicides different? In: Maris RW, Berman AL, Maltsberger JT, Yuffit RI (eds) Assessment and Prediction of Suicide. New York: Guilford, 1992.

33. Motto JA. An integrated approach to estimating suicide risk. In: Maris RW, Berman AL, Maltsberger JT, Yuffit RI (eds) Assessment and Prediction of Suicide. New York: Guilford, 1992.

34. Linehan MM, Goodstein JC, Nielsen SL, Chiles JA. Reasons for staying alive when you are thinking of killing yourself: the reasons for living inventory. J Consult Clin Psychol 1983;51:

276–286.

35. Westefeld JS, Cardin DC, Deaton WL. Development of the College Stuc
Inventory. Suicide Life-Threat Behav 1992;22:442–452.

36. Lewinsohn PM, Langhrichsen-Rohling J, Langford R, Rohde P, Seely
attitudes scale: a scale to assess adolescent life-enhancing and life-thr
cide Life-Threat Behav 1995;25:458–474.

37. Pokorny AD. Prediction of suicide in psychiatric patients: report of a prospective study. In:
Maris RW, Berman AL, Maltsberger JT, Yuffit RI (eds) Assessment and Prediction of Suicide.
New York: Guilford, 1992.

38. Pokorny AD. Suicide prediction revisited. Suicide Life-Threat Behav 1993;23:1–10.

39. Eyman JR, Eyman SK. Personality assessment in suicide prediction. In: Maris RW, Berman
AL, Maltsberger JT, Yuffit RI (eds) Assessment and Prediction of Suicide. New York: Guild-
ford, 1992.

40. Tanney BL. Mental disorders, psychiatric patients and suicide. In: Maris RW, Berman AL, Maltsberger JT, Yuffit RI (eds) Assessment and Prediction of Suicide. New York: Guilford, 1992.

41. Evaluation Criteria for the Certification of Suicide Prevention Centers and Crisis Programs.
Washington DC, American Association of Suicidology, 1976.

42. Jacobs D. Psychotherapy with suicidal patients: the empathic method. In: Jacobs D, Brown HH
(eds) Suicide: Understanding and Responding. Madison, CT: International Universities Press,
1989.

43. Mack JE. Adolescent suicide: an architectural model. In: Jacobs D, Brown HN (eds) Suicide:
Understanding and Responding. Madison, CT: International Universities Press, 1989.

44. Havens L. Clinical interview with a suicidal patient. In: Jacobs D, Brown HH (eds) Suicide:
Understanding and Responding. Madison, CT: International Universities Press, 1989.

45. Kahn A. Principles of psychotherapy with suicidal patients. In: Blumenthal SJ, Kupfer DJ (eds)
Suicide Over the Life Cycle. Washington, DC: American Psychiatric Press, 1990.

46. Lester D. Psychotherapy for Suicidal Clients. Springfield, IL: Chas C. Thomas, 1991.

47. Freeman A, Reinecke MA. Cognitive Therapy of Suicidal Behavior: A Manual for Treatment.
New York: Springer, 1993.

48. Richman J. Family Therapy for Suicidal People. New York: Springer, 1986.

49. Dunne EJ, McIntosh JL, Dunne-Maxim K. Suicide and Its Aftermath. New York: Norton,
1987.

50. Bongar B, Maris RW, Berman AL, Litman RE. Outpatient standards of care and the suicidal
patient. Suicide Life-Threat Behav 1992;22:453–478.

51. Bongar B, Maris RW, Berman AL, Litman RE, Silverman MM. Inpatient standards of care and
the suicidal patient, part 1: general clinical formulations and legal consideration. Suicide Life-
Threat Behav 1993;23:245–256.

52. Silverman MM, Berman AL, Bongar B, Litman RE, Maris RW. Inpatient standards of care and
the suicidal patient, part II: an integration with clinical risk management. Suicide Life-Threat
Behav 1994;24:152–169.

53. Robertson JD. Psychiatric Malpractice: Liability of Mental Health Professionals. New York:
Wiley, 1988.

54. Silverman MM, Felner RD. The place of suicide prevention in the spectrum of intervention:
definitions of critical terms and constructs. Suicide Life-Threat Behav 1995;25:70–81.

55. Silverman MM, Maris RW. The prevention of suicidal behavior: an overview. Suicide Life-
Threat Behav 1995;25:10–21.

56. Litman RE. Suicide prevention in a treatment setting. Suicide Life-Threat Behav 1995;25:
134–142.

57. Fawcett J, Scheftner W, Clark D et al. Clinical predictors of suicide in patients with major affective disorders. Am J Psychiat 1987;144:35–40.

58. Crammer JL. Symposium on suicides on hospital. Br J Psychiat 1984;145:459–476.

Clinical issues

Clinical problems in assessing suicide risk

D.J. Pallis

Graylingwell Hospital, Chichester, UK

Abstract. Although a clinician's task is to translate the statistical probabilities of suicide based on our understanding of risk factors into specific predictions about individuals, we are uncertain on how best to perform this task or on how to demonstrate that our assessment has been valid. Actuarial predictions are hampered by including too many false positives among those classed as high risk but clinical judgements are not demonstrably more accurate or cost-effective.

Rare events make prediction difficult and the odds of suicide occurring within the rather short periods of clinical engagement are much smaller. As proclivity to suicide varies over time, usually in accord with stressful events, personal predicaments or fluctuating mental states, any evaluation of risk is only a tentative forecast in need of being constantly revised. Assessment can be hazardous unless both the relevant procedures and the target populations are clearly defined and in accord with a reliable consensus of good practice. In focusing on what is both predictable and preventable, clinicians also need to make a more explicit commitment on whether risk should be assessed strictly within the context of restoring an individual's mental health or whether it should be part of a more ambitious aim of restoring meaning in people's lives.

Keywords: clinical judgement, mental illness, suicide prediction, suicide prevention.

Concept and criterion of risk

Any consideration of risk must begin with its definition. What do we actually mean by "suicide risk"? Although it would be simpler to define it as most of us understand it, i.e., as the likelihood of a person killing himself, in clinical practice — from which we draw our day to day experience of dealing with the suicidal — as well as in relevant research — from which we derive that formidable list of factors which can be shown to be statistically linked with "suicidal" outcomes — the criterion of risk appears to include a whole range of signs and behaviours, from the tangible, or at times, inferred suicidal ideas or inclinations to suicidal gestures or attempts, and finally to deaths which leave behind sufficient evidence to be pronounced as deliberately self-inflicted. Furthermore, as suicide often occurs at the end of a rather tortuous and protracted process, what we tend to imply when we talk of "risk" is a wide variety of signs or behaviours which reveal to us that the critical process may have just begun, that it may already be well on its way or that it is just about to be completed.

By highlighting this continuum, Table 1 also serves to illustrate the semantic and methodological difficulties of failing to make a sufficient distinction between

Address for correspondence: Dr D.J. Pallis, Old Lyminster House, Church Lane, Lyminster, Littlehampton, West Sussex, PO19 7QJ, UK.

Table 1. Spectrum of suicidal behaviours in relation to broadly defined categories of suicidal intent and to the main[a] and alternative[b] criterion of suicide risk.

Description of suicidal behaviour	Evidence of suicidal intent (from all available sources)	Current classification (by outcome)
Communicating suicidal ideas or intentions (directly or indirectly)	Unexpressed or inferred intent	?
	Unequivocably expressed	Suicidal ideation
Performing a nonfatal suicide attempt	Negligible, low or equivocal intent	Parasuicide
	Moderately high or serious intent	Attempted suicide
	Extremely high or unequivocal intent	Failed suicide[b]
Performing a fatal suicide attempt	Absent or inadequate evidence of intent	Accidental death
	Insufficient or equivocal intent	Open verdict
	Extremely high and unequivocal intent	Suicide[a]

the various types of suicidal and seemingly suicidal acts on the one hand and suicide risk on the other. Despite calls to improve conceptualisation in defining such behaviours [1] many writers still treat all kinds of suicidal acts and the concept of risk as synonyms, and the recent example of a meta-analysis which used a rating of suicidal ideation based on one item of a depression scale in order to draw inferences about the relative risk of patients treated with antidepressants [2] is a case in point. It should therefore be clarified that, throughout this paper, the term will be used to imply the likelihood of death by suicide, as defined after a coroner's inquest, although it could be argued [3] that the category of "failed suicide" provides us with a defensible alternative criterion of suicide risk.

Predicting suicide or identifying risk?

Recognising risk is essentially making a prediction and what concerns clinicians most is not only to identify those persons whose risk is highest but also to do so soon enough so that we could try our very best to ensure that our prediction will not come true. Inevitably, our focus is shifted backwards so to speak, from the prediction of actual death to the prediction of its antecedent "presuicidal" state. But if it is difficult enough to obtain proof of risk by relying on evidence of intent after a person's death, it is infinitely more difficult to define the mental state which coincides with the time at which someone is just about to end his life.

One gets a fairly good idea about the magnitude of the task by looking at the actual odds of suicide as they apply to the general population, to people with a diagnosis of depression and to those who have already made a suicide attempt (Table 2). It can be seen that as we focus on shorter time intervals, the odds become more and more forbidding. Even if we were to use a hypothetical and rather powerful scale which includes among its top 20% as many as 80% of future

Table 2. Odds of suicide for defined periods in three distinct populations and in their respective high-risk groups.

Populations and "high-risk subgroups"	Odds of committing suicide		
	In 20 years	In 1 year	In 1 month
General population	1 in 500	1 in 10000	1 in 125000
High-risk group	1 in 125	1 in 2500	1 in 33000
Depressives	1 in 10	1 in 200	1 in 2400
High-risk group	1 in 3	1 in 50	1 in 600
Attempted suicides	1 in 5	1 in 100	1 in 1200
High-risk group	1 in 2	1 in 25	1 in 300

suicides, one can see that, in the population of attempted suicides, for example, and for the period of 1 month, in order to be in a position to prevent one suicide we would need to identify — and consequently treat as highly suicidal — another 299 patients who had not intended to end their lives. For a prediction concerning the period of 20 years, on the other hand, the odds seem much more promising and "cost-effective", but then there is no guarantee that we could ever be in a position to intervene if we do not know the time at which that high-risk individual would be at the most critical state of mind.

Therefore logically, as well as empirically, we are forced to conclude [4,5] that it is almost impossible to make a valid and accurate prediction about individuals. As clinicians, however, this is precisely what we are expected to do. When we decide that someone must be closely supervised, because we think he is suicidal, or when we arrange his admission to hospital against his own wishes, there would appear to be little doubt that our implied prediction is both specific and unequivocal. Yet we have no means of proving that our assessment was correct, only the consolation in the hope that our colleagues would have done precisely what we did or that we have acted in good faith. If we are to be realistic therefore, the clinically meaningful task is not so much how to predict the suicide of an individual but how to identify, within populations known to be at risk, those special subgroups likely to contain the highest possible number of prospective suicides. The task is manageable, provided of course that such subgroups do not include an overwhelmingly large number of people who are erroneously classified (false positives), and this in turn brings us to the problem of assessing the relevance of the various risk factors.

Empirically derived risk factors

Table 3 summarizes the main bulk of empirical findings, as they apply to people in general, to four diagnostic groups known to be at high risk and to certain defined periods of time. Although it provides us with a valuable overall picture, there are several reasons why this list of "significant variables" may not be as impressive or as relevant as we would like to believe.

Table 3. Variables shown to increase the risk of suicide in the population in general (A) and among four major diagnostic categories of psychiatric problems (B) with reference to specific periods of high risk (C, next page).

(A)	Socio-demographic and personal data			Health record and suicidal history		
General high-risk features	– Older age (>40 years) – Male – Caucasian – Widowed, divorced, separated – Immigrant	– Unemployed, retired unoccupied – Living alone – Socially isolated – Social class: I (high) or IV and V (low)	– Living in urban or socially deprived areas – No strong religious affiliation – "Drop-outs"	– History of functional psychiatric illness, alcoholism and/or substance abuse – Abnormal personality, especially "antisocial"	– Serious or chronic physical illness (e.g., cancer, AIDS, epilepsy) – Family history of suicide, depression or alcoholism	– Previous suicide attempt – Multiple suicide attempts – Use of violent methods or medically serious attempt – Showing high intent to die – Suicidal ideas or threats

(B)	Depression	Schizophrenia	Alcoholism	Attempted suicide
Group specific high-risk features, symptoms and life events	– Long duration of illness – Many previous admissions – Severe depression – Previous suicide attempts – Alcohol abuse – Older – Male – Single, separated	– Chronic remitting illness – Relapsing course of illness – More severe illness – Younger when illness began and high educational status beforehand – Paranoid or schizo-affective disorder – Fears of "mental disintegration" – Previous depressive spells	– Long history of drinking or "established alcoholism" – Serious physical complications because of drinking – Poor physical health – Poor work record – Presence of depression – Critical age: 40–60 years	– Previous or current mental illness – Depression – Alcohol abuse – Long standing physical illness – Male – Older age (>40 years of age) – Higher social class – Loneliness

(cont.)

Table 3. Continued.

(B)	Depression	Schizophrenia	Alcoholism	Attempted suicide
Group specific high-risk features, symptoms and life events	— Living alone — Insomnia — Hopelessness — Depressive delusions — Loss of memory — Self-neglect — Agitation — Bereavement or separation — Financial or work problems — Accumulation of adverse events	— Previous suicide attempts — Male — Younger (<30 years of age) — Unemployed — Living alone or socially isolated — Hopelessness — Suicidal ideas — Anorexia or loss of weight — Akathisia — Abrupt stopping of drugs	— Suicidal ideas — Previous suicide attempt — Previous high suicidal intent — Previous psychiatric illness — Personality disorder — Breaking off or "interpersonal disruption" (broken love relationship, death or separation and/or estrangement from family)	— Previous suicide attempts or present attempt showing serious intent to die (e.g., precautions against discovery, suicide note) — Bereavement, loss — Lack of social cohesion, many changes in dwelling place or poor work record — Adverse life events in the presence of depression

(C)	Depression	Schizophrenia	Alcoholism	Attempted suicide
Time most at risk	— During a phase of depression when the illness (or treatment) begins — First 2 years of follow-up — After discharge from treatment	— First week after admission — During the first year of follow-up — First few weeks or months after discharge — 5–10 years after illness began — When depression is present	— In the 6 weeks following the break (or the disruption) of important relationships — Within 2 years of a break in relationships	— Within 6–12 months after the attempt — After multiple attempts of high suicidal intent — When intent increases with subsequent suicide attempts

First, a number of relatively "soft" items, such as those concerned with "illness", symptoms or mental states, are not only of questionable reliability but they also do not always refer to the crucial period preceding suicide. Data gathered from a suicide's relatives or "informants" on the other hand — usually some time after death — cannot be said to be strictly comparable with those reported by living patients who may have similar symptoms. Secondly, in view of the existing differences between countries in respect of the type and delivery of their psychiatric and allied services or between periods during which there may have been substantial changes in the overall pattern of care, it is questionable whether one should attach special significance to risks attributed to the timing of admission and discharge or indeed to a current or an earlier spell of psychiatric treatment. Thirdly, although the high risk assigned to certain diagnostic labels is perfectly justified, this information by itself could hardly enhance a psychiatrist's powers of detection since simply "being a psychiatric patient" or "having a record of suicidal behaviour" carries at least as much weight.

Reservations of this kind are by no means confined to clinical variables but are still relevant when we need to judge the contribution of the more robust sociodemographic factors. Our focus on the elevated risk of older age, for example, needs to be tempered by the knowledge that in many countries suicide is now rising among the young. Though it is widely accepted that being male carries a higher risk worldwide, recent reports indicate that Chinese women kill themselves more often than men — a considerable death toll given China's population and high suicide rate which, incidentally, is not higher in urban areas but in the countryside. Similarly, the mass suicide pacts by members of religious cults in recent years are in stark contrast with the widely held view that "religious affiliation" is a protective factor.

Any evaluation of the empirically derived factors, therefore, needs to be made with the understanding that any extrapolations from such findings should be confined to populations and treatment settings which are similar to those from which the original data were derived as well as with the recognition that factors of this kind tend to predict long-term rather than short-term risk. But having accepted that such information should be "interpreted with caution" [6] we are still left to cope with the assessment of short-term risk — the clinical "here and now" — and in doing so we need to construct our own unique list of high-risk factors, hopefully, by knowing well the person who stands before us.

Clinical judgement

Recognising that it is often hard and at times impossible to say whether a person is a "true danger" to himself, the clinician's task is to estimate that risk not only to the extent that it seems to arise from symptoms of illness or a specific psychopathology but also as it seems to emerge, or could be understood, within the total context of that patient's personal dilemmas and life circumstances. By focusing on risk factors which are potentially reversible, the clinician also is in a very good position to judge whether the mental illness is the crucial parameter which affects a person's attitude and reasoning about the value of being alive.

Judging whether a person will kill himself, or when he might actually do so, calls for the highest professional skills. Without genuine rapport we will never extract the true account of that person's private feelings, thoughts and plans. Someone who is desperate or suicidal is unlikely to undress mentally in our presence unless we transmit a caring attitude and a clear message that we are capable to understand and handle his problem. We will get no special prizes when things seem to go well but we can be sure to expect questions and inquiries when it seems that we have "failed". According to a British audit of inpatient suicides, their risk "was not fully appreciated" in as many as 75% of cases [7]. Judging risk seems so much easier with the benefit of hindsight.

One should add that, even when we have done our best, our assessment is nothing more than a tentative forecast which needs to be constantly revised. For people who are treated in hospital and for those who are in a critical stage of their illness, detecting risk demands constant vigilance and informed awareness by all members of the clinical team and an environment which offers the best possible quality of care. These points are underlined once more by the Royal College of Psychiatrists' latest confidential inquiry into a sample of 240 suicides by psychiatric patients in England [8].

The report indicates that, by and large, many patients who killed themselves were at the time thought to have a poor capacity to relate to others, to be unwilling to be involved in treatment and to be affected by a threat or an actual break up in important relationships; male suicides were judged to be irritable, aggressive, alienated and unpredictable while female suicides seemed more vulnerable, dependent or depressed. Drawing attention to the fact that a number of patients had killed themselves at a time when they were thought not to need supervision, or when their supervision was relaxed, the report underlines the need for improved assessment of suicide risk — especially at the time of changes in a patient's treatment — for better communication between professional groups as well as between staff and a patient's relatives and for other measures to ensure a better psychiatric service [8]. Although the report's conclusions are based on impressions after the event rather than on rigorous research, they nevertheless have important implications for our assessment of risk factors.

Predictability and preventability of suicide

Clinicians do not behave as detached scientists and although they may aspire to be objective, they are strongly biased by concentrating on what they can actually do. They ask: Is there a depressive illness to treat? Could a person's inner strength be reinforced in order to cope better with traumatic events and life's adversities? Is it possible to control some of the most distressing or incapacitating symptoms more effectively? Is there a safe environment within which deadly impulses could be contained? Is this person's hopelessness and alienation of a

Table 4. Showing eight subgroups of probable suicides according to the likelihood of being predictable, preventable or treated.

Target population	Likely to be predicted	Likely to be prevented	Likely to be treated	Target subgroups[a]
Probable suicides	Predictable	Preventable	Treated	A
			Untreated	B
		Unpreventable	Treated	C
			Untreated	D
	Unpredictable	Preventable	Treated	E
			Untreated	F
		Unpreventable	Treated	G
			Untreated	H

[a]Subgroups of a target population (probable suicides) which may have to be considered in evaluating the effectiveness of therapeutic interventions.

truly "malignant" kind? Prediction and prevention go hand in hand: we aim to predict suicide in order to prevent it but even when we do so it is impossible to generate the statistics of our success.

Finally, in any assessment of risk we need to consider not just what is predictable and preventable but what is treatable too, as well as the likelihood of a person receiving or accepting treatment (Table 4). In doing so, we must also ask ourselves whether detection of risk should be strictly confined within the specific task of restoring an individual's mental health or whether it should be extended to the wider and much more ambitious aim of restoring meaning in people's lives. There is good evidence to link suicide with mental illness and psychological distress but we must not underestimate the crucial role of social risk factors which have been established long ago and persist to the present day [9,10]. Indeed, it could be argued that the accumulated evidence concerning risk may not be as relevant to saving lives as we would like to believe because the great bulk of existing data has been derived from suicides most of which neither could be predicted and prevented nor could be treatable, in the medical sense. Often enough suicide comes as a surprise and there is no lack of evidence that some patients kill themselves after receiving what appears to be good or adequate psychiatric care. The conclusion, however, that such a state of affairs is generally applicable, i.e., that all predictable and preventable suicides are currently detected and averted, carries the assumption that our present psychiatric and allied services operate at their highest level of efficiency — an assumption which is certainly not justifiable from the findings of the latest confidential inquiry into suicides in England [8] and one doubts whether it would be any more justifiable for suicides in Greece or elsewhere.

References

1. Van Egmond M, Diekstra RFW. The predictability of suicidal behaviour: The results of a meta-

analysis of published studies. In: Diekstra RFW et al. (eds) Suicide and its Prevention: The Role of Attitude and Imitation. Leiden: E.J. Brill, 1989.

2. Beasley CM et al. Fluoxetine and suicide: a meta-analysis of controlled trials of treatment for depression. Br Med J 1991;303:685—692.

3. Pallis DJ, Gibbons JS, Pierce DW. Estimating suicide risk among attempted suicides: II. Efficiency of predictive scales after the attempt. Br J Psychiat 1984;144:139—148.

4. Rosen DH. Detection of suicidal patients: an example of some limitations in the prediction of infrequent events. J Consult Psychol 1954;18:397—403.

5. Goldstein RB et al. The prediction of suicide-sensitivity, specificity and predictive value of a multivariate model applied to suicide among 1906 patients with affective disorders. Arch Gen Psychiat 1991;48:418—422.

6. Williams R, Morgan GH. Suicide Prevention: The Challenge Confronted. A Manual of Guidance for Purchasers of Mental Health Care. NHS Health Advisory Service, Thematic Review. London: HMSO, 1994.

7. Morgan HG, Priest P. Suicide and sudden unexpected deaths among psychiatric inpatients: The Bristol confidential inquiry. Br J Psychiat 1991;158:368—374.

8. Steering Committee of the Confidential Inquiry into Homicides and Suicides by Mentally Ill People. Report of the Confidential Inquiry into Homicides and Suicides by Mentally Ill People. London: Royal College of Psychiatrists, 1996.

9. Gunnell DI et al. Relation between parasuicide, suicide, psychiatric admissions and socio-economic deprivation. Br Med J 1995;311:226—230.

10. Charlton J et al. Suicide deaths in England and Wales: trends in factors associated with suicide deaths. Pop Trends 1993;71:34—42.

Parasuicide: is it a distinct phenomenon?

Rene F.W. Diekstra

Municipal Health Department City of Rotterdam, Rotterdam, The Netherlands

Abstract. Despite a number of attempts towards standardization, contemporary scientific literature still suffers from a hodgepodge of terms when it comes to suicidal behavior. There are neither clinical nor research diagnostic criteria for phenomena such as suicidal ideation, nonfatal suicidal behavior and even fatal suicidal behavior, that are internationally endorsed in order to ensure comparability of clinical and epidemiological studies. In addition, there is also considerable terminological and conceptual confusion within the category of nonfatal suicidal behavior as witnessed by the fact that some authors use terms like parasuicide and attempted suicide (or suicide attempt) as synonyms while others use them to refer to distinct phenomena, and again others discard the one or the other term.

Since there is some evidence of developmental pathways running from self-harm ideation through nonfatal self-harming behavior to suicide, and since the risk of suicide is many times higher (up to 30 times) among those who engaged in nonfatal deliberate self-harm than in the general population, it seems safe to assume that a number of such acts are indeed suicide attempts in the motivational sense. However, since the patterns of recruitment from nonfatal self-harm to suicide are diverse and only a minority of persons engaging in such behaviors go over to kill themselves, while most acts of deliberate self-harms are and remain first-evers, the larger majority of such acts must be "para" suicides indeed. This has important research and intervention implications, particularly that a high-risk or problem-group approach in itself will have no demonstrable effect on population prevalence rates of suicidal behavior.

Keywords: attempted suicide, definitions, population vs. problem group approaches, prevention, suicide.

Introduction

Marcus Fabius Quitillianus (ca. 35–96 a.c.), famous writer and teacher in first century Rome, has his name recorded in the history of science first and foremost because of the following statement about science: "Scientia facit difficultates" (science creates difficulties). It is this statement or saying, that the author has chosen to be the lead of this paper, intended to create difficulties about the epidemiology of nonfatal suicidal behavior as it has been practiced by suicidologists of the present and of the past. This paper will create three kinds of difficulties. First of all, it will address some of the prevailing problems of terminology and definition. Second, it will address some fundamental deficiencies in our present state of knowledge regarding the descriptive epidemiology or, stated more simply,

Address for correspondence: Rene F.W. Diekstra PhD, Professor of Psychology, Municipal Health Department City of Rotterdam, P.O. Box 70032, 3000 LP Rotterdam, The Netherlands. Tel.: +31-10-715273725. Fax: +31-10-715146028.

it will deal with deficiencies in the available information on the nature and magnitude of nonfatal suicidal behavior. Finally, it will address some of the far-reaching implications that the first two issues have had and still continue to have for intervention in and prevention of suicidal behaviors.

Attempted suicide or parasuicide: what's in a name?

One of the first things that immediately strikes the eye when one scans the present scientific literature on suicidal behavior and nonfatal suicidal behavior in particular, is the terminological and definitional confusion that prevails everywhere. Many presenters at the conference where this book originated, as well as many authors in the suicidology literature, do present their work either as pertaining to the phenomenon of attempted suicide or to parasuicide, or sometimes even in one and the same contribution to one another. The question arises as to what is the significance of this hotchpotch of terms? Is it just a matter of triviality? Is it that although we might use different terms, we know from one another that we still mean one and the same thing? Is this understanding limited to a particular group of scientists within the field of suicidology, or is it the general understanding of all in the field of suicidology and even outside of it? Do policymakers as well as the general public also share the same semantic reactions to the terms "attempted suicide" and "parasuicide"? Are the social processes involved in the application of the labels and in the construction of their meanings the same in the case of attempted suicide as in parasuicide? And finally, are the social and emotional consequences the same whether either term is applied? Similar questions could be asked with regard to other terms that are used sometimes as synonyms of parasuicide and attempted suicide and sometimes not, such as deliberate self-harm, or intentional self-poisoning or nonfatal self-destructive behavior. In trying to find answers to these questions, let us first broaden the issue of terminology somewhat. Consider for a moment the term suicide and its definition. Most suicidologists and most lay people, at least in the European countries and on the North-American continent, only apply the term suicide in the case of behavior with a fatal outcome. By logical implication, the term attempted suicide, different from the term parasuicide, would refer to a behavior that implies an attempt, an effort, to bring about a fatal outcome. If we now say that we call certain behaviors attempted suicide — meaning an attempt to bring about a fatal outcome — but then hastily add what we truly mean happens always or most of the time, then we are already in the first stage of a terminological mess. Unfortunately, however, the mess is not merely terminological, it is also social and emotional. Take the example of an adolescent girl, who after a quarrel with a boyfriend swallows a limited number of benzodiazepines of low lethal potentiality. Let us attach to this behavior the term attempted suicide and not some other term such as parasuicide. Let us also suppose that the label becomes known both to the girl herself, her boyfriend, her parents and others in her inner circle, such as her teachers at school and her classmates, as well as to professional helpers to whom she might be referred to. Would it then be reasonable to assume that the semantic reactions attached to the label can or will have far-reaching consequences for:

1. How the girl is going to perceive and react to herself.
2. How others are going to perceive and react to her.
3. The kind of treatment approach she is likely to receive.

Several case vignette studies, including one that was carried out by the author and his colleagues a number of years ago [1], where the insertion of the term suicide or attempted suicide in further identical case descriptions was the independent variable which pointed out that the answers to these questions are clearly affirmative [2]. The term attempted suicide appeared to function more as a prescription than as a description. In two case descriptions where everything is the same except the presence or absence of the words attempted suicide, more pathology is attached to the etiology of the act described with the word attempted suicide than with the word left out. Also, the measures they proposed to be adequate in the case of the term attempted suicide were more severe and far-reaching, such as involuntary commitment. Of course, this semantic effect might be more pronounced in some languages, than in others such as in Dutch, where "zelfmoordpoging" actually stands for "attempt to self-murder", which is similar to the German word "selbstmortversuch". But the bottom line is, that it is in no way a matter of indifference what term is used. This is also from an international perspective rather important, the case with politicians as policymakers. In a study by sociolinguists [3], it was shown that the majority of politicians and policymakers have semantic reactions to terms that scientists use resembling more the reactions of the public at large than those of the scientific community. So, if for example, the public identifies suicide and therefore also attempted suicide with psychiatric disorder or mental illness, policymakers will do the same. And if the public identifies the word attempted suicide with the desire or the intention to die, policymakers and politicians usually will do the same. By implication, they will tend to consider suicidal behavior in general as a very specific problem belonging to a very specific realm of professional specialism and not so much, if at all, a target for public policy.

By conclusion, the terms we use in this field and we disseminate, have important social and political implications. There is no exaggeration in the statement that suicidologists have thus far not given this issue the attention it deserves. But, equally important, the terms used also have important research implications. For example, in the National Institute of Mental Health epidemiological catchment area studies in the USA [4], respondents were asked in order to assemble information on lifetime prevalence, of nonfatal self-destructive behavior, the question: "Have you ever attempted suicide?" [4]. Compare this method of data collection with methods used in surveys in other countries [5], who use so-called self-harming behavior questionnaires in which the terms "attempted suicide", "suicide attempt" or "parasuicide" are deliberately avoided. Instead respondents are asked questions like: "Have you ever because of social, emotional or other problems:...tried to hang yourself;...taken an overdose of...?, etc., or other possible self-harm methods". Whenever a respondent ticked one or more of these (potentially) self-harming behaviors, they were asked to provide further details on each episode as well as circumstantial evidence. Only those episodes reported, for which also a certain number of information criteria were met, were then scored as evidence for the occurrence of self-harming behavior. A slightly adapted version of this method is being used in the parasuicide monitoring study of the World Health Organization's Regional Office for Europe [5]. Clearly enough, for the same reasons as outlined earlier, either method will lead to very different prevalence rates. But, even more important, using the behavioral descriptive approach in descriptive epidemiological studies also has fundamental implications for where one is going to collect data on the true magnitude of such behaviors. If one approaches these behaviors first and foremost as behaviors for coping with negative affect states and social, interpersonal or physical adversities, in which case the term parasuicide would be more appropriate than attempted suicide, the place to look for and study them is not in hospitals, in-patient centers or in the doctor's office, but in their natural settings. That is to say, one would have to go "downtown" in order to identify any relevant persons and groups/settings within the community.

An interesting question is what researchers in actual effect are trying to collect information on nonfatal self-harming behavior in naturalistic settings. There are, unfortunately, only a limited number of studies to date that have used the population survey method, either by mail, street or household interview. As a literature review shows [5], what these studies generally point out is that the magnitude of the phenomenon under study seems to be far greater than service utilization studies reveal. Depending upon method, population, country and period studied, lifetime prevalence rates of parasuicide in general populations range from about 1 to 20%. Although one would expect year prevalence rates of parasuicide to be lower than lifetime prevalence rates, surprisingly this is not the case. A review of community survey studies [5] shows that the range of year prevalence of parasuicide runs from 2.4 to 20%. This clearly suggests that there are methodological flaws with regard to the accurate assessment of lifetime vs. year prevalence rates in many studies. But what interests us here in particular is the observation from two studies [1,6] that the larger majority of parasuicidal acts do not lead to health service contacts. It is surprising that both a study in The Netherlands [1] as well as a study in the USA [6] report the same ratio of parasuicides that do or do not result in service contacts, namely 1:3. This so-called tip-of-the-iceberg phenomenon has been observed for many somatic and mental illnesses and complaints, and was first described by the epidemiologist Morris in his publication "Uses of Epidemiology" [7]. Last [8] was the first to investigate in his article "The Iceberg" this phenomenon in general practice with regard to psychiatric disorders. Mechanic [9] summarized the major findings over the previous 20 years with regard to the iceberg phenomenon as follows:

"Patient-physician contacts involve symptoms and illnesses unevenly distributed in the population and more frequently untreated than treated," [9].

The tip-of-the-iceberg phenomenon in parasuicide: research questions and preventive implications

As Mechanic [9] pointed out, the tip-of-the-iceberg metaphor applied to the field of mental disorders, implies that only a small part of the total mass of mental disorders surfaces, i.e., becomes visible above the waterline. By far the larger part remains under water and eludes the eye of both the layman as well as the professional beholder. Hosman [10] summarized the main findings with regard to the ratio of the tip to the underwater part of the iceberg within the field of mental disorders and concluded that for most disorders the ratio varies between 1:4 and 1:10. Hosman also pointed out that even in populations where one would expect a high participation or utilization of health services such as college student populations, the ratio with regard to psychiatric disorders is still about 1:3. Later studies [11] provided similar data. Given the ubiquitousness of this phenomenon it is surprising indeed that within the field of attempted suicide or parasuicide hardly any attention has been given to it, apart from the two studies mentioned earlier. This is surprising especially because as Mechanic [9] points out, research with regard to the iceberg phenomenon has raised very relevant questions and provided also some very relevant answers pertaining to theory building in the area of mental disorders as well as to the development of intervention and prevention strategies. The first of those questions regards potential differences between those that constitute the tip of the iceberg and those that constitute the part underwater. Narrowing this down to parasuicidal behavior, the following questions have to be asked: are those two populations of parasuicides different with regard to demographic characteristics, behavioral characteristics, in particular characteristics of the parasuicidal behavior itself, and to risk factors for repetition of (para)suicidal behavior? It seems, for example, quite plausible to assume that those (para)suicidal persons who use so-called medically prescribed means, such as taking an overdose, have a higher probability to be seen by or treated by health-care services than those who use other methods, such as an acute overdose of alcohol or attempts to jump from high places or in front of moving vehicles, but are thwarted in their intention by the intervention of others. It cannot be excluded that the fact that the majority of those who form the tip are females, might partly be attributed to such differences in parasuicide methods. It cannot therefore be excluded that the typical sex differences in parasuicide might be found "under water". Another important issue that Mechanic [9] raises, pertains to the mechanisms of transport between the tip and the part under water. Important questions here are among others: are there persons who after a parasuicidal act get into contact with services and later on, after a subsequent suicidal act, do not get into contact with services again and how does this relate to the risk of a fatal outcome of subsequent acts? Important also is the question of whether those who made a parasuicidal act that did not lead to service utilization and after a subsequent parasuicidal act got in contact with health services, have a lower risk of further repetition than those who even after repeated suicidal acts remain under water? Still another important question is whether there are social class differences between the tip of the iceberg and the underwater part. Research with regard to other mental symptoms or disorders [10] shows that there is a predominance of the lower social classes under water.

A question is also whether those on the tip of the iceberg have arrived there not so much because of their parasuicidal behavior but because of the fact that they suffer from a clear-cut mental disorder, such as an affective disorder or schizophrenic disorder, therefore suggesting a stronger association between a mental disorder on the one hand and suicidal behavior on the other hand than would have been found had the total of the iceberg been included in the analysis. Another issue that Mechanic [9] raises regards the possible existence of developmental trajectories underlying the transport mechanisms from the part underwater to the tip of the iceberg and vice versa. It might very well be that the early instances of parasuicidal behavior in a person's lifecycle, in particular when they take place at a later age or early adolescence, because of low fatality or medical seriousness and also because of the fact that the perpetrator is usually still a dependent child whose behavior reflects upon the parents and the family at large, do not as often lead to contact with services as do parasuicidal behaviors that take place later in the lifecycle. That being the case, it might well be that prevailing intervention/prevention strategies focus on life stages and on groups of suicidal persons that are already relatively advanced in their para(suicidal) career and therefore less amenable to treatment/intervention efforts than would have been the case had they been contacted under water.

Clearly then, the issues raised with regard to the iceberg phenomenon have very important implications for intervention and prevention of suicidal behavior in general, both fatal and nonfatal. For if the tip is not representative of the much larger part under water, then the service-oriented approach to prevention and intervention — sometimes also called the problem group approach — can hardly be expected to have effects that will become visible at the general population level. This might indeed be one of the explanations for the fact that thus far intervention and prevention projects and programs have not been able, as far as the available literature shows, to affect suicide or parasuicide rates at the level of the general population or community.

General population vs. problem group approach in intervention

A publication by the World Health Organization on primary prevention of mental, neurological and psychosocial disorders [12] stated with regard to the prevention of suicidal behavior:

"..from a public health perspective, the main difficulty with activities for the prevention of suicide within the psychosocial approach is the lack of evidence in this respect. We do have several proposals and descriptions of promising programs for the prevention of suicide behaviors, but none of them have yet been in operation for a long period of time as to make evaluation possible. (Their evaluation is either missing or no indication of positive results.) One of the most widespread activities for the prevention of suicide in the health sector has perhaps been represented by suicide prevention centers. Unfortunately, however, even evaluation of this type of activity has not been able to show its effectiveness," [12].

An important question is whether these conclusions are related to the iceberg phenomenon described in the previous paragraph. There are important reasons to assume that the answer to this question must be in the affirmative. Rose [13] has explained an important principle in preventive medicine that is now commonly described as follows: The prevalence of deviance depends on the population mean. This principle is a highly important one but is also highly unpopular both among politicians and the public as well as among health professionals. The reason for this is that psychiatrists, psychologists and other mental health professions usually are inclined to concentrate their attention on the high-risk minority and to imagine that the majority of people have no need to worry or that there is no need to worry about them. The literature in the field of suicidology, indeed, is abundant with writings and research on high-risk populations and their characteristics and management but there is very little on the not-so-high-risk majority with regard to intervention in or prevention of parasuicidal behavior. As Rose [13] explains, there is a very peculiar mechanism active here that can be interpreted as the following: it is impossible to effectively prevent deviant behavior to a degree that is visible on a population level without influencing the behavior of that population itself. Stated with regard to parasuicidal behavior, according to Rose [13] the false assumption here would be that it is possible to decrease the incidence or prevalence of suicidal behavior to a degree that is visible on the level of the general population without influencing the behavior or condition of that general population, in addition to the behavior or condition of those that carry a heightened risk for parasuicidal behavior. The relevant question here is: what is the relationship between the population mean and the prevalence of deviance? Rose provides the answer with regard to alcohol intake, an important risk factor of suicidal behavior. His data comes from the Intersalt study, using data from 52 populations from around the world, collecting standardized measures of various health-related characteristics. From these data it is very clear that the prevalence of alcoholism, the deviant condition, is simply a function of the population mean alcohol intake: the correlation between both is 0.97. Analogous results have been found for overweight and blood pressure. Rose [13] suggests that it may be that this applies to many other conditions as well: he mentions depression, where the prevalence of psychiatric illness may be a function of the whole population's mood. He also mentions violence which possibly reflects the overall aggression in society. Rose's suggestion with regard to the mood disorders appears to be very well taken if one reads a recent publication of the Academia Europea, the European Academy of Sciences on psychosocial problems, among others depressive disorders, and suicidal behavior among young people in Europe over the course of this century [5]. The findings presented in this publication on secular trends in depressive disorders as well as in suicidal mortality support the hypothesis that a true increase in this phenomenon has occurred over the larger part of this century among the white urban adolescent and young adult populations of North America and Europe. This conclusion is corroborated by the fact that the data on depressive disorders and on suicide converge on the observation that this increase is particularly conspicuous among young males. Of further relevance here is evidence suggesting that the percentage of adolescent male suicides that suffered from a depressive disorder at the time of their death has increased over the past decades. In a comparison of psychological autopsies in studies of male suicides with an in-between distance of 25 years, it was found that the prevalence of disorders was higher among young males in the most recent series. It is difficult to assert, the report states, that the earlier age of onset of depressive disorders over the larger part of the century, is also reflected in an increase of suicide mortality at a lower age, given the problems with suicide statistics for early adolescence. But there is indirect evidence that suggests that this might be the case. There have been a number of community service studies assembling (retrospectively) data on lifetime prevalence of parasuicides both among the general population as well as among high-school student and adolescent populations. In the reasonable expectation that lifetime prevalence rates should increase with age since time augments risk, it is surprising that the lifetime parasuicide rates in general population studies do not exceed and even sometimes remain below the rates for adolescents. Assuming that recall of past episodes remains constant throughout the lifespan, one possible explanation for this finding is a lowering age of first-ever parasuicidal acts over the past decades. Since parasuicide is an important, presumably the most important precursor of suicide, a lowering of age of first-ever parasuicides can be expected to cause a lowering of age for suicides as well.

Concluding remarks

In conclusion, if we wish to see a large improvement in the reduction of the problem of parasuicide, attempted suicide and therewith of suicide, suicidologists and others active in this field must see suicidal behavior in its broader social, economic and environmental context. They must learn that the problem-group or high-risk approach has only a very limited effect on the magnitude of that problem. Societal factors shape the occurrence of mental ill health and disorder, and societal changes shape its control and prevention to a high degree. Society, the population at large, not suicidologists or preventionists, decide on how they wish to live and what their priorities are. Suicidologists can advice and assist, but they cannot make society's choices. They only have a shared responsibility.

Recently we have seen an astonishing growth in public concern about health, i.e., physical health. But at the same time we have not at all witnessed a moving up of mental health on society's priorities list. Most of the diseases that cause disability and mortality are intimately related to the increasing stresses that the organization of society and the accompanying lifestyles put upon people. Given the unequal distribution of vulnerability to such stresses and the unequal availability of robust patterns of coping, depending also upon such factors as standard of living and wealth, certain groups carry a higher risk for mental ill health, mental disorder and accompanying symptoms such as suicidal and related self-harming behavior. It is by assembling and sharing knowledge about relationships between these general processes, affecting the population at large, and specific manifestations of mental ill health in certain subgroups, and by raising the awareness that prevention is a societal responsibility and not the responsibility of a specific professional group, that we can hope to achieve reductions in suicide morbidity and mortality that become, in the most literal sense of the word, "epidemiologically" visible.

References

1. Diekstra RFW, van der Loo KJM. Attitudes toward suicide and incidence of suicidal behavior in a general population. In: Winnik HZ, Miller L (eds) Aspects of Suicide in Modern Civilization. Jerusalem: Jerusalem Academic Press, 1978;79—85.
2. Shneidman ES (ed) Suicidology: Contemporary Developments. New York: Grune & Stratton, 1976.
3. Wegner DM, Pennebaker JW (eds) Handbook of Mental Control. New Jersey: Prentice Hall, 1993.
4. Moscicki EK, O'Caroll PW, Rae DS, Roy AG, Locke BZ, Regier DA. Suicidal ideation and attempts: the epidemiological catchment area study. In: Report of the Secretary's Task Force on Youth Suicide. Department of Health and Human Services Publication: Rockville-USA, no. (ADM) 1989;89-1264:4-115/4-128.
5. Rutter M, Smith DJ (eds) Psychosocial Disorders in Young People: Time Trends and their Causes. Chichester: Wiley, 1995.
6. CDC-Centers if Disease Control Attempted Suicide among high school students — United States 1990, leads from the Morbidity and Mortality Weekly Report. JAMA 1991;266:14,911.
7. Morris W. Uses of Epidemiology. Edinburgh: Churchill Livingstone, 1957.
8. Last JN. The Iceberg. Lancet 1963;2:28.
9. Mechanic D. Illness behavior, social adaptation and the management of illness. J Nerv Mental Dis 1957;165:79—87.
10. Hosman CMH. Psychosociale problemen en Hulpzoeken (Psychosocial problems and helpseeking behavior). Lisse: Swets & Zeitlinger, 1983.
11. Sarason IG, Sarason BR. Abnormal Psychology, 7th edn. Engleworth Cliffs, NJ: Prentice Hall, 1993.
12. WHO (World Health Organisation). Guidelines for Primary Prevention of Mental, Neurological and Psychosocial Disorders: Report for Suicide. Geneva: WHO-MNH-MND-39.24, 1993.
13. Rose G. Doctors and the nation's health. Ann Med 1990;22(5):297—302.

Attempted suicide by violent methods

V.P. Kontaxakis and G.N. Christodoulou

Department of Psychiatry, University of Athens, Eginition Hospital, Athens, Greece

Abstract. *Background*. The aim of this study is to describe the differential characteristics of attempters using various violent methods (jumping, hanging, drowning, etc.) who were referred to the Outpatients Psychiatric Department, Eginition Hospital, Athens, as emergency cases.

Methods. Attempters by jumping, by hanging and by drowning were compared on sociodemographic and psychiatric parameters to those who had attempted suicide in a nonviolent way (drug overdosers).

Results. The differential characteristics of persons attempting suicide by jumping were the following: men, older in age, married, suffering from major psychopathology (i.e., affective psychosis-depressive type or schizophrenia). The characteristics of attempters by hanging were as follows: older in age, married, unemployed, living with their own family, suffering from major psychopathology. The characteristics of attempters by drowning were: older age and major psychopathology.

Conclusions. The common differential characteristics for all three groups of attempters by violent methods were: advanced age and major psychopathology.

Keywords: advanced age, affective psychosis, emergency cases, schizophrenia.

Introduction

Suicide and attempted suicide are two distinct forms of behaviour. Patients who attempt suicide without fatal consequences have been shown to differ in certain characteristics from those who actually commit suicide [1,2].

It has been claimed that subgroups of persons with high suicidal intention can be discerned within the larger group of suicide attempters and suicidal intention has been positively correlated to the seriousness of bodily harm caused by an attempt [1,3,4]. Attempters of suicide by violent methods constitute a small proportion of the whole group of attempters and tend to involve people with serious suicidal intent [1,5]. The aim of this study is to describe the differential characteristics of attempters using various violent ways.

Materials and Methods

During a 9-year period, 123 suicide attempters using various violent ways (46 by jumping, 44 by hanging and 33 by drowning) were referred to a general medical service at the Outpatients Psychiatric Department (OPD) Eginition Hospital, Athens, as emergency cases. The function and the staff composition of the OPD

Address for correspondence: Vassilis Kontaxakis, Assoc. Professor of Psychiatry, Eginition Hospital, 74 Vas.Sophias Av., 11528 Athens, Greece.

have been presented in detail elsewhere [6]. Attempters with different violent methods were compared on social-demographic and psychiatric-clinical parameters with a random sample of 106 attempters by drug-overdose (nonviolent way) who were referred during the same time period to the same department.

Any intentional self-injury where some degree of suicidal intent was expressed has been considered as a suicide attempt regardless of the modality of suicidal behaviour [7]. The psychiatric diagnoses of the attempters were made by psychiatrists of similar education and experience and the patients files were reassessed according to ICD-9 criteria [8]. Since most of the neurotic patients presented depressive mood, the Newcastle Diagnostic Scale for Depression [9] was also applied to exclude endogenous depression cases from the above group of patients.

The data of our study were collected from the standardized OPD files. For the statistical evaluation Student's t test and χ^2 test (with Yate's correction where needed) were used.

Results

Table 1 shows the comparison of suicide attempters using various violent methods (jumping, hanging and drowning) to suicide attempters by drug overdose on social-demographic parameters. All three groups of attempters by violent ways were of older age compared to overdosers. Attempters by hanging were more often married ($p < 0.01$), unemployed ($p < 0.01$) and were living with their own family ($p < 0.01$).

Table 2 shows the comparison of suicide attempters on psychiatric parameters.

Table 1. Comparison of suicide attempters using various violent methods (jumping, hanging, drowning) to suicide attempters by drug overdose (nonviolent way): social-demographic parameters.

	Jumping (n = 46)	Hanging (n = 44)	Drowning (n = 33)	Drug overdose (n = 106)
Age (mean)	40.0[b]	42.7[b]	38.9[a]	30.8
Sex (male)	61%[b]	57%	45%	41%
Marital status				
married	46%[a]	54%	33%	33%
single	41%	36%	49%	55%
other	13%	10%	18%	12%
Employment status				
employed	41%	47%	49%	60%
unemployed	30%	37%[b]	30%	14%
housewife	29%	16%	21%	26%
Living situation				
with parents	30%	27%	36%	40%
with their own family	41%	57%[b]	36%	35%
alone	13%	11%	6%	14%
other	16%	5%	22%	11%

[a]$p < 0.05$; [b]$p < 0.01$.

Table 2. Comparison of suicide attempters using various violent methods (jumping, hanging, drowning) to suicide attempters by drug overdose (nonviolent way): psychiatric parameters.

	Jumping (n = 46)	Hanging (n = 44)	Drowning (n = 33)	Drug overdose (n = 106)
Psychiatric morbidity				
Affective psychosis (depression)	37%	43%[b]	30%	25%
Schizophrenic psychosis	35%	21%	49%[c]	22%
Neurotic disorder	13%	9%	15%	23%
Drug dependence	0	2%	0	5%
Alcohol dependence	2%	7%	0	3%
Antisocial personality disorder	11%	9%	3%	12%
Other	0	2%	0	2%
No mental illness	2%	7%	3%	8%
Major psychopathology[a]	72%[c]	64[c]	79%[c]	47%
Previous suicide attempt				
Previous contact with	22%	43%	36%	28%
psychiatric services	38%	36%	39%	50%
Previous hospitalization	35%	43%	39%	30%

[a]Major psychopathology = Affective psychosis (depression) + Schizophrenic psychosis; [b]$p < 0.05$; [c]$p < 0.01$.

All three groups of suicide attempters using violent methods were suffering from major psychopathology compared to overdosers. Attempters by hanging were suffering more often from affective psychosis (depressive type) ($p < 0.05$) while attempters by drowning from schizophrenia ($p < 0.01$). There were no statistically significant differences between violent suicide attempters and suicide attempters by drug overdose with respect to previous suicide attempts, previous contact with psychiatric services (last 6 months) or previous hospitalization.

Discussion

Attempted suicide and suicide are closely related. An important percentage (20–30%) of those who commit suicide have made attempts in the past, while 1–2% of those who attempt to kill themselves succeed to die committing suicide 1 year later and 4–10% over a 10-year period [5,10,11].

Obviously, there is an overlap in the above two subcategories of self-destructive behavior. A number of individuals from those who attempt suicide can be regarded as high-risk candidates for a subsequent suicide.

Patients who injure themselves do not belong to a homogeneous group and can be classified into three subgroups on the basis of the type of injury inflicted: superficial self-cutting, (associated with little or no suicidal intent), self mutilation (which may result in disfigurement usually occurring in individuals with schizophrenia) and serious self-injury (such as hanging, jumping, drowning, etc.,

190

which are usually associated with serious suicidal intent) [1].

The aim of this study is to reveal the differential characteristics of this last group of attempters using violent methods (serious self-injurers).

The findings of our study indicate that the differential characteristics of attempters by jumping are the following: male gender, older age, married status and major psychopathology (affective psychosis-depressive type or schizophrenia). On the other hand, the characteristics of attempters by hanging are: older age, married status, living with their own family, unemployment, major psychopathology (mainly schizophrenia); while the characteristics of attempters by drowning are: older age and major psychopathology.

The common differential characteristics of all three groups of attempters using violent methods are advanced age and major psychopathology.

Other authors who have studied the characteristics of people with serious self-injuries or attempters using different violent methods have found controversial results [12—23]. This may have been due to differences in populations studied or differences in psychiatric diagnostic methods. However, most authors agree that the majority of attempters using violent methods suffer from serious psychiatric illness.

The characteristics of attempters using violent methods revealed by our study are positively correlated with the characteristics of attempters who actually later kill themselves [24,25]. This is in keeping with biological research, which points to similarities between attempters using violent methods and successful suicides, i.e., low 5-HIAA in CSF [26].

Thus, our study supports the heterogeneity of suicide attempters and underlines the strong relationship between the characteristics of suicidal attempters with violent ways and those of successful suicides.

In view of the fact that attempters carry a high repetition risk, special attention should be given to this group of people. Psychiatric consultation and treatment in a preventive framework is strongly indicated especially for attempters with violent methods.

References

1. Hawton K, Catalan J. Attempted Suicide. Oxford: Oxford University Press, 1987.
2. Kreitman N. Suicide and parasuicide. In: Kendell RE, Zealey AK (eds) Companion to Psychiatric Studies. Edinburgh: Churchill Livingston, 1983;396—411.
3. Pierce DW. Suicidal intent in self-injury. Br J Psychiat 1977;130:377—385.
4. Pallis DJ, Barraclough B. Seriousness of suicide attempt and future risk of suicide: A common on card's paper. Omega 1977;8:141—149.
5. Suokas J, Lonnqvist J. Outcome of attempted suicide and psychiatric consultation: Risk factors and suicide mortality during a five-year follow-up. Acta Psychiatr Scand 1991;84:545—549.
6. Vaslamatzis G, Kontaxakis V, Markidis M, Katsouyanni K. Social and resource factors related to the utilization of emergency psychiatric services in the Athens area. Acta Psychiatr Scand 1987;75:95—98.
7. Weissman MM, Fox K, Klerman JL. Hostility and depression associated with suicide attempts. Am J Psychiat 1973;130:450—454.

8. World Health Organization. Mental Disorders: Glossary and Guide to their Classification in Accordance with the Ninth Revision of the International Classification of Diseases. Geneva: WHO, 1978.

9. Carney MWP, Roth M, Garside RF. The diagnosis of depressive syndromes and the prediction of ECT response. Br J Psychiat 1965;111:659—674.

10. Cullberg J, Wasserman D, Stefansson GG. Who commits suicide after a suicide attempt? Acta Psychiatr Scand 1988;77:598—603.

11. Barraclough B, Bunch J, Nelson B, Sainsbury P. A hundred cases of suicide: Clinical aspects. Br J Psychiat 1974;125:363—378.

12. Beautrais AL, Joyce PR, Mulder RT, Fergusson DM, Deavoll BJ, Nightingale SK. Prevalence and comorbidity of mental disorders in persons making serious suicide attempts: A case-control study. Am J Psychiat 1996;153:1009—1014.

13. Robinson ADT, Daffy JC. A comparison of self-injury and self-poisoning from the Regional Poisoning Treatment Centre, Edinburgh. Acta Psychiatr Scand 1989;80:272—279.

14. Fox K, Weissman M. Suicide attempts and drugs: Contradiction between method and intent. Soc Psychiat 1975;10:31—38.

15. Lester D, Beck AT. What the suicide's choice of method signifies. Omega 1980;11:271—277.

16. Andreasen NC, Noyes R. Suicide attempted by self-immolation. Am J Psychiat 1975;132: 554—556.

17. Kontaxakis VP, Evripidou E, Havaki-Kontaxaki BJ, Christodoulou GN. Attempted suicide by burning. In: Ferrari G, Bellini M, Crepet P (eds) Suicidal Behaviour and Risk Factors. Bologna: Monduzzi Editore, 1990;449—452.

18. Prasad A, Lloyd GG. Attempted suicide by jumping. Acta Psychiatr Scand 1983;68:394—396.

19. Vieta E, Nieto E, Gasto C, Girera E. Attempted suicide by jumping. Euro Psychiat 1992;7(5): 221—224.

20. Cantor CH, Hill MA, McLachlan EK. Suicide and related behaviour from river bridges: A clinical perspective. Br J Psychiat 1989;155:829—835.

21. Katz K, Goyen N, Goldberg I, Mirjari J, Radway M, Yosipovitch Z. Injuries in attempted suicide by jumping from a high. Injury 1988;16(6):371—374.

22. Nayeem N. Attempted suicide by hanging. Injury 1992;23(1):61—62.

23. O'Donnel I, Farmer R, Catalan J. Explaining suicide: The views of survivors of serious suicide attempts. Br J Psychiat 1996;168:780—786.

24. Dingman CW, McGlashan TH. Characteristics of patients with serious suicidal intentions who ultimately commit suicide. Hosp Commun Psychiat 1988;39:295—299.

25. Hawton K, Fagg J. Suicide and other causes of death, following attempted suicide. Br J Psychiat 1988;152:359—366.

26. Asberg M, Nordstom P, Trackman-Bendz L. Biological factors in suicide. In: Roy A (ed) Suicide. Baltimore: Williams & Wilkins, 1986;47—71.

Counseling the suicidal person in the modern age

David Lester

Center for the Study of Suicide, Blackwood, New Jersey, USA

Abstract. In general, counselors should lay aside their personal biases and moral objections in order to counsel people effectively. Suicidal behavior is not necessarily irrational and, even if it were, so are many of the decisions we make. Today, with "how-to-do-it" books available for committing suicide and people advocating physician-assisted suicide, the responsible counselor should be prepared to discuss suicide as a viable option with clients rather than simply working to prevent the client's suicide. Direct decision therapy provides a good basis for this, since this form of therapy takes a pragmatic stance rather than a moral stance and helps clients make appropriate decisions from their perspective.

Keywords: appropriate death, assisted suicide, direct decision therapy.

In the USA, assisted suicide is no longer a hypothetical possibility — it is a reality. Not surprisingly, it has been discovered that physicians in the USA have been assisting patients to die for many years without publicity [1]. Thus, the issue facing us changes from "Should we permit assisted suicide?" to "Should we regulate assisted suicide?" There is much to be said for permitting and regulating a behavior instead of pretending that the behavior does not occur.

Humphry [2], founder of the Hemlock Society, recently published a "how-to" book on suicide which quickly rose to the top of the best-seller lists. Voices were raised both in support of the book and in opposition. Relevant to this, a perusal of the medical literature on attempted suicide indicates the diverse and severe ways in which people injure themselves seriously as a result of unsuccessful attempts to kill themselves. Plastic surgeons publish reports on the restoration to some semblance of normality of faces shattered by bullets. Burn specialists work to heal the skin of those who failed to die from self-immolation, and many patients live painful lives as a result of the severe internal damage inflicted by the overdoses they took. For example, Frierson and Lippman [3] found an incidence of 15% for colostomies after self-inflicted gunshot wounds, 6% for organic brain syndromes, 5% for seizures and 4% for amputations. Biering-Sorensen, Pedersen and Müller [4] have described a sample of spinal cord injuries after attempted suicide, 19% of whom had cervical lesions.

If there are about 10 attempts at suicide for every completed suicide, as we suspect, then about 300,000 people will attempt suicide in the USA this year. Many of them will make a medically harmless attempt and so suffer little damage. But

Address for correspondence: David Lester, Center for the Study of Suicide, RR41, 5 Stonegate Court, Blackwood, NJ 08012, USA.

a good proportion of the remainder, some of whom intended to die, will suffer grave and long-term consequences. Is that what we want?

More recently, Jack Kevorkian has built devices which enable people to kill themselves; and he has also been present and assisted them when they in fact make their fatal suicidal action. Michigan, which had no laws against such actions, has tried to convict Kevorkian for murder and other offenses, but failed. Kevorkian [5] believes that physicians should establish medical clinics where terminally ill patients could opt for death under controlled circumstances. Such an idea is not new. Indeed, Alfred Nobel, founder of the Nobel Prizes, suggested this many years ago [6]. Public opinion surveys by both Lou Harris and the Roper Organization have found that a majority of the general public support physician-assisted suicide [7].

The issues surrounding suicide and assisted suicide involve, among other things, decisions about the way in which a person dies. Lawmakers can decide which ways are legal, and philosophers can argue which ways are moral, but the way in which we die is also an issue that psychologists and psychiatrists should consider. Death is inevitable. Our choice is, therefore, not whether to die, but how to die. As psychologists, we can ask what makes a death psychologically appropriate? Since this concept should be instrumental in decisions regarding suicide and assisted suicide, Lester [8] examined some of the possibilities for an appropriate death.

The concept of an appropriate death

Weisman and Hackett [9] brought attention to the concept by specifying the conditions that they felt constituted an appropriate death. First, the death must be seen as reducing conflict, as a solution to abiding problems, or else the patient must see very few problems remaining. Then, death must be seen as being compatible with superego demands or else these demands must be reduced. Third, there must be a continuity of important relationships or a prospect of their being restored (as in typical reunion fantasies). Lastly, death must fulfill a wish for the patient.

Lester [8] suggested other ways of defining an appropriate death. Kalish [10] distinguished between four types of death. Physical death is when the organs of the individual cease to function and when the organism ceases to function. Individuals are psychologically dead when they cease to be aware of their own self and of their own existence. The individuals know neither who they are or even that they exist. Social death is when the individual accepts the notion that for all practical purposes he or she is dead. The final kind of death is anthropological death in which the individual is cut off from the community and treated as if he or she no longer existed. These four kinds of death can occur at different times in an individual's life. Lester suggested that a death could be considered appropriate when all four of these different kinds of death coincide in time. A person who falls into coma (psychological death) and physically dies much later has had an inappropriate death. The person placed in a nursing home and forgotten about (social death) does not die an appropriate death. Using this criterion, suicide and assisted suicide could be appropriate deaths.

Some writers judge a death to be appropriate insofar as the person played a role in his own death. A person struck down by chance factors, such as lightning, therefore, does not die an appropriate death. In contrast, a suicide plays the maximum role in his own death.

Some view a "natural" death as good, for in a natural death the body retains its integrity. An act of suicide, such as shooting oneself, destroys the body's integrity and is, therefore, inappropriate. From this point of view, any life that is prolonged by the use of transplants and medical intrusions into the body cannot be appropriate. A death from natural causes without medical intrusion alone is appropriate. Suicide and assisted suicide could be appropriate under this criterion if an appropriate method is used.

An appropriate death can be defined as one which is consistent with the person's lifestyle. For example, Ernest Hemingway's suicide by firearm in the face of growing medical and psychiatric illness was consistent with the death-defying lifestyle he developed. Again, both suicide and assisted suicide could be viewed as appropriate using this criterion.

Shneidman [11] suggested that the timing of a person's death was a relevant factor. Shneidman felt that one could sometimes discern an inner consistency in an individual's acts and ambitions so that, after a given point, any further life would be a defeat or a pointless repetition. Within a person's life, there may be specific points or crests when death would be appropriate and would give a self-consistent tone to the lifestyle of the person. Such a death can even heighten an individual's impact by making his memory more treasured. Suicide and assisted suicide could be consistent with this criterion.

It is perhaps one of the responsibilities of a counselor or therapist to ensure that a patient dies an appropriate death. To do this, we must first be aware of the alternative concepts for an appropriate death, and then we must identify the concept that the patient has. If death for our patient is more appropriate in one particular manner, then perhaps it is our duty to allow, and perhaps facilitate, the patient to die in that way. Psychologists and psychiatrists need to consider alternative criteria for an appropriate death so that discussion of this issue with clients can become more meaningful.

The role of the counselor

What should the role of a counselor be today when confronting a client who is considering suicide? Should the counselor be someone who believes that suicide is always the best option? Of course not! But should the counselor be someone who believes that suicide is never an acceptable option? Or should the counselor be someone whose role is to help clients decide what is best for them, be it life or death?

196

The purpose of this essay is to suggest that this third choice is the most appropriate in this modern world [12]. The role of the counselor or therapist in talking to suicidal clients is to assist them to make an appropriate choice for themselves — not for the counselor, not for the society, but rather for the clients themselves. The choice need not be moral, rational or healthy, but it should be appropriate for the client.

Is suicide irrational?

Objections to suicide based on its irrationality are difficult to sustain. Lester [13] argued that there is no evidence that suicidal people argue illogically. There is, however, a possibility that the premises of the suicidal person may be irrational.

In rational-emotive therapy [14] the pathological emotions and behaviors of clients are assumed to be the result of irrational beliefs (or premises). For example, if after your intimate relationship breaks up, you may say to yourself, "I'll never find someone to love and marry; my relationships always end after a short-time; I'll never be happy; I'm a failure." According to Ellis, these are irrational beliefs. You are labeling yourself as a failure after merely one or two experiences, and you do not know that you will never find someone to marry or always be unhappy. Thus, your beliefs are irrational. If you changed these irrational beliefs to rational beliefs, then your depression and anxiety would be considerably reduced.

Although in criminal trials, the defendant is presumed innocent until proven guilty, in rational-emotive therapy the client is presumed irrational until proven rational. I have known several people who never did find anyone to love and marry and who stayed alone all of their lives. I have known people who never found happiness. If these people had talked to a rational-emotive therapist earlier in their lives, they would have been accused of being irrational, whereas in fact they were correct.

Thus, when suicidologists claim that their suicidal clients are thinking and behaving irrationally, those suicidologists are being dogmatic and authoritarian, imposing their own view of the world on their clients. Such indoctrination is unethical and, if the client was not in a suicidal crisis, would not be tolerated in a counselor working in a nontotalitarian society.

A good death

Too many writers bandy about the word "euthanasia." We are supposed to die a good death if we consider the literal meaning of the word — a death with dignity, a death without suffering. This may be a goal, but it is certainly an unrealistic goal. How many of us lead a good life — one with dignity, one without suffering? How many of you reading this article are psychologically healthy? How many of you are free from depression, anxiety and anger?

If people have been irrational in their thinking much of their life, why expect them to be rational when dying? If you have raged all your life, then you will probably "rage, rage against the dying of the light" [15]. If you wondered whether "to be or not to be" at an earlier age, then you will probably be indecisive at the time of dying also.

The quality of life

Some practitioners have asserted that it is important to prevent all suicides. Whatever the circumstances of the case, they assert that everyone ought, in an ideal world, to be prevented from committing suicide. In an ideal world, everyone would be able to receive and benefit from good psychotherapy and appropriate medication. Therapy would be effective, there would be no incompetent therapists (as, for example, the therapist who had sexual intercourse with Anne Sexton in the years prior to her suicide [16]), there would be no side effects from medication, and there would be adequate insurance coverage for therapy.

Of course, the world is not ideal. Therapy often does not work, therapists are sometimes incompetent, medication does have side effects, and insurance coverage for therapy is being reduced in current health plans. Thus, suicidal clients may have little reason to expect a better life if they do not commit suicide. They are quite rational in expecting things to continue to be bad or to worsen.

The question of whether suicide can be appropriate or rational cannot be answered based solely on the issues raised above, such as the criteria for logical and rational decisions. The question has to take into account the alternatives open to the person — suicide vs. psychiatric hospitalization, or suicide vs. a lingering death from cancer treated by a medical profession in the USA which seems to care little for the comfort of the patient. (For example, until the development of new antinausea medications, the best medication for patients undergoing chemotherapy for cancer was marihuana, but the US government judged their "war on drugs" to be more important than the pain of cancer patients. Perhaps Ada Rollin [17] would have faced treatment for her cancer more willingly and not committed suicide if the medical profession had prescribed marihuana for her?)

What of survivors?

Several commentators have focused on the trauma caused by people's suicides on the friends and relatives of the deceased, the so-called survivors [18]. The implication is that we should not commit suicide because to do so would make others suffer.

A British bishop once declared that he would die content that he had made at least one person in the world happy — the woman he did not marry! I think a much greater case could be made that marriage and becoming pregnant make others suffer. Far many more spouses harm their mates and parents harm their children than the few suicides who harm their kin. Yet we do not forbid marriages or forbid people to have children. On the contrary, we counsel those who have been divorced, and we counsel those who come from dysfunctional families. So we need to provide counseling for survivors who request it, but their trauma does not make suicide immoral, irrational, or inappropriate for the suicidal individual.

Indeed, if we were to reorient our approach to suicidal people, it would be possible to provide family counseling for a family in which one member has decided to commit suicide. The family as a group could come to share, participate in and accept the decision of the suicidal member. For example, Betty Rollin, her husband, and her mother dying of cancer and refusing further chemotherapy could have been helped by a counselor, had one been available, so that they could have explored and worked through the myriad of feelings they went through as the mother was helped to commit suicide [16].

How to counsel the suicidal person

How then should a counselor approach a person who is seriously considering suicide? An obvious first step is to do what any good counselor does, i.e., to act as a person-centered counselor, namely to actively listen to the client [19]. The client's situation needs to be explored and the client's thoughts and feelings about the situation expressed. If family therapy is possible, then the position of everyone in the family must be explored until, at some point, the situation is clear both to the client and to the counselor.

The second step is for the counselor to explore the suicidogenic factors. What stresses has the client experienced (physical illnesses, losses, etc.)? What psychological factors are present, such as psychiatric illness, depression, cognitive distortions, and so on. What is the social situation of the client, and what are reasonable expectations for the future? Part of the task here is to educate the client about suicide — what we know of the causes and characteristics of the suicidal crisis.

The third step is to discuss options. The presence of a severe illness does not argue for or against suicide. If the client has not tried treatment yet, then trying treatment is a possible first option. Then the counselor and client can continue to meet to discuss the effects of the treatment. For example, Abbie Hoffman, a manic-depressive, did not like the effects of lithium on his body [20]. He tried instead to medicate himself with Prozac and Valium. His eventual suicide may suggest that his preferred medications were not appropriate, but discussion of all of the decisions that he made with a counselor may have enabled his choices to be informed choices and, therefore, better choices.

Each time that the client makes a decision, then the counselor's task is to help the client carry out that decision. If the decision is to try a new treatment, then the counselor should help the client go through the process. If the decision is to refuse treatment, and even to terminate life, then the counselor should help the client to carry out these decisions.

The client should be reminded that the decisions made are only decisions at that point in time and that decisions can be changed. A decision to undergo treatment can be reversed; a decision to commit suicide can, up to the final moment, be reversed.

The best framework for a counselor with these goals, is "direct decision therapy" proposed by Greenwald [21]. Direct decision therapy focuses on the decisions that clients make. The task of the therapist is to help clients make decisions to change their behavior and to help clients carry out these decisions.

Clients choose their problem, according to Greenwald. They choose to be afraid of heights, to be depressed, or to have an unhappy marriage. Once the therapist has helped the client become aware of these decisions, the next task is to identify the circumstances in which the decision was made. Once this is done, the decision no longer appears to be irrational.

Greenwald next helps the client to assess the advantages and the disadvantages of the decisions they have made in the past, and this must be done without criticizing the client. Then the client must devise or be presented with alternative decisions, and for each of these the client must be helped to assess the positive and negative gain. Clients must be helped to become aware of alternatives and their consequences.

However, it is the client, and the client alone, who must decide which alternative to choose. Once the client has chosen, then the therapist's final task is to help the client make that decision and accomplish his or her goals, though the therapist should make sure that the client realizes that a decision has to be reaffirmed continually and that decisions can be changed.

This approach to counseling would appear to be ideal for the person considering suicide.

Discussion

People commit suicide, and perhaps a small proportion of them will want to discuss their decision before they do so. It should be possible for a counselor to assist such a client. People are assisting loved ones to die in ever increasing numbers and, though counselors have the right to refuse to counsel such people, refusing to counsel such people does not make the problem go away. Rather it adds one more problem to which our society fails to respond appropriately or adequately. The hospice movement brought some dignity to the natural deaths of terminal patients. Perhaps we need a movement to bring some dignity to suicidal deaths?

References

1. Quill TE. Doctor I want to die. Will you help me? J Am Med Assoc 1993;270:870–873.
2. Humphry D. Final Exit. Eugene, OR: Hemlock Society, 1991.
3. Frierson RL, Lippman SB. Psychiatric consultation for patients with self-inflicted gunshot

wounds. Psychosomatics 1990;31(1):67—74.

4. Biering-Sorensen F, Pedersen W, Müller PG. Spinal cord injury due to suicide attempts. Paraplegia 1992;30:139—144.

5. Kevorkian J. The last fearsome taboo. Med Law 1988;7:1—44.

6. Sohlman R. Alfred Nobel and the Nobel Foundation. In: Schuck H (ed) Nobel: The Man and His Prizes. Amsterdam: Elsevier, 1962;15—72.

7. West LJ. Reflections on the right to die. In: Leenaars AA (ed) Suicidology. Northvale, NJ: Jason Aronson, 1993;361—376.

8. Lester D. Psychological issues in euthanasia, suicide and assisted suicide. J Soc Iss 1996;52(2): 51—62.

9. Weisman A, Hackett TP. Predilection to death. Psychosom Med 1961;23:232—256.

10. Kalish RA. Life and death. American Psychological Association meeting. New York, NY, 1966.

11. Shneidman ES. Sleep and self-destruction. In: Shneidman ES (ed) Essays in Self-Destruction. New York: Science House, 1967;510—539.

12. Lester D. Counseling the suicidal person in the modern age. Cris Interv Time Limit Treat 1995; 2:159—165.

13. Lester D. The logic and rationality of suicide. Homeostasis 1993;34:167—173.

14. Ellis A. Humanistic Psychotherapy. New York: Julian, 1973.

15. Thomas D. The poems of Dylan Thomas. New York: New Directions, 1971.

16. Middlebrook DW. Anne Sexton. Boston: Houghton-Mifflin, 1991.

17. Rollin B. Last Wish. New York: Simon & Schuster, 1985.

18. Rudestam KE. Survivors of suicide. In: Lester D (ed) Current Concepts of Suicide. Philadelphia: Charles Press, 1990;203—213.

19. Gordon T. PET: Parent Effectiveness Training. New York: Wyden, 1970.

20. Jezer M. Abbie Hoffman. New Brunswick, NJ: Rutgers University Press, 1992.

21. Greenwald H. Direct Decision Therapy. San Diego: Edits, 1973.

©1997 Elsevier Science B.V. All rights reserved.
Suicide: Biopsychosocial Approaches.
A.J. Botsis, C.R. Soldatos and C.N. Stefanis, editors.

Suicidal crisis: psychodynamic approaches

Béla Buda

Department of Communication, Semmelweis University of Medicine, Institute of Behavioural Sciences, Budapest, Hungary

Abstract. Traditional psychodynamic approaches to understanding the phenomenon of suicide included a wide variety of concepts ranging from guilt feelings and intents of revenge to efforts of self-reassertion and restoration of personal dignity. According to recent psychodynamic thinking, the emphasis is on the etiologic role of narcissistic traumas in life history and the occurrence of a narcissistic crisis and the consequent damage to self-esteem which is being dealt with by superego functions in a rigid and self-destructive way. Usually, there are typical crises behind self-destructive tendencies, while the main crisis arises through the intent of self-destruction per se. It should be noted that both crisis theory and the various psychodynamic approaches are based on experience with persons at risk for suicide or with suicide attempts. Thus, many completed suicides may involve different psychological mechanisms. On the therapeutic level, psychodynamic interventions range from classical psychoanalysis to a rather active and direct supportive psychotherapy. Generally, an integrative and eclectic approach is preferable. Crisis theories have considerably enriched the psychodynamic therapies, performed in a group setting because they utilize mobilization of interpersonal resources and immediate emotional support, they focus on the here-and-now and they aim at crisis resolution.

Keywords: crisis, psychodynamic approaches, self-destructiveness, suicide, theory.

Suicidal crisis and psychodynamic approaches to it are complex issues which need some conceptual clarification. Both issues are clinical, they are not based on research, but rather on therapeutical experiences. They have different roots in the history of psychiatry and psychotherapy, different representations in the "mainstream" of suicidology, e.g., in America only some roots are taken into consideration. In this mainstream of suicidology these issues seem to be more or less outmoded and underestimated. Many of their theoretical elements and methods are, however, implied in standard descriptions of suicidal processes and in the recommendations of therapeutic interventions [1,2].

Psychodynamic approaches rest upon many presuppositions which are useful for the clinician but hardly supported by studies, i.e., by "hard data".

First, the theory of crisis presupposes several tenets, such as:
— the existence of a specific psychological response pattern to unresolved acute problems of life, mainly to losses and traumas;
— the causal relationship of crisis to suicide; and

Address for correspondence: Béla Buda MD, Department of Communication, Semmelweis University of Medicine, Institute of Behavioural Sciences, Budapest, Hungary. Tel./Fax: +36-1-214-42-52.

— an opportunity to reach the suicidal person through the crisis and to induce
   beneficial changes in her or him, etc.

None of these presuppositions have really been proven, but crisis theory is, nevertheless, a good practical guideline for clinical encounters with suicidal persons.
Indeed, there are typical crises behind many suicides, while in many cases the
real crisis arises from the intent of self-destruction. In such cases the crisis is a
reflection of the inner conflict between suicidal forces, life-preserving motivations, anxieties, fears of pain and injury, as well as reality testing. In some cases
there is no crisis at all. For example, impulsive, violent action leading to suicide
may be observed in patients presenting with cognitive disturbances.

   Their inner conflicts in relation to the main problems inherent in the crisis or
to suicidal motivations lend themselves to psychodynamic explanations. Again
these explanations rely upon a series of presuppositions, such as:
— unconscious mind, unconscious motivations;
— structures in the personality, such as ego and superego;
— functioning of defense mechanisms;
— complexes;
— transferences; and
— determination of psychological mechanisms in the personality by early experiences and object relations, etc.

In terms of methodology, a psychodynamic approach means the use of empathy
in diagnosis and treatment, interpretations, establishing a helping relationship (a
therapeutic situation with specific rules), handling transference mechanisms in
an appropriate way, etc.

   This is the classical Freudian version of the psychodynamic approach. There
are many modifications of it, which, however, also include this classical, standard
approach, where understanding, emotional support, catharsis and strengthening
the ego are the main tasks in dealing with a suicidal crisis. Stekel — a pupil and
later a rival of Freud — insisted on a more direct approach to the suicidal person.
According to Stekel, suicidal crisis mainly consists of the individual's guilt feelings, intents of revenge, selfpunishment, wishes to escape from problems or dis-
torted perceptions of reality.

   Adler, equally a pupil and rival of Freud, pointed out the reactivation of the
reparative, reconstructive forces of the ego which is very weak and disturbed as
manifested in the suicidal decision and act. According to Adler, the ego tries to
protest against the environment and tries to reassess itself and restore its dignity.

   Adler's theory has mainly had an impact on European thought on suicidology,
in the form of a recommendation to accept the suicidal person's inner verdict
on his or her life and the definition of his or her situation as a basis of communication and contact. In Germany, the usefulness of this approach is demonstrated
by a study by Wedler [3]. This is also the viewpoint of Erwin Ringel, the founder
of IASP, whose theory of presuicidal syndrome is more or less forgotten in the
English-speaking world. According to Ringel, there is a narrowing, a restriction
of emotional and cognitive processes to the predominant problem, to the issue

of crisis, aggression is turned against one's own self and there is a preoccupation of a suicidal action in fantasy as a solution to the problem.

This syndromatic description of suicide risk stresses several points of intervention, targeting on each of the main processes involved in the model, that is the problem as reflected in emotions and cognitions, the aggressive impulses and the processes of fantasy [4].

Other psychodynamic approaches emphasize various psychological mechanisms, such as regression, specific sensitivities in object relations, magical fantasies of rebirth, denial of death as a consequence of self-destruction, etc. All these aspects have some relevance to the therapeutic work with suicidal persons.

New forms of psychodynamic approach highlight specific sensitivities and vulnerabilities of the ego; these are the theories of narcissism. They presuppose the etiological role of narcissistic traumas in suicide. These approaches put suicidal crisis in the context of the life history of the person and hypothesize that it is in essence a narcissistic crisis. According to this view, the developmental process of the ego is distributed and a pathological compensation of damaged self-esteem and negative self-image takes place. The emerging system of emotional self-regulation, where superego functions in a rigid and destructive way and there are grandiose delusions, idealized object relations, symbiotic relations to significant others, etc., make the ego vulnerable for narcissistic traumas.

These traumas, losses, frustrations, failures, rejections, etc. decompensate this system of emotional self-regulation, create a crisis in self-esteem and a sense of catastrophe in the narcissistic personality. If narcissism is strong, a crisis may arise in consequence of minor, but symbolically significant traumas. The decision of suicide reaction means in such cases as regression to an early, secure level of object relations and at the same time a pathological attempt of the reintegration of ego functions. The most elaborated form of this approach is found in Henseler's theory [5], in which several (10—12) dysfunctional mechanisms of emotional and cognitive processes are identified which play a part in the suicidal crisis and which yield themselves to psychotherapeutic intervention. The theory is a multifactorial, dynamic formulation, in which the constellation of factors and their impact explain the probability and outcome of the suicidal response to the traumatic situation. Henseler studied cases of parasuicide and pointed out the vulnerability of narcissistic personality structures to new traumas and thereby to new suicidal crises.

Later developments in the psychodynamic approaches also underlined the pathological narcissism of the personality and the role of a specific structure called borderline syndrome [6,7]. According to these theories borderline personalities are prone to repeated suicide attempts. In many occasions these attempts are clearly parasuicides and thereby they are means of interpersonal appeal, repetitions of early traumas and effort to restitute control over interpersonal situations. In some cases, however, these suicidal crises can lead to completed suicides in order to get rid of introjected, split parts of "bad ego" or to satisfy impulses of a rigid and punishing superego. Theories of borderline personality recommend special therapeutic interventions only in severe narcissistic pathology, while parasuicidal crisis can be treated in regular therapeutic framework. Parasuicidal reactions are often self-injuries, self-damages, obviously results of discharges of emotional tensions, not aimed to endanger life [8], while specific traumas, albeit symbolic ones, might elicit really dangerous suicidal crises. In borderline personalities, tensions and conflicts interfering with the therapeutic relationship may lead to parasuicidal reactions, and states of narcissistic transference may end in serious and dangerous suicidal crisis.

A new formulation of borderline personality theory [9] gives an even more elaborated description of the development and functioning of narcissistic disturbance of the ego. It stresses the central importance of close interpersonal relationship to the borderline personality and at the same time its inability to maintain them. The result is an emergence of unrelenting, unremitting crisis in the interpersonal field and a risk of suicide manifestations as attempts to control the situation and to act out aggressive impulses. An inhibited capacity of grieving makes these personalities unable to work through these relational problems. This complex theory is a very detailed guideline to therapeutic intervention. Interestingly, the recommended processes of therapy are mainly cognitive and behavioral techniques, which aim to make changes in the cognitive mechanisms of the ego functions and the acquisition of new skills in interpersonal behavior.

This later development shows that psychodynamic approaches tend to facilitate therapeutic interventions in general; nowadays they depart from the classical conceptual framework of psychoanalysis and go towards integrative, eclectic directions. Their complex nature makes research difficult but clinical studies and observations support their usefulness. They are also useful in elucidating the specific vulnerabilities of certain forms of personality development and functioning of the ego, and therefore in making sense of highly irrational manifestations and reactions concerning suicidal states. They have weaknesses in explaining suicidal crises in terms of classical crisis theory because of their concentration on intrapsychic processes and on the specific distortions of the therapeutic relation (transference). Their combination with the classical crisis theories bring obvious benefits, since these theories suggest assessment and mobilization of interpersonal resources, immediate emotional support, use of group forces in crisis resolution and therapy, recommend therapeutic work in the immediate problems of the crisis and on the here and now level of the encounter with the suicidal person. Recent developments of psychodynamic approaches, based on the concept of the borderline personality extend the therapy of such disorders to the use of different group therapies, in the frame of therapeutic communities [10,11].

Both crisis theory and psychodynamic approaches are based on experiences with persons at risk for suicide or with persons after a suicide attempt. It cannot be excluded that completed suicides involve different psychological mechanisms. In many cases there is an impression of an almost complete cessation of cognitive processes and a takeover of enormous affectual tension which enforces a violent action in order to escape from it or to get rid of it. A proponent of the psychodynamic approaches, Menninger described in his system theoretical elaboration of psychodynamics [12] that the breakdown of basic regulatory mechanisms threatens the person with annihilation and total loss of control, and therefore causes a vital panic. This might be the case in the large part of suicides which have not been known previously to professionals, and where mental diseases, such as schizophrenia or melancholia (depression) are believed to have an etiological role or where biological factors are suspected to have operated. In many of these cases, however, psychodynamic theories seem useful in psychological autopsies and retrospective studies, and they certainly give clues to understanding of failures in crisis interventions and other therapeutic efforts to counteract suicide. Both the crisis framework and the psychodynamic approaches, therefore, merit further elaboration and research and in the future they may hopefully contribute to the understanding of suicidal process.

Suicidal crises and manifestations seem to be today increasing in number, especially in cases of fatal illnesses. This tendency can have several explanations. More people live alone without sufficient support systems. Thus, serious chronic illness may be a great burden for them. There is less tolerance of suffering because of individualization and secularization. Personal autonomy is more important today than it has been previously. There is now a climate, a general attitude favourable for asserting the right of decision over one's own death and dying.

Fatal diagnosis is felt in general as a narcissistic trauma or a catastrophe. The disclosure of the diagnosis to the patient usually induces ideas of suicide, if denial is not too strong. Decisions concerning irradiation, operations or chemotherapy programmes usually increase ideas and fantasies of self-inflicted death. Those persons are suspected of having some fatal illness (most of them have had serious symptoms, pains or losses of functions before diagnosis) have an increased risk of suicidal crisis. The simple communication of diagnosis either to the patient or to the family is therefore not recommended, both from a practical and ethical point of view. It is frequently forgotten that disclosing a fatal diagnosis to the patient should be a sort of psychological operation. A previous assessment is necessary. Psychiatric status, existential situation, interpersonal resources, skills and positive experiences of coping, specific weaknesses and vulnerabilities, etc. have to be assessed. The communication of diagnosis, if necessary, can be a result of several meetings with the patient and the family and sometimes it requires techniques of psychotherapy or family therapy. The risk of suicide has to be taken into account, especially with narcissistic, impulsive, perfectionist personalities.

After diagnosis the majority of patients receive more support from family and friends while denial exerts a protective effect. Painful and incapacitating treatments after a shock may be followed by further denial. Again there is a need for careful psychological work with the patient and relatives. Use of self-help groups is beneficial and a decision of laryngectomy or colostomy cannot be viewed psychologically and ethically adequate, if a meeting with somebody who has been successfully rehabilitated after that condition is not arranged. Without a proper

206

support system patients before or after incapacitating or mutilating therapies are at great risk for suicide or suicide attempts which might warrant psychiatric intervention. Depressive states occur frequently in this stage. Conflicts with spouse and other family members in this phase can be very dangerous (but again, psychological help should be given).

After the long process of coping with symptoms, complications and treatment consequences of the illness, in a deteriorating state and with loss of many capacities and functions, depressive conditions might often develop without major conflicts or crises. This is the period, however, when relatives usually become exhausted and overburdened and the therapeutical relationship with doctors and nursing staff is strained. A prolonged period of illness and treatment is conducive to feelings of hopelessness and despair. In this phase, patients do not have access to means of suicide and therefore they tend to ask relatives and nursing personnel for euthanasia. If there is a lot of pain and the methods used for pain reduction do not bring success, this situation can be desperate for the patient and the family. Doctors frequently withdraw themselves from this phase, at least on the level of discussion of the problem. There are frequent overdoses due to the collection of medication by the patients themselves. On many occasions it is not discovered by the staff (the patient usually ingests smaller amounts of medicines trying to avoid detection), or it is benevolently overlooked in order not to hurt the turbulent therapeutic relationship any further. Deep regression, challenging behavior, and increased sensitivity can be observed frequently during this phase of illness and treatment. Later demands for symptomatic relief are voiced. On many occasions hidden attempts at suicide occur. Refusal of food, avoiding medication, e.g., by misinforming the subsequent shifts of staff, or manipulating with infusions or medical appliances belong to these attempts, for which responsibility is usually denied. These attempts are meant to be kept secret in respect of relatives. These may be a result of lack of communication between the patient and the family as well as between the patient and the staff. The diagnosis of depression is usually given in this phase and treatment is offered for it. The real intervention is the improvement of communication processes. This can be started on the nursing level. Increasing attention to the nursing and caring needs, small talk and preparations may be very beneficial. Open communication with religious counsellors or other related professionals may also be very helpful. On the basis of good contact and personal encounter the issue of suicide can be addressed directly. If possible, involving relatives so that they can help the patient through periods of despair and hopelessness can improve communication between the family and the patient; it may also contribute to an adequate solution to grief and the mourning reaction of the survivors later.

References

1. Shneidman ES, Farberow NL, Litman RE. The Psychology of Suicide. New York: Science House, 1970.

2. Shneidman ES. The Definition of Suicide. New York: Wiley, 1985.
3. Wedler H-L. Der Suizidpatient im Allgemeinkrankenhaus. Krisenintervention und psychosoziale Betrennung von Suizidpatienten. Stuttgart: F. Enke, 1984.
4. Ringel E. Selbstmordverhütung. Bern, Stuttgart, Wien: H. Huber, 1963.
5. Henseler H. Narcisstische Krisen. Zur Psycho-dynamik des Selbstmords. Hamburg: Rowohlt, 1974.
6. Gunderson GJ. Borderline Personality Disorder. Washington, D.C.: The American Psychiatric Press, 1984.
7. Kernberg O. Borderline Conditions and Pathological Narcissism. New York: Janson Aronson, 1985.
8. Sachsse U. Selbstverletzendes Verhalten. Psychodynamik — Psychotherapie (2. Auflage). Göttingen: Vandenhoeck und Ruprecht, 1995.
9. Linehan MM. Cognitive-Behavioral Treatment of Borderline Personality Disorder. New York, London: The Guilford Press, 1993.
10. Ammon G. Dynamische Psychiatrie. München: Kindler, 1980.
11. Ammon G. Der mehrdimensionale Mensch. Zur ganz-heitlichen Schau von Mensch und Wissenschaft. München: Pinel Verlag, 1988.
12. Menniner K, Mayman M, Pruyser P. The Vital Balance. The Life Process in Mental Health and Illness. Middlesex: Penguin, Harmondsworth, 1963.

Assessment of suicidal behavior in adolescence

Stavroula Beratis

Department of Psychiatry, School of Medicine, University of Patras, Patras, Greece

Abstract. Several factors should be taken into consideration in assessing suicidal risk in adolescence. These factors are:
1. The presence of a psychiatric disorder, especially major depression.
2. Various indices of psychopathology, such as previous suicide attempts.
3. Presence of stressful factors.
4. Feelings of hopelessness.
In evaluating Greek youngsters who attempted suicide, two factors were identified as the major risk factors leading to suicidal behavior. The first factor was the restriction of the youngster's personal freedom, imposed by the parents, and the second one was the presence of a psychiatric disorder, especially dysthymic disorder. In investigating all completed suicides by Greek individuals from 10 to 19 years of age, from 1980 through 1987, we found that risk factors were the presence of a psychiatric disorder, strained relationships between the young victims and their parents, and failed love affairs. It was shown that cultural factors and customs have an effect on suicidal risk and should be taken into consideration in assessing the suicidal behavior of Greek adolescents.

Keywords: evaluation of suicide, suicidal attempts, suicide.

Introduction

The adolescent period of human development, characterized by the growing individuation and autonomy, is particularly vulnerable to the appearance of suicidal ideation and behavior [1–3]. Completed suicide, being a rare phenomenon during childhood, increases significantly during adolescence [4].

Several factors should be taken into consideration in assessing suicidal risk in adolescence.

Presence of a psychiatric disorder

The relationship between psychiatric disorders and adolescent suicide is well-established. In psychological autopsy studies of adolescent suicide it has been found that Axis I psychiatric disorders are present in about 90% of suicide victims [5,6]. It has been shown by certain investigators that affective disorders in general and major depression specifically are the most significant risk factors for completed suicide in adolescents [6,7]. Also, bipolar disorder is related to adolescent suicide and according to certain studies bipolar disorder II is very

Address for correspondence: Stavroula Beratis MD, Department of Psychiatry, School of Medicine, University of Patras, 265 00 Rion, Patras, Greece. Tel./Fax: +30-61-994-534.

closely associated with suicidal behavior in general [6]. Other studies, however, have shown that substance abuse and antisocial behavior are the conditions mostly associated with youthful and adolescent suicide [8–11]. Also, various personality disorders, especially those with impulsive, dramatic and dependency trends [12], as well as antisocial, borderline and narcissistic [13] personality disorders, have been associated with adolescent suicide.

Suicidal attempts in adolescence have been linked to mood disorders [14,15], to alcohol and drug abuse [16], to conduct disorder [17] and to personality disorders, especially borderline personality disorder [18].

Other indices of individual psychopathology

Previous suicide attempts have been linked to completed suicides [19] and to suicidal attempts [20]. Also state and trait anxieties are considered risk factors for adolescent suicidal behavior, but only trait anxiety is independent of coexisting depression in its effect on suicidal behavior [21]. Academic difficulties have been associated with suicidal attempts [1,22].

Stressful factors

Youngsters who have experienced family stresses such as difficult parental divorce, death of a parent, sexual or physical abuse and suicidal behavior of family members, are potentially at risk for fatal and nonfatal suicidal behavior [23]. Also, it has been reported that suicide completers, the year before death, were more likely to have experienced conflicts with parents and boy or girl-friends, failed love affairs and legal or disciplinary problems [24]. The stressor of a physical illness may increase the possibility for the manifestation of suicidal behavior [25]. Family psychopathology in general, especially parental depression and alcoholism have been linked to adolescent suicidal behavior [23]. It has also been reported that children of parents with somatization disorders are at risk for demonstrating suicidal attempts [26].

State of hopelessness

Hopelessness has frequently been reported as being a good predictor of suicidal intention [27] or eventual suicide [28]. However, there are conflicting reports about the relationship of hopelessness to suicidal behavior in children and adolescents. According to certain investigators hopelessness was not related to suicidal ideation [29] and behavior, especially when depression was controlled [30]. Others have reported a positive association [31].

All the factors mentioned above place a youngster at risk for suicidal behavior and in assessing such youngsters we should evaluate them for suicidal thoughts and acts and for preoccupation with death.

Suicidal attempts by Greek adolescents

In a study of suicidal behavior of Greek adolescents, we evaluated youngsters up to 16 years of age who, because of a suicidal attempt, were brought to the emergency room of the Department of Pediatrics of the University of Patras Medical School. The suicidal youngsters were compared to a control group matched for age, sex and parental socioeconomic status. Of the 29 youngsters who attempted suicide, 27 were female and two were male.

The findings demonstrated that half of the adolescents who attempted suicide were subjected to severe restriction of their personal freedom, which they claimed as being the reason for the attempt. The youngsters' parents limited their independent activities outside the house to almost none, fearing that the adolescent individuation and growing autonomy would lead them to sexual delinquency and drug abuse. It should be noted that this parental oppressive behavior coincided with the beginning of adolescence and the blooming of sexuality. This restriction of freedom emerged as the major stressful factor leading Greek adolescent girls to suicidal attempts.

Although social isolation has been identified as a major characteristic of adolescents involved in suicide attempts [1], in the population we investigated, 57% of the attempters were severely isolated, but in 46% of them the isolation was imposed upon by their parents.

Quarrels and poor communication between the attempters and their parents were observed in two out of three cases, but in three out of four of them, the quarrels were the direct result of the restriction of personal freedom imposed on the adolescents by their parents.

At least one psychiatric disorder was identified in one out of two of the attempters studied, dysthymic disorder being the most frequent. The other half of the attempters demonstrated various relational problems and primarily parent-child relational problems.

Only one in four of the attempters had experienced broken homes through divorce, death, or separation of the parents. Also, parental drinking, child abuse, or previous suicide attempt by another family member, and physical ill health, or use of drugs by the attempters were noticed infrequently.

What seemed to be of importance for the manifestation of the suicidal behavior in these youngsters, in addition to the restrictions imposed by their parents, was their conviction that they could not find a way to get out of this situation. This conviction would lead to extreme frustration and despair. Also, the absence of hobbies and other interests would increase the possibility for the manifestation of suicidal attempts.

Completed suicides by Greek adolescents

We investigated all completed suicides in Greece of individuals between 10 and 19 years of age, from 1980 through 1987. During the 8-year period of the study,

3,044 cases of completed suicides were recorded. Of those who committed suicide, 118 were between 10 and 19 years of age.

Of the 118 individuals, 10–19 years old, who committed suicide in the whole country, 66 were boys and 52 were girls. The difference between boys and girls is not significant ($p > 0.3$). The average suicide rate per 100,000 adolescent population per year in the whole country was 0.98 (boys: 1.07, girls: 0.89). The suicide rates of the adolescent population in the metropolitan area of Athens and in the rest of the country except Athens were 0.48 and 1.19, respectively.

Boys showed a greater suicide rate than girls in both the metropolitan area of Athens and the urban areas, but this difference in the rate of suicide was not significant ($p > 0.2$ and $p > 0.3$, respectively). On the contrary, in the rural areas girls committed suicide more frequently than boys, but the difference again was not significant ($p > 0.5$).

It should be noted that the rate of suicide in the mixed population of boys and girls was significantly greater in the rural areas than in the area of Athens ($p < 0.001$) and the other urban areas ($p < 0.05$). In addition, girls committed suicide significantly more frequently in the rural areas than in the area of Athens ($p < 0.001$) and the other urban areas ($p < 0.02$). Similarly, boys committed suicide significantly more frequently in the rural areas than in the area of Athens ($p < 0.05$). However, the difference in the suicide rate between boys living in the rural areas and other urban areas but Athens was not significant ($p > 0.5$).

It is of interest that the adolescent suicide rate was lowest in the area of Athens and highest in the rural areas, as well as that there were differences in the relative rates of suicide between boys and girls among the populations of these areas. These observations may reflect existing differences among the population in the urban and the rural areas. These include differences in moral, social, and family values, in the attachment to traditional customs, in the degree of parental interference in the youngsters' life and in the ability of adolescents to find emotional outlets (frustrations may result from limited opportunities in the rural areas).

Psychiatric disorders were the most frequent reason for suicide recorded in the total population of the country, being significantly more frequent in boys than in girls ($p < 0.001$). This was particularly true for boys and girls living in the metropolitan areas of Athens and other urban areas. However, significant differences in the reasons for suicide were observed between the rural areas and the rest of the country (area of Athens and other urban areas). The most frequent reasons for suicide in the rural areas were family problems in the form of strained relationships between the young victims and their parents, romantic problems with psychiatric disorders ranking third. The impact of family problems on the frequency of suicide in the rural areas was significantly greater in girls than in boys ($p < 0.05$).

Although a failed love affair was a major reason for suicide in female adolescents throughout the country, its frequency was greatest in the rural areas. This factor was three times less frequent in male suicides, being again more frequent in boys from the rural areas than in those from the rest of the country. This observation seems to reflect the difference in ethical values regarding adolescent sexual freedom between the rural and urban areas, as well as the greater oppression of female youngsters, for whom premarital sexual relations are less accepted than for males.

The findings that psychiatric disorders were the most frequent cause of suicide in male adolescents underlines the different etiologies that lead to suicide in adolescents of the two sexes. It indicates that factors related to individual psychopathology may be more prevalent in boys, whereas stressful environmental factors may be more prevalent in girls.

Conclusions

Is assessing the suicidal behavior of Greek adolescents several issues should be taken into consideration:
1. Cultural factors and customs are determining the relevant importance of the causes that may lead adolescents to suicidal behavior.
2. A suicide attempt, in some cases, may be an alternative for the female youngster to indicate that she feels emotionally suffocated and is trying to find escape from parental oppression, which impedes her progress to autonomy and individuation.
3. A variability of factors exists within the country, having an effect on adolescent suicidal behavior, as illustrated by the different suicide rates, the different male to female suicide ratios, and the different relative importance of the reasons leading to suicide observed in the urban and rural areas of the country.

References

1. Rohn DR, Sarles RM, Kenny TJ, Reynolds BJ, Heald FP. Adolescents who attempt suicide. J Pediatr 1977;90:636−638.
2. Tabachnick N. The interlocking psychologies of suicide and adolescence. Adolesc Psychiat 1981; 9:399−410.
3. Brent DA, Kalas R, Edelbrock C, Costello AJ, Dulcan MK, Conover H. Psychopathology and its relationship to suicidal ideation in childhood and adolescence. J Am Acad Child Psychiat 1986;25:666−673.
4. Shaffer D, Fisher P. The epidemiology of suicide in children and young adolescents. J Am Acad Child Psychiat 1981;20:545−565.
5. Brent DA, Perper JA, Goldstein CE, Kolko DJ, Allan MJ, Allman CJ, Zelenak JP. Risk factors for adolescent suicide: a comparison of adolescent suicide victims with suicidal inpatients. Arch Gen Psychiat 1988;45:581−588.
6. Brent DA, Perper JA, Moritz G, Alman C, Friend A, Roth C, Schweers J, Balash L, Baugher M. Psychiatric risk factors for adolescent suicide: a case-control study. J Am Acad Child Adolesc Psychiat 1993;32:521−529.
7. Shaffer D, Garland A, Gould M, Fisher P, Trautman P. Preventing teenage suicide: a critical review. J Am Acad Child Adolesc Psychiat 1988;27:675−687.
8. Rich CL, Young D, Fowler RC. San Diego suicide study: 1 young versus old subjects. Arch Gen Psychiat 1986;43:577−582.
9. Rich CL, Sherman M, Fowler RC. San Diego suicide study: the adolescents. Adolescence 1990; 25:856−865.

214

10. Shaffer D, Garland A, Gould M, Fisher P, Trautman P. Preventing teenage suicide: a critical review. J Am Acad Child Adolesc Psychiat 1988;27:675–687.
11. Martunnen MJ, Aro HM, Henriksson MM, Lönnqvist JK. Antisocial behavior in adolescent suicide. Acta Psychiatr Scand 1994;89:167–173.
12. Brent DA, Johnson BA, Perper J, Connolly J, Bridge J, Bartle S, Rather C. Personality disorder, personality traits, impulsive violence, and completed suicide in adolescents. J Am Acad Child Adolesc Psychiat 1994;33:1080–1086.
13. Marthunen MJ, Aro HM, Henriksson MM, Lönnqvist JK. Mental disorders in adolescent suicide. DSM-III-R Axes I and II diagnoses in suicides among 13 to 19-year-olds in Finland. Arch Gen Psychiat 1991;48:834–839.
14. Pfeffer CR, Klerman GL, Hurt SW, Lesser M, Peskin JR, Siefker CA. Suicidal children grown up: demographic and clinical risk factors for adolescent suicide attempts. J Am Acad Child Adolesc Psychiat 1991;30:609–616.
15. Kovacs M, Goldston E, Gatsonis C. Suicidal behaviors in childhood-onset depressive disorders: a longitudinal investigation. J Am Acad Child Adolesc Psychiat 1993;32:8–20.
16. Garfinkel BD, Froese A, Hood J. Suicide attempts in children and adolescents. Am J Psychiat 1982;139:1257–1261.
17. Apter A, Gothelf D, Orbach I, Weizman R, Ratzoni G, Har-even D, Tyano S. Correlation of suicidal and violent behavior in different diagnostic categories in hospitalized adolescents patient. J Am Acad Child Adolesc Psychiat 1995;34:912–918.
18. Brent DA, Johnson B, Bartle S, Bridge J, Rather C, Matta J, Connolly J, Constantine D. Personality disorder, tendency to impulsive violence and suicidal behavior in adolescents. J Am Acad Child Adolesc Psychiat 1993;32:69–75.
19. Brent DA, Perper J, Moritz G, Baugher M, Allman C. Suicide in adolescents with no apparent psychopathology. J Am Acad Child Adolesc Psychiat 1993;32:494–500.
20. Pfeffer CR, Klerman GL, Hurt SW, Kakuma T, Peskin JR, Siefker CA. Suicidal children grow up: Rates and psychosocial risk factors for suicide attempts during follow-up. J Am Acad Child Adolesc Psychiat 1993;32:106–113.
21. Ohring R, Apter A, Ratzoni G, Weizman R, Tyano S, Plutchik R. State and trait anxiety in adolescent suicide attempters. J Am Acad Child Adolesc Psychiat 1996;35:154–157.
22. Hawton K, O'Grady J, Osborn M, Cole D. Adolescents who take overdoses: their characteristics, problems and contacts with helping agencies. Br J Psychiat 1982;140:118–123.
23. Pfeffer CR. Life stress and family risk factors for youth fatal and nonfatal suicidal behavior. In: Pfeffer CR (ed) Suicide Among Youth: Perspectives on Risk and Prevention. Washington, D.C.: American Psychiatric Press, 1989;143–164.
24. Brent DA, Perper JA, Moritz G, Baugher M, Roth C, Balach L, Schweers J. Stressful life events, psychopathology, and adolescent suicide: a case control study. Suicide Life-Threat Behav 1993; 23:179–187.
25. Weinberg S. Suicide intent in adolescence: a hypothesis about the role of physical illness. J Pediatr 1970;77:579–586.
26. Livingston R. Children of people with somatization disorder. J Am Acad Child Adolesc Psychiat 1993;32:536–544.
27. Dyer JAT, Kreitman N. Hopelessness, depression and suicidal intent in parasuicide. Br J Psychiat 1984;144:127–133.
28. Beck AT, Brown G, Berchick RJ, Stewart BL, Steer RA. Relationship between hopelessness and ultimate suicide: a replication with psychiatric outpatients. Am J Psychiat 1990;147:190–195.
29. Pfeffer CR, Lipkins R, Plutchik R, Mizruchi M. Normal children at risk for suicidal behavior: a two-year follow-up study. J Am Acad Child Adolesc Psychiat 1988;50:202–209.
30. Cole DA. Psychopathology of adolescent suicide: hopelessness, coping with beliefs and depression. J Abn Psychol 1989;98:248–255.
31. Asarnow J, Guthrie D. Suicidal behavior, depression and hopelessness in child psychiatric inpatients: a replication and extension. J Clin Child Psychiat 1989;18:129–136.

Suicide: Biopsychosocial Approaches.
A.J. Botsis, C.R. Soldatos and C.N. Stefanis, editors.

Suicide in children and adolescents

Alan Apter

Department of Psychiatry, Sackler School of Medicine, University of Tel Aviv; and Child and Adolescent Division, Geha Psychiatric Hospital, Petach Tikva, Israel

Abstract. Completed suicide is rare before the age of 12. Adolescents are generally more prone to suicidal behavior. Actual suicide is more common in boys, while attempted suicide is more common in girls. Girls are often using suicidal behavior as a way of asking for help, while for boys the underlying force is usually severe psychopathology. Concomitant psychopathology in suicidal children and adolescents may be: depression, obsessive-compulsive disorder, substance abuse, eating disorders, borderline and other personality disorders, problems with gender identity. The most frequent means of completed suicide among young people is use of firearms, while the common way of attempting suicide is self-poisoning and wrist slashing. Programs of primary prevention are of doubtful effectiveness; it is estimated that through such school-based programs only 16 out of 12,000 suicides can be prevented. Secondary and tertiary prevention strategies aim at reducing the suicide rate among youngsters who are at high risk for suicide. High risk for suicide is indicated by: male sex, previous attempts, history of aggressive disorder, substance abuse, major mental disorder, hopelessness, severe social adversity, unwanted pregnancy or intractable eating disorder. In general, adolescent suicide attempters should be hospitalized until the suicide risk is no longer present.

Keywords: adolescents, children, psychopathology, suicide.

Introduction

Suicidal behaviors in children and adolescents have become increasingly common and collectively they represent a growing public health problem. Surveys in schools have found that many young people think about suicide, make suicidal threats and gestures and even report having made suicide attempts. In addition, adolescent subculture as represented by heavy metal and heavy rock music are full of references to the attractions of death and suicide. In most countries suicidal behavior is among the most likely reason for a young person to receive psychiatric treatment or to be psychiatrically hospitalized.

There is a close relationship between age and suicidal behavior. Before the age of 12 completed suicide is rare, possibly due to the family support which is relatively common at this age and because a young child does not have the cognitive maturity to conceive and carry out a suicide plan even though many children

Address for correspondence: Alan Apter MD, Chairman, Department of Psychiatry, Sackler School of Medicine, University of Tel Aviv, Director, Child and Adolescent Division, Geha Psychiatric Hospital, P.O.Box 102, Petach Tikva, Israel 49100. Tel.: +972-3-9358286/240. Fax: +972-3-9241041. E-mail: apter@post.tau. ac.il

do wish that they were dead. Sex differences are also marked with actual suicide being much more common in boys and attempted suicide being much more common in girls. This may be due to the fact that girls use less violent and less fatal means of attempting suicide than boys, e.g., most girls are self-poisoners while most boys use guns in their suicide attempts. In addition, it appears that girls are much more likely to use the suicide as a way of asking for help while for many boys the motivation force is severe psychopathology and the wish to die.

In some children and adolescents suicidal ideation starts at an early age and is a constant burden to the young person, greatly interfering with their quality of life. These children often suffer from concomitant psychiatric illness such as depression, obsessive compulsive disorder or eating disorders. In others suicidal ideation is not a static phenomenon but tends to wax and wane over time. Many times the suicidal behavior is impulsive without much thought and is related to anger and emotional instability. Many of these young people have a history of multi-impulsive behavior including substance abuse, bulimia and problems with authority.

The outcome of the suicidal behavior is intimately related to the method used. There is a disturbingly significant correlation between parental ownership of guns, especially hand guns and completed suicide. Indeed the most common method of completed suicide in children and adolescents is through the use of firearms, which accounts for about two-thirds of suicides in boys and almost half of the suicides among girls. Boys also often use hanging as a method of suicide although sometimes this is a complication of the psychosexual disorder of hypoxyphilia and not a real suicidal act. Carbon monoxide is the third most popular method of fatal suicide but accounts for less than 10% of male suicides in the young. Most nonfatal suicides are due to self-poisoning and wrist slashing. Self-cutting is a very frequently observed behavior in disturbed adolescents but usually the motive is tension relief rather than suicidal.

Issues of gender identity such as homosexuality are also well-recognized risk factors for adolescent suicide [1].

Epidemiology

This topic has been reviewed by Diekstra [2,3] and Hollinger [1]. Many countries have shown a considerable to very strong increase in the frequency of suicide in the 15- to 29-year-old age group in the past two decades. Since this first became apparent in 1965, some authors have suggested that we are dealing with a cohort effect. Around that time, the children of the postwar "baby boom" were coming of age. Their numbers were so big that the law of critical mass in demography came into effect. These young people became a factor in political destabilization expressing itself in the student revolts of the late 1960s. The size of the youth population also increased intrageneration competition and stress related to finding jobs and establishing careers. It has been shown that there is a positive correlation between the rate of youth suicide and the percentage of youths in the population. The relationship is stronger in males than in females, which is perhaps due to the former being more vulnerable to unemployment.

The Netherlands and the USA have had two peaks in youth suicide this century, the 1980s and the 1910s. The first scientific meeting on suicide took place in 1910 at the Viennese Psychoanalytic Society. The meeting was chaired by Alfred Adler and one of the main discussants was Sigmund Freud. The subject was inspired by several school epidemics that had occurred at that time in Austria and other middle European countries.

Explanations for the 1910 peak are speculative and include: rapid urbanization, introduction of compulsory education (thus defining modern adolescence), changes in the status of women, turning from religion to socialism, rapid population growth and mass production of liquor.

Theories on the recent outbreak have focussed on those countries with the most dramatic increases in youth suicide such as Ireland. In this country the rise in suicide has parallelled rises in illegitimacy, crime, alcoholism, unemployment and a decrease in the marriage rate. Other social factors that correlate with youth suicide are: a high divorce rate, a low percentage of under 15 year olds (i.e., low number of families), high unemployment, high homicide rates, increase in the number of people over the age of 65 years, increase of the numbers of females in university, change in the percentage of women employed, and changes in church membership.

An interesting example of this is in Ireland which has experienced extremely high increases in youth suicide rates [4]. Between 1976 and 1977 over 60% of university places were filled by males. This had fallen to 50% by 1990. Because girls on the whole do better than boys in their matriculation exams, many high prestige subjects, such as medicine, now have a higher preponderance of female students than males; this puts extra pressure on boys.

Furthermore, there have been striking changes in the nature of adolescence over the past decades. The secular trend has shown a decrease in the age at when the biological manifestations of puberty occur. For example, menarche used to occur between 16 and 18 years of age, whereas today it is closer to between 12 and 13 years of age. Thus, biological changes occur at a much earlier age when the adolescent is not psychologically and cognitively able to deal with these challenges.

In addition, the psychosocial moratorium, as described by Ericson [5], means that in today's society adolescence is greatly prolonged. The age at which young people have to commit themselves to marriage and children as well as a definite career has been greatly extended. There are also more leeways for experimentation with different identities such as homosexuality and delinquency. This psychosocial moratorium is important for the development of complex industrial societies but takes its toll on the psychic endurance and stable identity of youth.

Risk factors

Psychopathology

One consistent theme in the literature is that suicide and suicidal behavior are linked to a wide variety of psychiatric disorders, including affective illness, substance abuse, conduct disorder and schizophrenia [6]. Over 90% of adolescent and adult suicide victims appear to have at least one major psychiatric disorder. There is also an excess mortality among former adolescent male psychiatric outpatients. Pelkonenn et al. [7] looked at a cohort of 156 males and 122 female Finnish adolescents 10 years after having received outpatient psychiatric care. They found that 16 male subjects but no female subjects had died. The mortality for any cause for males was 10.3% and that for suicide was 7.1%. Current suicidal ideation and suicide attempts, poor psychosocial functioning and a recommendation for psychiatric hospitalization during the index treatment were associated with male mortality and suicidality.

There has also been recent recognition of the very definite increased risk for suicide in girls with eating disorders [8]. The relationship between anorexia nervosa (AN) and depression is well-documented, however, the suicide potential of these adolescents has been neglected in the literature, perhaps because these youngsters use denial to a large extent and because it was felt that starvation was the suicidal equivalent to obviating the need for a direct self-attack in these patients. It also appears that suicidal behavior may be an important portent of poor prognosis AN. Patton [9] followed-up 460 patients with eating disorders and found that the increased standard mortality rate in anorectic patients was mostly due to suicide, with death occurring up to 8 years after the initial assessment.

Borderline personality disorder (BPD) is traditionally associated with nonfatal suicide attempts but there is increasing evidence that fatal suicide is common in these patients as well. The topic has been extensively reviewed by Linnehan [10]. Intentional self-damaging acts and suicide attempts are the "behavioral specialty" of these patients. About 9% of patients with BPD eventually kill themselves. In a series of BPD inpatients followed for 10–23 years after discharge, patients exhibiting all eight DSM III criteria for BPD at the index admission had a suicide rate of 36% compared to 7% of people who exhibited five to seven of the criteria. It should be noted that about 75% of patients with BPD are women.

Adolescent substance abuse and suicidal behavior

This topic has recently been extensively reviewed by Kaminer [11]. Many studies have reported an elevated risk ratio for adults diagnosed with psychoactive substance abuse disorder (PSUD). Although there has not been extensive research on this subject in adolescence, it is well known that conduct disorders and mood disorders are frequently comorbid with both substance abuse and suicidal behavior. Brent et al. [6] found the following odds ratios (OR) for adolescent (completed) suicide risk factors: major depression (OR = 27); bipolar disorder (OR = 9); PSUD (OR = 8.5) and conduct disorder (OR = 6).

The relationship between suicide, aggression and alcoholism may be especially relevant to subjects with type 2 alcoholism. These persons are characterized by high novelty-seeking, low harm avoidance and low reward dependence. Here alcoholism has an early onset and is characterized by a rapid course, severe psychiatric symptoms, fighting, arrests, poor prognosis and multiple suicide attempts. Low levels of serotonin in alcoholism, depression, suicide and aggression have been hypothesized as the biological, etiological correlate of these behaviors.

Suicidal thoughts are experienced by more than 25% of college students between 16 and 19 years of age; in general research findings support a general nonspecificity for adolescent suicidal thoughts. However, students with PSUD have more frequent and more severe suicidal thoughts than average, they are also more likely to have a prolonged desire to be dead. PSUD was also found to be associated with more severe medical seriousness of actual suicide attempts.

Studies of completed suicide in adolescents have shown that in Scandinavia, Canada and the USA, PSUD is commoner among victims than in the general adolescent population. There is some evidence that alcohol and cocaine may be especially dangerous with regard to suicide, but this is yet to be validated.

Adolescents with PSUD, especially males, are more likely to commit suicide with guns than are adolescents without PSUD. Adolescent suicide also seems to be related to more chronic PSUD in subjects who have not sought treatment. In one study PSUD was typically present for at least 9 years before the suicide.

Impulsive rather than planned suicides by adolescents have been reported in large numbers. Many adolescents manifest suicidal behavior after an acute crisis such as perceived rejection or interpersonal conflict, an acute disciplinary act, sexual assault, or immediate loss. Intoxication for the purpose of self-medication, which often follows a crisis, may trigger suicide in an adolescent who feels shame, humiliation or frustration.

For any age group, intoxication often precedes suicide attempts. It has been suggested that adolescents may use psychoactive substances to bolster their courage to carry out the suicide attempt. Intoxication may also lead to impaired judgement and decreased inhibition and thus may facilitate suicidal behavior.

Social factors

Children and adolescents are vulnerable to overwhelmingly chaotic, abusive and neglectful environments. A wide range of psychopathological symptoms may occur secondary to growing up in abusive or violent homes, including all kinds of self-destructive behaviors such as suicidal acts.

Familial clustering of suicide and suicide attempts

This topic has recently been extensively reviewed by Brent [12]. The familial clustering of suicide and suicide attempts is well known. The relatives of suicide completers show high rates of attempts and completions compared to the relatives of community controls, friends, nonsuicidal controls and adoptive relatives. Family studies of the Amish indicate that 73% of the suicides were clustered in 16% of the pedigrees. In addition, patients who attempt suicide have been found to have much higher rates of attempts in their relatives than medical, psychiatric, or normal controls. Recent family studies of adolescent suicide completers [12] have shown that their first degree relatives show more suicide attempts, affective disorders, conduct disorders, antisocial personality disorders and impulsive violence. Similar results have been shown for adolescent suicide attempters [12]. Both studies showed that the transmission of suicidal behavior was independent of the transmission of a psychiatric disorder. Although it is plausible that familial transmission occurs to some extent through psychosocial and environmental influences such as imitation and exposure to psychosocial adversity and dysfunctional processes, there is some evidence from adoption studies that familial transmission can occur without exposure to a suicide model and conversely that exposure to an adoptive relatives suicide does not lead to suicidal behavior.

Biological factors

There appears to be an intimate relationship between the serotonergic parameters of aggression, impulsivity and suicidal behavior especially in young people [13]. Brent et al. [6] reported that adolescent suicide completers had more impulsive aggressive personality disorders than controls and had higher aggression ratings on a parent questionnaire. This seems to hold true for suicide attempters and for the families of adolescent suicide completers and attempters. Apter et al. [8] have also shown that adolescents with aggression and conduct disorders may be suicidal even in the absence of depression. Suicidal adolescent inpatients also exhibited a range of interrelated psychological behaviors (aggression, impulsivity and anxiety) that are related to serotonergic functioning.

Thus, a compelling argument can be made that all biological and molecular psychiatric research needs to be performed with a greater emphasis on the different dimensions or components of behavior that contribute to psychopathology without regard to particular nosology. This especially appears to be the case with regard to suicidality [14]. Currently, the most plausible biological system related to suicidality, impulsive violence and anxiety is the serotonergic system [14].

Regardless of the etiology of suicidal behavior in young people suicide attempts and suicide are extremely rare before puberty. Ryan et al. [15] reported altered prolactin and cortisol response to L5HTP in prepubertal depressed children but did not find any correlation with either aggression or suicidality. Kruesi et al.

[16] examined correlates of low CSF 5HIAA and did not find any correlations with aggression in preadolescent boys. However, on follow-up, when the boys were around 14 years of age, a strong correlation was noted [16]. Brent [17] after reviewing the evidence, suggested that aggression, particularly impulsive or reactive aggression, predates suicidal behavior, but that until the child enters puberty and becomes at risk for other pathological conditions like depression or substance abuse the risk for suicidal behavior is latent.

We [18] recently examined 152 adolescent inpatients, assessing the correlation between serum cholesterol levels and emotions and suicidal behavior in addition to other emotions connected with adolescent suicidal behavior such as aggression, impulsivity, depression and anxiety. The suicidal adolescents showed a significantly higher level of serum cholesterol compared to the nonsuicidal adolescents. This difference was not accounted for by gender. In the suicidal group of adolescents, however, there was an inverse relationship between serum cholesterol levels and severity of suicidal behavior. None of the other psychological dimensions assessed correlated with cholesterol levels, a finding similar to other reports in hospitalized children.

The peripheral-type benzodiazepine receptor (PBR) is involved in cholesterol translocation from the outer mitochondrial membrane to the inner membrane and its activity is influenced by hormonal changes and steroidogenesis [19]. Upregulation occurs in acute stress, while downregulation occurs in chronic stress [20] and in conditions such as posttraumatic stress disorder and general anxiety disorder [21]. We [22] recently examined the PBR in a group of suicidal adolescent inpatients and compared them to a group of nonsuicidal inpatients. The PBR density in the suicidal patients was significantly lower in the suicidal than in the nonsuicidal group. In addition, there was an inverse and significant correlation between the severity of the suicidal behavior, as measured by the suicide risk scale and the PBR density. This finding is probably related to the influence of stress on suicidal behavior but may also be a part of the association between cholesterol and suicidal behavior described above.

Contagion

Some psychiatric disorders of adolescence appear to spread by contagion. Thus, clusters of eating disorders, substance abuse and paranoia may occur among adolescents who are friendly or who go to the same school. This phenomenon seems to be well-established for suicide and attempted suicide among young people. The mechanism seems to be via a form of identification and thus the suicides are called copycat suicides. Sometimes it is stories in the press or on television that precipitate the "epidemic" of suicidal behavior, especially when the stories are presented in a dramatic fashion. This phenomenon which is still not fully established or understood is called the "Werther effect", after the protagonist in Johann Wolfgang von Goethe's novel "The Sorrows of Young Werther". The novel in which the hero kills himself was banned in some European countries more than 200 years ago because of the rash suicides by young men who had read it [24].

The relationship between attempted suicide ("parasuicide") and suicide

One of the most common everyday tasks of psychiatrists dealing with adolescents is the evaluation and acute management of young people who have made a suicide attempt, yet knowledge about the natural course of adolescents following suicide attempts is limited [25,26]. On the one hand there is evidence to show that adolescent suicidal behavior should always be taken very seriously, on the other many clinicians believe that overtreatment of these cases is not cost-effective and may even be counterproductive.

Many clinicians believe that suicidal behavior is one of the most significant risk factors for completed suicide among adolescents [3]. These authors point out that adolescent suicide victims are much more likely than community controls to have had a history of a suicide attempt. Prospective studies have also indicated that the risk of completed suicide is substantially elevated in those who have attempted suicide.

Adolescent attempters are also considered to be at higher risk for nonfatal re-attempts, however, although there have been many studies that have followed-up adolescent suicide attempters, it has often been difficult to contact these individuals and thus these studies have involved many methodological problems [25]. Repetitions of attempts reported a range as wide as 6.3—51%, while reported risk for completed suicide following an attempt in adolescence ranged from 0 to 9%. Lower completed suicide and nonfatal repetition rates are seen in nonpsychiatrically hospitalized samples and in younger suicide attempters [25]. Male attempters subsequently complete suicide more often than do female attempters.

There are, however, those who oppose the view that attempted suicide in adolescence is necessarily a portend of a morbid prognosis, especially in youngsters who have no history of a psychiatric hospitalization. In Europe, the term "deliberate self harm" has replaced the term "attempted suicide" reflecting a large body of literature distinguishing attempter populations from completer populations [2,3]. These workers point out that the attempt is frequently impulsive, the result of an unpredictable acute interpersonal conflict and, unlike completed suicide, unrelated to illness and symptom severity. Shaffi et al. [27] found that Hungarian adolescent attempters were far less likely to reattempt or to actually commit suicide than adult attempters. In addition, follow-up studies suggest that approximately half of all adolescent suicide attempters improve psychologically following a suicide attempt [25]. Angle et al. [28] reported a favorable outcome for adolescent attempted suicide irrespective of lethality of intent, parental loss, depression, diagnosis, availability of support systems and specific therapy. It has also been suggested that suicide attempts in males have a graver significance than attempted suicide in females.

We [29] recently compared adolescent subjects who made a suicide attempt with matched controls on psychological and psychometric screening tests for the military service in the Israel Defense Force at age 16.5 years and on their performance during military service between ages 18 and 21 years. We also compared the prognosis of those attempters who received intensive psychiatric evaluation in a general hospital with those who received emergency room treatment only. The computerized military records of 216 adolescents who had been treated for attempted suicide in a general hospital emergency, prior to their induction into the army were evaluated for scores on tests for cognitive/educational performance and psychosocial adaptation; for psychiatric and physical health diagnoses and for performance during their military service. Although female attempters had slightly more problems in the military than controls their overall prognosis was surprisingly good. Male suicide attempters did very poorly in their subsequent military service. There was no long-term advantage for psychiatric evaluation in hospital than for brief emergency room evaluation. Most differences were for service performance rather than for cognitive and psychometric tests. We concluded that there may be marked sex differences in the significance and indications for intervention in attempted suicide.

In another study we (Apter et al., submitted for publication) compared national samples of consecutively ascertained 18- to 21-year-old male recruits who completed suicide, were surgically hospitalized for a near-fatal suicidal attempt, or were referred by a unit medical officer to the IDF Central Mental Health Clinic for evaluation of a suicide attempt or gesture or nonsuicidal psychiatric crisis.

Subjects completing suicide and those making near-fatal attempts resembled each other and differed from nonsuicidal psychiatric controls and those with less serious overt suicidal behavior in terms of the former's apparent higher pre-induction physical, cognitive and psychological fitness; more demanding assignment (reflecting higher adaptive competency ratings); and higher prevalence of major psychiatric disorder, especially major depression, as diagnosed at the time of the suicidal episode. Those with suicidal ideation, but no action, also had a high prevalence of depressive symptoms and disorder. In contrast, those with less lethal attempts, gestures and threats were more likely to have carried a diagnosis of an adjustment disorder, but not major depression.

Despite this contrast between the extremes of those with the most severe suicidal behavior and those with less severe or none, there also appeared to be a gradient, such that those with intermediate degrees of suicidal behavior showed intermediate levels of severity of depression (HAM-D), the number of prior suicidal events, and presence of a suicide note at the time of the index event.

The discrepancy between the high psychological fitness of the most severely suicidal subjects, as judged prior to induction, and their more severe psychopathology, as assessed at the time of the suicidal episode, is striking and may have several sources. Since the preinduction assessment of these subjects preceded their entry into active duty by at least 1 year and the suicidal episode occurred on average 15.1–19.9 months following induction, it is possible that in the interim these subjects developed a major psychiatric disorder that was not present at the time of preassessment screening. In contrast, the less suicidal and nonsuicidal psychiatric controls were judged as being less psychologically sturdy prior to induction, as reflected in their lower combat suitability scores. It is also possible that the inductees in the completed suicide and near-fatal attempt groups were less open in revealing their vulnerabilities in the preinduction assessment and that this reluctance may have also made them less likely to seek help when they later encountered difficulty.

The data from this study underline the heterogeneity of suicidal behavior with respect to psychological and social context and communicative intent. Completed suicides and near-fatal suicides were more likely than other subject groups to have been in stressful front-line units. The interactive effects of personality, military occupational assignment and stress exposure, however, are difficult to disentangle in this sample, since those exposed to the most potentially stressful (i.e., front line) assignments were those judged to be most adaptively competent and able to tolerate stress. Despite the availability of medical and mental health officers at all levels of command, such units often have an ethos of stoicism in the face of adversity.

In contrast, less lethal suicidal behaviors and nonsuicidal psychiatric crises were more likely to occur in subjects who were in less demanding, noncombat units and often occurred impulsively in the context of a transiently stressful situation.

The completed suicides occurred, on average, later in the subjects period of compulsory active duty than did nonfatal suicidal episodes or nonsuicidal psychiatric crises leading to clinical presentation. Whether this is due to a greater accumulation of stress among the completers, relatively greater reluctance to have signalled for help prior to the breaking point, or some other factor, is unclear. Preliminary data from an instrument assessing perceived stresses and coping resources in military life suggest that the intensity and type of perceived stress in recruits vary with duration of service, but differently for recruits in front-line and support units.

Although in retrospect many of the suicide completers and near-fatal attempters had made prior suicidal attempts or communications, these were either not revealed to others or were made in a way that was not taken seriously. In contrast, prior attempts of other subjects were more likely to be impulsive acts of higher visibility; these subjects current attempts, which reflected poor stress resiliency, were relatively public ones. The usual consequence of such attempts is, and is widely assumed by recruits-to-be, a re-evaluation of the recruit's assignment, with reassignment to a less stressful unit being the most likely outcome. An effort to communicate distress and to effect a change in placement thus seemed implicit in many of these less serious attempts.

In terms of implications for prevention, these findings emphasize the importance of remaining alert to signs of depression, even in apparently well-functioning subjects, and, if suspected, the necessity of serious inquiry about current and prior history of suicidal ideation or attempts. From the perspective of suicide research design, it appears that although some forms of suicidal ideation or behavior can be conceptualized as falling on a continuum, important discontinuities and contrasts also exist.

Treatment

Primary preventative measures are intended to change the attitudes of unaffected individuals that might predispose them towards suicide. The majority of such programs are school-based and appear to operate on the assumption that, given enough stress, there is a universal predilection for suicide and it is therefore appropriate to direct preventative interventions at unselected groups of young people. Such programs have become increasingly popular in the USA, and in 1986 over 100 such programs existed there, reaching approximately 180,000 students. This approach has been critically reviewed by Shaffer et al. [30] and criticized on the following grounds:

1. They follow a low risk strategy: given the low base rate of teenage suicide very few of the adolescents receiving the programs are ever likely to commit suicide. e.g., in 1984 the rate for all 15—19 year olds was nine deaths per 100,000 population. Thus, if all the school-based programs in the USA were completely effective (and this is highly questionable) only 16/2,000 suicides would have been prevented.
2. The only systematic controlled study of three such programs in the USA found that before exposure to the school program most students held views and had knowledge of suicide that would generally be considered sound. They knew many of the warning signs, took the view that mental health professionals were helpful, and were aware that suicidal disclosures should be taken seriously, that suicidal disclosures should be managed by consultation with responsible adults and that suicidal preoccupations were best shared. Thus, most students do not seem to need such programs.
3. Between 5—20% of pupils expressed views that would generally be considered inappropriate. They stated that under certain conditions suicide was an appropriate solution to problems and that they would not reveal a suicidal confidence of a friend or seek professional help if they felt troubled. However, the programs had very little effect on these attitudes.

Garland et al. [31] examined survey response data characterizing 115 youth suicide prevention programs with experience implementing school-based prevention curricula. The typical program reached 17 schools encompassing 1,700 students during the 1986—1987 school year. Most programs covered facts about suicide, warning signs of suicide, mental health resources available to the students and techniques for getting a troubled student in touch with help. The great majority of programs (95%) reported that their theoretical approach was patterned after the "stress model" wherein suicide is seen as a response to extreme stress, to which everyone is vulnerable. Only 4% subscribed to the view that suicide is typically the consequence of a mental disorder. The investigators warn that the prevailing assumptions are not supported by the available scientific evidence. Suicide rarely occurs in the absence of a documentable psychiatric illness. Most teenagers under severe stress do not contemplate or attempt suicide. Referring to evidence from other studies, the authors argue that high-school students who have not been exposed to prevention programs, already know about suicide warning signs and "have very reasonable and favorable attitudes about seeking help for suicide-related problems". They cite one of their own studies showing that high-risk students (e.g., those who have made suicide attempts in the past) have negative reactions to some traditional programs, raising a concern that the students we are concerned about, leave the experience unaffected or more disturbed than they were beforehand.

Secondary and tertiary interventions aim at reducing suicide among youngsters who are at high risk for suicide. In view of what has been said above these are the most effective and efficient means of preventing suicide, however, they depend on finding out just who is at high risk for suicide.

A major problem in the management of adolescent suicide attempters is the failure of adolescent attempters to attend and complete treatment and the efficacy of such treatments is as yet uncertain [25,32]. It has been suggested that about half the adolescent suicide attempters do not receive adequate psychotherapy following their attempt. This may be due to the fact that, unlike adult suicide attempters, most adolescents do not make a suicide attempt in order to obtain formal psychiatric care or that emergency room intervention is sufficient for most cases. In addition, parental denial and psychopathology may interfere with treatment planning. Some clinicians have attempted to deal with this problem by mandating the admission of all adolescent suicide attempters to a general hospital for brief therapy and evaluation [33]. Although this method of approach has not been shown to result in significantly increased posthospitalization care [33], this policy has been widely adopted and has recently been made compulsory by law in Israel.

Although the literature is replete with suggestions for the appropriate treatment of teenaged suicide attempters [25], no satisfactory studies that have systematically evaluated such treatment (i.e., comparing outcome over a reasonable period of time with other treated or nontreated groups, using standard measures before the start of treatment at follow-up and random assignment to different treatment groups or the use of placebo or dummy interventions) have been made. This is probably due to the very complex methodological issues involved (Hawton (In press)). Most studies that have been undertaken have been done on predominantly adult attempters. In a paper quoted by Spirito et al. [25] a nonrandomized study was performed wherein a social worker was assigned to each adolescent suicide attempter seen in the emergency room. The role of the social worker was to help the adolescent keep their follow-up appointments, to provide support and to explore potential services available to the adolescent. In addition, an educational curriculum for schools, social services workers, health care personnel and police, was also conducted in the target area. Results of this study showed that research subjects were twice as likely to keep their clinic appointments and comply with medical recommendations. However, repeat suicide was not diminished.

Since family relationship difficulties are extremely common in adolescent attempters, one might expect that family therapy might be the most productive way of helping suicidal youngsters. This approach appears, however, to be severely limited in effectiveness in many cases because of the high rejection rate by parents, as reflected by high levels of nonattendance at treatment sessions [34].

Recently there have been several attempts to develop systematic "manualized" therapies for adolescent suicide attempters based on evidence that shows deficiencies of problem-solving abilities in adolescents shortly after the attempt. Some of these therapies have been shown to be of value in controlled trials [35]. One can express the hope that new findings emerging from the studies of young attempters could be used to enrich treatment programs which would then need to be evaluated in randomized controlled trials.

In general, adolescent suicide attempters who are at high risk for committing suicide should probably be hospitalized until the suicide risk is no longer present. High risk is indicated by the presence of: male sex; previous attempts; a history of aggressive behavior or substance abuse; the presence of a major mental disorder; depression especially when accompanied by social withdrawal; hopelessness and lack of energy, severe social adversity such as running away or a neglectful or abusive family; unwanted pregnancy or severe intractable eating disorder.

References

1. Holinger P, Offer D, Barter J, Bell C. Suicide and Homicide among Adolescents. New York, London: The Guilford Press, 1994;9—22.
2. Diekstra RFW. Suicide and the attempted suicide: An International Perspective. Acta Psychiatr Scand 1989;80(Suppl 354):1—24.
3. Diekstra R. On the burden of suicide. In: Kelleher M (ed) Divergent Perspectives on Suicidal Behavior. Cork: O'Leary Ltd., 1994;2—27.
4. Kelleher M. (Suicide and the Irish Mercier Press Cork. In: Angle CR, O'Brien TP, McIntire MS (1983).) Adolescent self poisoning: A nine-year follow-up. Devel Behav Pediat 1996;4:83—87.
5. Ericson E. Identity and the Life Cycle. New York: Norton, 1980.
6. Brent D, Kolko D, Wartella M, Boylan M, Moritz G, Baugher M, Zlenak J. Adolescent psychiatric inpatients' risk of suicidal attempt at 6-month follow-up. J Am Acad Child Adolesc Psychiat 1993;32(1):95—105.
7. Pelkonen M, Marttunen M, Pulkkinen E, Koivisto A, Laippala P, Aro P. Excess mortality among former male out-patients. Acta Psychiatr Scand 94(1);60—66.
8. Apter A, Gothelf D, Orbach I, Har-Even D, Weizman R, Tyano S. Correlation of suicidal and violent behavior in different diagnostic categories in hospitalized adolescent patients. J Am Acad Child Adolesc Psychiat 1995;34(7):912—918.
9. Patton GC. Mortality in eating disorders. Psychol Med 1988;18(4):947—951.
10. Linehan MM. Cognitive Treatment of Borderline Personality Disorder. New York: Guilford Press, 1993.
11. Kaminer Y. Adolescent substance abuse and suicidal behavior. Child Adolesc Psychiatr Clin North Am 1996;5(1):59—71.
13. Apter A, Brown S, Korn M, van Praag HM. Serotonin in childhood psychopathology. In:

Brown S, van Praag HM (eds) Serotonin in Psychiatry. New York: Bruner Mazel, 1990.

14. van Praag HM, Kahn RS, Asnis GM, Wetzler S, Brown SL, Bleich A, Korn ML. Denosologiza-tion of biological psychiatry or the specificity of 5HT disturbances in psychiatric disorders. J Affect Dis 1987;13:1–8.

15. Ryan ND, Birmaher B, Perel JM, Dahl RE, Meter V, Al-Shabout M, Iyengar S, Puig-Antich J. Neuroendocrine response to L-5-hydroxytryptophan challenge in prepubertal major depression. Arch Gen Psychiat 1992;49:843–851.

16. Kreusi MJP, Hibbs ED, Zahn TP, Keysor CS, Hanburger SD, Bartko JJ, Rapoport JL. A 2-year prospective follow-up of children and adolescents with disruptive behavior disorders: Prediction by CSF% HIAA, HVA and autonomic measures? Arch Gen Psychiat 1992;49:429–435.

17. Brent DA. Familial factors in adolescent suicide. In: King R, Apter A (eds) Adolescent Suicide. Cambridge: Cambridge University Press, (In press).

18. Apter A, Dror S, Weitzman A. Cholesterol levels and suicidal behavior in adolescence. Paper presented at the Israel Psychiatric Congress, Tel Aviv, 1997.

19. Kreuger KE, Papadopoulus V. Peripheral benzodiazepine receptors mediate translocation of cholesterol from outer to inner mitochondrial membrane in adrenocortical cells. Biol Chem 1990;265:15015–15022.

20. Drugan RC, Basile AS, Crawly JN, Paul SM, Skolnick P. Characterization of stress-induced alteration in 3H Ro 5-4864 binding to peripheral benzodiazepine receptors in rat heart and kid-ney. Pharmacol Biochem Behav 1988;30:1015–1020.

22. Weizman A, Burgin R, Harel Y, Gavish M. Platelet peripheral type benzodiazepine receptor in major depression. J Affect Dis 1995;33(4):257–261.

23. Apter A, Sireni N, Weitzman A, Gavish M. Peripheral GABA receptor function in suicidal ado-lescents. Paper presented at the Israel Psychiatric Congress, Tel Aviv, 1997.

24. Kaplan HI, Saddok BJ, Grebb JA. Suicide: Synopsis of Psychiatry. Baltimore: Williams and Wilkins, 1994.

25. Spirito A, Plummer B, Gispert M, Levy S, Kurkjan J, Levander W, Hagberg S, Devost L. Ado-lescent suicide attempts: outcomes at follow-up. Am J Orthopsychiat 1992;62(3):464–468.

26. Spirito A, Brown L, Overholzer J, Fritz G. Attempted suicide in adolescence: A review and cri-tique of the literature. Clin Psychol Rev 1989;9:335–363.

27. Shaffi M, Carrigan S, Zonda T. A longitudinal follow-up study of 583 attempted suicides, based on Hungarian. 1991.

28. Angle CR, O'Brien TP, McIntire MS. Adolescent self poisoning: A nine-year follow-up. Devel Behav Pediat 1983;4:83–87.

29. Apter A. Follow-up of adolescent suicide attempters. Paper presented at the regional WPA Con-ference, Geneva, 1997.

30. Shaffer D, Garland A, Gould M, Fisker P, Trautman P. Preventing teenage suicide: A critical review. J Am Acad Child Adolesc Psychiat 1988;27:675–687.

31. Garland A, Whittle B, Shaffer D. A survey of youth suicide prevention programs. J Am Acad Child Adolesc Psychiat 1989;28:931–934.

32. Hawton K. Suicidal behaviors in young people. In: Kelleher M (ed) Divergent Perspectives on Suicidal Behavior. Cork: O'Leary Ltd., 1994;96–106.

33. Swedo SE. Postdischarge therapy of hospitalized adolescent suicide attempters. J Adolesc Health Care 1989;10:541–544.

34. Taylor EA, Stansfield SA. Children who poison themselves: I. A clinical comparison with psy-chiatric controls. Br J Psychiat 1984;145:127–132.

35. Trautman PD, Rotherham Borus MJ. Cognitive behavior therapy with children and adolescents. In: Rush J, Allen F (eds) Review of Psychiatry, vol 7. Washington DC: American Psychiatric Press, 584–607.

© 1997 Elsevier Science B.V. All rights reserved.
Suicide: Biopsychosocial Approaches.
A.J. Botsis, C.R. Soldatos and C.N. Stefanis, editors.

The suicidal patient and the antidepressant drugs

Andreas I. Parashos

B' Dept of Psychiatry of Aristotelian University, Psychiatric Hospital of Thessaloniki, Thessaloniki, Greece

Abstract. Suicidal thoughts and suicide attempts are among the most life-threatening symptoms of severe depression. A number of surveys regarding the specific causes of suicide suggest that depressed patients will often use antidepressants to attempt or commit suicide. A completed suicide through an overdose of antidepressants is mostly due to antidepressants inherent cardiotoxicity and neurotoxicity. Thus, the toxicity of antidepressants is an important risk factor for suicidality and must receive the greatest attention by the prescribing clinicians. The highest rates of cardiotoxicity and neurotoxicity of antidepressants are associated with tricyclic drugs due to their quinidine-like myocardial depressant action leading from sinus tachycardia to major arrhythmias. Respiratory depression, convulsions, coma with shock or agitation, bowel and bladder paralysis and delirium are central, also peripheral toxic effects mainly due to their anticholinergic action. Regarding the MAO-inhibitors overdose, lethality is due to episodes of paroxysmal hypertension, intracranial haemorrhage, pulmonary oedema and circulatory collapse. The new antidepressants such as SSRIs, SNRIs and NaSSAs have been proved to be much safer in overdoses and lethal cases with some of these drugs have scarcely been reported. Therefore, an essential preventive policy for clinicians prescribing antidepressants to suicidal patients includes: 1) preferring drugs with less cardio- and neurotoxicity; 2) prescribing nonlethal quantities; and 3) entrusting the drug administration to a relative or a good friend of the patient.

Keywords: antidepressants lethality, NaSSA, prevention, SNRI, SSRI, suicide, TCA, toxicity.

Introduction

One of the substantial problems in management of depressive patients is their liability to attempt suicide by self-poisoning. Self-poisoning is usually attempted by prescribed antidepressant drugs and sadly many patients succeed by taking overdoses of such drugs [1—3].

Lethality of antidepressant drugs is mainly due to their inherent cardiotoxicity and second to neurotoxicity, although toxic effects in other organs, like the liver and kidneys, may play an additional factor.

In this respect, it is very important in clinical practice to recognise depressive patients at high risk for suicide and to prescribe for these patients the less toxic antidepressant drugs and in nonlethal quantities. This policy does not mean that other preventive measures should be neglected. It would be wise, for example, if

Address for correspondence: Assoc. Professor Andreas I. Parashos MD, B' University Department of Psychiatry, Psychiatric Hospital of Thessaloniki, 36, Konstantinoupoleos Ave., Stavroupolis, GR 56429 Thessaloniki, Greece.

as a routine measure the prescription for the drug(s) as well as the dispensed pills were delivered to and kept by a relative or a friend who would undertake the care of the patient, and who should also be informed about the risk for suicide. With regard to such a preventive policy, it is important for the clinician to be informed of the toxicity of antidepressants, and for him to keep up-to-date with the relative international literature.

Unfortunately, past and more recent literature on this issue has been ambiguous, due to the type of data available with respect to which drug is more or less toxic, which drug is more or less popular in attempting suicide and how many depressive patients attempt or complete suicide using antidepressant drugs, mainly because of methodological difficulties [4—6].

In this paper we attempt to compile some recent information about the toxicity of the currently used antidepressant drugs as well as their suggested implication in attempted or completed suicide.

Tricyclic and tetracyclic antidepressants

Severely depressed patients are most likely to undertake serious suicidal attempts and tricyclic agents, used to treat such patients, have been proved to possess the highest risk of serious or even fatal intoxication when overdosed, while tetracyclics follow tricyclics in toxicity [5,7,8]. Lethal intoxication of these drugs is primarily due to their cardiotoxicity and secondary to their neurotoxicity [8—11].

Most of the older cyclic antidepressants have been classified according to their fatal toxicity index (FTI). The FTI represents the known lethal cases per million prescriptions of each drug. Cassidy and Henry [5], Henry [6] and Henry and Alexander [7], registering the known lethal cases from cyclic antidepressants in the UK, ranked the FTI of these drugs as follows: desipramine 148.9, dothiepin 59.6, amitriptyline 56.1, nortriptyline 42.3, doxepine 40.6, imipramine 30.0, trimipramine 30.0, maprotiline 18.8, trazodone 12.3, clomipramine 9.9, mianserine 7.8, protriptyline 6.5 and nomifensine 2.4. Some other similar studies, although suggesting some different indices with respect to each one drug, coincide in the estimation that tricyclics are more toxic than other classes of antidepressants [1,2,8—11].

According to Kessel and Simpson [11], the relative cardiotoxicity of cyclic drugs is attributed not only to these drugs as such, but also and mainly to their hydroxy-metabolites. These authors classified some of the cyclic antidepressants from most offensive to least offensive as follows: hydroxy-imipramine → other hydroxy-metabolites of cyclic antidepressants → amitriptyline → imipramine → clomipramine → doxepin, maprotiline and amoxapine, while the secondary amines nortriptyline and desipramine are less cardiotoxic. The inherent cardiotoxicity of these compounds is mainly attributed, although not clearly, to their detrimental actions on intrinsic and extrinsic determinants of cardiac function, i.e., 1) in the autonomic nervous system innervation of the heart and blood vessels; 2) in "dysregulation" of some humoral factors, mainly catecholamines; and

3) in disturbance of membrane function of the electrically active tissues (i.e., the ordinary muscle and specialised conducting tissue [11,12]).

The atropine-like action of tricyclics, which block muscarinergic postganglionic vagal terminals, liberate atrioventricular nodal regions from vagal control, and result in an immediate sinus tachycardia. On the other hand, the inhibition of reuptake of biologically active monoamines, especially the norepinephrine by norepinephrinergic postganglionic sympathetic terminals, increases monoamine concentration in respecting synapses and provokes additional acceleration of pacemakers, speeds-up the conduction velocity, increases myocardial irritability and finally, by these energy-consuming processes, the contractility of myocardium is critically exhausted. Blockage of $\alpha 1$-adrenergic receptors in the periphery is the suspected cause for the postural hypotension [11,12].

The most important intrinsic feature of tricyclics, responsible for their myocardial toxicity, is the ability to stabilise electrically excitable membranes through the inhibition of $Na^+:K^+ATPase$ pump. This inhibition of the $Na^+:K^+ATPase$ system retards the influx-exflux movement of respective ions, an indispensable requirement not only for membrane polarisation and excitation but also for energy metabolism regulation of myocardial and specialised conduction tissues. These intrinsically provoked electrometabolic disturbances are demonstrated by an electrocardiogram (ECG) as a QRS complex prolongation of more than 500 ms (prolongation of ventricular depolarisation) and/or as deviations of the ST segment from the baseline (changes in the synchronisation of ventricular muscle depolarisation) [12].

Toxic overdoses with amitriptyline (plasma level higher than 350 ng/ml) can develop a first-degree heart block, while higher plasma levels (as high as 1,000 ng/ml) show a persistent QRS prolongation greater than 100 ms [11–13].

The clinico-laboratory evaluation of overdosed patients shows sinus tachycardia and fibrillation (enhanced atrioventricular conduction), partial or complete atrioventricular block (prolongation of QT interval), severe myocardial depression with prolonged action potential, reduced effective refraction period, increased threshold of excitability (and thereby atrial, ventricular and Purkinje tissue hypofunction), decreased cardiac output which together with a peripheral vasodilatation (because of the $\alpha 1$-receptors blockade) lead to serious hypotension and finally to cardiac arrest [11–13].

Therefore, patients taking large tricyclic/tetracyclic overdoses having a plasma level higher than 3-fold that of therapeutic levels (450–900 ng/ml, regarding the drug taken) should be carefully monitored as the cardiotoxic effect could be serious and the outcome could be fatal.

The neurotoxicity of cyclic antidepressants is also plasma concentration dependent. It is usually manifested by the sequential clinical pictures of agitation, confusion, delirium, seizures, coma and respiratory arrest, and finally death. Aged patients and women are more prone to neurotoxic consequences. The neurotoxic consequences of cyclic antidepressants are mainly attributed, although not exclusively, to their pharmacodynamic property to block the central postsynaptic muscarinergic receptors. As all subtypes of muscarinergic receptors are widely distributed in many brain circuits it is now unclear which pharmacological subtype(s) of these receptors could be involved. However, as the pharmacological actions of these drugs on many other types of receptors, at least of monoamines and amino acids, in the central nervous system are also considerable, these actions are certainly involved in the neurotoxic consequences of the cyclic drugs.

Amitriptyline is again the most potent antidepressant compound of all muscarinergic receptors subtypes in vitro, with the following being second in order: protriptyline, clomipramine, trimipramine, dothiepin, doxepine and imipramine; third in order: nortriptyline, desipramine, maprotiline and mianserine; and the least potent: amoxapine and trazodone [11,14].

A clinical picture of neurotoxicity is characterized by temporary agitation, confusion, tendons hyperreflexity, disturbances of temperature regulation, bowel and bladder paralysis, mydriasis, delirium, convulsions, coma, respiratory arrest, and finally death. The lethal doses of these drugs depend on the plasma levels of the paternal drug and their hydroxy-metabolites, and has been generally estimated to be 10- to 30-fold that of their mean therapeutic daily doses.

The most frequent causes of death are the disturbances of cardiac rhythm such as tachycardia, atrial fibrillation, ventricular flutter and atrioventricular or intraventricular block [11–14].

Monoamine oxidase inhibitors (MAO-I)

The classical monoamine oxydase inhibitors, nonhydrazine (tranylcypromine) and hydrazine derivatives (isocarboxazid, iproniazid, nialamide and phenelzine) were accepted as effective antidepressants, but a number of medicated patients died either after a hypertensive crisis with cerebral haemorrhage or after acute hepatotoxicity. Lethal toxicity in overdose after a "latent" period of some hours is characterized by a progressive development of signs and symptoms [3,15]. Cardiovascular symptomatology includes precordial pain, rapid and irregular pulse rate, hypertensive crisis and/or serious hypotension, vascular collapse, respiratory depression and failure, cool and clammy skin, hyperpyrexia and diaphoresis [3,16]. Symptoms of central nervous system intoxication may include drowsiness, dizziness, faintness or hyperactivity, agitation, irritability which subsequently gets worse, with complications such as severe headache, hallucinations, rigidity, trismus, opisthotonus, convulsions and coma [16].

It hardly needs be pointed out that life-threatening symptoms of cardio- and neurotoxicity arise slowly, reaching a maximum 24–48 h after ingestion of MAO-Is. Immediate hospitalization with intensive care monitoring is therefore essential, especially for the critical period after consumption of a toxic overdose of such drugs. In studies of FTIs, classical MAO-I in overdose is ranked as somewhat less toxic than heterocyclics [5,6]. Moclobemide, the new reversible inhibitor of MAO-A, (RIMA) has shown a good tolerance and in a number of patients who had attempted suicide (maximal known ingested quantity was 7,200 mg) the recovery was complete, while one death is known after moclobemide overdose from a hypertensive crisis [16].

Serotonin-specific reuptake inhibitors (SSRIs)

Five SSRI compounds — fluoxetine, fluvoxamine, paroxetine, sertraline and citalopram — have been marketed in most European countries, the USA and many other countries over the last few years. These compounds are widely recognised as effective antidepressants. Although clinical experience with these drugs is rather limited in comparison to the oldest antidepressants, e.g., heterocyclics and classical MAO-I, and for this reason extensive FTI data are not yet available, these drugs are reasonably acknowledged as being more tolerable and safe in overdoses [3,17–19].

In premarket clinical trials with fluoxetine, three deaths are known among 38 attempted suicides, but in these three lethal cases other drugs (maprotiline, codeine, alcohol) were also ingested. In one case an attempter took 3,000 mg of fluoxetine alone, without long-term toxical consequences [20,21]. FTI data for fluoxetine indicate one death from overdose per million prescriptions [21].

According to available data, 354 cases of overdose of fluvoxamine are known and from this population there were 19 deaths. Only in two of these cases was fluvoxamine alone implicated, while in the remaining 17, other drugs were also ingested. The highest reported nonlethal overdose of fluvoxamine was 10,000 mg and this patient recovered fully with no consequences [22].

No deaths were reported with certainty following acute overdose with paroxetine alone or in combination with other drugs and/or alcohol, 18 cases with doses up to 850 mg have been reported during premarketing clinical trials. Adverse events that were reported since the introduction of the drug onto the market include: acute pancreatitis, liver dysfunction, with one case of lethal liver necrosis, neuroleptic syndrome and some other less life-threatening side effects, but it is not clear if the only implicated compound was paroxetine alone or, as in most such cases, if other drugs were also ingested [23]. Seventy-nine cases of nonfatal overdoses involving sertraline were reported to date in 1992, of which 28 were overdoses of sertraline alone and the remainder involved a combination of other drugs and/or alcohol in addition to sertraline. The reported doses ranged from 500 to 6,000 mg. Although there were no deaths reported when sertraline was taken alone, there were four deaths involving overdoses of sertraline in combination with other drugs and/or alcohol [24,25].

Citalopram is the only SSRI not marketed in the USA, although it is widely prescribed in most European and other countries. Six forensic investigated suicides with overdoses of citalopram were reported by Ostrom et al. [26] in Sweden when postmortem plasma concentrations of citalopram varied between 5.2 µg and 49 µg/g in blood of the femoral vein, while the therapeutic concentration has been reported as being as low as 0.3 µg/g, measured under similar conditions. As a possible mechanism of death, cardiac arrhythmias were implicated. In another Swedish study [27] the signs and symptoms of high overdoses of citalopram were reported in five attempted suicides. All these patients survived after successful treatment at the hospital. The main signs and symptoms included prolonged QT intervals in ECG, sinus tachycardia, severe hypokalemia, and generalised seizures. The highest serum concentrations were 40–350 times higher than that of a 20-mg therapeutic dose [26,27].

The commonly observed adverse effects regarding accidental or intentionally overdosed patients with SSRIs include: drowsiness, nausea, vomiting, dyspepsia and dizziness. Other less common signs and symptoms are headache, nervousness, agitation, anxiety, insomnia, asthenia, abdominal pain, anorexia and dry mouth. In severe cases of 20-fold and more of higher therapeutic doses, in most of which other drugs and/or alcohol were also ingested, toxic syndrome includes tachycardia, bradycardia, hypertension, QRS prolonged interval in ECGs, hypokalemia, loss of consciousness, convulsions and coma [17–20]. Lethal outcome of such serious cases was rare (1.7 deaths per million prescriptions of SSRIs, in contrast to 34 deaths per million prescriptions of heterocyclics in the UK [7]. Some earlier studies and anecdotal clinical observations have suggested that SSRIs might provoke de novo suicidal thoughts in depressive patients who had not experienced such thoughts before the treatment with various SSRIs. The meta-analyses of the database of SSRIs have been scrutinised and the evidence clearly suggests that, rather than provoking, the SSRIs protect against the emergence of suicidal thoughts [17,18,21].

Serotonine and norepinephrine reuptake inhibitors (SNRIs)

More recently, two new antidepressant drugs with selective reuptake inhibition of serotonin and norepinephrine have been marketed in the USA, most European and other countries: nefazodone, a trazodone relative and venlafaxine. Although these drugs exert a strong inhibition on presynaptic reuptake of serotonin and norepinephrine [28], actions in which their antidepressant effects are attributed, they have not affected, at least in a clinically significant level, other neurotransmitters receptors (muscarinergic, α1-adrenergic, histaminergic) and for this reason are suggested as being more tolerable and safe in comparison to the heterocyclics. There is a very limited experience with nefazodone overdoses. In premarketing clinical studies there were seven reports of nefazodone overdose alone or in combination with other drugs. The amount of nefazodone ingested in accidental or intentional overdose ranged from 1,000 to 11,200 mg. None of these overdosed patients died. The more significant symptoms of these patients were nausea, vomiting and somnolence [29].

The human experience with overdoses of venlafaxine involves 14 patients who ingested either venlafaxine alone or in combination with other drugs and/or alcohol. The highest quantity ingested in one case was 6.75 g and in two others 2.75 and 2.50 g, respectively. All 14 patients recovered after hospitalization without sequelae. The symptoms reported were increased blood pressure, somnolence, sinus tachycardia, generalised convulsions in one case, and a prolongation of QT interval in the ECG (500 ms) in the patient who ingested 2.75 mg of the drug [30].

Mirtazapine (NaSSa)

A new antidepressant compound recently marketed in European countries is mirtazapine. Mirtazapine is characterized as noradrenergic and specific serotoninergic antidepressant (NaSSA). This drug enhances the noradrenergic activity inhibiting $\alpha 2$ noradrenergic presynaptic receptors (autoreceptors) and also increases serotonin activity stimulating $\alpha 1$-presynaptic receptors of serotonin neurones and blocking their $\alpha 2$ heteroreceptors. At the postsynaptic level of serotoninergic synapses it activates the 5HT1 receptors and blocks the 5HT2 and 5HT3 receptors.

The antidepressant effect of mirtazapine is attributed to these selective actions, while the blockade of 5HT2 receptors is suggested as a protection to the serotoninergic side effects [31,32].

Toxicity and lethal events with mirtazapine are few and need more investigation.

Conclusions

Depression is a serious mental disorder in which suicidal thoughts, suicide attempts and completed suicides are the most life-threatening problems in the treatment of depressive patients.

Antidepressant drugs prescribed for the treatment and relief of depressive patients are often used by those who have overt or covered self-destructive ideas to kill themselves.

All antidepressants in clinical use can be lethal if taken in overdoses, but their inherent toxicity is widely ranged. The older cyclic antidepressants and classic MAO-I are characterised as potentially dangerous in contrast to the antidepressants of the new generation (RIMA, SSRIs, SNRIs and NaSSAs) which have been proved to be much more tolerable and safe.

Thus, it is an essential preventive measure for clinicians prescribing antidepressant drugs to severely depressive patients, to choose the most effective but also the less dangerous drug and to deliver nontoxical quantities.

References

1. Henderson A, Wright M, Pond SM. Experience with 732 acute overdose patients admitted to an intensive care unit over six years. Med J Aust 1993;158:28−30.
2. Meredith TJ. Epidemiology of poisoning. Pharmacol Ther 1993;59:251−256.
3. Pawer BM, Hackett PL, Dusci LJ, Ilett KF. Antidepressant toxicity, and the need for identifica-

tion and concentration monitoring in overdose. Clin Pharmacokinet 1995;29,3:154—171.

4. Buckley NA, Whyte IM, Dawson AH, McManus PR, Ferguson NW. Correlations between prescriptions and drugs taken in self-poisoning implications for prescribers and drug regulation. Med J Aust 1995;162(4):194—197.

5. Cassidy S, Henry J. Fatal toxicity of antidepressant drugs in overdose. Br Med J 1987;295: 1021—1024.

6. Henry JA. A fatal toxicity index for antidepressant poisoning. Acta Psychiatr Scand 1989;80 (Suppl 354):37—45.

7. Henry JA, Alexander CA, Sener EK. Relative mortality from overdose of antidepressants. Br Med J 1995;310/6974:221—224.

8. Kasper S, Schindler S, Neumeister A. Risk of suicide in depression and its implication for psychopharmacological treatment. Int Clin Psychopharmacol 1996;11(2):71—79.

9. Farmer RDT, Pinder RM. Why do fatal overdose rates vary between antidepressatns? Acta Psychiatr Scand 1989;80(Suppl 354):25—35.

10. Montgomery SA, Baldwin D, Green M. Why do amitriptyline and dothiepin appear to be so dangerous in overdose? Acta Psychiatr Scand 1989;80(Suppl 354):47—53.

11. Kessel JB, Simpson GM. Tricyclic and tetracyclic drugs. In: Kaplan HI, Sadock BJ (eds) Comprehensive Textbook of Psychiatry/VI, 6th edn. Baltimore: Williams and Wilkins, 1995; 2096—2112.

12. Myerburg RJ. Electrocardiography. In: Isselbacher KJ, Adams RD, Braunwald E, Petersdorf RG, Wilson JD (eds) Harrison's Principles of Internal Medicine, 9th edn. Tokyo: McGraw-Hill Kogakusha Ltd., 1980;999—1010.

13. Burke MJ, Preskorn SH. Short-term treatment of mood disorders with standard antidepressants. In: Bloom FE, Kupfer DJ (eds) Psychopharmacology: The Fourth Generation of Progress. New York: Raven Press, 1995;1053—1065.

14. Glassman AH, Roose SP, Giardina E-GV, Bigger JT Jr. Cardiovascular effects of tricyclic antidepressants. In: Meltzer HY (ed) Psychopharmacology: The Third Generation of Progress. New York: Raven Press 1987;1437—1441.

15. Bernstein JG. Handbook of Drug Therapy in Psychiatry, 2nd edn. Chicago: Year Book Medical Publishers, Inc. 1988;277—304.

16. Himmelhoch JM. Monoamine oxidase inhibitors. In: Kaplan HI, Sadock BJ (eds) Comprehensive Textbook of Psychiatry/VI, 6th edn. Baltimore: Williams and Wilkins, 1995;2038—2053.

17. Grebb JA. Serotonin-specific reuptake inhibitors. Introduction and overview: Fluvoxamine. In: Kaplan HI, Sadock BJ (eds) Comprehensive Textbook of Psychiatry/VI, 6th edn. Baltimore: Williams and Wilkins, 1995;2055—2056.

18. Montgomery SA. Selective serotonin reuptake inhibitors in the acute treatment of depression. In: Bloom FE, Kupfer DJ (eds) Psychopharmacology: The Fourth Generation of Progress. New York: Raven Press, 1995;1043—1049.

19. Leonard BE. Toxicity of antidepressants in overdose. Int J Clin Pharmacol Res 1989;9:101—110.

20. Schatzberg AF. Fluoxetine. In: Kaplan HI, Sadock BJ (eds) Comprehensive Textbook of Psychiatry/VI, 6th edn. Baltimore: Williams and Wilkins, 1995;2056—2062.

21. Kapur S, Mieczkowski T, Mann JJ. Antidepressant medications and the relative risk of suicide attempt and suicide. JAMA 1992;268:3441—3445.

22. Letizia C, Kapik B, Flanders WD. Suicidal risk during controlled clinical investigations of fluvoxamine. J Clin Psychiat 1996;57(9):415—421.

23. Debattista C, Schatzberg AF. Paroxetine. In: Kaplan HI, Sadock BJ (eds) Comprehensive Textbook of Psychiatry/VI, 6th edn. Baltimore: Williams and Wilkins, 1995;2063—2069.

24. Mendels J. Sertraline. In: Kaplan HJ, Sadock BJ (eds) Comprehensive Textbook of Psychiatry/VI, 6th edn. Baltimore: Williams and Wilkins, 1995;2069—2073.

25. Carracci G, Zinner SH. Unsuccessful suicide attempts by sertraline overdose. Am J Psychiat 1994;151:147—148.

26. Ostrom M, Eriksson A, Thorson J, Spigset O. Fatal overdose with citalopram. Lancet 1996;348:

339–340.

27. Grundamas L, Wohlfart B, Lagerstedt C, Bongtsson F, Ektundh G. Symptoms and signs of severe citalopram overdose. Lancet 1996;348:339.

28. Roy A. Suicide. In: Kaplan HI, Sadock BJ (eds) Comprehensive Textbook of Psychiatry/VI, 6th edn. Baltimore: Williams and Wilkins, 1995;1739–1751.

29. Barry JJ, Schatzberg AF. Trazodone and nefazodone. In: Kaplan HI, Sadock BJ (eds) Comprehensive Textbook of Psychiatry/VI, 6th edn. Baltimore: Williams and Wilkins, 1995;2089–2095.

30. Grebb JA. Venlafaxine. In: Kaplan HI, Sadock BJ (eds) Comprehensive Textbook of Psychiatry/VI, 6th edn. Baltimore: Williams and Wilkins, 1995;2120–2121.

31. De Boer T. The effects of mirtazapine on central noradrenergic and serotonergic neurotransmission. Int Clin Psychopharmacol 1995;10(Suppl 4):19–23.

32. Montgomery SA. Safety of mirtazapine: a review. Int Clin Psychopharmacol 1995;10:(Suppl 4)37–45.

Conceptual and ethical issues

The will to die: an international perspective

Antoon A. Leenaars and Rene F.W. Diekstra

University of Leiden, Leiden, The Netherlands

Abstract. The right to die (RTD) concept is complex and controversial. In spite of the ongoing debate, people do not have sufficient understanding of this concept. Yet, there is growing public support of the RTD worldwide. Thus, a large number of issues regarding RTD as well as suicide need to be addressed. Some of these issues, particularly the ones related to the psychological perspective, should be discussed in detail. Following such a discussion, the authors provide a set of criteria and rules of conduct for the decision making in assisted suicide. Based on their experience in The Netherlands, they defend the acknowledgment of dignified death as a viable solution or coping strategy with problems of life under certain terminal illness conditions. They strongly object, however, to the unconditional application of assisted suicide, e.g., to that practiced by Kevorkian.

Keywords: assisted suicide, ethical issues, psychological perspectives, right to die, suicide.

The right to die concept is one of the most controversial and elusive issues facing suicidology around the world today. The concept is complex, having many sub-controversies. Polls and research [1–6] have indicated growing support for the right to die process in the USA, Europe, Japan, Canada and elsewhere. The fact that the first national conference on suicide in Greece (Suicide: Biopsychosocial Approach, May 16-19, 1996) addressed the issue in a panel, suggests that the debate is far-reaching with many Eastern European and former Soviet Union nations addressing the issue as well. Yet, a persistent question that has been raised is whether people have a sufficient understanding of what they are considering. This observation is even broader because people lack in their understanding of suicide itself.

People are perplexed, bewildered, confused, and even overwhelmed when they are confronted with suicide, including the suicide of a terminally ill person. People do not understand suicide very well. The purpose of this chapter is to define suicide and to address some key questions in the debate. The chapter will attempt to provide a psychological perspective on the question, highlighting the steps in The Netherlands as an international perspective on the topic. The authors are simply too limited to present all the divergent perspectives across the world. These thoughts are, in fact, not meant to be exhaustive nor encompassing. The thoughts are presented only to raise some questions and to offer a few directions about some aspects of the right to die debate.

Address for correspondence: Antoon Leenaars PhD, Archives of Suicide Research, 880 Ouelette Ave., Suite 806, Windsor, Ontario, Canada N9A 1C7. Tel.: +1-519-253-9377. Fax: +1-519-253-8486.

Is rational suicide rational?

The headline of the 8 May 1996 in a local newspaper where the senior author lives read "Dr. Death linked to Bastable suicide" [7]. Austin Bastable, suffering from multiple sclerosis (MS), was assisted in his death by "Dr Death", Jack Kevorkian. Bastable was Kevorkian's first international victim on 6 May 1996. "Dr Death" has attended 27 suicides since 1990. Bastable's death occurred 1 week after a failed attempt to meet with Canada's Prime Minister, Jean Chretien to discuss assisted suicide. Bastable had campaigned to permit legal means for Canadians to commit suicide with professional help. Forlorn, Bastable then turned to Kevorkian and with more than one doctor present, he died.

The headline in the same newspaper of the 9 May 1996 read, "Suicide sparks cross-border problem" [8]. Friends of Bastable saw his death as peaceful, a final end to years of agony. Although MS is not a terminal illness, Bastable was not willing to accept the pain it caused. He felt "tortured", basing his decision to die on autonomy [9]. This view holds that autonomous individuals have a right to behave in any noncriminal way they choose. The alternative view is one of absolutes, such as "Thou shall not kill". The position of absolutes leads to opposition to assisted death whereas the autonomy view is utilitarian. People like Bastable argue for the utilitarian position, implying that the other is wrong. The conclusion simply follows, Bastable saw his suicide as rational. The individual in this view has a right to kill him/herself. Yet, can suicide ever be simply a rational choice?

According to Lester [10] there are two separate questions in the quest of "Is suicide rational?" First, "Is the reasoning of a suicidal person logical?" Lester argues that granted the premise (e.g., "No one will ever love me") of the suicidal person, the reasoning in most cases is logical. There is no logical error; thus, suicide is rational.

A second question concerned the rationality of the premises. Although a mental health professional may label some premise (such as the above) as irrational [11], the professional's beliefs are equally unproven. The patient, however, is considered irrational until proven rational. Why is the therapist correct? Lester has concluded, thus, the majority of suicides do reason logically. Suicide is rational.

Yet an a priori question is "Why do people kill themselves?" or more accurately "Why did Bastable or that individual commit suicide?" People are perplexed about this question. The suicidal person who takes his or her own life may, at the moment of decision, be the least aware of the essence of the answer. Was Bastable aware of the reason? Was it only relief of pain? Or were there other factors? It is known that he was depressed, becoming quite upset at the refusal of Chretien to meet with him, a rather unrealistic request. What was the mode of death?

What is suicide?

From a perception of mode, suicide is defined (by a medical examiner or coroner) as one of four possible modes of death. An acronym for the four modes of death is NASH: natural, accidental, suicidal, and homicidal. This classification has its problems — especially if used in the right to die discussions. Its major deficiency is that it treats the human being in a Cartesian fashion, namely as a biological machine rather than appropriately treating him/her as a motivated biopsychosocial organism, i.e., it obscures the individual's intentions in relation to his/her own cessation and, further, completely neglects the contemporary concept of mind, regarding intention, including the unconscious.

Psychological concepts about suicide, that are not simply reductionistic, are fortunately common today. The 10 most significant suicidologists in history are the following: A. Adler, L. Binswanger, S. Freud, C.G. Jung, K.A. Menninger, G. Kelly, H.A. Murray, E.S. Shneidman, H.S. Sullivan and G. Zilborg. From these discerning individuals, we learn that suicide is a multidimensional malaise [12,13]. We do not agree with those who point to an external stress as the cause of suicide. We also do not agree that the cause is simply pain. We tend to place the emphasis on the multideterminant nature of suicide. Suicide is intrapsychic. It is not simply the stress or even the pain, but the person's inability to cope with the event or pain. The goal of any scheme about human personality, such as personology [14], is one that makes an individual, an individual. It should be the study of the whole organism, not only the stress or pain. People do not simply commit suicide because of pain, but because the pain is unbearable, they themselves are often mentally constricted and they find they cannot cope [13,15].

In addition, from a psychological point of view, suicide is not only intrapsychic, it is also interpersonal. Individuals are interwoven. We live in a world. We disagree with those who point only to some intrapsychic aspects such as anger turned inward or primitive narcissism. Suicide occurs between people (or relationships to some ideal). Metaphorically speaking, suicide is an intrapsychic drama on an interpersonal stage. With these preliminary thoughts, suicide can be clinically understood from at least the following concepts [12,16—18].

Intrapsychic

Unbearable psychological pain

The common stimulus in suicide is unendurable psychological pain [13]. The enemy of life is pain, a psychache [15]. Although, as Menninger [19] noted, other motives (elements, wishes) are evident, the person primarily wants to flee from pain experienced in a bottomless trauma. The person may feel any number of emotions, such as boxed in, rejected, deprived, forlorn, distressed, and especially hopeless and helpless. The suicide, as Murray [20] stated, is functional because it abolishes painful tension for the individual. It provides relief from intolerable suffering.

Cognitive constriction

The common cognitive state in suicide is mental constriction (i.e., rigidity in thinking, narrowing of focus, tunnel vision) [13]. The person is figuratively "intoxicated" or "drugged" by the constriction; exhibiting at the moment before his or her death only permutations and combinations of a trauma (e.g., business failure, poor health, rejection by a spouse). The suicidal mind is in a special state of fixed purpose and of relative constriction. In the face of the painful trauma, a possible solution became the right solution. (Is one then rational?)

Indirect expressions

Complications, ambivalence, redirected aggression, unconscious implications, and related indirect expressions (or phenomena) are often evident in the suicidal mind. The suicidal person at the moment of the death is ambivalent. There are complications, concomitant contradictory feelings, attitudes, and/or thrusts, often toward a person and even toward life. The person experiences humility, submission, devotion, subordination, flagellation, and sometimes even masochism. Yet, there is much more. What the person is conscious of, is only a fragment of the suicidal mind [21]. There are more reasons to the act than the suicidal person is consciously aware of when making the final decision [16,21].

Inability to adjust

People with all types of problems, pain, losses, etc., are at risk for suicide. Although the majority of suicides may not fit best into any specific nosological classification, depressive disorders, manic-depressive disorders, anxiety disorders, schizophrenic disorders, panic disorders, borderline disorders, and psychopathic disorders, have been related to some suicides [16,22,23]. Depression may well be the most frequent disorder; however, it is unbearable pain, not always depression, that is the most frequent state in suicidal people. Indeed, suicidal people see themselves as unable to adjust. His/her state of mind is incompatible with an accurate discernment of what is going on.... and that is not rational. Considering themselves too weak to overcome difficulties, they do not survive life's difficulties.

Ego

The ego with its enormous complexity [14] is an essential factor in the suicidal scenario. The Oxford English Dictionary (OED) defines ego as, "the part of the mind that reacts to reality and has a sense of individuality". Ego strength is a protective factor against suicide. Suicidal people, however, frequently exhibit a relative weakness in their capacity to develop constructive tendencies and to overcome their personal difficulties [24]. The person's ego has likely been weakened by a steady toll of traumatic life events. This implies that a history of traumatic disruptions, especially pain, placed the person at risk for suicide.

Interpersonal

Interpersonal relations

The suicidal person has problems in establishing or maintaining relationships (object relations). There is frequently a disturbed, unbearable interpersonal situation. A calamity prevailed. A positive development in those same disturbed relationships may have been seen as the only possible way to go on living, but such a development was not seen as forthcoming. The person's psychological needs are frustrated, often the need for attachment, although other needs, often equally intrapsychic and interpersonal, may be equally evident (e.g., control, achievement, autonomy, honor). Suicide is committed because of frustrated or unfulfilled needs.

Rejection-aggression

The rejection-aggression hypothesis was first documented by Stekel in the famous 1910 meeting of the Psychoanalytic Society in Freud's home in Vienna [25]. Loss is central to suicide; it is, in fact, often a rejection that is experienced as an abandonment. It is an unbearable narcissistic injury. This injury is part of a traumatic event that leads to pain and, in some, to self-directed aggression [26]. The person is deeply ambivalent and, within the context of this ambivalence, suicide may become the turning back upon oneself of murderous impulses (wishes, needs) — it may be murder in the 180th degree [13].

Identification-egression

Freud [21,27,28] hypothesized that intense identification with a lost or rejecting person or, as Zilboorg [24] showed, with any lost ideal (e.g., health, youth, employment, freedom), is crucial in understanding the suicidal person. Identification is defined as an attachment (bond), based upon an important emotional tie with another person (object) [27] or any ideal. If this emotional need is not met, the suicidal person experiences a deep pain (discomfort) and wants to egress, i.e., to exit, to get away, to get away,... to be dead.

Endnote

In concluding, although the above observations are only a point of view, based on the perspectives of the 10 most noted suicidologists, these elements common to suicide are useful in understanding suicide. Suicide cannot be simply reduced to the NASH concept. The common ground at least highlights that suicide is not only due to external "stress", pain, or even reasoning. The issues of autonomy or absolutes are philosophical. Although they have a place in understanding human behavior, whether premises are rational or not misses the point from our view. To provide only philosophical speculations on the topic without considering the psychological reality of the malaise, also other realities, is wrong. The question should be "What is suicide?" and understanding suicide from a psychological view leads us to conclude that suicide is not rational. It is simply not a rational choice. Bastable's death was not simply a rational choice (Indeed when is any death simply rational?). The common consistency in suicide is, in fact, with life-long adjustment patterns [13], not a logical choice about loss, health, employment, or whatever. Suicidal people have experienced a steady toll of painful life events, i.e., threat, stress, failure, loss, and challenge that have undermined their ability to reason.

Regarding the question, "Are these suicidal people rational?", we can conclude that at the moment of taking his or her life the suicidal person is figuratively intoxicated with unbearable pain, overpowering emotions, and constricted logic. The pain is unbearable. Is anyone at such a moment capable of making an informed or "rational" choice"? Indeed, when is any human behavior simply rational.

Lester and others [29,30] argue about the right to die (e.g., rational suicide) from a pure theoretical-ethical stance, going as far as to state that, even if one does not believe in the view personally, the issues should be seen only from a logical view. Kevorkian [31] goes even further, stating that we should go ahead assisting suicide without discussion of the issues. No debate is necessary. He stated, "...all of these (issues) have been well debated in the past, and there is nothing new to learn" [31]. We disagree with Kevorkian. We need to talk about these real life issues. The discussion will have to be ongoing, not an end statement. The "practical" is people. Bastable is a person. We should begin with the practical... the lives of people.

Ethicists and all suicidologists need to be accountable. These are not merely theoretical, ethical issues. No person kills him/herself because of a theoretical argument. They do not kill themselves because of a premise nor because it's their civil right. They kill themselves because of pain, mental constriction, and so on. This is the suicidal mind. These are not only philosophical issues. We have to, in fact, be responsible for our statements (and in Kevorkian's case, his actions)...... to our suicidal people.

The case of Sigmund Freud

For those familiar with the right to die debate, the case of Sigmund Freud is important. Freud is a dramatic example in the issues at hand since his work in psychology is so influential. Freud's death has been called a suicide. Yet, was his death really a suicide? That should, in fact, be the first question in the debate: "What is a suicide?" What is a suicide beyond the reductionistic NASH concept?

The question is not "Is suicide rational?" but "What is a suicide and what is not?" Freud killed himself. Was it, as he stated, because of his terminal illness? Or was it because he had been severely depressed at the time? He had been overwhelmed by World War II and had notable problems in his adjustment to moving to England. Freud left Vienna in 1938, when Hitler took over Austria. Those years were troublesome for him not only because of the war, but because, since 1923, he had suffered from cancer of the mouth and jaw. The cancer had progressed to a degenerative stage; indeed, the smell was so bad that even his faithful dog refused to be in the same room with him. The pain was unbearable for him. In Moses and Monotheism [32], Freud himself says "....do not call me a pessimist." He died by his own wish with the assistance of his physician by lethal injection on 26 September 1939 at 83 years of age. Was Freud's suicide (or homicide) due only to his terminal illness? Does Freud's suicide, and by implication, those of other terminally ill people, differ in essence from other suicides? That should be a key question in the right to die debate.

To add a further thought for consideration about Freud, suicide has a history. As Shneidman [13] noted, the common consistency in suicide is with life-long adjustment patterns. It is easy to see that Freud was in unbearable pain, mentally constricted, depressed, forlorn over the loss of his attachment to Vienna, and so on. Yet, there is more. Freud had made a previous suicidal threat. Years before his suicide, he made an overt threat during his engagement to his wife to be, Martha Bernays [33,34]. According to Jones [35], Freud had decided to kill himself if he lost Martha. In a letter to Martha, Freud wrote, "I have long since resolved on a decision, the thought of which is in no way painful, in the event of losing you. That we should lose each other by parting is quite out of the question. You would have to become a different person, and of myself, I am quite sure. You have no idea how fond I am of you, and hope I shall never have to show it." [35]. Freud was quite attached to Martha and, as his history showed, to other ideals (e.g., Vienna, health).

Can Freud's suicide be best accounted for by pain, cognitive constriction, indirect expressions.... identification-egression? (Can Bastable's death be accountable for by these processes?) Or were there other processes occurring. The question is simply: Is this suicide? Is Freud's death best described as a suicide? If one goes beyond the NASH concept, we believe not. This may not be suicide. Indeed, would it not be more appropriate to call it "dignified death" or "assisted death" or "self-chosen death?" Such discussions are much more important than the question, "Is suicide rational?" and these are not merely semantics. Is Freud's (or Bastable's) death only due to logical choice? Freud himself did not see his death as rational but as a means to ease the pain of his cancer.

Once we stop asking the question of "Is suicide rational?", we can begin to address the real issues. To ask, "Is suicide rational?", is, in fact, to use a common metaphor, a red herring in the debate. Independent support for this view comes from a discussion about the suicide of Arthur Koestler by Goldney [36]. Ultimately, the question is "What is suicide?" There are fundamental questions that people need to address in the debate on the right to die. For example, is Freud's death suicide or homicide? Or is Freud's death better seen as self-chosen death?

The case of Nico Speijer

For those familiar with the right to die debate, the case of Nico Speijer is equally important. Nico Speijer was The Netherlands leading suicidologist. He was 76 years of age, Emeritus Professor of Social Psychiatry at the University of Leiden, and an honorary member of the International Association for Suicide Prevention (IASP). An internationally recognized suicidologist, a preventionist, ending his life by self-chosen death.

The death of Speijer confronts us directly with some of the fundamental issues regarding terminal illness, suicide and euthanasia. First of all, if "self-chosen death" as in the case of Speijer is intimately related to the experience of severe and irreversible loss of physical health due to terminal illness, it seems nothing more than a natural and unavoidable consequence of our biopsychosocial disposition that: 1) self-determined death mortality increases with age; and 2) the elderly contribute disproportionally to the population of "suicides" for which no psychiatric disorder per se but rather irreversible and severe loss of physical, mental and social wellbeing are principal factors.

A second issue, and related to the previous one, pertains to the common tendency to describe "suicide" as the tragic and untimely loss of human life. Does this description also fit the case of Speijer (or Freud) or, stated more broadly, to what extent does it apply to suicide in the terminally ill in general, or is this even suicide? The third issue is: if some self-chosen deaths are not to be considered suicides as described earlier, if they are to be seen as the lesser of all possible tragedies, how are we to recognize beforehand those deaths-to-be and how should we react to them, as fellow human beings, as health professionals, as volunteer helpers, as society in general? Should we simply ignore them, turn our backs against them?

What if Nico Speijer had not been a doctor himself who could therefore easily lay his hands on the preferred method, i.e., drugs, for his death? What if he then would have seen a doctor and asked him or her to prescribe a drug? What if that doctor would have been willing to assist him? How should he have had to go about it professionally? Should he have consulted with colleagues? Should he just act like Kevorkian? What about legal aspects? Should he have reported his assistance to the appropriate authorities? Should he be punishable by law for providing Speijer with a method for bringing about his own death?

What if a doctor approached by Speijer for assistance with his death would have refused the request? Imagine that Speijer, not having been able to find another doctor or another way to obtain the desired mode of death, one day would have walked into a railway station — a station which even at midnight is crowded — and in despair jumped in front of a departing train, being killed instantly. Or, what even if the doctor assisted but followed his or her own decisions? All too often these decisions are, in fact, made by doctors themselves and across the globe, often stating that they administered a lethal dose to relieve pain. This is what happened with Bastable. Kevorkian followed his own principle. Indeed, in the case of Bastable, subsequent reports [37] indicated that the Canadian doctor that was supposed to have been present and signed the death certificate was not even there. Indeed, he was completely surprised by his association to the death. What if we allow doctors like Kevorkian to simply go ahead and do what they want, not willing to follow any rules of conduct nor law of the land. Questions, as one can see, are easily asked, but clear-cut answers are immensely difficult to give. We are touching here upon some of the most central themes in our present thinking about life and death: the value of human life, the right to autonomy, the right to die in dignity.

Remarkably, it was to a certain extent precisely through the death of Speijer that some of the questions raised about came to be put in the limelight of public and political debate in The Netherlands and received answers that in the end resulted in the acceptance in The Netherlands of assisted death provided a set of rules and regulations are carefully observed.

About 1 year before his demise Speijer co-authored a book [38] entitled "Assisted suicide: A study of the problems related to self-chosen death". In this book, which was the first to address exclusively the issue of assisted death from ethical, legal and professional perspectives, the authors outlined a set of criteria for assisting with self-chosen death by health-care professionals in cases of unbearable physical illness without reasonable perspective for improvement or for recovery of an acceptable quality of life. The book initially received little attention but the death of Speijer brought a drastic change in this respect. Speijer, in fact, had followed the rules of conduct in the book for his own demise. Three months after the event, in December 1981, the Court of the City of Rottedam convicted a female lay volunteer who had helped an elderly chronic psychiatric patient to die by feeding her at her request a chocolate pudding in which barbiturates had been mixed. The court sentenced the volunteer to a suspended imprisonment stating that in providing the assistance at the request of the deceased she had not (as she could not have because of the simple fact that she was a volunteer) acted carefully, which was then operationalized by reference to the rules of conduct as formulated in "Assisted suicide". By implication the court asserted that had the assistance been carried out in accordance with those rules, the act may have gone unpunished.

As a matter of fact, jurisprudence throughout the country ever since has complied with the verdict of the Rotterdam Court, no health-care professional that has been known to have assisted with death and that carefully observed the rules of conduct has been persecuted or been put on trial, despite of the fact that in the formal sense assistance with death is punishable by law. However, there are cases in The Netherlands, e.g., the Assen case, that are objectionable to the senior author. In that case, a psychiatrist assisted a depressed 50-year-old female with her suicide after the death of her son, arguing that her pain was understandable and untreatable. There is, of course, the issue of the slippery slope [10] and other issues that warrant caution in how we approach all of these issues.

The case of Bastable is quite different from Freud and the case of Speijer is even more different. Bastable was not terminally ill. Freud was terminally ill, so was Speijer; however, Speijer, unlike Freud, followed some pre-established rules of conduct that serve as guidance for assisted death. Bastable, on the other hand, allowed Kevorkian to assist him in death, without any rules of conduct (What mode of death is this? Homicide?).

Definition, criteria and rules of conduct

In "Assisted suicide" [38], the authors first of all make clear that allowing for assisted death within the health-care system does not at all imply "promotion" of "suicide" nor does it testify to a general failure to prevent suicidal deaths. Suicide, as they assert, is by itself not an easy death. On the contrary, in the light of the theory of suicide outlined (and available empirical evidence), a large majority of suicides are to be considered sorrowful deaths. Most suicides appear to be preventable, since there are usually means and methods available for improving the quality of life of the suicidal persons involved, to such a degree that pain, and thus life, might become bearable (again).

It can, however, also not be denied, both from an empirical as well as a subjective point of view (i.e., from the point of view of the subject's experience), that a certain percentage of "suicides" (estimates vary from 5 to 10% but have to be taken with great caution) should be considered "eu-thana-toi", good deaths — indeed, we would question if these should be labelled as suicides. We are here concerned with persons who suffer from a chronic, incurable physical illness and who are in a terminal condition. There will probably be less and less disagreement with the health-care system about this assertion internationally over time. But there is, and there will also continue to be, discussion concerned with persons who are not physically ill in the strictest sense and who are not in terminal condition, but who suffer from a chronic or episodic disorder such as in the case of Bastable. There is considerable disagreement concerned with this group of people. The current authors themselves disagree about these concerns, the first being opposed and the second in agreement.

Definition

In "Assisted suicide" the following definition of self-chosen death is given: *"...when someone deliberately performs or refrains from actions towards another person at this latter person's request, in order to enable this person to implement his/her decision, taken voluntarily and compos mentis before the request was made, to end his/her own life in a manner determined and desired by him/herself, and when the death occurs in the desired way indeed"* [38].

Is this an appropriate definition about the mode of death at hand? Do we need an alternative view? At the least, this definition is a beginning and has a number of important implications.

Since space will not allow us to address many of the implications, let us cite the following critical one. The definition of assisted suicide — or more accurately assisted death — does not simply comprise providing means or methods (such as drugs) or technical information on means or methods to enable a person to end his or her life. Assistance with death also can mean the removal of obstacles for the implementation of a plan, such as discharge from hospitalization in order to allow for a death to occur (often terminally ill people wish to die in dignity in their own home). Assistance with death can mean refusal of treatment or withdrawal of treatment. But assistance with death can also mean simply being present "until the very end", i.e., remaining with the person up to the moment that he or she actually carries out the fatal act. Finally, giving advice to a person with regard to certain precautions to be taken and certain final actions to be carried out, such as making a will, settling bills, informing/preparing others, for example, the person's relatives, also fall within the definition of assisted death.

Criteria and rules of conduct

The criteria and rules of conduct for assisted "suicide" formulated on the base of the definition are shown in Table 1 and will be elaborated upon in the following paragraphs.

Of course, these are the criteria written by Speijer and Diekstra. It can be asked, are they sufficient and accurate, etc. Indeed, the senior author believes that the first criteria should be: diagnosed terminal illness with nearness to death.

Based on the criteria in Table 1, the decision to assist with death already requires a very careful consideration and examination of a number of characteristics of the person and his or her situation/condition. First of all (Table 1 (1)), the help has to be asked for voluntarily and explicitly by the person. The request has to be personally (face-to-face) addressed to the potential helper, who should be a qualified/certified health-care professional. The great danger Speijer and

Table 1. Assisted suicide criteria.

1. Request made voluntarily and directly by actor.
2. Sufferer of sound mind at time of request.
3. Wish to end life is longstanding.
4. Presence of unbearable suffering (subject).
5. No reasonable perspective of improvement (object).
6. Remaining treatment alternatives uncertain/only palliative (offered but rejected).
7. Helper is acknowledged professionally.
8. Helper has used intercollegial consultation (1—6) (actor has been seen/examined by colleague(s)).
9. Avoidance of preventable harm/damage to others.
10. Decision-making process and steps taken documented for professional and legal evaluation.

Diekstra foresaw here is that doctors gradually would be put in the role of "the great justifiers" and therewith in many instances become the actual "cause of death", a situation that all too often exists around the world. Often the doctor states the intent to assist death as a relief of pain. Yet despite the stated manifest intent, the result is the same. The doctor's intent should not be a criteria; this is especially true because depending on such issues as religion, social status, etc., differences occur in physician's behavior. Speijer and Diekstra, in fact, feared a development in which both individual patients as well as society in general would "medicalize" assisted death, turn it into euthanasia, and therewith avoid taking responsibility for what is in essence an individual and social and not so much a medical issue under the motto: "if the doctor approves of it and also does it, we can rest assured that it is alright."

Second (Table 1 (2,7,8)), the helper has to establish in a reliable way that the person concerned is compos mentis at the time of the request. This means that the helper should have asked for a second opinion (collegial examination of help-seeker as well as intercollegial consultation) with regard to the mental state of the person. It is of crucial importance here to note the following considerations.

First of all, the desire to end one's life should never per se be taken as sufficient proof of mental illness. It might be a symptom of a florid mental disorder and it might not. The fact that the person concerned has (had) a psychiatric diagnosis does not necessarily imply that the two (psychiatric diagnosis and wish to die inclination) are casually related. (Was Freud psychologically disturbed?)

Next (Table 1 (3)), the wish to end life should be an enduring one. This criterion is of utmost importance. The very fact that a person expresses the wish to end his/her life is in itself never a sufficient justification for assistance with his/her death. Many conditions/situations that evoke suicidal tendencies are transient and many suicidal tendencies are also transient, even in stable (unfavorable) conditions. (Is this what occurred with Bastable, after Chretian did not meet him?) The helper should, therefore, ascertain that the wish to die inclination of the person concerned has been present for many months (at least 6) and its presence should have been continuous during that period. In addition, the helper should make sure that the wish is not exclusively associated with a specific condition (such as a depressive episode) that in the past has always been proven to be amenable to intervention.

Related to the previous point, it is of paramount importance (Table 1 (4 and 5)) that the helper "has had established" that the person is suffering unbearably (subjective statement) and that there is no reasonable perspective/chance for improvement (objective evidence). This implies that both the helper him/herself as well as informed others/colleagues (called in for consultation) have assembled evidence that: 1) the person concerned experiences his/her suffering as unbearable (repeated statements with such a content suffice); and 2) nor the helper nor at least one other health professional with expertise relevant to the person's condition have been able to identify accessible and acceptable methods/treatments for reducing his or her suffering to any significant degree (or have ascertained that significant reduction of the suffering leads to a significant and unacceptable loss of quality of life). It is quite all right and even obligatory, as we shall see later, for a helper to point out or offer to the person possible alternatives to death and even to confront the person with the position that no assistance with death can be given unless these alternatives, if scientifically substantiated, accessible and practical, are tried adequately. But health professionals should be aware of an important ethical dilemma involved in offering all possible alternatives to death. This dilemma, phrased in terms of a question, is the following: might it not be ethically dubious and professionally questionable if a helper demands of a person to try all possible alternatives to death but still refuses any involvement in assistance with death when all these alternatives are tried out by the terminally ill patient long and seriously enough but without tangible results? Speijer and Diekstra [38] did answer this question in the affirmative, but others (Nederlandse Vereniging voor Vrijwillige Euthanasie (NVVE) [39]) do not. Recently, however, the Chief Inspector for Health in The Netherlands [40] wrote a public letter in which he supported the position expressed by Speijer and Diekstra (1981) by stating that physicians not willing to provide assistance with death in any way to one of their patients requesting such assistance and meeting the criteria outlined in Table 1, are at least obliged to provide this patient with information about where he/ she can find a physician that might indeed be willing to provide the assistance requested. In case they would also refuse to provide such information disciplinary action (by their professional organization) should be taken against them.

Next (Table 1 (9)), the helper must ascertain that, wherever possible, preventable harm or damage to others as a consequence of the death is prevented. This means, among other things, that those near and dear to the person are, as much as possible, adequately informed and prepared. The helper has to play an important role both in raising the awareness of the person regarding preventable emotional, social and practical consequences for survivors as well as in assisting both the person and survivors in dealing with and communicating about these issues.

Finally (Table 1 (10)), the helper has to keep a detailed record of the whole assistance process, and to make the record accessible for legal and professional evaluation afterwards.

Conclusion: the future of death and suicide

It seems that the countries around the world are in need of a revaluation of death. This is especially true about one mode of death: suicide. The darkness of secrecy and evil that has surrounded this mode of death for so long is slowly being forced away. We are forced to this insight, almost despite ourselves. This is necessary because people's understanding of suicide — and death more generally — is limited. People are perplexed, bewildered, and confused including about the self-determined death of the terminally ill person. Often in the past, such deaths were called suicide. Indeed, suicide, assisted suicide and euthanasia are often terms used wrongly. This was especially evident in the use of the oxymoron, rational suicide.

Dignified death and the right to die concept is one of the forefront issues today in suicidology. It is a controversial issue around the world. Yet, the increased control we have gained over biological life because of the progress of medical science and technology makes a confrontation with the subject inescapable. After all, we are capable of prolonging biological life to beyond the point where life, in a psychological and social sense, may become experienced as meaningless for the dying. With the increase of the control over life, the questions to the meaning of prolonging the lives of the terminally ill will increase accordingly. Concomitantly, more and more often the question will be posed whether life or death is the most humane choice in the terminally ill.

However paradoxical it may seem, the increase in human ability to control the length of life may make self-chosen death the way of death of the future for some terminally ill individuals. This was true for Speijer, and maybe Freud. This development in turn will cause a fundamental change in our view of human life and our concepts of normality and morality and force upon us a fundamental change in attitudes towards dignified death. The issue will no longer be only what suicides can and must be prevented, but also what is a suicide and what is not.

There are, of course, considerable risks attached to this development. Maybe the most important danger is that when self-chosen deaths are the results of no rules of conduct such as in the case of Bastable. By allowing Kevorkian to behave as he does, we may actually perpetuate the lack of "rational" processes in society. If we are to face dignified death, then we need to debate the issues. In this sense, Kevorkian is simply wrong, and the real sadness of people like Bastable are that they take one moment in history rather than helping us in the discussions and the development of insights and actions.

As the experience in The Netherlands shows, if a society acknowledges dignified death as a viable solution or coping strategy with problems of life under certain terminal illness conditions, then health-care systems of that society make themselves more approachable and attractive for those who consider death, erroneously or not, the only way to egress. Therewith, we positively maximize our preventive potential and begin to sort out the perplexing and confusing issue of death, suicide, self-chosen death and the right to die. Of course, this is not to suggest that we should simply transpose the protocol of The Netherlands around the world. As we stated at the beginning, they are presented here as a perspective that we know best (as opposed to a foreign commentator on another land). Each nation, in fact, has to examine its own needs — as keeping their head in the sand is no longer possible internationally.

As a final footnote, the authors of this paper do not agree about all issues in the debate on the right to die. We do not see ourselves like a Kevorkian who seems to suggest that all debate is unnecessary. We also do not see ourselves like a Szasz who believes that all these issues should be addressed from a pure theoretical stance. Yet, we also do not see ourselves as alike. Our separate previous writings show that we differ considerably about many issues in the debate. However, the outline in this paper are some preliminary areas that we can agree on — with key disagreements — at this time in the discussions. We offer these partial insights in this paper as a sort of prototype of how the issues need to be addressed, namely by discussion.

References

1. American Association of Suicidology. Report of the Committee on Physician-Assisted Suicide and Euthanasia. Washington, D.C., 1996.
2. Battin M. The Least Worst Death: Essays in Bioethics on End of Life. New York: Oxford University Press, 1994.
3. Diekstra R. Suicide and euthanasia. Ital J Suicidol 1992;2:71—78.
4. Diekstra R. Dying in dignity: On the pros and cons of assisted suicide. Psychiat Clin Neurosci 1995;49(Suppl):139—148.
5. Domino G, Leenaars A. Attitudes toward suicide among English speaking urban Canadians. Death Stud 1995;19:489—500.
6. Special Senate Committee on Euthanasia and Assisted Suicide of Life and Death. Ottawa, 1995.
7. Dr. Death linked to Bastable suicide. The Windsor Star 1996;May:1A.
8. Suicide sparks cross-border problem. The Windsor Star 1996;May:1A.
9. Beauchamp T, Childress J. Principles of Biomedical Ethics. New York: Oxford University Press, 1979.
10. Lester D, Leenaars A. The ethics of suicide and suicide prevention. Death Stud 1996;20:162—184.
11. Lester D. The logic and rationality of suicide. Homeostasis 1993;34:167—173.
12. Leenaars A. Suicide: A multidimensional malaise. (The Presidential Address). Suicide Life-Threat Behav 1996;26:221—236.
13. Shneidman E. Definition of Suicide. New York: Wiley, 1985.
14. Murray H. Exploration in Personality. New York: Oxford University Press, 1938.
15. Shneidman E. Psychache. Northvale, NJ: Aronson, 1993.
16. Leenaars A. Suicide Notes. New York: Human Sciences Press, 1988.
17. Leenaars A. Suicide across the adult life-span: An archival study. Crisis 1989;10:132—151.
18. Leenaars A. Are young adults' suicides psychologically different from those of other adults? (The Shneidman Lecture). Suicide Life-Threat Behav 1989;19:249—263.
19. Menninger K. Man Against Himself. New York: Harcourt, Brace & Co., 1938.
20. Murray H. Death to the world: The passions of Herman Melville. In: Shneidman E (ed) Essays in Self-Destruction. New York: Science House, 1967;7—29.
21. Freud S. Mourning and melancholia. In: Strachey J (ed & Trans.) The Standard Edition of the Complete Psychological Works of Sigmund Freud, vol 14. London: Hogarth Press, 1974;239—260 (original work published in 1917).
22. Sullivan H. Schizophrenia as a human process. In: Perry H, Gorvell N, Gibbens M (eds) The Collected Works of Harry Stack Sullivan, vol 2. New York: W.W. Norton, 1962.
23. Sullivan H. The fusion of psychiatry and social science. In: Perry H, Gorvell N, Gibbens M (eds), The Collected Works of Harry Stack Sullivan, vol 2. New York: W.W. Norton, 1964.
24. Zilboorg G. Suicide among civilized and primitive races. Am J Psychiat 1936;92:1347—1369.
25. Friedman P. On suicide. New York: International Universities Press, 1967 (original work published in 1910).
26. Shneidman E, Farberow N. Clues to Suicide. New York: McGraw-Hill, 1957.

27. Freud S. A case of homosexuality in a woman. In: Strachey J (ed & Trans.) The Standard Edition of the Complete Psychological Works of Sigmund Freud, vol 18. London: Hogarth Press, 1974;147—172 (original work published in 1920).

28. Freud S. Group psychology and the analysis of the ego. In: Strachey J (ed & Trans.) The Standard Edition of the Complete Psychological Works of Sigmund Freud, vol 18. London: Hogarth Press, 1974;67—147 (original work published in 1921).

29. Szasz T. The ethics of suicide. Intellect Dig 1971;2:53—55.

30. Szasz T. The case against suicide prevention. Am Psycholog 1986;41:806—812.

31. Kevorkian J. The last fearsome taboo: Medical aspects of planned death. Med Law 1988;7:1—14.

32. Freud S. Moses and monotheism. In: Strachey J (ed & Trans.) The Standard Edition of the Complete Psychological Works of Sigmund Freud, vol 23. London: Hogarth Press, 1974;243—258 (original work published in 1939).

33. Leenaars A. Unconscious processes. In: Leenaars A (ed) Suicidology: Essays in Honor of Edwin Shneidman. Northvale, NJ: Aronson, 1993;126—147.

34. Litman R. Sigmund Freud on suicide. In: Shneidman E (ed) Essays in Self-Destruction. New York: Aronson, 1967;324—344.

35. Jones E. The life and work of Sigmund Freud. New York: Basic Books, 1953—1957.

36. Goldney R. Arthur Koestler: Was his suicide rational? Crisis 1986;7:33—53.

37. Physician denies witnessing Bastable death The Windsor Star 1996;May:5A.

38. Speijer N, Diekstra R. Hulp bij zelfdoding: Problemen in de Hulpverlening bij zelfgekozendood. (Assisted suicide: A study of the problems regarding help with self-chosen death). Deventer: van Loghum Slaterus, 1980.

39. NVVE (Nederlandse Vereniging voor Vrijwillige Euthanasie). Rapport inzake hulp bij zelfdodingsvragen. (Report regarding questions on Assisted Suicide) Amsterdam: Dutch Association for Voluntary Euthanasia, 1991.

40. Diekstra R, DeLeo D. The Anatomy of Suicide. A Treatise on Historical, Social, Psychological and Biological Aspects of Suicidal Behaviours and their Preventability. Dordrecht: Kluwer Academic Publishers, 1994.

Civilisation, suicide, physician-assisted suicide and euthanasia

M.J. Kelleher

National Suicide Research Foundation, Cork, Ireland

Abstract. The right of self-determination and by inference the right to die can be viewed within the concept of personhood, which is ultimately defined as the capacity to value one's own existence. Euthanasia, however, has many medical, legal and ethical implications. Therefore, it should be considered cautiously taking into account its various facets: psychological, sociological, economic, moral, philosophical, etc. Although, these facets remain largely controversial, there is a growing trend towards acceptance of physician-assisted suicide under the condition of implementing safeguards. In this context, a recent survey of 49 countries showed that in 23 countries passive euthanasia is already being practiced, while in 12 countries active euthanasia is said to occur secretly. This is in spite of the existence of strict laws in 45 of these countries, characterizing assisted suicide to be a crime. Clearly, there is an urgent need to establish worldwide rules and criteria for euthanasia.

Keywords: assisted suicide, criteria, euthanasia, safeguards, suicide.

Introduction

Ultimately our humanity is determined by intention. It defines what we are, where we have come from and where we are going. It presupposes deliberation and choice. In choosing any end we must also select the means which ought never to be an end in itself, only an instrument for achieving a goal. Up to the recent past most people assumed that death was something to be avoided, or at least, actively delayed. However, this may no longer be so.

Rather than delaying death, it is being brought forward in time. Control, or the semblance of control, can be demonstrated in that way. Death may now be less feared than previously. Time was when European culture was preoccupied, to its economic disadvantage, with the four last things of eschatology — death, judgement, heaven and hell. Once heaven and hell were swept away, judgement became irrelevant and death itself became, as it ever was in reality, nothing.

Dying and the manner of dying, however, increased in importance. Technological medicine has lengthened the process. The time distance between the initial diagnosis of a potentially fatal or terminal illness and the final advent of death, may be truly great. In medieval Europe the cost of dying, at least for the wealthy devout, was truly enormous [1]. The money was spent on the obsequies and in particular on the church services for the dead, sometimes numbering as many as 1,000 on the day of death, which was sufficient to keep a number of religious communities going. One result was that estates found it difficult to meet the costs

Address for correspondence: Michael J. Kelleher MD, National Suicide Research Foundation, 1 Perrott Avenue, College Road, Cork, Ireland. Tel.: +353-21-277499. Fax: +353-21-277545.

and the rise of capitalism in medieval Europe was delayed as a result [2]. Needless to say, such extravagance is unlikely to be incurred today!

Dying, nonetheless, in recent times may have come to be construed as absorbing disproportionate amounts of capital — a modern, as opposed to a medieval sin. There are three sources of this money handed over during the time of dying. Each source may have a vested interest in shortening the period thereby saving costs. Firstly, there are the resources of the dying person himself, which may be eyed by his potential benefactors; there is a loss to the health insurance plan of which he is a member; and lastly, there are the outgoings of the health care service of his country of residence. The latter, perhaps covertly, has welcomed the development of euthanasia in modern times.

Some reasons given for euthanasia

One reflective advocate of limited euthanasia, John Harris, bases his ideas on the concept of personhood, which he says is defined by the individual's capacity to value his own existence [3]. As part of this valuing, one has a right to self-determination which in a civilised society should not be taken from the individual. Societies, however, vary in their civility. Some are ruthless in pursuing their own economic ends which was what happened in Germany in the 1930s and 40s with the rise of national socialism. The programme leaned heavily on the Hoche and Binding concept of a life unworthy of life [4,5].

This inhuman perspective was in turn linked to crude economics and in the absence of professional ethics among the doctors and nurses involved, as well as the failure of the judiciary and the executive legal arm to implement existing laws. Thus, the euthanasia programme was born which largely wiped out the seriously mentally ill as well as the mentally handicapped and some addicts. The methodologies developed were subsequently used in the holocaust, Europe's greatest crime in this century. The latter programme, however, was driven by delusional concepts such as racial purity. The popularity of the programme, however, was imbued with ideas of economic advantage. In all of this the value of the life of a patient or a Jew was seen as infinitesimally small compared to the level of resources required to keep them in existence.

The question of value underlies modern euthanasia practices as well. This may be particularly so in The Netherlands where the civil law in matters relating to the preservation of life is not, at present, implemented. By comparison with other countries, money may be saved by failure to develop a hospice movement. The working party of the British Medical Association reviewing matters on euthanasia commented that palliative care in The Netherlands is not as advanced as in Britain [6]. It has also been noted that many Dutch doctors are inadequately experienced in good pain management [7]. The World Health Organisation is in no doubt that proper pain management, rather than selective euthanasia, is the pathway to follow in the management of the terminally ill. It states: "Now that a practicable alternative to death in pain exists, there should be concentrated efforts to implement programmes of palliative care, rather than a yielding to pressure for legal euthanasia." [8].

A Dutch response to these criticisms is to state that their general practitioner services are, comparatively, very well developed. The doctor knows his patient and the patient knows his doctor over very many years. This may be so. However, euthanasia, like suicide, is a rare event. Most general practitioner services see a case of suicide about once in several years. Such an infrequent occurrence makes acquisition and maintenance of appropriate skills difficult. Furthermore, the Dutch argue that they are simply doing what the patient wants and added to this they have imposed upon themselves a wide range of voluntary controls [9]. Civilisation, however, is based on the implementation and development of publicly sanctioned laws. If the laws are not right, they should be changed following public debate, legislation and judicial decision.

Ultimately the taking of life is a question for ethics and morality. In medieval Europe the church was the ultimate authority in these matters. The Reformation initially and secularisation more gradually have reduced this clerical control. A new secular "priesthood" has established itself in medical practice in recent years. This is the moral philosopher who may be a member of a particular school but is expected to derive his advice and recommendations from matters of principle which it is assumed are self-evident once clearly exposed. Unfortunately, once rival schools of philosophy seek centre stage this clarity becomes less apparent.

In the euthanasia debate, the two main philosophical approaches have been either utilitarianism or deontology. The former judges the situation by the outcome or consequences while the latter judges it by the intention. If economists have a philosophy it is more likely to be utilitarianism.

The law, however, particularly the criminal law concerns itself with matters of clear consciousness and justified intention. Therefore, the euthanasia debate is clouded by the dichotomy between two significant domains of the public sphere, economics and law.

Comparisons between suicide, physician-assisted suicide and euthanasia

In suicide, physician-assisted suicide (PAS) and euthanasia death is brought forward in time. They may differ in methods used. In suicide, particularly in males, these may be hard, painful and unpleasant. In PAS and euthanasia this is less so. There may also be differences in intention. In suicide the individual intends his own death. In PAS the intention is shared with the doctor as it is in true voluntary euthanasia. This is not so, however, in nonvoluntary and involuntary euthanasia.

Intention presupposes knowledge, deliberation, choice and implementation. Juries routinely assess its importance in criminal matters. According to the select committee of the House of Lords (1994) the "prohibition of intentional killing" is "the cornerstone of law and social relationships" [10]. They rejected unanimously any proposal to "cross the line which prohibits any intentional killing, a line which we think essential to preserve" [11]. Morality, the choice of good or evil, is dependant on intention. The taking of human life is always a moral matter. Hence the importance of ethics in this regard [12].

The morality of suicide

Do we have we have a right to commit suicide? We certainly have the capacity but do we have a positive right? Society condones or even sanctifies some political suicides [13]. However, even here Judaism, Christianity and Islam lay down stringent restrictions on the circumstances [14—16]. At a minimum the individual should seek to preserve his life and not wantonly provoke the killing authority.

Many jurists believe that we do not have a positive right to kill ourselves [17]. To date, civilised society saw itself as having an obligation to prevent suicide. At the beginning of this century, in London, chaplains successfully encouraged magistrates to imprison suicide attempters in order that they might counsel them appropriately [18]. This Draconian procedure was no more successful than modern-day interventions. The obligation to prevent suicide, however, fell traditionally on everyone but, in particular, lay on doctors and nurses, the members of the healing professions who are now covertly, in some countries and overtly in others, encouraged to change their professional stance and become death-inducing agents.

At its narrowest, the argument centres on whose life it is. Hume [19] more or less said that since God gave existence as a gift to the individual, it is for him to do with it as he would. But is this really so? Does one own one's life exclusively, even in the absence of or disbelief in God? Clearly not. Individuals share ownership of life through contractual relationships with others. These include parents, partners, children, friends, colleagues, patients and clients. Each has a hold. All are affected by the individual's death. Indeed the collective, both societal and global, is lessened by the loss of each individual life as each life is a component of the whole.

As the poet John Donne put it, "No man is an island, entire of itself: every man is a piece of the continent, a part of the main. Any man's death diminishes me, because I am involved in mankind." [20].

Each suicide diminishes us all. It makes a statement about life that influences other lives. A noble life ennobles others. A mean life or a furtive death takes from our value. The manner in which we face the inevitability of death is instructive as all must face it in their time. Society should never prolong the passage pointlessly or foreshorten it ruthlessly.

Suicide is now legal in many countries. A survey of 49 of the 51 countries affiliated to the International Association for Suicide Prevention (IASP) found it to be so in 43 countries. In virtually all of these countries attempted suicide is also not a crime, with a few exceptions, e.g., if it occurred within the armed forces of one country or where a public nuisance is likely to be caused, such as a breach of the peace (M.J. Kelleher et al., in preparation). It may be presumed, however, that most suicides, even in countries where it is legal, are immoral in the sense that they prematurely fracture relationships and leave others to find solutions to unresolved problems which may be of a social, interpersonal or economic nature.

Assisted suicide

Most countries, while tolerating suicide, actively distribute resources for its prevention. Despite toleration of suicide, these countries set their faces against assisted suicide which is seen as a crime to be pursued with the full vigour of the law through the courts, if necessary, with a view to prevention. This is important because physician-assisted suicide and euthanasia are subsets of this concept of assisted suicide.

Assisted suicide takes two forms: one distinguished by the giving of advice, the other by provision of means. The attitude of the assistant is important. Many are ambivalent about the choice of death and dying. Chance plays a part in the fatal outcome of suicide. Often the individual is confused within himself. If agents of society, as opposed to society's laws, are also ambivalent, then the one may influence the other. The main concern in outlawing assisted suicide is the prevention of homicide. The hinterland between assisted suicide and murder may not be clearly marked. It is easy to cross boundaries once it is assumed that an individual has the positive right to commit suicide and in so doing has a right to seek assistance. The person most likely to be called upon to give such assistance is a doctor.

This is not a recent phenomenon. Medicine, from the time of Hippocrates, has collectively set itself the task of relieving suffering and preserving life. However, there were exceptions. Stoic philosophy provided a counterweight. If one fell out with the Emperor Nero, he was likely to enquire whether suicide had been considered [21]. If not, he recommended it. If one still hesitated, he offered the services of his physician who would call by appointment!

Patients are vulnerable in illness. The doctor is in a privileged position and most patients do what they are told. If this was not so, surgery, in particular unnecessary surgery, would never have blossomed in the way that it did. In the past it was bleeding and purging. Most recently, tonsillectomies, appendectomies and hysterectomies have been performed more frequently, particularly in private medicine. Some such operations are necessary, many are not. If the doctor is disposed to surgical intervention, the patient will comply. So also, if the doctor leans towards euthanasia, the patient will do likewise.

The buttressing of patient autonomy, on the surface, is a safeguard for two reasons. Intention must always be determined in "unnatural" death. Secondly, if the privacy of a patient is to be invaded by medicine, the doctor has a duty to fully explain both the choices and the consequences.

The concept of "unnatural" death

Biostatisticians believe that we die for one of two sets of reasons — internal or external. The former are seen as "natural" and the latter as "unnatural". As Fig. 1 shows, there are a number of different types of unnatural deaths. In each, intention by selection of means or ends plays a part. All are brought about by one human being upon another, or in the case of suicide and many accidents by the individual upon himself. There are many overlaps as the diagram shows.

Fatal accidents occur more frequently in those with a history of accidents or risk-taking behaviour. A few apparent accidents are genuine suicides. More often the intention is less clear but the risk-taking has its equivalent in a type of roulette in which the stakes are dangerous thrills vs. possible death.

Suicide and euthanasia share the human choice of death. In the former, as stated above, the individual ends his own life. In the latter, another does so with his agreement and, at least in theory, following his explicit and persistent request. Many have questioned how often the theory is implemented in the Dutch practice [22]. The Dutch government itself was concerned about this matter and as a result instituted the Remnelink Commision [23].

This report provided essentially two things, raw data and an interpretation of this data. The data itself was used by some [24] to show that the practice of

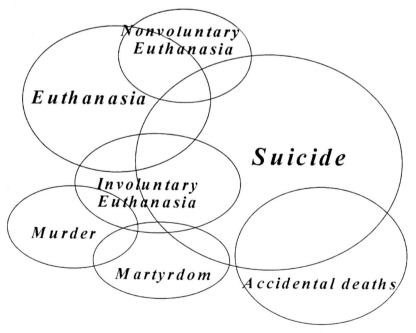

National Suicide Research Foundation

Fig. 1. Death from "external causes". Relationship between suicide and euthanasia.

euthanasia in The Netherlands was very widespread and that many deaths occurred in breach of the guidelines. The authors of the report reject these criticisms as unfair, preferring their own more anodyne account. These differences in interpretation may reflect a more profound difference in perspective of the inherent or incoherent goodness of mankind.

Fundamentally there are two or perhaps three moral concepts of man — the good, the fallible and the bad. Traditionally the law in democracies favours the second. We have inalienable rights although we may err in our day to day activities. The law arbitrates these on the basis of intention. If you do an evil, intentionally, you are guilty in the eyes of the law. If it was unintended, you are not. National socialism and apartheid were based on the concept that there were good people, Aryans and Whites, and bad, Jews and blacks. Those who argued for apartheid were convinced of this natural goodness in themselves until the very end of the system. Central to this belief is the idea that a good man can do no evil. Such a utopian perspective befits a perfect society of good men and women where there is no want or no distressing division of resources.

How voluntary is euthanasia?

A patient may be unable to state, demonstrate, or understand intention. Where this incapacity exists and when euthanasia occurs, it is described as nonvoluntary euthanasia. How frequent is this occurrence in The Netherlands? The official commentary of the Remnelink Report states that it is infrequent while some of those who have studied the raw statistics provided within the report state otherwise [25].

In arguing this issue battles are fought over who commands language, in particular the English language. If Lewis Carroll [26] was alive today, Humpty Dumpty might well have had something to say to Alice in his appraisal of the use of words relative to euthanasia. "When I use a word I mean it to mean, what I mean it to mean, nothing more or nothing less" he haughtily told Alice. So also the Dutch would have us confine the use of the term euthanasia to what they see as its ideal usage namely the explicit and persistent request for life to be terminated on medical grounds. The English language, however, will not allow itself to be so confined. Furthermore, most other jurisdictions, e.g., the Select Committee of the House of Lords (1994) and the New York Task Force on Life and the Law [27] are happy to divide euthanasia in three — voluntary, nonvoluntary and involuntary.

In nonvoluntary euthanasia, the individual has lost the capacity to decide and choose. This may be because of dementia, unconsciousness or clouding of consciousness. Someone else decides for him "in his own best interest". If there is only one decision-maker it is invariably the doctor [28]. A notorious example of this was Lord Dawson, physician to King George V, who ended his life illegally, by injection, in January 1936 [29].

If there is more than one decision-maker as is recommended in The Netherlands, a relative or friend is likely to be the other applicant. The question must be raised as to who gains by these decisions or as is said in law, cui bono? The doctor clearly gains. In Lord Dawson's case it was practice convenience. Planned timing of birthing is also a boon to the medical profession. It is easier to end a patient's life than to support him, at inconvenient times, in his final travail. Relatives may also benefit by either early access to bequests or the preservation of these against the drain of costly treatments.

The situation is different again in involuntary euthanasia. Here the individual has the capacity but lacks the information which would allow him to consider and choose. A couple of years ago a Japanese surgeon killed his friend and patient whose intractable pain he no longer felt competent to treat [30]. In the doctor's view the patient would be better off dead. He therefore proceeded to kill him.

Distinguished American jurists are of the opinion that all types of euthanasia are wrong [17,31]. Judicial decisions must relate to what has legally gone before and foreshadow or foresee the future possible legal and social consequences. Anything that undermines the citizens inalienable right to life is an evil. To date, the Dutch legislature and the German one before it has abided by this principle. For a brief period the legislature of the Northern Territories of Australia abandoned this notion but in a matter of months the Australian Senate overturned this decision by the narrowest of majorities. Most recently the American Supreme Court has restated the general principle that there is no fundamental right to assistance in committing suicide [32]. The Dutch maintain that there is a decrease in nonvoluntary and involuntary euthanasia [33]. Others, however, maintain that there has been an increase in these phenomena [34].

Widening the criteria

Those critical of the Dutch policy in euthanasia fear two things. Firstly, that the criteria will widen or be patchily applied, resulting in a numerical increase. Secondly, these practices may take root in other countries less advanced, in this regard, than The Netherlands. These concerns are sometimes bundled together as representing the slippery-slope argument. Undoubtedly there has been qualitative widening of the criteria (Fig. 2).

What was originally projected as a medical treatment for the terminally ill in great suffering was widened to include those physically suffering who were not terminally ill. There may have been logical reasons for doing this. Terminal illness could only be diagnosed with certainty after death has occurred. Furthermore, there is confusion as to whether the term "terminal" includes both cases who were given treatment and those who were not given treatment. Prognosis which is a particular type of diagnosis taking outcome into consideration is notoriously unreliable. This being the case, why allow the confusion? It is easier to lump both together. More recently the distinction between physical and psychological pain and suffering has been blurred, which again is logical [35]. There is only

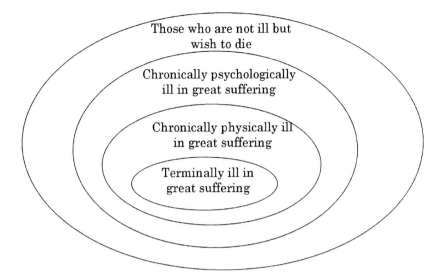

Fig. 2. Euthanasia, narrowly and broadly defined.

one person who expresses himself through mind and body. It is the person who suffers. This formed the basis of the Chabot case.

But why should the process stop there? If physician-assisted suicide is a right (or at least condoned in The Netherlands), why is it necessary to be ill to avail of the service? Two patients known to the author, neither of whom was treated by him, highlight this dilemma. The first, like the Chabot case, was bereaved. She did not wish to go on living. Her relatives had her compulsorily placed in a mental hospital. Although depressed the doctors felt she was incorrectly detained under the Irish Mental Treatment Act as she was insufficiently ill. The relatives thought otherwise and threatened to sue if she was released while still retaining her suicidal intentions. Eventually she was discharged and she did kill herself. The second case was a university student who made a serious attempt on his life following which he was compulsorily admitted to a mental hospital. No evidence of depression or other mental disorder or addiction was identified. Nevertheless he was treated as if depressed with antidepressants and psychotherapy. It made no difference to his intention. He saw no point in life. Discharge was followed by suicide.

Both these cases demonstrate the illogicality and conceptual danger of deviating from the principle that individual existence is an inalienable right. There are no medical grounds for intentionally ending innocent life. If such grounds are allowed, they will and have been proven to be elastic, stretching to include all cases of medical business. If the principle is allowed that we have the right to kill ourselves or to allow ourselves to be killed, why should this right be restrained to patients? Surely personal autonomy allows ourselves to be protected from this indignity? Freedom of choice should allow that you do not have to be an invalid to be killed.

The other conceptual danger of allowing innocent killing has already been alluded to. It is the imperceptible bridge between voluntary, nonvoluntary and involuntary euthanasia. Although expressed categorically, in practice the distinction is dimensional. Many of us are ambivalent about the important decisions of life. There can never be certainty. Perhaps the most important decision is the selection and choosing of a partner to share one's life with. Many who do this change their minds. Most at the time of decision, however, think the choice is right. Retrospectively they may regard themselves as having acted on the emotion of the moment. The same may occur in the choice of dying. Here the patient is weak while the doctor and the relatives are strong. In such circumstances, the boundary between voluntary, nonvoluntary and involuntary may become blurred. Finally, the burden placed on the conscientious may be great and of increasing weight. Like the folklore account of the elderly Innuit who, in times of deprivation, remained behind to starve while the family camp moved on, the act may not be entirely voluntary. There is, or was, cultural pressure to do the noble thing — much as there was economic pressure put on Hindu widows to die by suttee. So also if one is no longer productive and if one is drawing on expensive resources, the most convenient thing for all would be to choose assisted suicide or euthanasia.

Safeguards

The Dutch make much of the safeguards they have built into their procedures. They may be making too much of these because there is no proper policing, only threats, on failure to report. Underreporting is, however, widespread [24], although officially satisfaction is expressed that the level is falling [33]. There are much more serious problems with the Dutch concept than the official position recognises.

The first of these relates to the timing of the reports and the second to the representation of the deceased. On the question of timing, the patient is well dead by the time this occurs. Nothing can then be done that would save his life. On the question of representation, he has none. No one puts his case. It is assumed that he can do that himself even though essentially he is ill and suffering. This is unacceptable in law. Most of us seek the counsel of lawyers when we come to distribute our worldly goods. How much more do we need a lawyer when we are literally about to give up the ghost? A good lawyer would satisfy himself that his client knew what he was doing before his death. If he did not, his lawyer could cogently argue his case before a tribunal to be held prior to and not after death has occurred. It would be reassuring to the international community if such services were available to the dying in The Netherlands.

Active and passive euthanasia

The distance between active and passive euthanasia is disputed, particularly by ethicists [3,36,37]. Rightly perhaps, they see no logical difference in conse-quences. Only the means differ. In the latter a treatment is either not commenced or if so, is discontinued. In the former an intervention is put in place, e.g., the giving of an injection, with the declared purpose of ending life. Doctors who, needs be, are pragmatists, intuitively feel that there is a difference which for them is of great professional significance. This has in effect, if not in name, been recognised by the English courts in deciding two cases in recent years. The names of the two patients were Lillian Boyes and Tony Bland.

Lillian Boyes suffered great pain from chronic rheumatoid arthritis. Her long-term doctor, Nigel Cox, did his best to relieve these pains but failed to do so to her satisfaction. Earlier she had got a commitment from him to shorten her life should the pain get out of control. Eventually he did that by injecting potassium chloride which probably stopped her heart. He was tried and found guilty of attempted murder and given a suspended sentence. The judgement hinged on whether he intended to kill his patient or not. As the body had been cremated by the time an investigation occurred, it could not be proven that the injection had indeed stopped her heart. Before returning to medical duties the General Medical Council recommended that he underwent training in pain relief.

In the second case, neither the words euthanasia or murder were used. It con-cerned the ending of the life of Tony Bland who had been for 4 years a brain-dead survivor suffering a persistent vegetative state (PVS), following a crowd crush at Hillsborough football stadium in 1989. He was fed artificially through a tube. Much play hinged on whether this was a medical treatment or a natural right. In deciding it was a treatment, it was concluded it was not of benefit to the person (that was) of Tony Bland. It was discontinued and the patient died. In plain language, Lillian Boyes died by active euthanasia while Tony Bland died as a result of passive euthanasia.

Some would disagree with the latter description, in particular the English judi-ciary. At all costs, they wished to preserve the principle of the inalienable right to life of the innocent individual. The intention was to remove or discontinue a treatment unlikely to restore Tony Bland to himself. The foreseen outcome and the one desired by his parents and the hospital authorities was the cessation of his life, so that the family could conclude the business of grieving. Most doctors recognise the distinction between these two types of cases and most would con-cur with the decision of the court in these circumstances.

Double effect

The doctrine of double effect is a bone of contention among moral philosophers [38,39]. Emotion and personal insult are integral to this debate as it was in the invited criticism of the Dutch television film "Death on Request" [40–42]. Essen-tially the paradigm distinguishes between foreseen but unintended outcomes and outcomes which are intended. If a patient is in severe pain, the doctor may choose an appropriate level of medication to limit or remove the pain even in the likelihood that life will be foreshortened. No one, other than the patient perhaps, can find fault with this approach. One patient who did was Aloys Fleischmann, Emeritus Professor of Music at University College Cork, who declined pain relief when terminally ill with cancer because it was clouding his mind, thereby preventing the completion of his life's work, namely, compiling a repertoire of Irish musical airs.

The IASP study

There are 51 countries affiliated to IASP. Each of these was sent a questionnaire dealing with suicide, assisted suicide and euthanasia. Eventually after various degrees of "arm twisting", 49 countries replied through their national representatives. The questions were brief, written in English and demanded a "yes or no" response. Verbal comments on each answer were invited. The main deficiencies of the study were that the questions had to be brief and few (20 in all) as well as the fact that English was the first language of only a minority. Nevertheless, in the absence of other information, the responses were of some value.

The main findings were that worldwide there is an openness in law with regard to passive euthanasia. In almost half of the surveyed countries (23 out of 49) it is legal and in over half, nonvoluntary, passive euthanasia is practised. However, in most countries (42 out of 49) active euthanasia would be prosecuted while in 12 countries it is said to occur secretly. For most countries (45 out of 49) assisted suicide is a crime and in a similar proportion, the Medical Council, or its equivalent, will prosecute its members for providing such assistance. A further study is presently underway clarifying some of the issues raised in this study.

The psychological needs of the dying

The psychological needs of the dying would benefit from further study. Many of those present in hospices for the dying speak of their desire for death and fear of dying. Some ask for euthanasia. Once treated, however, and once they realise that they can gain mastery over their symptoms, these distressing fears are banished and euthanasia is no longer requested [43].

One study done in Cork of 100 hospice cases found 28 who answered positively to the following general question: "If a patient was suffering and close to the end of their life, do you believe in the right to chose the time of one's passing?" Some of these cases feared their symptoms would get out of control and others were diagnosed as suffering from depression. Eight, however, had neither symptom (A. Payne et al., (In press)). These matters are being researched further.

Final remarks

In conclusion, this essay began with a consideration of intention and its place in all forms of arranged or accidental death. The emphasis has been on what doctors, lawyers and ethicists have said and found. However, this is a limited approach. Many people throughout the ages have looked into the abyss and considered man's place and behaviour on the conduit joining being to nonbeing, existence to nonexistence. How we die may not define our afterlife, as St Augustine believed. There may be none. It does define, however, our life before death. The value we place on our lives should characterise how we die. In doing so, we elevate not only our own lives but also the lives of others. On such is our civilisation built.

References

1. Aries P. The Hour of our Death. Oxford University Press 1991. (Translated by H. Weaver.)
2. Le Gouff J. La civilisation de l'occident medieval 1964. (As quoted by P. Aries, The Hour of our Death, p. 192.)
3. Harris J. Euthanasia and the value of life. In: Keown J (ed) Euthanasia Examined. Cambridge: Cambridge University Press, 1985;6—23.
4. Hoche A, Binding R (1920). Die Freigabe der Vernichtung lebensunwerten Lebens. Leipzig: Verlag Von Felix Meiner. In: Keown J (ed) Euthanasia Examined. Cambridge: Cambridge University Press, 1995.
5. Binding R, Hoche A. The release or destruction of life devoid of value. California, Life Quality, 1975. (Translation of above.)
6. British Medical Association. Euthanasia. London, 1988;49.
7. Dorrepaal KL, Aaronson NK, Van Dam Fsam. Pain experience and pain management among hospitalised cancer patients. Cancer 1989;63:593—598.
8. W.H.O. Cancer, pain relief and palliative care, Geneva. 1990. Technical Report Series No. 804.
9. Royal Dutch Medical Association (K.N.M.G.). Guidelines for euthanasia. (Translated by W. Lagerwey.) Issues Law Med 1989;2:429.
10. The Report of the House of Lords Select Committee on Medical Ethics 1994. H.M.S.O., Paragraph 237.
11. The Report of the House of Lords Select Committee on Medical Ethics 1994. H.M.S.O., Paragraph 260.
12. Kelleher MJ. Suicide: some ethical implications. Irish J Psychol Med 1996;13(4):162—163.
13. Mircea E, Martyrdom. The Encyclopedia of Religion. New York: MacMillan & Free Press, 1988;9:230—238.
14. Encyclopaedia Judaica. Jerusalem: Keter, 1971;15:490—491.
15. St. Augustine, De Civitate Dei, 1: 17-27.
16. Umri J. Suicide or termination of life. Islam Comp Law Quart 1987;7(2):136—145.
17. Kamisar Y. Physician assisted suicide: the last bridge to active voluntary euthanasia. In: Keown J (ed) Euthanasia Examined, Cambridge: Cambridge University Press, 1995;225—261.
18. MacDonald M, Murphy TR. Sleepless Souls: Suicide in Early Modern England. Oxford: Clarendon Press, 1990.
19. Graham G. Suicide and voluntary euthanasia: a moral philosophical perspective. In: Kelleher MJ (ed) Divergent Perspectives on Suicidal Behaviour. Proceedings of the fifth European symposium on suicide. Cork, D. & A. O'Leary, 1995.
20. Donne J (1647), Biathanatos (1/24), part 2, distinction 3, section 1, lines 2710—2715.
21. Van Hooff AJL. From Autothanasia to Suicide: Self-Killing in Classical Antiquity. London: Routledge, 1990.
22. Keown J. The law and practice of euthanasia in The Netherlands. Law Quart 1990;108(Review 51):51—57.
23. Van der Maas PJ, van Delden JJM, Pijnenborg L, Looman CWN. Euthanasia and other medical

decisions concerning the end of life. Lancet 1991;338:669—674.

24. Keown J. Euthanasia in The Netherlands. In: Keown J (ed) Euthanasia Examined. Cambridge: Cambridge University Press, 1995;261—296.

25. Van der Wal G, Van der Mass PJ, Bosma JM et al. Evaluation of the notification procedure for physician-assisted death in The Netherlands. N Engl J Med 1996;335:1706—1711.

26. Carroll L. Through the Looking Glass: and What Alice Found There. London: MacMillan & Co., 1948;113—114.

27. The New York State Task Force on Life and the Law. When Death is Sought: Assisted Suicide and Euthanasia in the Medical Context, 1994.

28. Finnis J. A philosophical case against euthanasia. In: Keown J (ed) Euthanasia Examined. Cambridge: Cambridge University Press, 1995;23—35.

29. Ramsay R. Feature column entitled: "A king, a doctor and a convenient death.". Br Med J 1994; 308:1445.

30. News feature entitled: "Outrage in Japan over euthanasia without consent." Br Med J 1996; 312:1627.

31. Battin MP. What does the supreme court's decision on physician-assisted suicide mean to us?" Am Assoc Suicidol — Newslink 1997;3:4.

32. Churchill LR, King NMP. Physician assisted suicide, euthanasia or withdrawal of treatment. Br Med J 1997;315:137—138.

33. Van der Maas PJ, Van der Wal G, Haverkate I, Carman M, Kester JGC, Bregj ED et al. Euthanasia, physician assisted suicide and other medical practices involving the end of life in the Netherlands 1990—1995. N Engl J Med 1996;335:1699—1705.

34. Hendin H, Rutenfrans C, Zylicz Z. Physician assisted suicide and euthanasia in The Netherlands: lessons from the Dutch. J Am Med Assoc 1997;277:1720—1722.

35. Kelleher MJ. Euthanasia and physician assisted suicide. Med-Legal J Ireland 1997;2(3):77—79.

36. Rachels J. The End of Life. Oxford: Oxford University Press, 1986;Chapter 10.

37. Dworkin R, Life's Dominion. London: Harper Collins, 1993;Chapter 3.

38. Harris J. In: Keown J (ed) Euthanasia Examined. Cambridge: Cambridge University Press, 1995;Chapters 1, 3 and 5.

39. Finnis J. In: Keown J (ed) Euthanasia Examined. Cambridge: Cambridge University Press, 1995;Chapters 2, 4 and 6.

40. Kelleher MJ. Review of "Death on Request". Crisis 1995;16(2):92—94.

41. McKhann C. Comments on Dr Kelleher's review of "Death on Request". Crisis 1996;16: 141—143.

42. Nederhorst M, Schenk L. Reaction to Michael Kelleher's review of "Death on Request". Crisis 1995;16.

43. Twycross RG. Where there is hope, there is life: a view from the hospice. In: Keown J (ed) Euthanasia Examined. Cambridge: Cambridge University Press, 1995;Chapter 11.

Expanding our conceptual horizons on the future of suicide research

Robert Plutchik

Albert Einstein College of Medicine, Bronx, New York, New York and University of South Florida, Sarasota, Florida, USA

Abstract. Most of the published research on suicide has focused on a relatively small number of variables. However, suicide research has gradually revealed a large number of factors correlated with the risk of suicide. In order to carry out a program of research that measures large classes of variables, we need an approach to measurement that is efficient and parsimonious. Although the proclivity of psychiatrists is to use clinical interviews and judgments as a basis of measurement, such judgments are neither efficient nor parsimonious. In contrast, an alternative approach is to use carefully constructed self-report psychometric scales. Rather than to make descriptive differences between individuals the basis for new diagnostic labels, it seems more fruitful to develop a theory of the interaction of the many variables that determine suicidal behavior. With this idea in mind, we have developed the "two-stage model of countervailing forces" as a theory for the study of suicide. The study of suicide now appears to be going beyond the descriptive level and it is entering a phase of theory construction. The present time provides an exciting opportunity to participate in this development.

Keywords: measurements, suicide research, theoretical models, variables.

What has suicide research accomplished up to the present time and what is likely to be the direction of future research? Most of the published research on suicide has focused on a relatively small number of variables: sociological factors such as age, race, sex, occupation and nationality; and psychiatric variables such as diagnosis and depression. However, suicide research has gradually revealed a large number of factors that appear to be correlated with the risk of suicide. A recent list included 37 risk factors [1] and further reviews have now revealed at least 55 risk factors for suicide [2]. These include such variables as troubled early school experiences, soft neurological signs, history of menstrual problems, also medical and neurological problems in one's immediate family.

There are at least two points to be made about these observations. First, it is evident that sociological variables have little predictive power. Knowing that someone is male, white, middle class and Norwegian reveals very little about the probability of suicidal behavior. This fact is unlikely to change in the future.

Second, although psychiatric variables are of more interest and predicative power, they still represent only a small part of the relevant psychological factors

Address for correspondence: Dr Robert Plutchik, 4505 Deer Creek Blvd., Sarasota, FL 34238, USA. Tel.: +1-941-925-7409. Fax: +1-941-912-0221. E-mail: Proban@aol.com

that contribute to the risk of a suicidal act. Examples of other important but understudied variables are: impulsivity, number of life problems, dyscontrol scores, passivity as a personality trait, and poor reality testing. In fact, at least 10 classes of variables have been identified. These include: psychiatric history, personality traits, personality disorders, current life events, current and past losses, historical stressors, coping styles, ego defenses and current environment.

In order to carry out a program of research that attempts to measure samples of these large classes of variables, an approach to measurement that is efficient and parsimonious is required. Although the proclivity of psychiatrists is to use clinical interviews and judgements as a basis of measurement, such judgements are neither efficient nor parsimonious. Clinical judgements require extensive training and corresponding high costs of research. Too often, the task of rating is given to junior members of a research team or to nonmedical research assistants. Reliability has to be assessed for every clinician involved in the research. All of this is time-consuming, expensive and still not guaranteed to produce valid and reliable predictions.

In contrast, an alternative approach is to use carefully constructed, self-report, psychometric scales. Considerable evidence now shows that computerized, self-report testing produces more personal information in an initial interview than clinical evaluations [3]. Once a good psychometric scale has been developed, its reliability, validity, sensitivity and specificity can be easily obtained and these have usually been found to be adequate. Such self-report scales can be quickly administered and they do not require highly trained evaluators. I expect that future research will rely to an increasing degree on such self-report scales.

Many clinicians make fine distinctions between diagnostic categories, e.g., between major depression, masked depression, dysthymia, vital depression and manic depression; or between anxiety, general anxiety disorder, masked anxiety, phobias and social phobias. Although such categorizations are made in clinical practice the distinctions are subtle and often difficult to assess reliably.

An example of this tendency is the distinction that is often made between suicide and parasuicide. It is evident that some individuals make superficial suicidal gestures and rarely show high-risk suicidal behaviors. Does this imply that we are dealing with two distinct phenomena and two distinct populations?

In contrast to this view, there is considerable evidence that a continuum exists that ranges from "normal" individuals who have rare, fleeting thoughts of suicide, to individuals who make threats or superficial gestures; to those who make serious attempts and to those who succeed in killing themselves [4]. Given the fact that there are many factors which influence and determine the presence of a suicidal act, we can easily imagine the complex interaction of these variables in such manifold ways as to produce the range of behaviors actually seen. Rather than make descriptive differences between individuals the basis for new diagnostic labels, it would seem to be more fruitful to develop a theory of the interaction of the many variables that determine suicidal behavior.

This idea is related to the model that my colleagues and I have developed that we call a "two-stage model of countervailing forces". This theory assumes that the study of suicide is an aspect of the more general study of aggression and violence. It postulates the existence of amplifiers of the aggressive impulse and attenuators of the aggressive impulse. These interact at all times and in all individuals to determine a threshold level needed for overt behavior; the vectorial resultant of forces then determines the direction of expression of the aggression, i.e., inward or outward. This theory has guided many research studies which have identified both amplifiers and attenuators of aggression. This distinction is similar to the idea of risk and protective factors, but has the advantage of being part of a theoretical system in contrast to a simple description. Future research will undoubtedly be concerned with more detailed studies of both risk and protective factors and their interactions.

Another advantage of this theoretical model is that it places the study of suicide in a much broader context, i.e., as an aspect of evolutionary biology. In that forum it is appropriate to ask about the inclusive fitness and genetic implications of suicidal behavior. It is also appropriate to recognize the functional value of aggression in humans and lower animals and to inquire into the possible functional significance of suicides as well.

An interesting implication of this kind of theoretical approach to understanding suicidal acts is that the model suggests a relation between the study of suicides and the study of emotions in general. For example, both suicidal behavior and emotional behavior function for the individual as a way of regulating interpersonal relations. Both represent transient efforts at adaptation to difficult or emergency situations [5—7]. I believe that future research and theory will see suicide, violence, aggression and emotions as aspects of the same basic domain, the domain of interpersonal relations. As a consequence, medications that will be developed and used will be narrower in focus and will act to change the balance of emotions that exist in an individual. Thus, for example, it is conceivable that antiaggression medications will have as potent an effect in decreasing suicidal behavior in some patients as antidepressants now do.

Finally, I believe that an ability to make risk predictions for suicide or violence will increase somewhat but will always, in the foreseeable future, be far from perfect. This is simply because of the large number of interacting variables in an individual's life that influence the direction of his or her aggressive impulses. Although some variables are relatively fixed (e.g., excessive physical punishment as a child), others are extremely variable or unstable (e.g., current illness, psychotic reactions, environmental stresses). And because not all relevant variables can be measured and because trivial events may have large consequences (as chaos theory implies), our ability to predict future behavior will always be limited.

The study of suicide now appears to be going beyond the descriptive level and is entering a phase of theory construction. The present time provides an exciting opportunity to participate in this development.

References

1. Plutchik R. Outward and inward directed aggressiveness: The interaction between violence and suicidality. Pharacopsychiatry 1995;28(Suppl):47—57.
2. Plutchik R. Suicide and Violence: The Two Stage Model of Countervailing Forces, Paper presented at the conference on "Suicide: Biopsychosocial Approaches", Athens, Greece, May, 1996.
3. Plutchik R, Karasu TB. Computers in psychotherapy; an overview. Comput Hum Behav 1991;7: 33—44.
4. Pfeffer CR, Plutchik R, Mizruchi MS, Lipkins R. Assaultive behavior in child psychiatric inpatients, outpatients, and non-patients. J Am Acad Child Adolesc Psychiat 1987;26:256—261.
5. Plutchik R. Emotion: A psychoevolutionary synthesis. New York: Harper and Row, 1980.
6. Plutchik R. The psychology and biology of emotions. New York: Harper/Collins, 1994.
7. Plutchik R. The circumplex as a general model of the structure of emotions and personality. In: Plutchik R, Conte HR (eds) The Circumplex Model in Emotions and Personality. Washington, DC: American Psychological Association Press, 1997.

Index of authors

Keyword index